Religious Policy and
Practice in Communist China

RELIGIOUS POLICY AND PRACTICE IN COMMUNIST CHINA

A Documentary History by
DONALD E. MACINNIS

THE MACMILLAN COMPANY, NEW YORK, NEW YORK

COLLIER-MACMILLAN LTD., LONDON

W 4292.82/53

Grateful acknowledgment is made for permission to reprint from:

A Documentary History of Chinese Communism by Brandt, Schwartz and Fairbank: copyright © 1967 by Franz Schurmann and Orville Schell. By permission of the Harvard University Press.

Red Star Over China by Edgar Snow: copyright © 1938 Random House. By permission of Grove Press, Inc. and Victor Gollancz Ltd.

Revolutionary Immortality: Mao Tse-Tung and the Chinese Cultural Revolution by Robert Jay Lifton: copyright © 1968 by Robert Jay Lifton. By permission Random House, Inc.

The Hundred Flowers by Roderick MacFarquhar: copyright: International Association for Cultural Freedom. By permission of the International Association for Cultural Freedom.

Political Thought of Mao Tse-Tung by Stuart R. Schram: copyright © 1963 by Frederick A. Praeger, Inc. By permission of Praeger Publishers Inc.

China Observed by C. Mackerras and N. Hunter: copyright © 1967 by Thomas Nelson (Australia) Ltd. By permission of Praeger Publishers, Inc.

Anti-Memoirs by Andre Malraux: copyright © 1967 by Holt, Rinehart and Winston, Inc. By permission of Holt, Rinehart and Winston, Inc.

The Macmillan Company
866 Third Avenue, New York, N.Y. 10022
Collier-Macmillan Canada Ltd., Toronto, Ontario

Library of Congress Catalog Card Number: 74–182020

FIRST PRINTING

Printed in the United States of America

TO HELEN

sine qua non

Contents

PART III   IDEOLOGY AND THE MAOIST VISION:
           THE RELIGIOUS ANALOGIES

SECTION 1.   REFORMING OLD RITES AND CUSTOMS   312

DOCUMENT

SECTION 2.   NEW LITURGICAL FORMS   330

DOCUMENT

Preface

The purpose of this work is to bring together in one volume a representative selection of published materials, primarily from original Chinese sources, dealing with religious policy and practice in the People's Republic of China. Other excellent books deal with the religions of China through the centuries. Numerous accounts by Westerners and others who lived in China but left the country in the early 1950's are also in the public record. This volume however, brings to readers outside China the views, in their own words, of China's leaders, theoreticians and others on questions of religion. Aside from Part III, Section 3 (Religious Analogies), virtually all of the 116 documents and excerpts included here appeared first in the Chinese press.

The editorial introductions are intended for clarification only; interpretation of the *intent* of the original writers and the accuracy of the material in the documents is left to the reader's judgment. This is, first of all, a collection of primary source materials.

One strives for scholarly detachment and objectivity in producing such a work. But, as the conclusion demonstrates, I have my bias: it is my earnest hope that China's leaders will soon again follow the counsel of their Party leader, Mao Tse-tung, and the implications of Article 88 of the state Constitution by implementing in *practice* the religious *policy* so clearly and frequently enunciated—to allow adherents of all religions to freely and openly practice their faith.

xviii *Preface*

In preparation for this study I have been greatly helped by reading the books and writings of C. K. Yang, Kenneth Chen, Holmes Welch, Francis P. Jones, Father Léon Trivière, M. Searle Bates, and others of that small band of scholars interested in the religious beliefs and practice of the Chinese people. I'm especially indebted to Richard C. Bush and M. Searle Bates for their critical reading of the manuscript, and for their help and counsel in many ways. This books, in a very real sense, is a sequel to Dr. Bush's RELIGION IN COMMUNIST CHINA (Nashville, Abingdon, 1970), providing full documentary sources for much of the material covered in that excellent historical survey of China's religions since 1949.

Few scholarly works on China would be possible today without the screening and translating efforts of various agencies and individuals. Among those noted in the List of Documents by Source I'm especially indebted to the Union Research Institute (Hong Kong), the Foreign Languages Press (Peking), and the editors and translators of SCMP, SCMM and JPRS. The staff and library of the Universities Service Center (Hong Kong) generously provided essential help and resource material.

Thanks are due to my employers, the National Council of Churches of Christ in the USA, for authorizing a one-year assignment in Hong Kong, 1970–71, which made the completion of this book possible. But opinions expressed or implied here are fully my own responsibility, as are any errors of fact or interpretation.

I am grateful to my colleagues, the Rev. and Mrs. Raymond L. Whitehead and Mr. Joseph Chang, for their help; and to Miss Donna Ng and Miss Donna Yoder for typing portions of the manuscript. My greatest debt of gratitude is to my wife, Helen, who has given full encouragement and support through the long months of research, writing, and editing, down to the final reading of galley proofs.

Introduction

SINCE THE ABRUPT and forcible closing by Red Guard militants of all places of religious worship still open in autumn 1966, no direct word has been received from China's religious leaders, nor have recent visitors to China been able to meet with them. Until the report in mid-November, 1971 by an Italian journalist that the Roman Catholic cathedral in Peking had resumed observance of the daily mass, the only place of worship known to be holding services was a single mosque in Peking, apparently kept open primarily for visitors from Moslem nations. Aside from that, for the first time in centuries, there was no known open practice of any religion in China.

Since this happened with no revocation of the constitutional guarantee of freedom of religious belief, nor the issuing of any new public policy directive on religion, the present situation may be considered temporary, one which could revert to the situation prevailing before the Cultural Revolution when limited practice of public worship and personal freedom of religious belief were tolerated. The Red Guard action against religion in 1966 appeared to be part of a broad-scale, emotionally charged response to the Chinese Communist Party's (CCP) Central Committee communiqué summoning "revolutionary young people" to lead the Cultural Revolution against revisionist bureaucrats, bourgeois reactionaries, and "all other parts of the superstructure that do not correspond to the socialist economic base." Religion, for a generation of politicized youth with no personal religious experience, seemed superfluous and irrelevant, a hiding place for slackers and reactionaries.

The Cultural Revolution has now moved beyond the initial phase of militancy, and the Red Guards themselves are seldom mentioned in the Chinese press. Since the convening of the Ninth Party Congress in 1969 it seems evident that Chinese leaders are striving to consolidate the political and sociocultural gains of the Cultural Revolution while at the same time moving ahead with nation building. Recent moves in international relations suggest that ideology is no longer the determining factor in leadership decisions.

The Chinese Communists are thoroughly Marxist in their view of religion, seeing it at best as a useless excrescence of primitive or bourgeois society, and at worst as the instrument used by feudalistic oppressors, foreign imperialists and counter-revolutionaries to subvert and exploit the Chinese masses. In their early years, as will be seen by some of the documents in Section I, there was no room for religion in the Communist areas. But since 1937, when united front resistance to the Japanese took first priority in the northwest border region, the CCP has held to a stated policy of "freedom of religious belief." Party and government documents since that time, statements by Mao Tse-tung and other leaders, and discussions by theoreticians and writers in the Chinese press as recently as August 1969 hold consistently to the constitutional guarantee of freedom of religious belief. If that same guarantee is included in the new constitution, not yet approved by a People's National Congress but now circulating in draft form inside China,[1] it can be assumed that some degree of freedom of religious belief in practice as well as in word and document, however limited, may one day again be permitted.

1. No official version of the new draft constitution has yet been released to the world press. However, an unofficial text, generally believed to be authentic, has been circulated outside China. Under Section III, "Fundamental Rights and Duties of Citizens," Article 28 reads: "Citizens have freedom of speech, correspondence, the press, assembly, association, travel, demonstration and strike, the freedom to believe in religion or not to believe in religion, and the freedom to propagate atheism. . . ."

But freedom of religious belief has not meant, in the years up to 1966, separation of church and state in the Western sense, nor did organized religious groups have unlimited freedom to practice and propagate their faith. First priority for the new regime in 1949 and years following was national unification and construction. Religious groups, with all other social, ethnic and cultural units, were mobilized for united action under appropriate Party and government leadership. In the eyes of the leaders, the struggle to build a strong and independent new China in the face of threats from without and resistance from within demanded a caustic scrubbing out of pernicious vestiges of the old China and the building of a new China through the collective effort of the revolutionary masses. Then as now, the traditional religions were seen as strongholds for indigenous reactionary forces, while Protestant and Catholic Christianity, with strong financial and emotional ties to mission agencies in Western countries, was an obvious affront to the powerful mood of independence, liberation and national rebirth that swept the nation. In 1949, after the final victory over the Nationalist forces, Mao Tse-tung proclaimed, "The Chinese people have stood up!" Since that time the theme of self-reliance has been a fundamental determinant in major policy decisions, including policy toward religion.

In the first months of the new regime steps were taken toward the Christian churches, in what was known as the three-self movement,[2] which led to the total severance of relations with overseas mission agencies. In subsequent years all religions, indigenous as well as overseas-related, were brought firmly under the administration of the Religious Affairs Bureau of the central government and its regional and local offices. It was through these channels that religious policy was implemented.

The three main sections of this book all focus, in different ways, on a limited but important aspect of the subject of reli-

2. The "three autonomies" were: self-support, self-government and self-propagation.

gion in China today: the expressed policy of state and Party, of leaders, theoreticians and others on religion, and the actual implementation in practice of that policy. As with any attempt at scholarly appraisal of events in China, there are obvious physical and political obstacles in studying the internal situation. There is a considerable body of literature from the early 1950's, largely subjective accounts by expatriate Chinese believers or former missionaries, which relates personal experiences, some of them grim indeed. But, since that material is available elsewhere, this book, while citing in a few instances from the reports and analyses of recent foreign visitors or scholars, will draw for its documentation from a surprisingly large body of Chinese sources published originally in the official secular or religious press. In a country with a controlled press, like China, this approach has obvious limitations, since everything published there presumably has its purpose, whether for overseas or domestic readers. With that *caveat* in mind, these documents and excerpts, nearly all of them published first in Chinese and intended for domestic consumption, can be understood to reflect the official interpretation in practice of the policy of freedom of religious belief at any given stage in this period of Chinese history.

As has been traced elsewhere,[3] that interpretation changed during the twenty years from 1949 to 1969, growing progressively more restrictive on religious believers (with the exception of the brief "hundred flowers" period in 1957) until the total suppression of open religious practice by the Red Guards in 1966. It is important to see the particular treatment of religious believers and organized religion at any given time in the overall context of Party and state domestic policy or international relations at that same time. Church properties and buildings, for example, were expropriated or nationalized during the initial land reform period that affected all landholdings above a minimum size, and all foreign-owned properties. Reli-

---

3. Francis P. Jones, *The Church in Communist China*, Friendship Press, New York, 1962.
   Richard C. Bush, *Religion in Communist China*, Abingdon, Nashville, 1970.

gious believers were mobilized, along with all other sectors of society, for the "Resist-America, Aid-Korea" movement during the Korean war. Religious believers, especially monks, nuns and clergy, were brought out of religious sanctuaries for participation with everyone else in the mass production campaigns of the Great Leap Forward, where they have presumably remained to the present.

At the same time religious believers and leaders, for reasons of class status, relative wealth and privilege, education, or former connections with foreign "imperialists," were subjected, especially in the anti-rightist campaign following the "hundred flowers" period (1957), to the same intensive indoctrination and thought reform through study, labor camps, struggle-criticism-transformation meetings, etc., as non-religious Chinese with the same backgrounds. The constitutional guarantee of freedom of religious belief gave no protection to suspected revisionists, reactionaries, imperialist lackeys, counter-revolutionaries, neo-capitalists and intellectual elitists.

Periods of high-energy political activity and ideological emphasis allowed neither time nor place for tolerance of religious or intellectual deviation. The suppression of all visible practice of religion during the Cultural Revolution was only one part (and that part never explicit) of the total campaign to wrench the nation out of a course perceived by the Maoist group to be leading backward. The revolutionary revival of 1966–69, led by Chairman Mao against heretics among his own Party leadership, could no more stand dissent or non-conformity than could the great religious revivals of years past—in Cromwell's England, Savonarola's Florence, Saladin's Islam. The issues are perceived in each case to be the same by the believers, whether religious or ideological: the survival of the faith, of the nation, indeed, of mankind's very future. Yet political revival, like religious revival, holds its peaks of intensity only briefly; in the periods of denouement and rationalization, tolerance for a wider spread of views and practice—for pragmatic reasons, if none other—returns. This, it can be hoped, will be the case in China.

The Maoist vision of a new man and new society can be seen

in Mao's writings, in many of the Chinese goals for social and personal transformation, and in the enthusiasms of the Cultural Revolution, as secular equivalents for ethical goals and values of the various religions. But the question persists: can new and living culture patterns develop fully while totally cut off from the rich and meaningful heritage of old China and the spiritual vitality and spontaneity of authentic personal religious experience?

PART I

*Religious Policy: Leaders'
Views and Official Statements*

WHILE THEIR UNDERSTANDING of the origins, life and death of religion is thoroughly Marxist, repeatedly documented from the writings of Marx, Engels, Lenin and others, the policy expressed through the years by Chinese Communist leaders, writers, and theoreticians toward religious believers has consistently reflected Mao's own unhurried view, first published in 1927: "It is the peasants who made the idols, and when the time comes they will cast the idols aside with their own hands" (see Doc. 2).

Mao's remarks on religion in his speech "On the Correct Handling of Contradictions" delivered thirty years later, while more sophisticated in style and ideology, merely amplify the earlier view. "We cannot abolish religion by administrative decree nor force people not to believe. . . . The only way to settle questions of an ideological nature . . . is by the democratic method, the method of discussion, criticism, persuasion, and education, and not by the method of coercion or repression" (see Doc. 7). Religion, for Mao, was a non-antagonistic contradiction *among* the people which the people could handle themselves without recourse to higher authority or naked power.

Although he believed religion, from his own observation in the rural areas, to be one of the "four thick ropes" binding the peasants (see Doc. 2), he recognized the importance religion played in the lives of many. In his childhood he had been deeply influenced by his

3

mother's Buddhist piety, but had abandoned religious faith under the influence of a primary school teacher who sought to convert the temples into schools, a practice which Mao observed later in the Hunan peasant movement in 1927. The peasants' attack on religious traditions in that same movement convinced him that the people themselves would do away with religion; "there is no need for anyone else to do it for them prematurely."

Marxist analysis and his own experience convinced him that religion would wither and die in the process of socialist construction and socialist education. The short-term survival of religion during the transition period was of no real concern to him. "Whether you believe in religion or not and whether you believe in this religion or that religion, all of you will be respected," he told a Tibetan delegation in 1952.

There is no evidence that Mao had direct experience at any point with Western missionary institutions, nor does he make more than passing reference to missionary religious work in China in his writings. However, he often spoke of the two burdens on the backs of the Chinese people, the twin "mountains" of imperialism and feudalism. A textbook he helped write in 1939 speaks of the ceaseless efforts of imperialist powers to poison the minds of the Chinese people through missionary work, hospitals and schools, newspapers, and study abroad. Cultural imperialism by Western missionaries in China was repeatedly denounced in the Chinese religious and secular press in the years 1950–66. Indigenous religions and superstitions which belonged to feudalism, the second "mountain," it was assumed would quietly disappear along with all other feudal institutions.

From the evidence of his writing, religion was simply not a major concern of Mao's. In his discussion of old and new culture in *On New Democracy*, religion is not even mentioned, nor is it specified in the attack on the "four olds" (old habits, ideas, customs, and culture) which a Mao-dominated Central Committee launched with the sixteen-point Cultural Revolution *Decision* of August, 1966 (see Doc. 86). Mao was so confident that religion would wither and die from internal decrepitude that he could write in 1940: "Let us rather have a contest [with religion and other ideologies]. If Communism is beaten, we Communists will admit defeat in good grace . . ." (see Doc. 6).

Mao believes in no supramundane God or gods. In his revision of the old fable of the foolish old man he wrote, "Our God is none other than the masses of the Chinese people" (see Doc. 11). And to André Malraux in 1965 he said, "Chinese Marxism is the religion of the people. . . . When we say, 'We are the Sons of the People,' China understands it as she understood the phrase 'Son of Heaven.' The People has taken the place of the ancestors. The People, not the victorious Communist party" (see Doc. 12).

"Gods are all right for the rich. The poor have the Eighth Route Army" (see Doc. 12).

Section 1. Mao Tse-tung and Religion

DOC. 1. *Childhood Influences (as told to Edgar Snow)*

MY FATHER, Mao Jen-sheng, was in his early days, and in middle age, a skeptic, but my mother devoutly worshipped Buddha. She gave her children religious instruction, and we were all saddened that our father was an unbeliever. When I was nine years old I seriously discussed the problem of my father's lack of piety with my mother. We made many attempts then and later on to convert him, but without success. He only cursed us, and overwhelmed by his attacks, we withdrew to devise new plans. But he would have nothing to do with the gods.

My reading gradually began to influence me, however; I myself became more and more skeptical. My mother became concerned about me, and scolded me for my indifference to the requirements of my faith, but my father made no comment. Then one day he went out on the road to collect some money, and on his way he met a tiger. The tiger was surprised at the encounter and fled at once, but my father was even more astonished and afterwards reflected a good deal on his miraculous escape. He began to wonder if he had not offended the gods. From then on he showed more respect to Buddhism and burned incense now and then. Yet, when my own backsliding grew worse the old man did not interfere. He only prayed to the gods when he was in difficulties.

Another influence on me at this time was the presence in a local primary school of a 'radical' teacher. He was 'radical' because he was opposed to Buddhism, and wanted to get rid of the gods. He urged people to convert their temples into schools. He was a widely discussed personality. I admired him and agreed with his views.

DOC. 2. *Overthrowing the Clan Authority of the Ancestral Temples and Clan Elders, the Religious Authority of Town and Village Gods, and the Masculine Authority of Husbands* (*1927*)

A MAN IN China is usually subjected to the domination of three systems of authority: (1) the state system (political authority), ranging from the national, provincial and county government down to that of the township; (2) the clan system (clan authority), ranging from the central ancestral temple and its branch temples down to the head of the household; and (3) the supernatural system (religious authority), ranging from the King of Hell down to the town and village gods belonging to the nether world, and from the Emperor of Heaven down to all the various gods and spirits belonging to the celestial world. As for women, in addition to being dominated by these three systems of authority, they are also dominated by the men (the authority of the husband). These four authorities—political, clan, religious and masculine—are the embodiment of the whole feudal-patriarchal system and ideology, and are the four thick ropes binding the Chinese people, particularly the peasants. How the peasants have overthrown the political authority of the landlords in the countryside has been described above. The political authority of the landlords is the backbone of all the other systems of authority. With that overturned, the clan authority, the religious authority and the authority of the husband all begin to totter. Where the peasant association is powerful, the clan elders and administrators of temple funds no longer dare oppress those lower in the clan hierarchy or embezzle clan funds. The worst clan elders and administrators, being local tyrants, have been thrown out. No one any longer dares to practice the cruel corporal and capital punishments that used to be inflicted in the ancestral temples, such as flogging, drowning and burying alive. The old rule barring women and poor people from the banquets in the ancestral temples has also been broken. The women of Paikuo in Hengshan County gathered in force and swarmed into their ancestral temple, firmly planted their backsides in the seats and joined in the eating and drinking, while the venerable clan bigwigs had willy-nilly to let them do as they pleased. At another place, where poor peasants had been excluded from temple banquets a group of them flocked in and ate and drank their fill, while the local tyrants and evil gentry and other long-gowned gentlemen all took to their heels in fright. Everywhere religious authority totters as the peasant movement develops. In many places the peasant associations have taken over the temples of the gods as their offices. Everywhere they advocate the appropriation of temple property in order to start peasant schools and to defray the expenses of the associations, calling it "public revenue from superstition." In Liling County, prohibiting superstitious practices and smashing idols have become quite the vogue. In its northern districts the peasants have prohibited the incense-burning processions to propitiate the god of pestilence. There were many idols in the Taoist temple at Fupoling in Lukou, but when extra room was needed for the district headquarters of the Kuomintang, they were all piled up in a corner, big and small together, and no peasant raised any objection. Since then, sacrifices to the gods, the performance of religious rites and the offering of sacred lamps have rarely been practiced when a death occurs in a family. Because the initiative in this matter was taken by the chairman of the peasant association, Sun Hsiao-shan, he is hated by the local Taoist priests. In the Lungfeng Nunnery in the North Third District, the peasants and primary school teachers chopped up the wooden idols and actually used the wood to cook meat. More than thirty idols in the Tungfu Monastery in the Southern District were burned by the students and peasants together, and only two small images of Lord Pao were snatched up by an old peasant who said, "Don't commit a sin!" In places where the power of the peasants is predominant, only the older peasants and the women still believe in the gods, the younger peasants no longer doing so. Since the latter control the associations, the overthrow of religious authority and the eradication of superstition are going on everywhere. As for the clan system, superstition, and inequality between men and women, their abolition will follow as a natural consequence of victory in the political and economic struggles. If too much of an effort is made, arbitrarily and prematurely, to abolish these things, the local tyrants and evil gentry will seize the pretext to put about such counter-revolutionary propaganda as "the peasant association has no piety towards ancestors," "the peasant association is blasphemous and is destroying religion," and "the peasant association stands for the communization of wives," all for the purpose of undermining the peasant movement. A case in point is the recent events at Hsianghsiang in Hunan and Yanghsin in Hupeh, where the landlords exploited the opposition of some peasants to smashing idols. It is the peasants who made the idols, and when the time comes they will cast the idols aside with their own hands; there is no need for anyone else to do it for them prematurely. The Communist Party's propaganda policy in such matters should be, "Draw the bow without shooting, just indicate the motions." It is for the peasants themselves to cast aside the idols, pull down the temples to the martyred virgins and the arches to the chaste and faithful widows; it is wrong for anybody else to do it for them.

While I was in the countryside, I did some propaganda against superstition among the peasants. I said:

If you believe in the Eight Characters, you hope for good luck; if you believe in geomancy, you hope to benefit from the location of your ancestral graves. This year within the space of a few months the local tyrants, evil gentry and corrupt officials have all toppled from their pedestals. Is it possible that until a few months ago they all had good luck and enjoyed the benefit of well-sited ancestral graves, while suddenly in the last few months their luck has turned and their ancestral graves have ceased to exert a beneficial influence? The local tyrants and evil gentry jeer at your peasant association and say, 'How odd! Today, the world is a world of committeemen. Look, you can't even go to pass water without bumping into a committeeman!' Quite true, the towns and the villages, the trade unions and the peasant associations, the Kuomintang and the Communist Party, all without exception have their executive committee members—it is indeed a world of committeemen. But is this due to the Eight Characters and the location of the ancestral graves? How strange! The Eight Characters of all the poor wretches in the countryside have suddenly turned auspicious! And their ancestral graves have suddenly started exerting beneficial influences! The gods? Worship them by all means. But if you had only Lord Kuan and the Goddess of Mercy and no peasant association, could you have overthrown the local tyrants and evil gentry? The gods and goddesses are indeed miserable objects. You have worshipped them for centuries, and they have not overthrown a single one of the local tyrants or evil gentry for you! Now you want to have your rent reduced. Let me ask how will you go about it? Will you believe in the gods or in the peasant association?

DOC. 3. *Mao Tse-tung: Dialectical Materialism—Notes of Lectures, as published in K'ang-chan ta-hsueh (War of Resistance University Magazine) (April–June, 1938)*

I. Idealism and Materialism: The origin of the inception and the development of materialism

THE RECOGNITION THAT matter exists independently and apart from consciousness in the external world is the foundation of materialism. Man created this foundation through practice. . . .

Obliged to submit to natural forces, and capable of using only simple tools, primitive man could not explain the surrounding phenomena and hence sought help from spirits. This is the origin of religion and idealism.

But in the long-range process of production, man came into contact with surrounding nature, acted upon nature, changed nature, and created things to eat, to live in, and to use, and adapted nature to the interests of man and caused man to believe that matter has an objective existence.

The history of science furnishes man with proof of the material nature of the world and of the fact that it is governed by laws, and helps man to see the futility of the illusions of religion and idealism and to arrive at materialist conclusions.

II. Dialectical Materialism: On movement (on development)

DIALECTICAL MATERIALISM's theory of movement is in opposition first of all with philosophical idealism, and with the theological concepts of religion. The fundamental nature of all philosophical idealism and religious theology derives from their denial of the unity and material nature of the world, and in imagining that the movement and development of the world takes place apart from matter, or took place at least in the beginning apart from matter, and is the result of the action of spirit, God, or divine forces. The German idealist philosopher, Hegel, held that the present world results from the development of the so-called "world idea." In China the philosophy of the *Book of Changes*, and the metaphysics of the Sung and the Ming [dynasties], all put forward idealist views of the development of the universe. Christianity says that God created the world; Buddhism and all of China's fetishist religions attribute the movement and development of all the myriad phenomena (*wan wu*) of the universe to spiritual forces. All of these doctrines which think about movement apart from matter are fundamentally incompatible with dialectical materialism. . . .

DOC. 4. *The Chinese Revolution and the Chinese Communist Party: On Religious Cultural Aggression*

THE STATEMENTS in this document are from a textbook "written jointly by Mao and several other comrades in Yenan in the winter of 1939." This is the ninth in a list of the "military, political, economic and cultural means of oppression by the imperialist powers" in China.

THE IMPERIALIST POWERS have never slackened their efforts to poison the minds of the Chinese people. This is their policy of cultural aggression. And it is carried out through missionary work, through establishing hospitals and schools, publishing newspapers and inducing Chinese students to study abroad. Their aim is to train intellectuals who will serve their interests and to dupe the people.

DOC. 5. *On Religion and the United Front (1940)*

COMMUNISTS MAY FORM an anti-imperialist and anti-feudal united front for political action with certain idealists and even with religious followers, but we can never approve of their idealism or religious doctrines.

DOC. 6. *On Religion and Democratic Methods (1940)*

IX. Refutation of the Diehards

MOREOVER, THE "one doctrine" theory is an absurdity. So long as classes exist, there will be as many doctrines as there are classes, and even various groups in the same class have their different doctrine. Since the feudal class has feudal doctrine, the bourgeoisie a capitalist doctrine, the Buddhists Buddhism, the Christians Christianity and the peasants polytheism, and since in recent years, some people have also advocated Kemalism, fascism, vitalism, the doctrine of "distribution according to labor," and what not, why then cannot the proletariat have its communism? . . . Let us rather have a contest. If communism is beaten, we Communists will admit defeat in good grace. . . .

DOC. 7. *On the Correct Handling of Contradictions (1957)*

IN ADVOCATING FREEDOM with leadership and democracy under centralized guidance, we in no way mean that coercive measures should be taken to settle ideological questions or questions involving the distinction between right and wrong among the people. All attempts to use administrative orders or coercive measures to settle ideological questions or questions of right and wrong are not only ineffective but harmful. We cannot abolish religion by administrative decree or force people not to believe in it. We cannot compel people to give up idealism, any more than we can force them to believe in Marxism. The only way to settle questions of an ideological nature or controversial issues among the people is by the democratic method, the method of discussion, of criticism, of persuasion and education, and not by the method of coercion or repression.

Our Constitution lays it down that citizens of the People's Republic of China enjoy freedom of speech, of the press, assembly, association, procession, demonstration, religious belief, and so on.

DOC. 8. *On Coalition Government* (*1945*)

[ON] THE PROBLEM of racial minorities . . . the CCP is in complete accord with Dr. Sun's racial policy . . . to assist the broad masses of the racial minorities, including their leaders who have connections with the people, to fight for their political, economic, and cultural emancipation and development, as well as for the establishment of their own armed forces that protect the interest of the masses. Their languages, customs, habits, and religious beliefs should be respected. . . .

All religions are permitted in China's Liberated Areas, in accordance with the principle of freedom of religious belief. All believers in Protestantism, Catholicism, Islamism, Buddhism, and other faiths enjoy the protection of the people's government as long as they are abiding by its laws. Everyone is free to believe or not to believe; neither compulsion nor discrimination is permitted.

DOC. 9. *To the Tibetan Goodwill Mission* (*1952*)

THE COMMUNIST PARTY adopts the policy of protecting religion. Whether you believe in religion or not and whether you believe in this religion or that religion, all of you will be respected. The Party respects religious belief. This policy, as presently adopted, will continue to be adopted in the future.

DOC. 10. *Communism Replaces Religion*

NOT TO HAVE a correct political point of view is like having no soul.

DOC. 11. *The Foolish Old Man Who Removed the Mountains*

"THE FOOLISH OLD MAN Who Removed the Mountains" is one of the "Three Often-Read Articles" by Mao Tse-tung constantly read and pondered by everyone in China (see Doc. 109). The other two are "In Memory of Norman Bethune" and "Serve the People."

THERE IS AN ANCIENT Chinese fable called "The Foolish Old Man Who Removed the Mountains." It tells of an old man who lived in northern China long, long ago and was known as the Foolish Old Man of North Mountain. His house faced south and beyond his doorway stood the two great peaks, Taihang and Wangwu, obstructing the way. He called his sons, and hoe in hand they began to dig up these mountains with great determination. Another greybeard, known as the Wise Old Man, saw them and said derisively, "How silly of you to do this! It is quite impossible for you few to dig up these two huge mountains." The Foolish Old Man replied, "When I die, my sons will carry on; when they die, there will be my grandsons, and then their sons and grandsons, and so on to infinity. High as they are, the mountains cannot grow any higher and with every bit we dig, they will be that much lower. Why can't we clear them away?" Having refuted the Wise Old Man's wrong view, he went on digging every day, unshaken in his conviction. God was moved by this, and he sent down two angels, who carried the mountains away on their backs. Today, two big mountains lie like a dead weight on the Chinese people. One is imperialism, the other is feudalism. The Chinese Communist Party has long made up its mind to dig them up. We must persevere and work unceasingly, and we, too, will touch God's heart. Our God is none other than the masses of the Chinese people. If they stand up and dig together with us, why can't these two mountains be cleared away?

DOC. 12. *Mao Talks with André Malraux (1965)*

"THE FIRST PART of our struggle was a peasant revolt. The aim was to free the farmer from his overlord; to win not freedom of speech, voting or assembly, but the freedom to survive. Fraternity rather than liberty! The peasants had tackled it without us, or were on the point of tackling it. But often in a state of despair. We brought hope. In the liberated areas, life was less terrible. Chiang Kai-shek's troops were so well aware of this that they put it about that the prisoners and peasants who came over to us were buried alive. That is why we had to organize a war of slogans, having the truth propagated by people who were known to those who listened to them. And only by those who had left no relatives on the other side. It was in order to sustain hope that we developed guerrilla warfare as much as we could. Much more than for punitive expeditions. *Everything arose out of a specific situation*: we organized peasant revolt, we did not instigate it. Revolution is a drama of passion; we did not win the people over by appealing to reason, but by developing hope, trust, and fraternity. In the face of famine, the will to equality takes on a religious force. Then, in the struggle for rice, land, and the rights brought by agrarian reform, the peasants had the conviction that they were fighting for their lives and those of their children."

". . . The thought, culture, and customs which brought China to where we found her must disappear, and the thought, customs, and culture of proletarian China, which does not yet exist, must appear. . . ."

"Proletarian China," Mao goes on, "is no more a coolie than it is a mandarin; the People's Army is no more a partisan band than a Chiang Kai-shek army. Thought, culture, customs must be born of struggle and the struggle must continue for as long as there is still a danger of a return to the past. Fifty years is not a long time; barely a lifetime—our customs must become as different from the traditional customs as yours are from feudal customs. The basis on which we have constructed everything is the real toil of the masses, the real struggle of the soldiers. Anyone who does not understand that puts himself outside the Revolution. It isn't a victory, it is a mixing of the masses and the cadres over several generations."

"What is expressed in that commonplace term 'revisionism' is the death of the revolution. What we have just done in the army must be done everywhere. I have told you that the revolution is also a feeling. If we decide to make of it what the Russians are now doing—a feeling of the past—everything will fall apart. Our revolution cannot be simply the stabilization of a victory."

"Doesn't the Great Leap Forward seem much more than a stabilization?" I ask.

Its edifices surround us as far as the eye can see.

"Yes. But since then . . . There is what one sees, and what one doesn't see. Men do not like to bear the burden of the Revolution throughout their lives. When I said, 'Chinese Marxism is the religion of the people,' I meant—but do you know how many communists there are in the countryside? One per cent!—I meant that the communists express the Chinese people in a real way if they remain faithful to the work upon which the whole of China has embarked as if on another Long March. When we say, 'We are the Sons of the People,' China understands it as she understood the phrase 'Son of Heaven.' The People has taken the place of the ancestors. The People, not the victorious Communist party."

The revolution freed the wife from her husband, the son from his father, the farmer from his overlord. But for the benefit of collectivity. The individualism of the West has no roots among the Chinese masses. The hope of transformation, on the other hand, is a very powerful sentiment. A husband must stop beating his wife *in order* to become a different man, who will be a member of the party, or simply of his people's commune, or of those which the army will set free: "Gods are all right for the rich; the poor have the Eighth Route Army."

Section 2. Statements by Party, State and Leaders

DOC. 13. *Constitution of the [Chinese] Soviet Republic (November 7, 1931)*

PAR. 2) . . . under the Soviet regime the workers, peasants, Red Army soldiers and the entire toiling population shall have the right to elect their own deputies to give effect to their power. Only militarists, bureaucrats, landlords, the gentry, village bosses, monks—all exploiting and counter-revolutionary elements—shall be deprived of the right to elect deputies to participate in the government and to enjoy political freedom.

Par. 4) All workers, peasants, Red Army soldiers, and all toilers and their families, without distinction of sex, religion or nationality . . . shall be equal before the [Chinese] Soviet law, and shall be citizens of the Soviet Republic.

Par. 13) The Soviet government of China guarantees true religious freedom to the workers, peasants, and the toiling population. Adhering to the principle of the complete separation of church and state, the Soviet state neither favors nor grants any financial assistance to any religion whatsoever. All Soviet citizens shall enjoy the right to engage in anti-religious propaganda. No religious institution of the imperialists shall be allowed to exist unless it shall comply with Soviet law.

DOC. 14. *Land Law of the [Chinese] Soviet Republic (November, 1931)*

ARTICLE 6: All lands belonging to religious institutions or to temples and all other public lands shall be unconditionally delivered into the possession of the peasants by the Soviet government. However, in disposing of these lands, it shall be essential to obtain the voluntary support of the peasants, so that their religious feelings may not be offended.

DOC. 15. *Edgar Snow's Observations (1937)*

IN KIANGSI THE [Chinese] Soviet carried on extensive "anti-God" propaganda. All temples, churches, and church estates were converted to State property, and monks, nuns, priests, preachers, and foreign missionaries were deprived of the rights of citizenship, but in the northwest a much milder policy of religious toleration was practiced. Freedom of worship was a primary guarantee, in fact. All foreign mission property was protected and refugee missionaries were invited to return to their flocks. The Communists reserved the right to preach antireligious propaganda of their own, holding the 'freedom to oppose worship' to be a democratic privilege like the freedom to worship.

DOC. 16. *The Common Program (Adopted September 27, 1949)*

ARTICLE 3: Rural land belonging to ancestral shrines, temples, monasteries, churches, schools, and organizations, and land owned by public bodies, shall be requisitioned.

ARTICLE 5: The people of the People's Republic of China shall have freedom of thought, speech, publication, assembly, association, correspondence, person, domicile, change of domicile, religious belief, and the freedom of holding processions and demonstrations.

DOC. 17. *Constitution of the People's Republic of China (Adopted 1954)*

ARTICLE 88: Every citizen of the People's Republic of China shall have freedom of religious belief.

DOC. 18. *Decisions on Some Problems in Agrarian Reform*

PROFESSIONAL RELIGIONISTS: Those who have principally depended upon religious or superstitious occupations—such as pastors, Catholic fathers, Taoist priests, Buddhist monks, vegetarian hermits, geomancers, fortune-tellers, etc.—to make a living for three full years preceding liberation are called religious or superstitious professionals.

DOC. 19. *Agreement on Measures for the Peaceful Liberation
of Tibet*

(Signed May 23, 1951, by Ngapo Ngawang Jigme on Behalf of the
Tibetan Local Government)

. . . . WITHIN THIS BIG FAMILY of nationalities of the People's
Republic of China, national regional autonomy is to be exercised
in areas where national minorities are concentrated, and all
national minorities are to have freedom to develop their spoken
and written language and to preserve or reform their customs,
habits and religious beliefs, and the Chinese People's Government will assist all national minorities to develop their political,
economic, cultural and educational construction work. . . .

Number 7 of the seventeen-point agreement reads as follows:
The policy of freedom of religious belief laid down in the
Common Program of the Chinese People's Political Consultative
Conference will be protected. The Central Authorities will not
effect any change in the income of the monasteries.

DOC. 20. *Liu Shao-ch'i, Vice-chairman of the Central Committee: Report to the Eighth National Congress of the CCP
(September, 1956)*

WITH REGARD TO THE QUESTION of freedom of religious belief
in national minority areas, we must carry out with perseverance
the long-term policy of freedom of religious belief, and should
not interfere [with such freedom] during social reforms. As for
difficulties in livelihood for religious professionals, we should
help them to obtain proper solutions.

DOC. 21. *Chang Chih-yi, Deputy Director of the United Front Work Department: Concerning the Problem of Religious Policy (1958)*

IDEOLOGICAL DIFFERENCE on the question of God is tolerable. The policy on freedom of religious belief tolerates such difference and facilitates the correct handling of such kinds of contradiction among the people. The policy on freedom of religious belief, therefore, is a long-term basic policy of the Chinese Communist Party and the state to cope with the religious problem. . . .

It means that the state treats various religions on an equal basis without discrimination and accords protection to believers and disbelievers and believers of different religions alike, their faiths respected. The protective policy is adopted towards religion today and will be continued in the future. On this ground the state protects the legitimate religious activities of believers and forbids any act injurious to their religious feeling.

DOC. 22. *Liu Shao-ch'i: Report on the Draft Constitution of the People's Republic of China (1954)*

OTHER FOREIGN COMMENTATORS find it strange that while we safeguard freedom of religious belief for our citizens, we punish those imperialist elements and traitors who don the cloak of religion, but in effect engage in counter-revolutionary activities. Of course, anyone who expects us to protect the freedom of imperialist elements and traitors who carry out subversive activities against the Chinese people's democratic power is likewise bound to be disappointed. As provided in the Draft Constitution, our state will, as it has done in the past, effectively safeguard freedom of religious belief for the citizens. But safeguarding freedom of religious belief is quite a different matter from safeguarding freedom of counter-revolutionary activities; these two just cannot be mixed up. Nor, similarly, will our constitution and laws ever provide the slightest facility for those elements who engage in counter-revolutionary activities under the cloak of religion. There is nothing difficult to understand in this reasoning.

DOC. 23. *Chou En-lai Speaking to Chinese Christians on the Christian Share in the Revolution (1950)*

So WE ARE going to go on letting you teach, trying to convert the people. . . . After all we both believe that truth will prevail; we think your beliefs untrue and false, therefore if we are right, the people will reject them, and your church will decay. If you are right, then the people will believe you, but as we are sure that you are wrong, we are prepared for that risk. . . .

DOC. 24. *Regulations Governing All Organizations Subsidized with Foreign Funds: Edict of the Sixty-fifth Session of the State Administrative Council, Chou En-lai, Chairman, Peking (December 29, 1950)*

1. IN ORDER TO CONTROL effectively the funds from foreign sources sent into China for the support of Cultural, Educational, Relief, and Religious work, the following regulations are promulgated.

2. The regulations are for those who receive foreign funds for the support of Cultural, Educational, Relief, and Religious work, and especially for the Chinese groups which receive these funds whether they be as gifts or as fixed budgets, and regardless of whether they are given by private sources or social groups, or whether they be for partial support or for full support. The groups are as follows:

a. Universities, Colleges, High Schools, Primary Schools, Kindergartens, Blind and Deaf and Dumb Schools and others.

b. Hospitals, Sanatoriums, Leprosariums, Ambulance Corps, and other medical units.

c. Religious Bodies and their affiliated organizations.

d. Orphanages, Old People's Homes, Children's Homes, and other social services.

e. Printing Houses, Publishing Societies, and Book Stores.

f. Libraries and Broadcasting Stations.

g. Cultural Groups and Study Organizations.

3. In regard to the above-mentioned organizations and their work, they must follow the regulations promulgated by the Government, each according to the various type of work. Each must register under their respective bureau, as for example schools under the Educational Bureau, and medical, social service, and industrial work under their respective bureaus. Besides this they must be registered with a Special Committee of the Local, City, and Provincial People's Government. In making this registration the important thing in each type of work is: the organization's name and location; the name of the responsible leader, his age, his nationality, his history, his capital, as well as his subsidies with their amount and their source; the nature of work and conditions for use of funds, as well as a detailed concrete plan.

4. In order to facilitate the registration of the groups mentioned above, a Special Registration Office shall be set up under the Municipal or Provincial People's Government to give special attention to all receiving and handling funds and foreign grants for Cultural, Educational, Relief and Religious work.

5. Each group specified under Paragraph Two must be obedient to the rules of the Common Program, and to all the laws of

the Government, and must not do anything that is in opposition to the people. They must observe the following:

a. Every six months they must submit in writing to the Special Committee of the respective Municipal and provincial People's Government a report of the subsidies and funds received for the support of Cultural, Educational, Relief, and Religious work, as well as a statement of the manner in which the funds are used.

b. If funds intended for one place or one type of work are remitted or used for work in some other place, or whenever funds arrive from a foreign land, such matters must be reported in advance to the Local, Municipal, and Provincial Committee which is authorized to handle gifts and grants for Cultural, Education, Relief, and Religious work.

6. Whoever violates the above regulations or secretly does not notify the proper authorities, or makes a false report, and is later discovered by the authorities, shall be punished. If the offense is regarded as grave, the taking over, reorganization, or forced closure shall be effected upon the ratification of the upper-level People's Government.

7. If after three months following the promulgation of these regulations it is found that the above-mentioned organizations or groups have not registered, they shall be subject to investigation by the local authorities and liable to penalty by the local People's Government.

8. All Cultural, Educational, Relief, and Religious Organizations registered according to the stipulations of the present regulations, who have truly severed all connections with foreign countries and shall have reported that to the Special Committee of the Local, Municipal, or Provincial Committee, shall be released from the regulations governing the special registration.

9. Measures for the enforcement of the present regulations shall be formulated separately by the Committee on Cultural and Educational Affairs of the State Administrative Council.

10. The Regulations shall be enforced upon promulgation by the Premier's Administrative Council of the Central People's Government.

DOC. 25. *Regulations of the Administrative Affairs Yuan on the Method of Controlling Christian Organizations That Have Received Financial Help From America, Issued by Chou En-lai to a Conference of 151 Protestant Leaders in Peking (April 16–21, 1951)*

THIS YUAN IN ITS sixty-fifth meeting on December 29, 1950, issued a ruling on churches and other institutions receiving aid from America, and authorized Vice-premier Kuo Mo-jo to make a statement that all religious institutions should be self-supporting and that the government would assist them in this movement. The following regulations are now issued regarding institutions which have received American help:

1. Chinese Christian churches and other organizations should immediately sever all relations with American Mission Boards, and with Mission Boards which receive a major part of their funds from America. Such Mission Boards shall immediately cease all activities in China.

2. Americans who are now working in Chinese Christian churches and other organizations shall be treated according to the following rules:

(1) Those who by word or deed work against the People's Government shall be dismissed from their work, and given appropriate punishment by the Government.

(2) Those desiring to leave the country may do so.

(3) Those who are not reactionary and whom the church or other organizations wish to employ and support may continue their work, but may not hold any administrative position.

3. Self-supporting churches and organizations which have been carrying on service projects, such as medical and benevolent organizations, may, if their finances are sufficient, continue these activities. But a Board of Managars must be organized, which will be responsible for ensuring that government regulations are obeyed. A list of the members of such a Board shall be

submitted to the government for approval. If their finances are not sufficient, they may petition the government either to make them a grant or to take over the institution. But colleges, middle schools and primary schools established by churches (not including schools of religion) shall be separate from churches. In principle the property used by such schools should belong to them, but if in any cases property is used jointly by schools and churches, the local government shall make an equitable division according to the merits of the case.

4. Foreign mission boards which desire to turn over their property in China (not including land) to Chinese Christian churches and organizations may do so, with Government approval, and such churches and organizations may receive all or a part of such property. But these gifts must be entirely unconditional.

5. Self-supporting churches and Young Men's and Young Women's Christian Associations may have taxes remitted on their churches and offices directly used for their work.

6. Buildings offered for rent by Chinese Christian churches and organizations shall be rented in accordance with Government regulations and an appropriate tax paid. If any buildings are used by the Government, a lease may, if demanded, be worked out on the basis of the local situation and the needs of the church.

7. Any church which is self-governing, self-supporting, and self-propagating, may make application to the government for permission to bring into the country any balances which they had on deposit abroad on and before December 29, 1950. The application must show the source and intended use of such funds. If there is any concealment, misstatement, or other attempted fraud in the application, the persons concerned must bear the legal responsibility.

8. Every church and organization which has received financial help from abroad shall, in accordance with the "Regulations for Registering all Cultural, Educational, Benevolent, and Religious Bodies Which Receive Foreign Subsidies," make the proper registration, without delay or neglect for any reason; if such organization has already become self-supporting, a conceling note may be added to the registration.

DOC. 26. *Lu Ting-yi, Chairman of the Administrative Yuan's Committee on Culture and Education: Speech to 151 Protestant Leaders Meeting in Peking (April, 1951)*

TODAY THE CURTAIN goes up on the Conference Dealing with Christian Groups Receiving Subsidies from America called by the Religious Affairs Office of the Committee on Culture and Education of the Administrative Yuan of the Central People's Government. The purpose of this conference is to deal with Christian groups receiving subsidies from America in accord with the decisions of the Administrative Yuan December 29th last year to encourage the movement within Christianity for self-government, self-support, and self-propagation, so as to transform them into groups completely run by Chinese Christians. . . .

[This Conference, he says, is necessary because the American imperialist manipulation of subsidies has created difficulties for the Chinese clergy.]

You all know that following the publishing of the December 29th decisions of the Administrative Yuan of the Central People's Government, the many conferences already called by the Central People's Government and local People's Governments to deal with cultural, educational and relief agencies receiving subsidies from America have all achieved fine results. The method adopted by the Government has been, when dealing with this question, to call together all related parties, state policy, discuss it together, and then carry it out. This time in relation to Christian bodies receiving subsidies from America, the Religious Affairs Office has already made a draft copy of methods for dealing with them, has invited representatives of religious bodies all over China to meet and discuss it together, and then wil request the Administrative Yuan to approve and carry it out.

The address today will be divided into three parts: first, about patriotism; second, the conspiracy of American imperialism of using Christianity to carry on aggression against the whole world and against the new China; third, what is expected of Christians.

1. On Patriotism

To DEAL WITH CHRISTIAN groups receiving subsidies from America is definitely not a technical question; it is a struggle. The goal of the struggle is to wipe out the influences of the past more than a hundred years of imperialistic cultural aggression towards our country. In this struggle it is necessary for patriotic Christians from the various religious groups to unite with the government in a common effort under the supervision of the People's Government led by the Chinese Communist Party. In order to achieve this unity a common political foundation is imperative. American imperialist elements within the church are continuously saying to Chinese Christians that it is impossible for the Communist Party to have such a common foundation with Christians because Communist Party members are materialists and Christians are idealists. True, the world view of the Communist is materialistic while the world view of the Christian is idealistic; these two world views are contradictory. Communists hold to dialectical materialism which is the world view of the Marxist-Leninist Party, and dialectical materialism and historical materialism form the theoretical basis of communism. We also hold that members of the Chinese Communist Party and patriotic Chinese religionists, including Christians, have a basis for unity in the political realm, namely the magnificent Common Program adopted by the People's Political Consultative Conference. This Program was approved by the common vote of representatives of the Communist Party, representatives from religious circles and representatives from all other walks of life. On that basis we can unite and deal effectively with religious groups receiving subsidy from America and wipe out the influences of American imperialism's cultural aggression.

Now let me read to you the several articles from the Common Program which have a relationship to this meeting:

The Preface of the Common Program: "The Chinese People's Political Consultative Conference unanimously agrees upon New Democracy and People's Democracy as the political foundation on which the People's Republic of China shall be built and further sets forth the following Common Program which shall be commonly observed by all parties participating in the People's Political Consultative Conference, the People's Governments at all levels, and all of the people of China."

Article 5: "The people of the People's Republic of China have freedom of thought, expression, publication, assembly, forming organizations, communication, person, habitation and moving, religious belief and public demonstration." The freedom of religious belief spoken of here means that the Government cannot interfere with anyone who belongs to the people of the new China, no matter whether he accepts or opposes religion, no matter what religion he believes in.

Article 8: "The people of the People's Republic of China all have the duty of protecting the fatherland, obeying laws, respecting labor discipline, respecting public property, accepting public duty and military duty and paying taxes." That is to say, both Christians and non-Christians have the above-mentioned duties, primarily the duty of protecting the fatherland. It is not permitted to be unpatriotic because of belief or non-belief in religion.

Article 42: "To promote love of country, love for the people, love for labor, love for science, love for public property is the public morality of the entire body politic of the People's Republic of China." Responsibility for promoting this public morality rests on believers and non-believers alike.

Article 7: "The People's Republic of China must suppress all counter-revolutionary activities, severely punish all Nationalist counter-revolutionary war criminals who are in league with imperialism, traitors to the fatherland, oppose the People's Democracy and other obdurate and irreclaimable leading counter-revolutionary elements. As for ordinary reactionary elements, feudalistic landlords and bureaucratic capitalists, after disarming them and destroying their special power, their political privileges must also be taken away in accord with law for a period of time, and they themselves must become new persons through physical labor. If they continue to carry on counter-revolutionary activities they must be restrained with severity." Both believers and non-believers have equal responsibility for assisting the government in suppressing counter-revolution.

Article 54: "The principles of foreign policy of the People's Republic of China are the preservation of the independence, freedom, and complete territorial integrity of this nation, the support of international lasting peace and friendly cooperation between the peoples of all nations, and opposition to the aggressive and war policies of imperialism."

Article 41: "The culture and education of the People's Republic of China shall be a new democratic, nationalistic, and scientific culture, and the education of the masses. The main duties of the cultural and educational work of the People's Government should be to raise the cultural level of the people, to develop personnel for national reconstruction, to wipe out feudalistic, compradore, fascist thinking and extend 'serve-the-people' thinking."

Gentlemen, we can see from the Common Program that, beyond the question of world view and religious faith, in which the Government cannot by administrative order interfere, there are many other matters concerning which we have a common responsibility for united effort. To say that between us there is no common basis for unity and cooperation is only the rumor-mongering of imperialists.

Our world views are different but we are all Chinese, we all love the fatherland, we all want to oppose imperialism and the reactionary party, we all want to struggle for the independence, democracy, peace, unity and prosperity of China.

Every Chinese ought to love the fatherland; Chinese Christians are also duty bound to be patriotic. We love the fatherland not only because we ourselves were born and reared in China, our ancestors were in China and our sons and grandsons will live in China, but still more because the China of today is already the China of the people themselves; there is a qualitative difference between today's China and the China of the past, and therefore it has become more lovable than in any previous period. . . .

III. What is Expected of Christians

WE EXPECT Chinese Christians to march under the flag of opposition to imperialism and love of the fatherland, and under the direction of the People's Government to join up with the People's Government to work together to build the new China on the foundations of the great Common Program.

1. At present in the process of being carried out on a nation-wide scale are three large movements: The Oppose-America-Assist-Korea Movement, agrarian reform, and suppression of counter-revolution. It is expected that Chinese Christians actively approve of and participate in these three movements. The goal of Oppose-America Assist-Korea is to enable our country to have an international environment for peaceful reconstruction, because if our nation finds itself under the threat of armed attack by imperialism there is no possibility of carrying on peaceful reconstruction. At the same time Oppose-America Assist-Korea is also to win world peace, to oppose the policy of war and aggression of American imperialism. In order to gain victory in the Oppose-America-Assist-Korea Movement, in addition to the brave front-line fighting of the Chinese Volunteer Armies and the Korean People's Army, there is much work to be done in the rear. One of the tasks is to carry Oppose-America-Assist-Korea propaganda to each place and to every person, and amongst church members to be especially careful to wipe out the "fear America, worship America, fawn on America" thinking, and learn to hate, despise, and vilify American imperialism.

The aim of agrarian reform is to destroy the feudalistic land ownership system, to raise production enthusiasm of the peasants who constitute 80% of the population of China, to develop farm production and improve the livelihood of the peasants; only by so doing can the industries of China expand favorably. Suppression of counter-revolution, the cleaning out of such injurious pests as special agents, bandits, local tyrants, and unrepentant counter-revolutionists is a pressing obligation of consolidating national defense, protecting production, and stabilizing the social order. Christians have a responsibility to assist the government in exposing these counter-revolutionary elements, especially such as wear the cloak of religion, like Ku Jen-en.

2. The [Christian] Manifesto, "The Direction of Endeavor for Chinese Christianity in the Construction of New China,"

(see Doc. 51) has already been signed by 180,000 persons; this is good. It is imperative to extend the name-signing movement amongst Christians. But more important is to fulfill in practice, not only in word, the self-government, self-support and self-propagation of Christian bodies.[1] First of all church bodies receiving subsidies from America must immediately undertake this duty. The People's Government will certainly encourage and help you to do it. The present draft copy of "Method for Dealing with Christian Bodies Receiving Subsidies from America," made by the Religious Affairs Bureau of the Culture and Education Commission of the Administrative Yuan, is precisely for this purpose.

Patriotic Christians, more intimately join up with the People's Government and work together to make our fatherland stronger and more prosperous!

DOC. 27. *Chou En-lai: Report on the Work of the Government at the First Session of the Third National People's Congress (December 21, 1964)*

WE SHALL CONTINUE to pursue the policy of freedom of religious belief correctly and to uphold the integrity of state power and the separation of religion from the state. We must prohibit all illegal activities. We hope that people in religious circles will continue to take a patriotic stand against imperialism, persist in the principle of the independence and self-administration of their churches, abide by government laws and decrees, intensify their own remolding and actively take part in the socialist construction of our motherland.

1. The Three-Self Movement, which brought all Protestant churches under the administrative "umbrella" of the Religious Affairs Bureau of the central government, was formally organized by 151 Protestant leaders meeting in Peking in the spring of 1951. The "three autonomies" were self-support, self-government, and self-propagation.

Section 3. Chinese Theoreticians Debate
Religious Policy, Theory, and Tactics

WHILE NUMEROUS ARTICLES on Chinese religious theory and religious practice appeared throughout the period from 1949 to 1966, the most important and illuminating articles were a series, of which we have seen eleven articles, which appeared between the years of 1963 and 1965 in such prominent journals and newspapers as *People's Daily* (*Jen Min Jih Pao*), *Red Flag* (*Hung Ch'i*), and *New Construction* (*Hsin Chien She*). In these eleven articles, Party intellectuals debated such topics as the distinctions between religion and superstition and the limits of a policy of freedom of religious belief, as well as the proper tactics for promoting the death of religion within the limits of such a policy. The writers of these articles, who drew heavily on classical Marxist sources and who seldom departed from the standard, dogmatic views of the origins, development, and decline of religion, center their debate on the tactics to be used with religious believers during the period of transition to full Communism.

Their differences of opinion on the definition of religion, and the distinctions between religion and superstitious practice, are important for the Party's determination of tactics to be used in dealing with religious believers under the constitutional guarantee of freedom of religious belief. Ya Han-chang sees no value to the state or the people in protecting superstitious practices. But he writes that legitimate religion can continue to exist if it is free from counter-revolutionary and imperialist influences. "After the nationwide liberation, the condition of religions serving as a tool for the ruling class in ruling the people, and for imperialism in aggression against our country has basically changed." For Ya, religious practice can and should be tolerated during the transition period.

His opponents make no fine distinctions between religion, the theist idea, and feudal superstition. With regard to the solution of the religion problem (namely, how to deal with religious believers in ways which will serve national construction without impeding the decay and death of religion) these three are all ideological deviations to be dealt with as sociopolitical problems. While these writers also support the Party's policy of freedom of religious belief, they define sharp limits, and stress the tactics to be used in hastening the end of religion. Peaceful coexistence with religion, except for purposes of a temporary united front, is unacceptable. They charge Ya with prettifying and defending religion, a charge which would surely place him with the revisionists as the internal stresses of the impending Cultural Revolution ended this public debate in late 1965.

The nature of these debates, and the prominence given them in leading publications, raises important questions. Why did the debate take place at this particular time, a period of rectification among intellectuals following the "second Hundred Flowers" period in 1962? Paradoxically, it was also a time when Confucian scholars could meet and discuss the contributions of China's greatest sage, as they did at the Forum of Confucian Scholars in 1962, and when there were, for a brief time, other indications of a freer intellectual climate.

But, as we know now, this was also a time of increasing political emphasis in the armed forces, and of behind-the-scenes Party struggle between the "two lines," a struggle that was to break into the open in 1966. Ya Han-chang represents the moderate line later to be identified with Liu Shao-ch'i and Teng Hsiao-p'ing. His intellectual opponents represent a more militant line, less subtle, less "reasonable" toward religious believers. By the time of the final published essay in this debate, several writers were lined up against Ya. In December, 1965, Liang Hao and Yang Chen charged that he "sometimes goes so far as to plead directly for religion." While Ya's own atheistic position is specifically set forth in several places, the charge might well be inferred from his own writing. Surely he had friends in high places, supporting his right to express these views. But the political polarization of the Cultural Revolution silenced the voices of both Ya Han-chang and his friends; as in the Maoist view of the Soviet Union, it was revisionist error to assume that socialist revolution brought an end to class struggle and class differentiation. Ya's view that the revolution had ended the conditions whereby religion served the imperialists and the ruling class was unacceptable.

DOC. 28. *Ya Han-chang: On the Question of Religious Superstition*

IN A LENGTHY ARTICLE in Peking's leading newspaper, *People's Daily*, Ya Han-chang gives a condensed analysis, based on Marx and Engels, of the genesis and growth of "spontaneous religions" and "artificial religions," pointing out that the first type arises in response to natural phenomena, while the second is the product of class society, in which the exploiting classes manipulate the masses with deceptive religious explanations of oppressive social phenomena. He traces the evolution of both types of religion in Chinese history, giving a descriptive account of traditional "superstitious" activities and noting the distinction between religion and superstition. The trades depending on superstition, according to Ya, do not qualify for protection under the policy of freedom of religious belief, for they are not genuine religion and their practitioners swindle money from the people and become tools for reactionary forces. They make no contribution to socialist construction and must be eliminated forthwith.

The struggle against authentic religion, on the other hand, is an ideological struggle and only "pure ideological weapons" may be used. Such weapons are positive education in atheism, mobilization for study of Marxist teachings, and propaganda efforts to raise the consciousness of the masses. It is not permissible to use coercive means, and it is necessary to take care "not to hurt the feelings of believers." In tactics, the principle of voluntarism must be followed.

However, when religion is used by imperialism or feudal reactionary forces for carrying out counter-revolutionary activities then the method of dictatorship must be employed. In conclusion, it is necessary to enforce the Party's policy of freedom of worship: "We must absolutely not interfere with others' worship or tamper with proper religious activities. . . ."

I. Religion and superstition have their similarities. They also have their differences. All religious activities are superstitious activities. This is their similarity. But not all superstitious activities are religious activities. This is their difference. Among the people of our country, especially people of the Han nationality [of pure Chinese ethnic background] such superstitious activities as fortune telling, physiognomy, and geomancy were quite prevalent in the past. While these, of course, are superstitions, they are not religious, being neither the activities of any religion nor any religions in themselves. Among the people of the Han nationality in our country, those who really believe in any religion and are the followers of any religion are numerically in the minority. But, among the peasants especially, those who believe in the existence of spirits and gods, in fate, and in such superstitions as fortune telling, physiognomy, and geomancy are still quite numerous. In view of this, we must be good not only at struggling against religious superstitions but also at struggling against all other kinds of ordinary superstitious activities.

For the extensive development of the superstitious activities mentioned above, there is, apart from the most basic reason that the reactionary ruling class advocated and fostered them, another very important reason, which is that in the old society a great number of people lived by swindling money and goods from the laboring people with these superstitious activities and formed specialized occupations of them. They included, for instance, physiognomists, geomancers, fortune tellers, priestesses, godly men, and priests. Apart from serving the interests of the exploiting class, these themselves constituted a part of the exploiting classes. After the nationwide liberation, educated and transformed by the Party and the People's Government, some of these people have really changed their occupations and trades and become part of the laboring people. But there are also many who have not yet been thoroughly transformed. When an opportunity presents itself, they will overtly or covertly resume their old trades and take advantage of the remnant superstitious thoughts of the masses of the people, mainly the peasants, in continuing their activities of swindling the masses of their money and goods and continuing to exploit the people. What deserves attention is that these people engaging in superstitious trades, who have not been successfully transformed, are often liable to be utilized by counter-revolutionaries and feudal forces and become their tools in carrying out reactionary activities in the rural areas. They will then do even greater harm.

Among the people of our country, especially the peasants, theist ideas are still quite widespread. To varying extents, they still believe that after a man has died, he becomes a ghost. So the thought that ghosts are terrible is still comparatively widespread. Because of this thought, when a man has died, they will burn imitation money, paper clothes, paper horses, paper houses, etc. for him so that his soul may use them in another world—the under world. On the Chinese New Year's Day and on festive occasions, as well as on death anniversaries, they still go to cemeteries to offer sacrifices. Some, when they fall sick, will "send off the ghosts," or go to a temple to "make vows." And so forth. These superstitious activities are spontaneous and as a rule have no direct connection with those engaging in superstitious trades. We must strictly distinguish between the people's theist ideas and spontaneous superstitious activities and the activities of those engaging in superstitious trades who swindle money and goods from the people through superstition. . . .

III. The struggle against religious superstitions is a struggle between atheism and theism. By nature, it is an ideological struggle. So we must employ the methods of ideological struggle. In the article *Socialism and Religion*, Lenin said, "Our

Party is an alliance of conscious, advanced warriors striving for the liberation of the working class. Such an alliance cannot and should not be indifferent to such an expression of unconsciousness, ignorance, and stupidity as religion. We demand the complete separation of the Church from the State and the use of pure ideological weapons and only ideological weapons, the use of our press and our discourses, for struggling against the mist of religion." Here, Lenin made it clear that in struggling against religion, only "the use of pure ideological weapons and ideological weapons alone, the use of our press and our discourses" was permissible. This is extremely important. Since the struggle against religious superstitions is a kind of ideological struggle, it should be waged only by the methods of ideological struggle. It is impermissible to wage the struggle by means of administrative orders or by other coercive means.

How should "pure ideological weapons" be used in struggles against religious superstitions? It is necessary, under the correct leadership of the Party, to conduct long-term, systematic, positive education in atheism among the broad masses of the people —especially the peasants. To do this work well, it is necessary to mobilize more comrades to study the atheist teachings of Marxism, have more articles and pamphlets written for conducting propaganda on atheism, and, where possible, make speeches and reports to the masses in conducting similar propaganda so as to raise their degree of consciousness gradually and release them gradually from the fetters of theist ideas and religious superstitions.

Both in writing articles and making reports in struggles against religious superstitions, it is necessary to take care not to hurt the feelings of the "believers." This was pointed out by Lenin in *The Draft Party Program of the Russian Communist Party (Bolsheviks)*. He said, "The Party tries to destroy completely the relations between the exploiting classes and the religious propaganda organizations and at the same time to liberate the laboring masses actually from religious prejudices, and, for this purpose, it organizes the most extensive scientific education and anti-religious propaganda work. It is necessary, at the same time, to take care to avoid hurting the feelings of the believers, for hurting their feelings will only consolidate their blind belief in the religions." Conducting education in atheism means struggling against people having theist ideas and religious superstitions. Ideologically speaking, this struggle is one between two antagonistic thoughts which are as irreconcilable as fire and water. However, from the point of view of the concrete persons, our objects are the board masses of the people, mainly the peasants. Our purpose in conducting education in atheism is to persuade them to give up their theism and religious superstitions and gradually become atheists. So we must take the attitude of "honest advice and proper guidance." If we hurt their feelings, they will then not listen to us however sound our reasoning may be. To avoid hurting the feelings of others, we must adhere to the principle of voluntariness. It is is up to a man himself to choose between giving up and not giving up his theist ideas and religious superstitions and between accepting and not accepting the atheist thought. Nobody else may apply pressure to force him. Comrade Mao Tse-tung pointed out clearly in *On Correct Handling of Contradictions among the People*, "We may not use administrative orders in eliminating religion or force people not to believe in religion. We may not force people to give up idealism or force them to believe in Marxism. All problems of an ideological nature, all controversial problems within the ranks of the people, can be solved only by democratic means and by means of discussion, criticism, and persuasive education. No attempt may be made to solve them by means of coercion and suppression."

As for the utilization of religious superstitions by imperialism in carrying out counter-revolutionary activities, by feudal forces in carrying out activities for a comeback, and by superstitious professionals in swindling money and goods from the people and exploiting the people, these are not problems of thought and understanding or problems of worship, but problems of class struggle and problems of contradictions between the enemy and us. In respect of the reactionary activities carried out by imperialism and feudal forces by making use of religious superstitions, the method of dictatorship must be employed. They should be hit forcefully on the basis of conclusive, true evidence. In *Report on the Draft Constitution of the People's Republic of China*, Comrade Liu Shao-ch'i said, "Safeguarding the freedom of worship and safeguarding the freedom of counter-revolutionary activity are two things which absolutely must not be confused with each other. Our Constitution and all our laws, similarly, will never give any facility to those elements who carry out counter-revolutionary activities while wearing the cloak of religion."

The utilization of superstitious activities by superstitious professionals in swindling money and goods from the people and exploiting the laboring people should also be prohibited strictly. In the socialist country, no phenomenon of exploitation of man by his fellow in any form can last for a long time, because it is not permitted by the socialist system.

In struggles against religious superstitions, in conducting education in atheism among the broad masses of the people as well as in struggling against the reactionary activities carried out by counter-revolutionaries and exploiters by making use of religious superstitions, it is necessary to enforce the Party's policy of freedom of worship and impermissible to set the struggle against religious superstitions and the policy of freedom of worship against each other. In other words, in conducting propaganda on atheism or opposing religious superstitions, we must absolutely not interfere with others' worship or tamper with the proper religious activities of the believers. On the other hand, the believers and theists, for their part, must not interfere with our conducting education in atheism or our opposing religious superstitions. Only this is the correct attitude.

DOC. 29. *Ya Han-chang: On the Difference Between the Theist Idea, Religion, and Feudal Superstition (A Reply to Comrades Yu Hsiang and Liu Chun-wang)*

IN THIS ESSAY Ya replies to two writers, Yu Hsiang and Liu Chun-wang, criticizing them for their failure to note the differences between the theist idea, religion and feudal superstition, and denouncing them for espousing the "bourgeois theory of religion" which he finds inapplicable to the Chinese situation past or present. In contrast to European "Christendom," the religious situation in China is too complex for such a simple theory. Among those who hold theist beliefs there are those who believe in religion and those who believe in ghosts, spirits and other superstitions. These latter, which he calls "feudal superstitions," are not religion; because of their socially nonproductive and exploitative nature "all these activities must be repressed" and their practitioners made to reform and "earn an honest living."

Religion, by which Ya means the developed religions with organized activities and doctrine, is quite different and cannot be so suppressed. While he does not deal with tactics in this essay, in later writing he clearly advocates a "democratic" policy toward religious believers. For now (he writes here), "This situation imposes on us a task, and that is that a struggle must be waged in the study of theories of religion to eliminate all influence of the bourgeois 'theory' of religion." That will require the combined efforts of all theoreticians "including Comrades Yu Hsiang and Liu Chung-wang"!

I. Recapitulation of views of Yu and Liu

WITH REGARD to the similarity and difference between the theist idea, religion, and feudal superstition, the author has already made a more or less detailed exposition in his essays "The Origin of the Theist Idea" and "On the Question of the Extinction of the Theist Idea" as well as "On the Question of Religious Superstition," and there should have been no necessity of further discourse on the subject. In the September, 1963, issue of *Hsin*

Chien-She, however, Comrade Yu Hsiang and Liu Chun-wang wrote an essay entitled "Several Questions of the Marxist-Leninist View on Religion," in which they put forward a new and different view for my consideration. As a result, I feel duty bound to write this article in reply to the questions raised by the two comrades.

Comrades Yu Hsiang and Liu Chun-wang also maintain in their essay that "Speaking from scientific definition, religion and superstition (meaning in this article feudal superstition—author) are the same concept with completely the same intention and extension. Both of them mean people's belief in supernatural, mystic forces, and are a reflection of the illusion of the objective world in the mind of man." And "in analyzing the relationship between religion and superstition, the first thing that should be pointed out is that they are the *same thing*." They also say: "The exact way of putting it is that 'not all superstition is systematized religion.'" (They [Yu Hsiang and Liu Chun-wang] hold that religion can also be divided into "systematized religion" and "primitive religion.") Accordingly, they hold that feudal superstition and religion are also the "same thing," that they are both "religion," and that the only difference is that some of them are "systematized religion" and some "primitive religion." They do not agree with the view that there are both similarity and difference between the theist idea, religion, and feudal superstition.

According to the view of Comrade Yu Hsiang and Liu Chun-wang, the fact that some children believe that there are ghosts and are afraid of them also constitutes "religion." The fact that peasants in the countryside burn joss paper when someone dies, ask an expert of geomancy to choose sites [for graves], get a sorceress to seize evil spirits when someone falls ill, and believe in such things as physiognomy, fortune-telling, divination by the lot, the casting of horoscopes, etc. also constitutes a religion. According to this view, there is no such thing as the theist idea or feudal superstition in the world, but only "religion" (or the religious idea). Comrades Yu Hsiang and Liu Chun-wang go further by declaring their above-mentioned view "the Marxist-Leninist view on religion," meaning that any other view which does not agree with theirs is a non-Marxist-Leninist view of religion. Is the view of these two comrades really "the Marxist-Leninist view of religion"? I think it will do some good to clear up the question.

II. *Superstition is not religion*

THEISTS SHOULD INCLUDE believers in religion, because there is no one among religious believers who is not at the same time a theist. However, not all theists believe in religion. Among our people, especially among the Han people, there are many who still believe in spirits and fate but who do not believe in any religion. Even some children and primary school pupils believe in spirits, are afraid of ghosts, and dare not sleep alone at night. These people may be called theists (or we may say that varying degrees of the theist idea exists in their mind), but may not be called religious believers.

There are still many among the broad masses of our people, especially among the Han people, who do not believe in any religion, but who have varying degrees of such superstitious beliefs as casting of horoscopes, fortune-telling, physiognomy, geomancy, the curing of illnesses through exorcising of evil spirits by sorceresses, mystic practices of secret societies, etc. Such people are still very numerous in rural villages. These people can only be called theists or people with varying degrees of feudal superstition, but cannot be called religious believers.

If all those who merely believe in and are afraid of ghosts, as well as those who merely hold such feudal superstitious beliefs as fortune-telling, physiognomy, casting of horoscopes, geomancy, etc., are described as believers in "religion," then probably quite a large number of our population of 650 million still believe in such "religion." What sort of "religion" do these people believe in? Are those who believe that there are ghosts and are afraid of them believers in the "religion of ghosts" or the "religion of ghost-phobia"? Are those who hold such feudal superstitious beliefs as fortune-telling, casting of horoscopes, physiognomy, geomancy, etc. believers in the "religion of fortune-telling," "religion of horoscopes," "religion of physiognomy," and "religion of geomancy"? If not, then what after all is their religion? [These questions are asked] because all religions are concrete and none of them is abstract. As Comrades Yu Hsiang and Liu Chun-wang say in their essay: "There are various kinds of religion in the world. According to different bases and from different angles, religion may be divided into polytheist and monotheist, primitive and systematized, foreign (or exotic) and native (or indigenous), etc." May I ask: Do those who believe that there are ghosts and are afraid of them, and those who hold such feudal superstitious beliefs as fortune-telling, the casting of horoscopes, physiognomy, geomancy, etc. belong to a "polytheist" or "monotheist" religion, to a "primitive" or "systematized" religion, to a "foreign" or "native" religion? Comrades Yu Hsiang and Liu Chun-wang have not answered these questions in their essay.

It may thus be seen that the contention that the theist idea and religion are the "same thing," that religion and feudal superstition are the "same thing," and that both the theist idea and feudal superstition are "religion," will not hold water in the practical life of the broad masses of our people.

III. Theism, superstition, and religion compared

My UNDERSTANDING IS that the theist idea, religion, and feudal superstition have their similarities as well as their differences.

Generally speaking, the theist idea, religion, and feudal superstitions are all idealist, unscientific things. That is their common character. Therefore, essentially speaking, the theist idea, religion, and feudal superstitions are similar, all being superstition. However, the theist idea, religion, and feudal superstitions also have their different characteristics and different meanings. That is their difference. Therefore, we cannot deny their difference just because they are essentially similar. We cannot regard them as the "same thing." Nor can we consider them all to be "religion."

Specifically speaking, the theist idea means the ideas in people's minds that believes in souls, spirits and gods, and God. Because they are only ideas, they are called the theist idea. The essence of the theist idea is the belief that all things in this world are created, arranged, and determined by supernatural spirits and gods (including God, the Creator, Providence). Whether one is "wealthy and noble or poor and humble," "long-living or short-lived, unlucky or lucky," is also arranged and determined by the spirits and gods. Everything is preordained.

Religion not only believes in souls, spirits and gods, and God, but has its organizations, groups, and activities. For instance, different religions believe in different gods and have different doctrines, different names, different organizations, groups and leaders, and different religious activities. Some religions require their novices to go through certain initiation rites, make their followers responsible for payment of certain sums of money, mete out punishment to those who have violated their own rules, etc. Of course, "spontaneous religions" and "man-made religions" are not entirely the same, and one religion is different from another, but the basic things are the same.

Since the theist idea and religion are not the "same thing," it follows that theists and religious believers are not entirely the "same thing." Generally speaking, all religious believers are theists, but not all theists are religious believers.

Religion and feudal superstitions are still less the "same thing."

Generally speaking, both religion and feudal superstition presuppose the existence of souls, spirits and gods, God (or Providence). That is their similarity. But religion and feudal superstition also have their different characteristics and different meanings. That is their difference.

Religion may roughly be divided into two kinds, "spontaneous religion" and "man-made religion." (This division was made by Engels. In bourgeois "theories" of religion, it is generally divided into "polytheist religion" and "monotheist religion." Such a division reflects some reality of religion, but is quite unscientific. In some religions, such as Taoism in our country, there is one God (the Jade Emperor) and at the same time many minor gods. It is difficult to say whether they are "polytheist" or "monotheist.") "Spontaneous religion" is early religion. Such religion has, generally speaking, no written tenets and no close-knit religious organization, and novices are not required to go through any religious rites at first. "Man-made religion," on the other hand, is the religion of class society. Generally speaking, it has written tenets, close-knit religious organization, and special initiation rites for novices.

Feudal superstition is different from religion. Feudal superstition is varied (meaning principally superstition in regions inhabited by the Han people). For instance, such practices as ancestral worship, asking for the guidance of gods, curing disease by exorcising evil spirits, choosing of auspicious times for certain acts, fortune-telling, physiognomy, geomancy, choosing good sites for buildings, the worship of minor gods at their temples (such as temples of the mountain god, temples of the god of earth, temples of the dragon king, etc.), and the activities of reactionary secret societies all belong to the category of feudal superstition. As these superstitious activities were generally formed in the edge of feudal society in our country, were exploited by the feudal ruling classes, and served the interests of the feudal ruling classes, we call them feudal superstitions, to distinguish them from the theist idea and religion. Broadly speaking, both the theist idea and religion are superstitions.

Feudal superstitions, though having their organizations, groups, and activities, have no religious doctrine and do not have the characteristics of religion. Feudal superstition is not religion. It is not "spontaneous religion" or "man-made religion."

Before the liberation of the whole country, we had a number of professionals of feudal superstition in our country (including sorceresses, sorcerers, professors of geomancy, fortune-tellers, etc.) who carried out their own activities by making use of feudal superstitions. They not only poisoned the mind of the laboring people and swindled them of their money and goods, but also regularly caused loss of life to the laboring people. In particular, sorceresses and sorcerers, professing the healing of the sick by exorcising evil spirits, often ill-used the sick in all conceivable ways, so that sick people who might have got well of their own accord were often killed by their healers.

IV. Implications for tactics in dealing with religion

AFTER THE ESTABLISHMENT of the People's Republic of China, all these activities must be repressed. In general, the method of reform through education has been adopted with regard to professional practitioners of feudal superstition. Under mass supervision, they are made to do labor and earn an honest living by their own efforts, so that they may be gradually reformed to become laborers. This policy is completely correct.

We comrades engaged in theoretical studies should make it clear on the basis of theory that feudal superstition is not religion. In their essay, however, Comrades Yu Hsiang and Liu Chun-wang declared that religion and feudal superstition are the "same thing," maintaining that feudal superstition is also "religion" (part of which is systematized religion and part primitive religion). That is wrong. True, Comrades Yu Hsiang and Liu Chun-wang state in their essay that "systematized religion" and "primitive religion" should be "separately and correctly dealt with," but they have not shown in their essay how "systematized religion" and "primitive religion" should be "separately dealt with."

On the basis of the dissertation above, it is very difficult to say that the view advanced by Comrades Yu Hsiang and Liu Chun-wang, who maintain that the theist idea and religion (or religious idea) are the "same thing," that religion and superstition (feudal superstition) are also the "same thing," and that the theist idea and superstition (feudal superstition) are both "religion or the religious idea," is a "Marxist-Leninist view of religion," because no grounds whatever can be found in the classical works of Marxism-Leninism and in relevant documents of our Party and State to substantiate the claim that such a view is a Marxist-Leninist view of religion.

As for the bourgeois "theory" of religion, which regards the theist idea, religion, and superstition (feudal superstition) as one thing and treats them all as "religion," such a viewpoint is obviously wrong. But this bourgeois "theory" of religion still exerts a certain measure of influence on our people, and even within the revolutionary ranks there are still some who are poisoned and harmed by it without knowing it. This situation imposes on us a task, and that is that a struggle must be waged in the study of theories of religion to eliminate all influence of the bourgeois "theory" of religion. That is certainly not a light and easy matter. It will require the combined efforts of all comrades engaged in the study of Marxist theory (including Comrades Yu Hsiang and Liu Chun-wang).

DOC. 30. *Yu Hsiang and Liu Chun-wang: Religion and Class Struggle in the Transition Period*

IN HIS IMPORTANT 1957 position paper, "On the Correct Handling of Contradictions," Mao distinguished "antagonistic" contradictions— that is, those posed by enemies of the people and therefore subject to correction by force—from "non-antagonistic" contradictions *among* the people, which may be resolved only by the "democratic" methods of "discussion, criticism, persuasion and education." Mao alluded to religion only within the context of the latter. In addition, he referred to religion as one of the freedoms guaranteed by the constitution. For Mao, religion was one of a number of contradictions to be resolved by "democratic methods." In this context his remark on methods for dealing with religion has been frequently cited by Chinese writers on religious questions: "We cannot abolish religion by administrative fiat nor oblige people not to believe. . . . Questions of an ideological nature . . . cannot be resolved by coercive and authoritarian methods."

As with the previous essay, important questions arise from a reading of this paper six years after its publication. The writers here state flatly that class struggle, reflected in religion, will continue throughout the period of transition from capitalism to pure communism—a period that Mao himself has said may take generations. During this time, aside from reactionary and other unlawful activities "using the cover of religion," religion will be dealt with as a non-antagonistic contradiction, and religious followers "should be given the freedom to engage in proper religious activities." After sufficient education of the masses the roots of religion will be removed and the masses can "free themselves gradually and consciously from the bonds of religion." Since China was obviously still in the transition period, why was it necessary in 1966 to terminate abruptly the policy Mao himself endorsed? Surely counter-revolutionary elements among religious believers were not, at that late date, numerous enough to offer any threat.

Class struggle in religion, for these writers, involves both a struggle against imperialist and reactionary forces using religion for counter-revolutionary activities (antagonistic contradictions), and a strategy for dealing with non-antagonistic contradictions between the proletariat and the "religious patriotic elements" [religious professionals] within the people's united front. The first requires study and recognition of the history of the use of religion by imperialism and of the "schemes and tricks," such as offers of material and spiritual aid, with which foreign mission boards dress up their "ideological infiltration." The second demands a constant internal vigilance to detect dissatisfaction and ideological backsliding among the religious patriotic elements.

Drawing on the Maoist theory of contradictions, they write: "It is our object to win over and rally all patriotic religious persons. . . . [Therefore] we must adopt the principle of uniting with and at the same time struggling against them, . . . educating them and reforming them." Generally speaking, the writers conclude, the contradictions between the proletariat and the religious circles can be resolved by "discussion, criticism, and persuasive education."

1. Class struggle and religion

THROUGHOUT THE WHOLE PERIOD of transition from capitalism to communism, class, class contradictions, and class struggle will continue to exist. Class struggle in the period of transition will necessarily be reflected in religion.

In the period of transition, with the intensification of the socialist revolution, the development of socialist construction, and the incessant rise of the consciousness and level of knowledge of the popular masses, religion appears to be weakening steadily as a general trend. However, the roots of religion are not yet completely removed in the transitional period and religion will continue to exist. Under the conditions of dictatorship by the proletariat, religion does not change its essential nature. It is still the opiate that drugs the people and a tool in the hands of the exploiting classes in the class struggle during the period of transition. When imperialism and the reactionary classes are carrying out subversive activities designed to restore them to power, and when the bourgeoisie are engaged in class struggle with the proletariat in the political, economic, and ideological fields, they will not forget to make use of religion, the weapon which they have appreciated so much for so long. Of course, under different conditions before and after the seizure of state power by the proletariat, the form of utilization and fostering of religion by the exploiting classes and the degree of such utilization are different. But that does not mean that after seizure of state power by the proletariat, religion will have lost its support from the [exploiting] classes.

On the other hand, having seized state power, the proletariat must carry through revolution to the end, consolidate the proletarian dictatorship, carry out socialist revolution on the economic, political, and ideological fronts, and˙ develop socialist construction. In leading the people in the struggle for revolution and construction, the proletariat and their party will inevitably have to struggle with the effort of the exploiting classes to use religion to maintain their class interests and with their activities aimed to uphold, consolidate, and expand the power and influence of religion, so as to reduce as far as possible the resistance from religion to the cause of socialism.

Seen from the aforementioned two aspects, class struggle during the period of transition will inevitably be reflected in religion. Accordingly, all revolutionary cadres must not be indifferent to or careless or negligent about the class struggle in religion, or even ignore the existence of class struggle in this respect or avoid it. They should study the concrete form and characteristics of class struggle in this respect and its concrete situation in every period, master the laws of class struggle in this respect, lead the people correctly in accordance with the policies of the Party in waging this struggle, and strive to the utmost to direct class struggle in this respect toward a direction favorable to the proletariat.

II. Use of religion by imperialists and reactionary classes

THE USE OF RELIGION by imperialism and the reactionary classes in carrying out reactionary political activities and their contradiction with the popular masses: religion in our country has for a long time been a tool with which imperialism and the reactionary classes upheld their class interests and ruled the popular masses. After the liberation of the whole country, the rule of imperialism, feudal landlords, and bureaucrat compradores was overthrown by the popular masses, but the influence of these three major enemies in religion has not been immediately eliminated. They continue to try vainly to use religion as a tool with which to bring about their restoration to power.

The Catholic and Protestant Churches in our country, long under the direct control of imperialists, are tools with which they used to carry out aggression against our country. In other religions, a small number of reactionary elements also worked hand in glove with the imperialists. In the early days of the liberation of the whole country, imperialist elements still controlled the principal powers of the Catholic and Protestant Churches in our country, doing unlawful and vile acts under the cloak of religion and carrying out all sorts of sabotage activity to subvert the new China. The criminal activities of the imperialist elements aroused great indignation and wrath among the people and patriotic Christians of China. For the sake of severing relations between the Protestant churches in our country and the imperialist missions and shaking off the control exercised by the Vatican on the Catholic Church in China, patriotic Protestants and Catholics launched one after the other the Protestant "three-self" patriotic movement and the Catholic anti-imperialist patriotic movement. With powerful support from the people of the whole country, an important victory was won in this struggle. All imperialist elements under cover of religion are now driven away from China. However, the imperialists, unwilling to admit defeat, are prepared always to come back. They have used all underhanded schemes and tricks, put forward slogans of "material aid" and "spiritual aid," and adopted financial bribery, ideological infiltration, and other methods, in a desperate attempt to nullify the fruits of the anti-imperialist patriotic movement of the Catholic and Protestant Churches in our country, and dreaming of restoring the old, colonial and semi-colonial appearance of the Catholic and Protestant Churches of our country. This is an acute, complex class struggle, a reflection in religion of the struggle between imperialism and the people of our country. So long as imperialism exists, this class struggle will not cease.

There are still concealed in various religions some counter-revolutionary remnants, and there are also some local nationalists in religious clothing and some bourgeois rightists, who hope vainly to use religion for carrying out reactionary political activities aimed to divide the Motherland and oppose the Party, the people, and socialism. There are also some bad elements in various religions who carry out unlawful activities under cover of religion by swindling the masses of their money, endangering the lives of the masses, raping women and girls, and disturbing the peace.

We should also realize that, while utilizing religion for their reactionary political activities, the imperialists and the reactionary classes have not forgotten to weaken the ideological positions of socialism by means of expanding the forces and influence of religion.

To wage a tit-for-tat struggle against imperialist and reactionary forces in religion and to smash their underhanded schemes is an essential condition for the consolidation of the proletarian dictatorship and for the smooth prosecution of socialist revolution and socialist construction.

III. Contradictions between religious adherents and the proletariat

THE CONTRADICTIONS in the political and ideological sphere between the proletariat and the religious patriotic elements within the people's democratic united front: the religious patriotic elements within the people's democratic united front cherish a certain degree of patriotism and have contradictions with the three major enemies. Some of them also more or less want to have democracy and oppose imperialism. As a result, it is possible to rally them and put them practically in the people's democratic united front. However, politically and ideologically they still have contradictions with and are even hostile to the proletariat. Politically and ideologically they are deeply influenced by imperialism and the reactionary classes within the country, and some of them are even unable to draw clearly a line of distinction between friend and foe. To varying degrees they doubt, resent, and are dissatisfied with the Party's lines, principles, and policies. A considerable number of them have expressed dissatisfaction with the increasing tendency of decline of religion as a result of the development of the socialist cause, and are trying by all means to expand the forces and influence of religion. Under certain conditions, especially when the activities of reactionary elements become rampant, some of them have reversed their positions considerably on major issues of right and wrong. This is the principal content of the class struggle that exists between the proletariat and the religious people within the people's democratic united front. This class struggle will persist throughout the whole period of transition.

IV. Tactics for dealing with religion

CLASS STRUGGLE IN RELIGION during the period of transition is an objective existence. All revolutionary cadres should correctly know and deal with this class struggle. For this reason:

First, a high-degree class vigilance of the proletariat must be maintained, and religious problems in the period of transition must be observed from a positive proletarian class stand and class viewpoint and by means of methods of class analysis.

It must always be remembered that in the period of transition, there exist in religion classes, class contradictions, and class struggle. It must be remembered when the class struggle becomes more or less acute as well as when it becomes milder. It must be remembered when attention is concentrated on class relations in this regard as well as when dealing with concrete problems concerning religion in day-to-day work. The struggle between reactionaries in religious clothing and the popular masses should be noted as well as that between the proletariat and religious patriotic elements within the united front. The struggle between religious patriotic elements and the proletariat in the political, ideological respect should also be noted as well as the contradiction and struggle between these religious elements in their expansion of the forces and influence of religion and the proletariat in their leadership and undertaking of building socialism.

It is not enough to know merely that class struggle exists in religion, but the concrete characteristics of this class struggle must be understood. Class struggle in religion, apart from conforming to the general laws that govern class struggle, also has its own characteristics. These are principally the following: (1) Such class struggle often goes on under cover of the cloak of religion. It has an "outer shell" and a coat of "protective coloring," and as a result it is more or less hidden and not easily detected. (2) The contradiction that arises out of belief and disbelief in religion within the ranks of the laboring people is often interwoven in an intricate manner with the class struggle in religion. And within the class struggle in religion itself, two different kinds of class struggle, that among the people themselves and that between the enemy and ourselves, are also intricately interwoven. Therefore, the situation is highly complex. Only when the characteristics of class struggle in religion are grasped will it be possible to see clearly, through the exterior appearance of religion, the substance of this struggle and to distinguish contradictions among the people from class struggle and class struggle among the people from struggle between the enemy and ourselves, when observing and dealing with class struggle in this respect.

It is still not enough to know that class struggle exists in religion and to understand the characteristics of such struggle, but the concrete situation of class struggle in religion in different periods must be clearly grasped too. Class struggle in religion, like class struggle in other respects, rises and falls from time to time. The concrete situation of this struggle varies in different periods. Therefore, it is necessary to make intensive investigations, take possession of large amounts of information that conforms to reality, constantly grasp the class trends in this connection, and make comprehensive analyses with reference to the international and domestic situation of class struggle as a whole. Only in this way will it be possible to make correct judgment in good time of the concrete situation of the class struggle in this respect in different periods, and therefore to formulate correct guidelines, policies, measures, and plans.

Second, the popular masses must be correctly led, in accordance with the policies of the Party, in waging class struggle in this respect. Everything must be done to make every result of this struggle favorable to the proletariat and to the cause of socialism.

In order to prosecute the class struggle in this respect correctly, it is first necessary to distinguish correctly, in accordance with Comrade Mao Tse-tung's teaching concerning the two different kinds of contradiction, the two kinds of contradiction as reflected in religion, to distinguish class struggle in religion from the contradiction among the people that arises from belief and disbelief in religion, to distinguish the class contradiction among the people from contradiction between the enemy and ourselves both within the class struggle in religion, and to deal with them correctly by adopting different methods in each case. In prosecuting the class struggle in this respect, religious followers who are working people form the force on which we can rely. They may have contradiction with other working people over the question of the existence or nonexistence of God, but their basic political and economic interests are identical with those of the other working people. Similarly, they may have something in common in the matter of religious belief with members of the exploiting classes who are religious followers, but an irreconcilable contradiction exists between the two in the matter of class interests. Therefore, it is necessary during the struggle to consolidate the unity with them [working class believers], strengthen the unity between them and working class non-believers, patiently give them class education and education in scientific and cultural knowledge, lead them to take an active part in practical struggles of revolution and construction, incessantly raise their class consciousness and level of knowledge, remove the political-ideological influence exercised over them through religion by the exploiting classes, and help them to free themselves gradually and consciously from the influence of religious superstition.

It is our object to win over and rally all patriotic religious persons. But since contradiction exists between them and the proletariat in the political-ideological sphere and in the dissemination of religion, we must adopt the principle of uniting with and at the same time struggle against them and implement a policy of uniting with them, educating them, and reforming them. Generally speaking, the contradiction between the proletariat and the religious circles, so long as the latter remain politically anti-imperialist and patriotic and observe the laws of the state, is a class contradiction among the people. It should be resolved according to the "unity-criticism-unity" formula and by means of discussion, criticism, and persuasive education, and not by coercive, oppressive means.

In the struggle, the reactionaries in religious clothing are the target of our blows. Their contradition with the popular masses, which arises as a result of their reactionary political activities and other unlawful activities conducted under cover of religion, is a contradiction between the enemy and ourselves and must be dealt with by dictatorial means. Of course, in dealing with them concretely, we should make distinctions of each case according to the magnitude of their crime, the gravity of their actions, and their good or bad attitude.

In order to deal with class struggle in religion correctly, it is also necessary to adopt the policy of freedom of religious belief in dealing with people's religious beliefs. In the struggle, it is necessary to deal blows to the reactionary and other unlawful activities conducted under cover of religion by reactionaries in religious clothing. With regard to religious activities which come into conflict with the interests of the State, society, and the collective as well as with other freedoms and rights of the citizens, the State should also take suitable administrative measures so as to keep these activities under the necessary control.

Meanwhile, however, religious followers should be given the freedom to engage in proper religious activities. This will be favorable to uniting the popular masses who believe in religion, to mobilizing their activism for serving the socialist cause, and to the struggle against the enemy. Meanwhile, it is only by adopting the policy of freedom of religious belief and by developing the cause of revolution and construction and raising the degree of consciousness and the level of knowledge of the popular masses that we can truly effectively remove by degrees the roots of religion and enable the popular masses to free themselves gradually and consciously from the bonds of religion. In his "On Correct Handling of Contradictions Among the People," Chairman Mao admonishes us thus: "We cannot destroy religion by an administrative order or force people not to believe in religion." To coerce people not to believe in religion instead of adopting the policy of freedom of religious belief in dealing with religious beliefs will be unfavorable to the effort to rally all possible religious believers for service to the socialist cause and also unfavorable to the struggle against such an ideology as religion.

DOC. 31. *Yu Hsiang and Liu Chun-wang: The Correct Recognition and Handling of the Problem of Religion*

FOR YU HSIANG and Liu Chun-wang religion cannot exist in an "isolated manner." It is not simply a private affair, as Ya Han-chang holds, but is in fact a sociopolitical problem belonging to the ideological realm and cannot be exempted from class struggle. Yu and Liu challenge Ya's stress on institution and organization as the distinguishing marks of religion, saying that this "idealistic" view overlooks the primary social and political contradictions inherent in religious belief.

They begin this essay by citing three areas of sociopolitical contradictions, concluding that the Party must form a united front with all patriotic religious elements in the struggle against foreign and domestic class enemies hiding under the "cloak of religion." To adopt this strategy will "gradually promote the death of religion." They allege that imperialist and reactionary elements under cover of religion are guilty of espionage, spreading false rumors, sabotage, fomenting insurrection, swindling believers of money, raping women, disturbing the social order and impeding production. They call for "intensive work": first the mobilization of the masses with patriotic religious believers into a united front; then, by class analysis, the exposure of the true facts and nature of the enemy. Through this strictly political alliance the Party will lead religious adherents to educate themselves, to learn to identify the enemies in their midst, and to rid themselves of their influence.

In another thrust at Ya, Liu and Yu allege that "peaceful coexistence" between the Party and. religious elements without going through struggle is an impossibility. However, only by the "thorough implementation of the policy of freedom of religious belief" can the masses achieve the awareness required to take the initiative in promoting the death of religion. On the instructions of Chairman Mao, coercive means may not be used. The decline of religion, they say, will be a long, slow, but inexorable process.

I. Two kinds of contradictions

RELIGION IS A social ideology, "the fantastic reflection in men's minds of those external forces which control their daily life" (Engels: *Anti-Dühring*). On this significance, religion is a problem which belongs to the ideological realm. The ideology of religion, like other social ideologies, is not something that exists in an isolated manner. It is expressed in the belief of millions and millions of people, and people with religious belief must carry out religious activities in society. The fantastic interpretations by religion of natural phenomena, social phenomena, and especially of class oppression and class exploitation, play the role of paralyzing the minds of the working people, and disintegrating their combat will. Moreover, religion is the spiritual weapon used by the exploiting class for the control of the working people. In this way, the problem of religion cannot but involve social life and class relations, and produce important effects on class struggle and the struggle for production. Accordingly, the problem of religion is an important sociopolitical problem.

Comrade Mao Tse-tung's theory on two kinds of social contradictions different in nature is of important guiding significance to us in our analysis of the problem of religion. In the problem of religion, there are likewise two kinds of contradictions different in nature.

The reactionary classes exploit religion to preserve their class interests and come into contradiction with the masses of the people. This is contradiction between the enemy and us. Under China's modern conditions, imperialism, the feudal landlord class, and the bureaucratic bourgeoisie exploit religion to preserve their reactionary interests, and come into contradiction with the masses of the people. This is contradiction between the enemy and us. This is the primary social contradiction during the period of China's democratic revolution in the religious area. Contradictions of this nature continue to exist during the period of the socialist revolution, and they are principally expressed in the continued exploitation by the imperialists and the remnant reactionary forces in the country, not content with their defeat, of religion to carry out all kinds of sabotage activities, in the futile attempt to overthrow the proletarian dictatorship, and to realize their restoration.

Before liberation of the whole country, China's Catholicism and Protestantism were principally controlled by imperialism, and were tools of imperialism in the aggression against China. Buddhism, Islam, and Taoism were principally controlled by domestic reactionary classes, used as tools for the preservation of their reactionary rule. After liberation of the whole country, the rule of imperialism, the feudal landlord class, and the bureaucratic bourgeoisie had been overthrown by the masses of the people. Nevertheless, their forces in religion have not been completely eliminated with such development, and they continue to attempt to fight the people on the religious front. Imperialist elements and other reactionary elements hiding under the cover of religion often collect intelligence for imperialism, fabricate rumors, and even organize insurrections and carry out other current counter-revolutionary activities. They spread reactionary views which are hostile to new China, oppose the Communist Party, and slander the socialist system. They exploit religion to obtain money under false pretenses, rape women, cause loss and injury of life, and upset the social order and the production order.

In carrying out the struggle against the reactionary class enemy who dons the cloak of religion, it is necessary to carry out intensive work on various sides. The most basic task is the mobilization of the broad masses, particularly the masses of religious followers, uniting with them to form the patriotic united front. . . . But the religious cloak of the reactionary class enemy must be taken off, and his ugly face fully exposed so as to educate the masses and raise their level of consciousness.

Completely possible is the formation of a patriotic united front between the Marxist-Leninist political party and the religious followers. This is because differences in ideological belief among people do not exclude cooperation on a given political foundation.

Religious adherents among the working people believe in religion and come into contradiction with the other working people. Such are contradictions among the working people. They are the reflection within the inner ranks of the working people of the contradiction between religion and the Marxist-Leninist world outlook, the contradiction between theism and atheism. These contradictions are large in volume and during the long historical period of the existence of religion, will continue to exist.

Professional religious practitioners who are politically patriotic and possess a democratic tint, and religious adherents of the upper strata who in practice make the dissemination of religion their professional activities (these shall be referred to as religious circles hereinunder), in their political and ideological beliefs and in the dissemination of religion, also come into contradiction with the working class, and with the other working people. Under China's conditions, generally speaking, these contradictions also belong to contradictions among the people. This is the major social contradiction of China's transitional period—the contradiction between the working class and the bourgeoisie—reflected in the religious area.

In actual life, the two kinds of contradictions different in nature, reflected on the problem of religion, are interwoven together in a complex manner. Accordingly, in dealing with the problem of religion, the proletarian political party must employ the Marxist-Leninist method of class analysis for a penetrating investigation and research, and handle them correctly in accordance with their different nature.

In accordance with the above analysis, in revolution and in construction, the Marxist-Leninist political party must unite with all religious adherents who can be united with to build a patriotic united front, to struggle resolutely against the reactionary class enemy who puts on the cloak of religion, and to eliminate the forces and influences in religion of the domestic and foreign reactionary class enemies. At the same time, it must also correctly handle the contradiction between the ideology of religion and the Marxist-Leninist world outlook, gradually awaken the effects of religion among the masses of the people, and gradually promote the death of religion.

II. On the united front

THE PRIMARY TASK of the Marxist-Leninist political party on the problem of religion is this: unite with all religious adherents who can be united with (including professional religious practitioners who can be united with) under the revolutionary and construction causes, and carry out a struggle against domestic and foreign reactionary class enemies, eliminating their forces and influences in religion.

For the most extensive unity with the broad masses of religious adherents and the isolation and attack of the enemy, in each concrete struggle we must strictly differentiate the two kinds of contradictions different in nature, separating the problem of ideological belief from the problem of politics; separating the proper religious activities of the adherents from the reactionary activities of counter-revolutionaries who exploit religion in carrying them out; separating the backward elements from the counter-revolutionaries, and separating general religious organizations from reactionary organizations that don the cloak of religion.

In carrying out the struggle against the reactionary class enemy who dons the cloak of religion, it is necessary to carry out intensive work on various sides. The most basic task is the mobilization of the broad masses, particularly the masses of religious followers, uniting with them to form the patriotic united front. To mobilize the broad masses of religious followers fully, it is necessary, in the course of the struggle, to get hold of true facts about the counter-revolutionary activities, and carry out their exposure and accusation among the masses with proper leadership. The religious cloak of the reactionary class enemy must be taken off, and his ugly face fully exposed so as to educate the masses and raise their level of consciousness.

In revolution and in construction, a proletarian political party should unite with all religious followers who can be united with to form a patriotic united front. The formation of this united front is fully in keeping with the interests of the proletariat. A Marxist-Leninist political party sees clearly that the religious followers constitute a social force. The majority of them are working people. When they are united with, we can develop their positive role in the revolution and in construction. At the same time, the religious followers among the broad masses of the working people can only rid themselves of the oppression and exploitation of imperialism and the reactionaries by positive participation in the revolution and in construction under the leadership of the Marxist-Leninist political party. Only then may they achieve thorough liberation politically, economically and ideologically.

Completely possible is the formation of a patriotic united front between the Marxist-Leninist political party and the religious followers. This is because differences in ideological belief among people do not exclude cooperation on a given political foundation. As we all know, in the democratic revolution, the socialist revolution, and socialist construction, the Chinese Communist Party had already formed a patriotic united front with all patriotic religious followers. Participants in this united front were, first of all, religious followers among the working people. The world outlook of the Marxist-Leninist political party is basically different from the world outlook of the religious followers among the working people. Nevertheless, the revolution and construction cause led by the Marxist-Leninist party represent the basic interests, politically and economically, of the religious followers among the working people. This point fundamentally decides the fact that religious followers among the working people can join the other working people and be united around the Marxist-Leninist political party. In China, generally speaking, religious circles possess patriotism to varying extents, and a portion of these people also have a definite amount of progressive democratic demands. Accordingly, it is also possible to unite with them under the patriotic united front.

Religious adherents among the working people constitute the mainstay of the patriotic united front between the Party and religious adherents, and the foundation of this united front. The alliance with patriotic religious circles is the auxiliary but also important alliance in this united front. Both alliances cannot be neglected, and they promote each other. Religious circles exert a definite amount of influence over the religious adherents among the working people. So winning over patriotic religious circles is conducive to unity with religious adherents among the working people. Nevertheless, in the final analysis, only on the foundation of unity with the religious adherents among the working people may we truly achieve unity with the patriotic religious circles under the patriotic united front.

With reference to religious adherence among the working people, we must first see the fact that they are working people and have the urgent demand for participation in the revolution and construction. At the same time, we must also see the fact they they are religious adherents, easily susceptible to the negative political influence, exerted by the upper strata of religion, and even the ideological poisons of domestic and foreign reactionaries, thereby obstructing the awakening of their class consciousness.

Accordingly, we must patiently, repeatedly, and continually carry out political and ideological education among the religious adherents among the working people, gradually raise their awakening, mobilize them into participation in the practice of the revolution and construction, and making them educate themselves in the midst of such practice, distinguish between the enemy and ourselves, gradually rid themselves of the negative influences of the upper strata of religion and even the political influences of domestic and foreign reactionaries, and join the other working people in being firmly rallied around the Party.

Though the patriotic religious circles can participate in the united front, nevertheless, ideologically they have been deeply influenced by imperialism and the domestic reactionary classes, and some of them cannot demarcate clearly the boundaries between the enemy and ourselves. They entertain to varying extents suspicion, conflict and dissatisfaction over the Party's line, directives and policies. They vigorously attempt to expand the force of religion, and through the foundation of religion deepen their own influence among the religious adherents among the working people.

In accordance with such a situation, in dealing with the patriotic religious circles, the Party must practice the principle of both uniting with them and struggling against them, continually pushing them to carry out political and ideological reform, gradually making them rid themselves of the political influences of domestic and foreign reactionaries, and helping them to catch up with the development of the general situation. If it is considered that the Party and the patriotic religious circles can achieve "peaceful coexistence" politically and ideologically, if it is considered that by merely relying on a certain agreement and without going through a definite struggle, unity with them can be realized, it will be a mistake. Acting in accordance with such a viewpoint will not achieve the formation and consolidation of a united front with the patriotic religious circles.

For the formation and consolidation of the above-mentioned patriotic united front, a Marxist-Leninist political party must also adopt a correct policy toward the people's religious belief. This is the policy of freedom of religious belief. That is to say, there must be freedom for belief in religion or non-belief in religion; belief in this religion or that religion; belief in this sect or that sect of the same religion; belief in religion in the past and non-belief now; and non-belief in religion in the past and belief now.

Facts have proved that only with the thorough implementation of the policy of freedom of religious belief, may we, within the ranks of the people, correctly handle the relations between religious adherents and the state, between religious adherents and non-adherents, and between adherents of different religions or different sects of a religion, and thereby strengthen the internal unity of the people.

III. On eliminating religion

ANOTHER TASK of a Marxist-Leninist political party on the question of religion is as follows: the development of the revolution and construction, the continual strengthening of the ideological education of religious adherents in order to gradually eliminate the roots giving rise to religion, and the gradual weakening of the influences of religion among the masses of the people to promote the death of religion.

The Marxist-Lennist political party advocates the building of a patriotic united front with religious adherents on a given political foundation, and consistently adopts the policy of freedom of religious belief. However, this does not in the least imply that it can adopt a neutral attitude toward religion, that it can "coexist peacefully" with religion in the realm of ideology, and that it can remain unconcerned with the bondage imposed on the masses by religion.

A Marxist-Leninist is the most thorough atheist and is opposed to all religion. In the history of the international workers movement, opportunists had opposed Marxism-Leninism on this question. They held that religion is a "private affair," which does not concern the Marxist-Leninist political party. Lenin resolutely opposed this opportunist viewpoint.

Fundamentally speaking, the active leadership of the masses in class struggle and production struggle is of decisive significance for the elimination of religion. This is the basic channel for the promotion of the death of religion. This is because in order to promote the death of religion, we must first eliminate the roots by which religion is given birth and exists—the pressure from natural forces and social forces. Only with the abolition of class and exploitation and the extensive development of the capacity to control nature, and on this foundation raising the people's degree of awakening and level of knowledge, may the death of religion be brought about. Comrade Mao Tse-tung pointed out that the removal of the religious superstitions of the masses 'is the natural result after victory in the political struggle and the economic struggle." For this reason, the Party should first lead the masses in carrying out the political struggle and the economic struggle.

Religious concepts exist in the minds of people, and the concepts in people's minds can only be transformed with the changes in the material living conditions of society and through the self-consciousness of the people.

Comrade Mao Tse-tung had stated at a very early date, "Idols are set up by the peasants. When a definite time is reached, the peasants will use their own hands to discard these idols, and other people need not do the job for them."

As a matter of fact, the use of administrative orders and other methods of compulsion in the struggle against religion not only will fail to achieve results, but will, instead, lead to the dissatisfaction of the religious adherents, and dampen their activism for the revolution and construction. At the same time, the situation may be exploited by the reactionary class enemies to incite their feelings for the protection of their religion and lead to religious fanaticism. This is non-beneficial to the revolutionary and construction cause, as well as [the goal of] ridding the people of the bondage of religion.

In the struggle against religion, the opposition to the use of administrative orders by a Marxist-Leninist political party definitely does not imply that in actual work we can disregard the struggle to promote the extinction of religion, and adopt the attitude of waiting for the extinction of religion, and even permitting the uninterrupted expansion of religious influences. China's experience has proved that with the development of the proletarian revolution and construction, religion must unavoidably be gradually weakened. This is the general trend.

However, even under the condition of the proletariat holding state power, the weakening of religion is not a vertical drop. In the general decline trend, there must be undulations. A Marxist-Leninist political party should recognize and control the law governing the birth, development and death of religion, use the favorable conditions for social development, actively carry out work, strengthen the propaganda of atheism, popularize scientific and cultural knowledge, so that the masses of the people may self-consciously abandon the concept of religious superstition.

DOC. 32. *Liang Hao and Yang Chen: Religion Has Always Been the Opiate of the People*

IN THIS ESSAY, published just months before the outbreak of the Cultural Revolution, two new writers enter the debate. At the same time as the Party's top leadership were locked in behind-the-scenes struggle, the attack on Ya Han-chang's moderate line in religion intensified. Ya is charged with prettifying and defending religion by singling out organized religion for special treatment and denying that all religion is the opiate of the people. Citing such arguments of "modern revisionists" [Ya and others?] as "Religion transcends politics" and "Religion does not always function as an opiate," the writers affirm that all forms of religion and superstition are opiates and poisonous to society. Ya, they say, casts away the social character of religion and the concept of class oppression as its principal root cause. Religion, they conclude, makes no contribution to class society and can only impede the people from knowing and transforming the world. Comrade Ya has forsaken these fundamental truths; his viewpoint, they say, is not a casual mistake, but a systematic one.

COMRADE YA HAN-CHANG has in recent years published a series of articles on religious problems. Quite a number of comrades have made known their divergent views on some points of argument advanced in these articles. We feel that since Comrade

Ya Han-chang's articles touch upon many important theoretical problems of religion, it is necessary to carry on with the discussion. It is the intention of this article to set out our view on the reactionary nature of religion for discussion with Comrade Ya Han-chang, and we hope he will criticize and correct us.

I. Religion is always an opiate

IN THE ARTICLE "My Understanding on Some Theoretical Problems of Religion," Comrade Ya Han-chang suggests that Marx's well-known saying that religion is the opiate of the people "deals not with religion in general, much less with the religion of primitive society, but with the revolutionary task confronting the German proletariat at that time." How does Comrade Ya Han-chang interpret religion? He thinks that religion is "theism plus organized activity." Moreover, he has created a complete system of classification for religious superstition and artificially treated theism, religion and feudal superstition as three independent parts. He declares that this is the hallmark of Marxist atheism becoming a branch of science.

We are of the opinion that it is rather improper for Comrade Ya Han-chang to hold these views.

We are of the opinion that religion is of course a reflection of man's illusion of the objective world and is a fallacious world outlook of man. But if we merely describe religion up to this point and see not its poisonous role toward the people, then we have not made known its essence. This is because man's knowledge of the objective world is erroneous in many ways, and his erroneous knowledge and mistaken world outlook are not religious ones in all cases. In what way religion differs from other erroneous knowledge and world outlook and what its own particularity is should be clearly explained.

The old and modern revisionists also try always to remove the theoretical cornerstone of Marxism on the problem of religion. They say: "Religion does not always function as an opiate." They say: "If religion is opiate, then a small dose of it can be useful and beneficial because it can calm people and mitigate their agony."

Now, there is nothing strange for the enemy of Marxism to raise such a hue and cry. However, Comrade Ya Han-chang who is engaged in research of Marxist theory looks upon religion merely as "a form of misinterpretation of Nature."

He does not point out that it is poisonous to society, but warns other people by saying: You must in no case misunderstand the basic theory of Marxism on religion. Religion of primitive society is not the opiate of the people. Nor is the ordinary religion of class society. It appears that only the religion of Germany in the 18th century functioned as the opiate of the people.

The above viewpoints are definitely not distributive mistakes in wording in Comrade Ya Han-chang's articles, but are his basic viewpoints.

Our view is contrary to Comrade Ya Han-chang's. We hold that religion is consistently the opiate of the people and all religions are the opiate of the people. Where there is religion, there the people are stupefied by it. Before religion is extinguished, its function as opiate will never change. Like the exploiting class, its exploitative character will never be eliminated until it is sent to the tomb.

Comrade Ya Han-chang is of the opinion that primitive religion is not "the opiate of the people." This is not in conformity with historical facts relating to the evolution of mankind. From the data of surveys made of some minority nationalities and tribes which are still in the economic state of primitive clannish society, we can cite the following points:

First, the religion of primitive society stupefied the people of that time, and wore away their determination to fight against Mother Nature. It made people believe that a bumper harvest in fishing, hunting or farming was a favor bestowed by the "gods," and that famine, poor harvest or failure to capture wild animals due to certain natural causes symbolized the wrath of the "gods."

Second, primitive religion propagated various kinds of taboos which restrained man's power of fighting against Nature. Primitive people must waste a lot of time to hold religious ceremonies. Even at harvest, fishing or hunting time, they had to wait for the dreams or prayers of their priests or chieftains, thus letting farming seasons or hunting opportunities slip away. All this, in effect, greatly hampered production.

Third, the budding culture—such as medicine, fine art, music, etc.—of primitive society was restrained by religion. Primitive religion limited these forms of culture over a long period of time to a narrow sphere of serving religion.

Fourth, primitive religion tended to oppose culture and to create many undesirable customs harmful to the physical and mental health of the people—such as fasting, tattoos, and even "head-hunting."

Fifth, at the last stage of primitive society, the role of religion was to uphold and consolidate the inherent relations of production and hamper the forward movement of society.

It can be seen that since the emergence of human society, religion has always been "the opiate of the people." By professing that primitive religion is not "the opiate of the people," Comrade Ya Han-chang has precisely provided those professional religionists and theologians—who safeguard religious influence—with a theoretical basis.

These people have always left no stone unturned to prettify religion. They say that "religion honors gods, benefits people," and "transcends politics." They tax their brains to find many beautiful figures of speech to deny that "religion is the opiate of the people," or that religion is the tool of the reactionary ruling class in class society.

However, once the criminal activities performed by religion to serve the reactionary class are brought to light, thus arousing the indignation of the masses and giving the lie to the claim that religion "transcends politics," they would make this plea: "Religion is originally good but has been exploited and discredited by the reactionary class. With the dirt removed and its true identity restored, religion itself is still good."

Seen in this light, there is nothing novel in the argument that primitive religion is not "the opiate of the people," and that religion is turned into the opiate of the people only after "it is manipulated" by the ruling class in class society. Such an argument has long been used by the apologists of religion.

As to the allegation that "religion in general" is not the

opiate of the people" in class society, this is entirely prepos-
terous.

II. Religion, theism, and superstition are the same

HAVING CAST AWAY the social character of religion and its essence as the opiate of the people, and having refused to ac-
knowledge that class oppression is the principal root cause of
religion in class society, Comrade Ya Han-chang has therefore
advanced a set of unique views on religion. He arbitrarily slices
religion into three parts: (1) theism, (2) religion and (3) feudal superstition. He says that such a division "is the hallmark
of describing Marxist atheism as a branch of science."

A whole thing is thus artificially cut into several pieces, and
each piece is made to stand in isolation. As a consequence,
there is no way to explain clearly their inner connections and
the relationships of developments and changes.

Comrade Ya Han-chang says: "Theism basically contains
three things: (1) spirit and ghost, (2) deity and (3) God."
This view cannot be established. As a matter of fact, the idea of
religion is in a general sense not divorced from the idea of
"ghost" and "deity." How can Comrade Ya Han-chang dovetail
his arguments when he arbitrarily divides "diety" and "god"
into two groups?

Actually theism and religion cannot be separated, but Comrade Ya Han-chang solemnly declares that he "is discussing the
problem of extinction of theism and not that of the extinction
of religion." How can religion exist when the idea of ghost and
deity is destroyed? Can it be said that without the idea of ghost
and deity there is any religion?

Comrade Ya Han-chang confuses things by severing theism
and religion into separate groups. On top of this, he juxtaposes
feudal superstition with theism and religion. As the name
suggests, feudal superstition naturally owes its origin to feudal
society, but Comrade Ya Han-chang juxtaposes the concept
which marks the various historical periods of mankind (theism
and religion) with the concept of a single historical period—
feudal society (feudal superstition). This is obviously not a
method of conducting "scientific" research.

Apart from this, we must also ask: Does superstition in feudal society include the religion of feudal society or not? According to Comrade Ya Han-chang's system of classification, in the feudal society of China which lasted several thousand years, only fortune-telling and physiognomy came under feudal superstition, while the religion of feudal society was not feudal superstition. This does not make sense.

Is religion better than feudal superstition? Comrade Ya Han-chang can only make use of symbolic parables to explain the relationships between theism, religion and feudal superstition. He says: "Both feudal superstition and religion are born of theism and are brothers from the same womb." In another article he says: "Theism and religion can be called twins." He also says: "Superstition is a general concept like that of 'animal,' while theism, religion and feudal superstition are specific concepts like those of man, dog and flea. . . ." In this way, both concept and logic are confused.

To defend himself, Comrade Ya Han-chang asserts that the consideration of theism, religion and feudal superstition as one and the same thing is not found in any classic works of Marxism, or in any relevant Party and State documents.

As a matter of fact, when Marx, Engels, Lenin, Stalin and Comrade Mao Tse-tung discussed religious problems, they have never arbitrarily separated religion and superstition, much less said that superstition includes three parts—theism, religion and superstition.

Concerning the policy documents of the Party and State, we want only to quote a few lines: "(10) Professional Religionists: Those who have principally depended upon religious or superstitious occupations—such as pastors, Catholic fathers, Taoist priests, Buddhist monks, vegetarian hermits, geomancers, fortune-tellers, etc.—to make a living for three full years preceding liberation are called religious or superstitious professionals." (*Decisions on Some Problems in Agrarian Reform*, People's Publishing House, 1964 edition, p. 28)

It can be seen from the above quotations that in both the classic works of Marxism and the policy documents of the Party and State, religion and superstition belong to one group of things and are not arbitrarily separated as Comrade Ya Han-chang claims. To be sure, "a fortune-teller" is not "a pastor" nor a "Catholic priest" a "vegetarian hermit." This is common sense. However, analyzed on the basis of the Marxist viewpoint, although they are expressed in different forms, yet their essence and their functions in society are basically the same.

Comrade Ya Han-chang draws a distinction between theism, religion and general superstition (later changed to feudal superstition). This runs precisely counter to the materialistic viewpoint of history. He does not proceed from the development of history by stages to analyze the differences in religion at different stages of development, but emphasizes the division of theism, religion and general superstition since primitive society. He even holds that the "origin" of religion is not the same as that of superstition.

We are of the opinion that theism is religious superstition and that the two cannot be separated basically from each other. As to the relationship between religion and supersition, this is more complicated.

In primitive society, religion and superstition are entirely one and the same thing and cannot be separated from each other.

In terms of the continuity of ideology, the religions of modern society are evolved from the foundation of those of primitive society, and are the conglomerations of all ideas of religious superstition in past history. Religion is a more systematic and finer form of superstition, while general superstition is piecemeal, crude religion. Judged by the extent to which man's thought is poisoned, it is of course true that the more systematic and finer a religion is the more dangerous it is.

Comrade Ya Han-chang says: "Religion not only preaches belief in the existence of souls, ghosts, deities and God, but has its organizations, groups and activities." He gives us here a formula—religion is the idea of ghost and deity plus organized activity.

It should be pointed out that this "definition" of Comrade Ya Han-chang's likewise rejects the social character of religion and makes no mention of the fact that religion is "the opiate of the people." It makes use of some superficial phenomena to cover up the essence of religion.

This is not all. Comrade Ya Han-chang sometimes goes so far

as to plead directly for religion. He says: "Judged by the materialistic viewpoint of history . . . the idea of God is especially a product which has raised man's power of thinking to a certain level. It has provided in the abstract some conditions for the subsequent development of sciences (natural science and social science). Consequently, it should be admitted that the evolution from 'animism' to the 'idea of God' is man's great progress in knowing Nature."

We know that religion is a reflection of man's mental illusion of the external forces which dominate man. Although the idea of God can come into being only after man's power of thinking has developed to a certain level, yet it is essentially unscientific and basically cannot furnish any conditions for scientific development.

How was man's scientific thinking, leading to a correct knowledge of the world, developed? Chairman Mao taught us by saying: "Where do man's correct ideas come from? Do they drop from the sky? No. Are they inherent in one's head? No. Man's correct ideas can come only from practice in society, from the three kinds of practice—struggle for production, class struggle and scientific experiment—in society."

The special point about religion is precisely to negate man's social practice, to distort the forces which dominate man and to reflect them as superhuman forces. The religious idea of God in class society especially endeavors to hide the true picture of class exploitation from the oppressed people so that they may indefinitely rest content with the lot of the oppressed and the enslaved and stay forever in the realm of ignorance. It can only impede man from knowing and transforming the world.

Comrade Ya Han-chang has forsaken these most fundamental truths. He holds that the birth of the idea of God (to be sure, also the birth of Christianity which consistently stands on the side of reactionary forces) has furnished some conditions for the development of sciences—including social science. Interpreted in this way, religion is no longer "the opiate of the people," but simply a tonic to the life of the people.

Summing up, Comrade Ya Han-chang has forsaken the theory of historical materialism concerning social ideology and the social character of ideology. He has negated the essence of religion as the opiate and glossed over the reactionary class attribute of religion in class society. He only explains religion according to superficial phenomena and has also founded a complete set of metaphysical methods of classification with regard to religious superstition.

Since Comrade Ya Han-chang has deviated from the theoretical orbit of Marxism-Leninism on the problem of religion, he has, as a result, prettified religion. All this reflects Comrade Ya Han-chang's viewpoint not as a casual mistake, but as a systematic one.

Not long ago, Comrade Ya Han-chang admitted in an article entitled "Draw a Clear Line of Demarcation with the Bourgeois 'Religious Science'" that the saying "Religion is the opiate of the people" was also applicable to primitive society. However, we are of the opinion that Comrade Ya Han-chang's system of mistaken theories cannot be corrected in this fashion.

DOC. 33. *Yu Hsiang and Liu Chun-wang: Problem of Understanding Religion—For Consultation with Comrade Ya Han-chang*

IN DOCUMENTS 31 and 32, Yu and Liu continue the debate on the "divergence of principle" with Ya. After an initial recapitulation of Ya's position, based on his writings, they launch into a long theoretical analysis supporting their position (omitted here). In a bitter and personal rebuttal of Ya Han-chang's criticism of their position, the writers depart from their earlier style of scholarly detachment, relating their argument directly to tactics and Party policy. "We are not the ones who bring harm to practice. Comrade Ya Han-chang is precisely the one who does it." In his opinion, they say, the struggle against religion is directed only to feudal superstitions and does not include the religious beliefs in the minds of the Roman Catholics, Protestants, Buddhists, Moslems and Taoists. "These points deserve serious thinking on the part of Comrade Ya Han-chang!"

But Ya is not yet silenced. Fighting back in a long article in *Kuang-ming Jih-pao* (the last of his published views) he charges Liu and Yu with following a non-Marxist viewpoint that belongs to the Western bourgeois science of religion. Since this is not applicable in the Chinese context (he writes), such views are harmful to the Party's struggle in the sphere of religion and superstition. Published in June, 1965, Ya's minimal reference to the Party's policy of freedom of religious belief and the rights of legitimate religious adherents, in contrast to his earlier writing, suggests the increasing pressures on Ya and other advocates of a moderate position.

I. Recapitulation of the debate

FROM 1963 ONWARD Comrade Ya Han-chang has initiated a series of debates with us on the problem of the Marxist-Leninist view on religion. Both sides have written a number of articles, setting forth each other's respective points of view. To the questions put to us in his article published in *Hsin Chien-she* (No. 2, 1964), we replied in the *Wen-hui Pao* on April 21 and May 5, 1964. In the same issues of the paper we also raised a few questions to discuss with him. Afterward, he published more articles in the *Tientsin Jih-pao* (June 17, 1964) and the *Wen-hui Pao* (September 11, 1964), reiterating his views and making a new attack on us.

There is a divergence on principle between Comrade Ya Han-chang and ourselves on a series of problems relating to the Marxist-Leninist view on religion. It seems to us that further discussions are called for.

We believe that in many ways Comrade Ya Han-chang's understanding of religion has left the track of the basic principles of Marxism-Leninism. It has formed a system of religious outlook of his own. In brief, it covers the following fields:

First, the problem of what constitutes religion and of the resulting relationships between religion, theism, and superstition. Comrade Ya Han-chang denies that religion is an ideology. His opinion is that a religion must have tenets, church rules and professional religionists. It must be something having organized public bodies to carry out its activities. Comrade Ya looks upon the idea of theism as a kind of isolated, self-existent thinking. He confines religious superstition to feudal superstition. Therefore, he believes that religion, theism, and superstition are not the same thing.

Second, the problem of the source from which religion has sprung. Comrade Ya Han-chang negates the objective material source which has produced religion as an ideology. He believes that all religions are derivatives of the idea of theism. This idea is the mother of religions and religions are children of the idea. He believes that the source engendering the idea (soul, ghosts, spirits, God) is different from the source of religion. Theism "owes its origin mainly to man's inability to understand the relationships between a dream, the corporal body and spirit as well as the laws of natural and social development" (see Ya Han-chang: "On the Problem of the Extinction of the Idea of Theism," *Hsin Chien-she*, No. 7, 1963). "The concept of spirits originally evolved from the concept of ghosts and further developed into the concept of *Shangti* [God, or the Supreme Being]" (see Ya Han-chang: "Origin of the Theist Idea," *Hsin Chien-she*, No. 1, 1963). In short, his formula for the origin of religion is: Errors in knowledge—the theist idea—religion, i.e., consciousness [led to] consciousness.

Third, the problem of the essential role of religion. Comrade Ya Han-chang denies that "religion is an opiate of the people," as put forward by Marx, but rather is a universal truth applicable to all religions at various periods. He believes that this famous Marxist saying is applicable only to class society and refers only to the harmful role of religion in class struggle. Thus, he negates the harmful role of religion in primitive society and in man's struggle against nature.

Fourth, the problem of how to struggle against religion and speed up its extinction step by step. Comrade Ya Han-chang practically regards atheist propaganda as the primary, and even the only way to promote extinction of religion.

II. Problem of defining religion

THE PROBLEM ON WHICH we are arguing with Comrade Ya Han-chang is: Whether or not, in a broad sense and as a matter of scientific definition, religion and superstition are the same thing. For this reason, we have not said much in our articles about the distinction between systematized religion and other religious superstitions.

In our view, the principal points of distinction between the two are: Systematized religion came into being in class society; it has a comparatively complete form of manifestation. Religious superstitions have their origin in, and are legacies of, primitive society; their form of manifestation is not as complete as that of systematized religion. It is because of these very points of distinction that people sometimes are in the habit of giving the name of religion to systematized religion and the name of superstition to all beliefs in supernatural forces with the exception of systematized religion. In a general sense, however, this cannot be interpreted to mean that only systematized religion is religion and other superstitious beliefs in supernatural, mystic forces are not religions or religious superstitions.

Comrade Ya Han-chang insists that religion and superstition are not the same thing. He sums up his view on this point in one sentence: "Religion is superstition but not all superstitions are religion" (see Ya Han-chang: "Religion Is Superstition But Not All Superstitions Are Religion," *Tientsin Jih-pao*, June 17, 1964).

In our view, this judgment is correct only on condition that the term "religion" used in the above sentence denotes systematized religion. If this term denotes religion in general and in a broad sense, then, the judgment would amount to saying:

"Religion is superstition—

"Blind beliefs in supernatural, mystic forces are blind beliefs in supernatural, mystic forces.

"But not all superstitions are religion—

"But not all blind beliefs in supernatural, mystic forces are blind beliefs in supernatural, mystic forces."

The above sounds unusually strange. This is precisely the queer logic on which Comrade Ya Han-chang wants to insist. It is imaginable that only under conditions of the simultaneous existence of systematized religion and other superstitions would we say, in order to distinguish between the two, that "religion is superstition but not all superstitions are religion." Otherwise, we would not say so.

In primitive society, for instance, no systematized religion existed for a very long time. There was only belief in such supernatural, mystic forces as the soul, ghosts and gods. At that time, what was manifested as man's religious belief was precisely the thing we specially call superstition in a narrow sense today.

On the basis of the conditions in primitive society, we would not say: "Religion is superstition but not all superstitions are religion."

III. Implications for tactics

COMRADE YA HAN-CHANG has attacked us, saying that our views "are harmful to the struggle against feudal superstition" (see Ya Han-chang: "Feudal Superstition and Religion Are Not the Same Thing," *Wen-hui Pao*, September 11, 1964). In this connection, we wish to point out once more in all seriousness that in his article in *Hsin Chien-she*, No. 2, 1964, he adopted the method of "quoter's notes" to substitute arbitrarily the concept, "feudal superstition," for the concept, "superstition," which we used in our articles.

He also arbitrarily—with severe criticism—changed our view that as a matter of scientific definition religion and superstition were the same thing into the view that religion and feudal superstition were the same thing. This method of resorting first to distortion and then to opposition is very bad. He even obstinately and unreasonably defended this apparent distortion by saying:

"They (referring to us, Yu Hsiang and Liu Chun-wang) believe that religion and superstition are 'the same thing.' Then, fortune-telling, physiognomy, geomancy and so on, like feudal superstition and religion, must also be 'the same thing.' Then, feudal superstition must be a religion, too. This is quite obvious and unlikely to be distorted" (see Ya Han-chang: "Feudal Superstition and Religion Are Not the Same Thing," *Wen-hui Pao*, September 11, 1964).

Naturally, it would be reasonable if Comrade Ya Han-chang,

on the basis of our views, puts the following question to us: "Since religion and superstition are the same thing, then is feudal superstition a religion?" But, it is plain distortion for him to say that we believe religion and feudal superstition to be the same thing. It is because our view that religion and superstition are the same thing means that their extension and intension coincide to form an identical concept.

He need not concur with us in this point. At any rate, he cannot twist our view to mean that religion and feudal superstition are the same thing and the same concept.

We cannot be charged with the alleged harm that our views would do to the struggle against feudal superstition. This is because simultaneously with pointing out that "as a matter of scientific definition religion and superstition completely coincide in their extension and intension to form an identical concept," we also say in our articles:

"In customary parlance, the term 'religion' is often used specially to denote systematized religion. . . . The belief in supernatural, mystic forces . . . is called superstition. . . . To make a distinction between systematized religion and superstition is of practical significance. It facilitates our giving discriminating and correct treatment to our work in accordance with Party and state policies."

As to whether feudal superstition is a religion and whether the Party policy on freedom of religious belief is applicable to feudal superstition, we shall have to carry our concrete analysis because feudal superstition, as it is usually referred to, covers a comparatively wide range of fields, such as certain superstitious ideas and activities of the masses, the activities of professional workers of superstition and the activities of organizations of feudal superstition. If feudal superstition is spoken of as the blind belief of the masses in certain supernatural forces, it is, in a broad sense, also a religious idea or religious superstition. For this very reason, we treat the superstitious beliefs of the masses in ghosts, spirits, fate and so forth on the same principle as we do the beliefs of the Roman Catholics and Christians in God, of the Moslems in Allah, of the Buddhists in Buddha and of the Taoists in fairies and genii.

Through our work in various fields, we should intensify atheist propaganda so as to release the masses from the shackles of religious superstition step by step. In this regard, we should not specially tighten our grip on the masses because they believe in the kitchen god or the door god. Nor should we relax our grip because they believe in God, Buddha or genii. We can only deal with their religious superstition by means of persuasion and education. We must not ban it by the issue of administrative orders.

In so doing, we give no special or preferential treatment to the believers in God, Buddha, and so on. Neither do we do anything to inflict feelings of discomfort on the believers in the kitchen and door gods.

However, as far as certain specific policies and measures of the Party and the State are concerned, the differences in various concrete conditions practically render them applicable only to the systematized religions existing in our country today and not to other religious superstitions. But this does not warrant any conclusion to be drawn that, in a broad sense, only those—to which these specific policies and measures are applicable—can be called religions.

We are not the ones who bring harm to practice. Comrade Ya Han-chang is precisely the one who does it.

His vigorous insistence that religion, the theist idea and superstition are not the same thing objectively plays the role of beautifying religion to the detriment of the struggle against religion. In his opinion, the struggle to speed up the extinction of religion is aimed at the extinction not of religious ideas in the people's minds but of religious "organizations, public bodies and activities." In his opinion, when religions with "organizations, public bodies and activities" have died out, then—regardless of how many people still believe in the soul, in ghosts and spirits and in God—it will be time to proclaim the extinction of religion, will it not? Hence, there will be no more task to fight against religion, will there?

In his opinion, the struggle against religion does not embrace the fight with the idea of theism and superstition in the people's minds. In his opinion, the struggle against the theist idea only denotes the fight with the belief in, and the fear of, ghosts in the minds of remnant theists in general. And, in his opinion, the struggle against superstition only denotes the fight with feudal superstition. All these struggles do not include those against the religious concepts in the minds of the Roman Catholics and Christians, the Buddhists, the Moslems and the Taoists.

These points deserve serious thinking on the part of Comrade Ya Han-chang.

DOC. 34. *Ya Han-chang: Drawing a Dividing Line With the Bourgeois 'Science of Religion'*

1. How the Debate on the Problem of Religion Began

BETWEEN THE YEARS of 1959 and 1964, I had several articles about atheism published in the press. Scientifically, these articles are not of a very high order, but I think I have nevertheless expounded in them the basic principles of the Marxist teaching of atheism and that theoretically they contain no error in principle.

Upon the publication of these articles, Comrades Yu Hsiang and Liu Chun-wang also had three articles published at various times between 1963 and 1964, criticizing me on a number of points.

Because their criticisms were erroneous, I accordingly wrote some counter-criticism. It was in this way that the debate over the problem of religion started.

Comrades Yu Hsiang and Liu Chun-wang again wrote in the *Kuang-ming Jih-pao* of March 7–8 this year a long article entitled "Question of Understanding Religion—For Consultation With Comrade Ya Han-chang," in which they made fresh criticisms of my several essays published in the past. They said: "We think that many of Comrade Ya Han-chang's ideas about religion have departed from the orbit of the basic principles of Marxism-Leninism, and formed a religious system of his own."

In their long article, Comrades Yu Hsiang and Liu Chun-wang criticize me for "having departed from the orbit of the basic principles of Marxism-Leninism" with regard to four points. The most important issue, however, is that of the relationship among the idea of deism, religion, and superstition (feudal superstition). They criticize me for thinking that the deist idea, religion, and superstition (feudal superstition) "are not the same thing."

On this question, there really exist two irreconcilable, antagonistic viewpoints. On my part, I maintain that the deist idea, religion, and feudal superstition are not the same thing, that the three have things in common but also their own particularities, that although they are interrelated with one another, they are also distinct from one another.

Comrades Yu Hsiang and Liu Chun-wang, on the other hand, hold that the deist idea, religion, and feudal superstition are "the same thing," and that they are all "religion."

Superficially, the debate appears to concern only the relations among the deist idea, religion, and feudal superstition. But as a matter of fact it is not confined to the relations among the three. Because Comrades Yu Hsiang and Liu Chun-wang have distorted the relationship among the deist idea, religion, and feudal superstition and the Marxist teaching of atheism, therefore in this article I cannot help touch upon many aspects of the Marxist teaching of atheism. In particular, I cannot help writing on the struggle between the Marxist theory of atheism and the bourgeois "science of religion."

*II. To Declare That the Deist Idea, Religion, and
Superstition Are the "Same Thing" Is a
Viewpoint of the Bourgeois "Science of
Religion"*

COMRADES YU HSIANG AND LIU CHUN-WANG declare repeatedly in their article that the deist idea and religion are "the same thing," that religion and feudal superstition are also "the same thing," and that the deist idea, religion, and feudal superstition are all "religion." That is their "theory." Such a "theory" is neither a Marxist viewpoint nor one which they themselves have created, but a viewpoint that belongs to the "science of religion" of the Western bourgeois countries.

The bourgeois "science of religion" is basically not a science at all. This is because religion belongs to the superstructure of society, it is a form of expression of ideology, and its genesis, development and extinction are in the final analysis determined by the economic base. This is a basic principle of historical materialism. Since bourgeois "religionists" know nothing at all about historical materialism, they cannot know anything about the objective law of the genesis and development of religion.

According to the bourgeois "science of religion," religion was first born in the mind of man. It was born because in his life man needed some sort of spiritual support and solace. That is completely a viewpoint of historical idealism and is basically wrong.

Another basic error of the bourgeois "science of religion" comes from a basic ignorance of the relationship among these three—the deist idea, religion, general superstition (now called "feudal superstition" in our country). Bourgeois "religionists" do not understand that the deist idea, religion, and general superstition (feudal superstition) have their common characteristics and their particularities (differences), their interrelations and distinctions. Bourgeois "religionists" hold that the deist idea and religion are the "same thing," that religion and general superstition (feudal superstition) are also the "same thing," and that the deist idea, religion, and general superstition (feudal superstition) are all "religion."

Accordingly, "nature worship," "fetishism," "totemism," "spirit worship," "ancestor worship," "pantheism," "witchcraft," and such practices or beliefs of primitive society are all called "primitive religion" by bourgeois "religionists." (In their essay, "Relationship Between Religion and the Deist Idea and Superstition," Comrades Yu Hsiang and Liu Chun-wang also completely affirm this viewpoint.)

Following the entry of Western culture into China, bourgeois "science of religion" was also introduced to our country from the West early in the twentieth century. Many of the old generation of bourgeois intellectuals of the old China, especially those who made a study of "sociology" and "science of history," accepted in its entirety the "theories" of the bourgeois "science of religion," and concretely applied them in the results of their scientific research.

For example, in his "Ancient History of China," Hsia Tseng-yu, a historian of the last years of the Manchu dynasty and the early years of the Republic, completely followed the set theories of the bourgeois "science of religion" by labeling the deist idea, religion, and general superstition (feudal superstition) of ancient China indiscriminately as the "ancient religion of China."

Similar instances are quite common in histories written by bourgeois intellectuals of the old China. It may thus be seen that the bourgeois "science of religion" exerted a profound influence on learned circles in the old China.

However, social conditions in our country were different from those in Western countries. In our history, both Taoism and Buddhism had their heyday, but neither of them had ever attained such a ruling position as that attained by the Christian Church in Western countries. In our history, therefore, there was formed a long time ago an intricate, complex situation in which the three religions, Confucianism, Buddhism, and Taoism, existed side by side with one another (as a matter of fact, Confucianism cannot be called a religion), religion existed side by side with feudal superstition, and religion and feudal superstition existed side by side with the idea of spirits and gods in general. That is a peculiarity in our history which made the situation in our country completely different from that of the Western countries, where there was only one religion (the Christian Church), one god (the Christian God), and one superstition (Christian miracles, etc.).

As a result, the introduction of the bourgeois "science of religion" into China met with different response from the bourgeois intellectuals of our country. Although most of them accepted the viewpoints of the bourgeois "science of religion" in their entirety, a small number of them rejected these viewpoints from the West.

For example, in his book *History of Changes of Learned Thinking in Ancient China*, Liang Ch'i-ch'ao maintained that "there was one thing that distinguished us from other countries, and that is that we had no religion." Thus Liang Ch'i-ch'ao held the view that there was no religion at all in ancient China.

Although Liang Ch'i-ch'ao rejected the viewpoints of the bourgeois "science of religion," his viewpoint was equally erroneous, because China was not a "religionless" country, but one with many religions. The difference is that in China, no one single religion had ever attained a ruling position throughout the whole country as the Christian Church had in the Western countries.

Both Hsia Tseng-yu and Liang Ch'i-ch'ao were representatives of the bourgeois intellectuals of the old China in the last years of the Manchu dynasty and the early years of the Republic. They represented two extreme viewpoints: Hsia Tseng-yu indiscriminately labeled as "religions of ancient China" the deist idea, religion, and feudal superstition that had existed in our history. On the other hand, Liang Ch'i-ch'ao obliterated with a single stroke of the pen all the religions that had existed in our history, claiming that ours was a "religionless" country. Both these viewpoints were erroneous and non-Marxist.

III. Implications for Tactics

IN OUR COUNTRY ESPECIALLY, it is extremely harmful to speak of deist "religion." This is because among the broad masses of our people, there have been in history, and are still at present, many who do not follow any religion, and yet they believe in "spirits" and "fate." These people are numerous. If we admit that the deist idea and religion are "the same thing" and that all deist ideas are "religion," then we must necessarily admit that all those who believe in "spirits" and "fate" are "religious believers." In this way many who are not religious believers will be counted as such, and this will greatly magnify the forces of religion in our country. This is obviously disadvantageous to our struggle against religion and superstition and to the class struggle in the sphere of religion and superstition.

It is not only erroneous in theory, but also harmful in practice, to regard religion and feudal superstition as "the same thing" and maintain that feudal superstition is also "religion," because sorceresses, priests, soothsayers, geomancers, etc. still exist openly or covertly in large numbers in our countryside.

If we admit that religion and feudal superstition are "the same thing" and that feudal superstition is also "religion," then we shall also have to admit that the Party's policy of freedom of religious belief also applies to all forms of feudal superstition, that repressive measures cannot be taken against them, and that those who practice them should be allowed to enjoy the "freedom of religious belief." Such a "theory" is obviously advantageous to feudal superstition and to those who practice it professionally, but disadvantageous to our struggle against feudal superstition.

On the basis of the three points enumerated above, it is obviously impossible for Comrades Yu Hsiang and Liu Chun-wang to identify their views with the "Marxist-Leninist view on religion" by quoting certain passages from Marxist-Leninist works. It will be seen that the views of Comrades Yu Hsiang and Liu Chun-wang, when carefully analyzed, are not the Marxist-Leninist view on religion, but those of the bourgeois "science of religion."

PART II

Religious Policy in Practice

THE TOTAL ABSENCE of official pronouncement on religious policy and practice since the closing down of all public religious activity by Red Guard activists in 1966 contrasts sharply with earlier years. As late as December, 1965, Party theoreticians were engaged in extensive public debate in the nation's leading journals on questions related to implementing religious policy. From the very beginning of the communist regime considerable attention was given to policy and tactics for dealing with religion, with frequent reference to the constitutional guarantee of freedom of religious belief and to statements by Mao Tse-tung and others on the necessity for persuasive rather than coercive tactics in dealing with religious believers.

At the same time, Party leaders and writers left no doubt as to their personal positions or the proper position of a communist toward religion: as orthodox Marxist-Leninists, they were convinced that religious belief and superstitious practices would die natural deaths as socialist education and national reconstruction transformed the lives and thinking of the people. For this reason, taking their cue from Chairman Mao, they seemed in no hurry to force prematurely the death of that which was already doomed.

Even so, the implementation of the constitutional freedom of religious belief was never allowed to interfere with higher priority goals of the state and Party. Whether or not in conflict with his religion, *every* loyal citizen was required to render patriotic service.

This might mean giving military service or civilian support in the Korean War, signing a patriotic covenant, or taking part in anti-American demonstrations. To many believers it meant joining in mass accusation meetings to denounce their own religious leaders charged with unpatriotic or subversive behavior, and accepting leaders authorized by the Religious Affairs Bureau. The united front policy demanded that sectarian differences—and unique, often precious doctrines and practice—be abandoned for the collective cause. Study campaigns brought clergy and leaders of all religions together for indoctrination in right thinking which stressed patriotic duties at the expense of religious distinctions, and sought to enlist all believers in common commitment to the national effort. Labor campaigns, such as the Great Leap Forward, demanded time and energy of religious adherents regardless of conflict with sabbath days and scheduled worship services.

Minority groups with minority voices had no place in the China of the 1950s and '60s. Religious minorities enjoyed freedom of religious belief only if they spoke with the voice of the national majority and shared the common burdens, goals and vision. Recalcitrant, dissenting or stubbornly independent leaders were singled out, harassed, publicly denounced and removed from office. Ordinary believers found the limits on religious practice steadily tightened throughout this period.

Institutional activities also were curtailed so that by the mid-1960s even the handful of religious journals that had survived ceased publishing. In 1965 only one Protestant theological seminary with fewer than 100 students remained open, while there was none for the Roman Catholics. Even this closed in 1966, along with the remaining religious studies institutes of the Moslems and Buddhists.

Patriotism, anti-imperialism, self-reliance, united front, socialist construction—these themes dominated the collective effort of a nation fragmented and devastated by eight years of war with Japan, and four more years of civil war followed by total mobilization for the Korean War less than a year later.

While the external threat from imperialism was being faced in Korea, the internal threat from lingering traces of imperialist-tainted thinking and counter-revolutionary or revisionist elements came under attack within religious groups as well as elsewhere. Because of their missionary origins and links with Western nations, the Christian groups, particularly the Roman Catholics, were highly suspect and subjected to rigorous scrutiny and ideological reorientation. Remnant "bad elements" were denounced in public meetings by their fellow believers, underwent thought reform by political study and manual labor or, in some cases, suffered imprisonment and even death. All direct ties with foreign mission agencies were cut by the end of 1951.

The drive for universal patriotic allegiance uncovered alleged subversion and reactionary thinking among China's traditional religions as well. Although the crimes of Buddhist, Moslem, and Taoist leaders came under the rubric of revisionist "feudalism" rather than "imperialism," the message was the same: believers could quietly practice their faith if they joined, without reservation, the common effort for socialist construction under the leadership of Party and government. They must abandon superstitious customs, sectarian divisiveness, and religious practices that interfered with production or the united effort. Above all they must root out all counter-revolutionary, revisionist or feudal-reactionary "poisonous weeds hiding under the cloak of religion."

The documents selected for this section (aside from Section 12) are taken from the official press and therefore reflect, in nearly every instance, official policy and practice. Even so, much can be inferred about the vitality of religious groups, their confrontation and accommodation with the new government and ideology, and the roles played by various religious leaders at different stages in the period 1950–66. For example, the outspoken statements of religious leaders during the brief "Hundred Flowers" period stand in startling contrast to the published views of these same men during later periods of tighter control.

Section 1. Patriotism and United Front

FREEDOM OF RELIGIOUS BELIEF and practice was tolerated (until 1966), as these documents clearly set forth, only within the state- and Party-defined context of patriotic service in the common cause. While it might be argued that, strictly speaking, freedom of *private* religious belief was, and still is, possible, the conditions for continuing public religious practice were clearly laid down by Lu Ting-yi, chairman of the Committee on Cultural, Religious and Educational Affairs of the Administrative Yuan, in 1951, and in subsequent statements by religious leaders and government officials. He told religious leaders (see Doc. 28) that all citizens, including religious believers, had certain patriotic duties, including military service, paying taxes, and obeying laws. They should oppose imperialism; they should love country, people, labor and public property. Old thinking and old culture should be wiped out and replaced with a new proletarian culture. Reactionary, unreformed elements were subject to loss of all civil rights.

The 1954 address by Y. T. Wu, Chairman of the Protestant Three-Self Movement, makes explicit the proper posture of the church: Christians should show a new spirit on the basis of "Love-country Love-church," stressing patriotism, nation-building, anti-imperialism, self-support, church unity, and purification of the church.

Writing four years later, the deputy director of the United Front Work Department prescribes conditions for participation in the people's democratic united front by religious believers: they must be patriotic, law-abiding and travel the road of socialism.

There is no need to persecute believers, the director of the Bureau of Religious Affairs told an Australian visitor in 1956, as long as they are patriotic and do their share of work in national reconstruction. While acknowledging the mishandling of some cases involving Christians, he declared that the arrest and imprisonment of Christian leaders was due in every case to charges of political offenses and had nothing to do with their religious activities—an interpretation obviously questioned by his Australian interlocutor (see Doc. 40).

DOC. 35. *United Declaration of the Delegates of Chinese Christian Churches, Issued by a Conference of 151 Protestant Church Leaders Convened by Chou En-lai in Peking (April 16–21, 1951)*

WE, THE REPRESENTATIVES of all Protestant churches and organizations in China, gathered in the capital city, Peking, to attend a conference of Protestant Christian organizations receiving American financial aid, called by the Central Government's Committee on Cultural and Educational Affairs, issue the following statement—to fellow Christians in China, and in the whole world:

At this time when the strength of peace is growing among the people of the world, imperialism has already reached its last days. The encroachment of American imperialism in Korea and Taiwan is a final show of strength before death. American imperialism is now arming Japan and Western Germany, preparing to attain its aggressive objectives, once again preparing to kill multitudes of people, but it will not attain its objective. In Korea it has already met the force of the people of China and Korea—it will yet experience in the end defeat and death.

We strongly oppose this American imperialistic aggressive plan, we strongly oppose the use of atomic weapons, we oppose a separate peace treaty with Japan and oppose rearming Japan, oppose rearming Western Germany. We wish to unite with all Christians in the world who love peace and oppose all schemes of American imperialism to break up peace programs.

But most Christians in the world are good. It is the wicked imperialists who use the church as their tool of aggression. In July, 1950, the Executive Committee of the World Council of Churches met in Toronto, Canada, and passed a resolution concerning the war in Korea, branding the North Korean government as an aggressor, and appealing to the United Nations to exhort member nations to take part in 'police action' in Korea, and opposing the signed appeal of 500 million people (The Stockholm Peace Appeal) against the use of atomic weapons.

This resolution distorts truth. It is contrary to the desires of peace-loving people of the world. This resolution of the World Council of Churches echoes the voice of the United States Congress. If one examines this truth-distorting resolution of the World Council, one can see that the World Council is the tool of Wall Street, and of that instigator of the Korean War, Dulles. We express our wish to expose U.S. imperialism, which during the past period of over a hundred years has made use of the church's work in evangelism and cultural activities to carry out its sinister policy. In our Manifesto of September, 1950, we emphasized the breaking off of relations between the church in China and imperialism, the purging from the church of all imperialistic influences. We feel that the breaking off of all imperialistic connections and the purging of all imperialistic influences is the direction that should be energetically pursued by the church in China and all Christians in the world. We must cleanse the Holy Temple of God, and preserve the purity of the church.

On December 29, 1950, the Legislative Yuan of the Central People's Government published the "Plan to control cultural, educational and relief organizations and religious bodies receiving American financial aid." At this present meeting, we have discussed the draft proposed by the Government concerning the plan to be adopted by Protestant religious bodies receiving

American financial grants. We have also heard the reports of Government leaders and had detailed discussions. We recognize that the plan of the Central People's Government for the protection of the Protestant church is certainly careful, complete and very satisfactory. The Fifth Article of the Common Platform guarantees the people's freedom of religion and belief; moreover, we have received freedom of religion and belief, and this state of affairs has greatly encouraged and strengthened Protestant Christians in self-government, self-support and independent evangelism. In regard to these government arrangements, we not only gladly accept them, but we also express the gratitude of our hearts. American imperialism wishes to use the method of freezing assets to cause those Protestant churches and enterprises dependent upon foreign funds to fall into despair. But the People's Government has helped us to progress toward a bright future. We believe that the Chinese Protestant church, relying upon God, and under the eminent guidance of Chairman Mao, and with the encouragement and help of the Government, will be able to make full use of its own strength to raise up a purer, fitter and more perfect Christian enterprise to serve the people.

We call upon fellow-Christians in the whole country:

(1) To resolutely support and carry out the Central Government Legislative Yuan's "Plan of control for all cultural, educational and relief organizations and religious bodies receiving American financial aid," also the regulations concerning registration for cultural, educational and relief organizations and religious bodies receiving foreign financial aid and having transactions in foreign exchange, together with the resolutions received from the Legislative Yuan and passed by the full meeting concerning 'the method of control for Protestant Christian bodies receiving American financial aid.' And finally, *to thoroughly, permanently and completely sever all relations with American missions and all other missions, thus realizing self-government, self-support and self-propagation in the Chinese church.*

(2) To enthusiastically take part in the 'Oppose-America, Support-Korea' Movement, strongly support the resolution of

the Executive of the World Peace Movement concerning the Five Nations Peace Treaty, support all decisions of the 'Oppose-America, Support-Korea' People's Central Organization, also make known and definitely carry out the patriotic program: *Every local church, every church body, every Christian publication must implement the 'Oppose-America, Help-Korea' propaganda and make this propaganda known to every Christian.*

(3) To support the Common Program, support the Government land reform policy and support the Government in the repression of anti-revolutionaries, obey all Government laws, positively respond to the Government commands, and exert every effort in the reconstruction of the nation. We want to be more alert, to resolutely reject the blandishments of imperialism, *to assist the Government to discover and punish anti-revolutionary and corrupt elements within the Protestant church*; to resolutely oppose the secret plans of imperialists and reactionaries who wish to destroy the Three-Self Movement; also encourage and spread the movement in each church and Christian organization and denounce imperialists and anti-revolutionary evil elements.

(4) To increase patriotic education, greatly enlarge the study movement in order to increase the political consciousness of Christians. Finally, we call upon all Christians to continue to promote and enlarge the campaign to secure signatures to revolutionary documents and firmly resolve to make effective the Three-Self mission of the church, and with the highest enthusiasm welcome the unlimited, glorious future of the People's Republic of China.

DOC. 36. *Methodist Patriotic Covenant*

THE PATRIOTIC COVENANT was sent out to all Methodist churches in April, 1951, to be signed by individual church members.

Chinese Christian Methodist Church Patriotic Covenant

1. WE SINCERELY SUPPORT Chairman Mao, the Chinese Communist Party, the People's Government, the Common Platform, and all the laws and actions of the People's Government.

2. We will unite all Christians in supporting world peace, and in opposing American imperialist re-arming of Japan, and will take part in the movement to oppose America, aid Korea, and protect our homes and our country.

3. We will promote the Reform Movement in the Christian Church, complete the work of Self-government, Self-support, and Self-propagation, and do well the work of religion among the Chinese people, so as to serve them.

4. We will help the People's Government to get rid of spies and special agents, and be on the alert to prevent reactionary elements from using the church in their destructive activities. We will clear the church of all renegades, so as to preserve the purity of religion.

5. We will forever cut off all relations with American imperialism, and will completely wipe out of our church all the influences of American cultural imperialism.

6. We will increase our study of current events, and our understanding of the government. We will take part in the labor movement, practice simple living, and strengthen the unity of the Chinese people.

> Each person accepting the Covenant should sign here.

DOC. 37. *Report to Protestant Leaders (1954)*

THESE EXCERPTS ARE FROM the report of Y. T. Wu, Chairman of the Protestant Three-Self Movement Preparatory Council, to 232

Protestant delegates from all over China who met in Peking for sixteen days, from July 22 to August 6, 1954. By action of this conference the China Protestant Three-Self Patriotic Movement was constituted.

(3) CHINESE CHRISTIANS as a result of the Three-Self Reform Movement have raised their patriotic consciousness, and have taken part in various patriotic movements and in the movement for world peace. These patriotic movements include the Oppose-America Help-Korea Fund, Comfort to the Volunteers, assistance to the families of martyred soldiers, the purchasing of government bonds, and the formulation of patriotic manifestos. There also appeared among the Christians many model workers, as well as others who loved both country and church, and many Christians were elected as people's representatives at various levels. . . .

(4) The churches of New China on the basis of "Love-country Love-church" are showing a new spirit.

We thank the Lord that during the past four years, by the grace of the Lord and the determination of both laymen and pastors, the Chinese Church has not only made progress in its spiritual work, but has attained a sense of solidarity which it never had before.

Today believers love their church more than ever and are willing to take responsibility for it, giving generously of both money and time. Many pastors have a firmer faith, seeing more clearly God's upholding providence, and are more zealous in caring for their flocks, rightly divining the word of truth, and training Christians in the spirit of Love-country Love-church. Accordingly the sense of fellowship between pastors and laymen is constantly growing.

The partitions which imperialism had raised between the churches are gradually being destroyed, and members and workers of different churches who formerly had little or nothing to do with each other are now increasing in fellowship. Nanking, Peking, Shanghai, Hangchow, Tientsin and Wuhan have all held church workers' retreats. The Christian young people of Shanghai, Peking, Wuhan, Canton, Amoy and Nanking have had interdenominational summer and winter conferences and Christmas and Easter programs. We have truly come to realize what a pleasant thing it is for brethren to dwell together in unity.

From the accomplishments of these four years we have gained the following experience: First, the road of opposing imperialism and loving country and church represents the demand and desire of the vast majority of Chinese Christians, which shows that Christians love truth rather than iniquity. Under the banner of opposing imperialism and loving the country, all the Christians of China can and should unite. Second, loving country and loving church are not inconsistent with each other. Our Lord Jesus loved His own country. Patriotism is the duty which we Chinese Christians owe our country as citizens, while devotion to the church is the expression of a precious faith. Since the church has been used, influenced and defiled by imperialism, so in order to purify the church it is necessary for us to oppose imperialism and show our love for our country. Third, we can understand the mutual relationships of opposing imperialism, loving country and loving church if we will devote ourselves to sincere study and align ourselves with the people.

The unity which we Christians have already achieved on the platform of loving country and church is unprecedented both in scope and degree, and is much to be prized. The widely representative character of the brethren met in this Conference is one proof of this fact. But the experience of the past four years shows us that imperialism is constantly maligning and trying to destroy our unity. Whatever increases our unity we must endeavor to do; whatever tends to break up that unity we must point out and endeavor to change.

For the sake of unity we must be more humble, not thinking of ourselves more highly than we ought to think, and must be ready to help our brothers and sisters with love and patience. We should turn away from unchristian pride and impatience, and learn to work and think together.

For the sake of unity we must recognize each church and each sect and each theological viewpoint, and accept firmly the principle of mutual self-respect.

In the development of our Three-Self Patriotic Movement, we should do the following things:

(1) Call upon all Christians to uphold the Constitution of the Chinese People's Republic and work for the establishment of a socialist society. . . .

(2) Call upon all Christians to oppose aggressive imperialism and work for an enduring world peace. . . .

(3) Continue patriotic studies by church members and church workers, and wipe out imperialistic influences. . . .

(4) Consolidate church organization in the spirit of self-government. . . .

(5) Study the problems of self-support and find out how to solve them. . . .

(6) Under the principle of mutual respect, study the work of self-propagation, get rid of imperialistic poison, and preach the true gospel. . . .

(7) In the spirit of love-country love-church promote patriotism and law observance, and thus purify the church.

If only we will be patriotic and law-abiding, the government under the guarantee of religious liberty will protect the church, its lawful activities and its proper interests. As to those churches which are still in difficulties, we will continue in accordance with the concrete situation to mediate between the churches concerned and the organs of government and work for a satisfactory settlement. The solution of these difficulties will help the whole church to a more prosperous development on the basis of the Three-Self Patriotic Movement.

The above proposals are for the purpose of purifying and conforming the church, and of making a good witness to the gospel of Christ. They are interrelated and cannot be separated; to carry them all out will be to love church and love country, and make progress in the work of the Three-Self Patriotic Movement.

DOC. 38. *Chang Chih-yi: Atheists and Theists Can Cooperate Politically and Travel the Road of Socialism (1958)*

III. Concerning the Problem of Religious Policy

THE CHINESE COMMUNIST PARTY and the state are now engaged in the framing of a religious policy on the basis of the nature of religion, its present and historical conditions and the needs of the socialist undertaking of the Chinese people. The policy aims at the correct handling of the contradictions among the people and those between the people and their enemy, and the provision of a common political basis to enable the believers to join the people throughout the country in a grand union and render services to socialism. This common political basis is anti-imperialist and patriotic and follows the road of socialism. This must be achieved or we must "overcome the opposition" or "convert the opposition." Religious circles, therefore, must conduct the anti-imperialist patriotic movement and the socialist educational movement. Ideological difference on the question of God is tolerable. The policy on freedom of religious belief tolerates such difference and facilitates the correct handling of such a contradiction among the people. The policy on freedom of religious belief, therefore, is a long-term basic policy of the Chinese Communist Party and the state to cope with the religious problem.

On the basis of the policy the state demands religious circles to conform to the constitution, be patriotic and law-abiding, support the people's democratic dictatorship under the leadership of the Chinese Communist Party and travel the road of socialism. The state does not resort to administrative procedure to interfere in religious affairs, concerning which religious circles make their own decisions independently. So long as they do not run counter to the interests of the socialist cause, the government does not interfere, but it also forbids any religion to interfere in state affairs under any pretext. All religions are accorded equal treatment by the government, and none is granted any special privilege. Our government has continually publicized the reasons for freedom of religious belief among the broad mass of people and protected the legitimate religious activities of believers and the establishments where such activities are conducted.

Concerning the religious life of the believers, the masses of the Catholics and the evangelistic rallies and Sunday schools of the Protestants are conducted as usual; the Buddhists chant sutras as before; the Islamites continue to worship, fast and go on pilgrimage in their traditional pattern. There has been no change in the post-liberation period, while the state has accorded religious organizations protection and certain facilities. State organs, public bodies, school enterprises and producers' cooperatives have also offered necessary and possible help to believers in their respective units in regard to their religious activities. Churches, temples, Taoist monasteries and cultural relics related to religion have been accorded protection. There are newly built churches in some places. The state has appropriated money for the repair of famed monasteries or mosques and religious relics involving Buddhism, Taoism or Islam. A number of such structures in Peking, Hangchow, Kansu and Loyang have been renovated by the People's Government during the post-liberation period.

IV. United Front Work Concerning Religious Circles

IDEOLOGICAL DIFFERENCES do not exclude political cooperation. . . . Socialist construction in our country being a herculean task, we must rally all those that can be rallied in a united effort to build it into a powerful, great socialist state. The united front policy of the Chinese Communist Party and the state towards religious circles, therefore, is of a long-term nature.

The united front has two allies, who are also present as regards the united front in religious circles. The broad mass of working people among the believers are the first ally, forming the cornerstone of our united front in religious circles. The sacred functionaries or professional religionists in religious circles and a portion of non-working people among the believers —chiefly the middle and upper reaches of the democratic patriotic elements—represent our second ally, and are the major objectives of our united front work in religious circles. Such middle and upper reaches of religious circles maintain definite contacts with believers and the masses and enjoy certain prestige among the latter. The living Buddhas among the lamas and the spiritual overseers of the Islamites are regarded as holy by their believers. The proper carrying out of united front activities among these people is of great help to winning over, rallying, and indoctrinating the believers.

The people's democratic united front prescribes certain conditions for religious circles. This is to say, they must be anti-imperialist, patriotic, and law-abiding and travel the road of socalism; these conditions form the political basis of unity and cooperation. The talk of a united front is futile in the absence of such conditions.

To love the country (to love socialism and the fatherland) is the sacred duty of every Chinese citizen, believers of course not excepted. . . . The patriotic movement of the Chinese Catholics and the self-administration patriotic movement of the Protestants represent the conscious patriotic movement of the believers aiming at converting Catholicism and Protestantism in China into self-administered religious undertakings, so that they will no longer become tools of imperialist aggression against China. It is a revolutionary movement seeking a thorough solution of the contradictions between the people and the enemy in respect to the religious problem and helping the mass of believers draw a sharp line of demarcation between the people and the enemy on the political and the ideological front. But the Vatican and the imperialist or counter-revolutionary elements in China under its command have made every attempt to intervene and prevent Chinese believers from participating in this movement and buffet the holy functionaries and the mass of believers. This is something which no patriotic Chinese, no patriotic religious followers can tolerate.

To be patriotic, one must abide by the law of the country.

To abide by the law is a concrete manifestation of patriotism and is the duty of all citizens, religious people not excepted. Every believer should do his bit to fulfill the general program of our country for the transition period. To build our country into a prosperous and strong socialist country, the people in our country have through the National People's Congress promulgated the constitution and various laws and statutes and the people's government has framed various policies and decrees. Every Chinese citizen is obliged to uphold them. The people's government does not interfere with religious activities, but it does not tolerate clandestine illegal activities and unequivocally bans rumor-mongering, misrepresentation of government policy, attempts to sabotage production and all other activities counter to the decrees of the government.

To be patriotic, one must love socialism and the New China under the leadership of the Chinese Communist Party. This is to say, one must love the socialist fatherland and travel the road of socialism, which is the only road enabling China to attain independence, strength, prosperity and happiness. We oppose travelling the road of capitalism, which must inevitably bring China back into the blind alley of semi-colonialism or colonialism. Without the leadership of the Chinese Communist Party there can be no socialism and no New China. We therefore demand that religious people support the Chinese Communist Party and the people's government and travel the road to socialism. Only by following such a course can religious undertakings obtain protection and can there be a future for the religious people.

DOC. 39. *Tsinghai Provincial Conference on All-out War War Closes (1959)*

THE CONFERENCE FURTHER AGREED: To keep on strengthening work on religions, and fully carry out the party policy of religious freedom, is a permanent work of importance in united front work. After the 1958 socialist revolution, counter-revolutionaries wearing the religious cloak were mostly cleared out, feudal privileges and the oppressing exploiting system of religious temples were cancelled, and the party policy of religious freedom was further put into effect. However, at this time many of the multitude still believe in religion. This is a matter of their thoughts and beliefs. At any time, we can only use the method of convincing and instructing, solving the problem by gradual raising of their ideas and feelings, and their level of science and culture; we certainly cannot use the way of enforcing by administrative order.

For this reason the conference emphasized: The policy of religious freedom is the party's fundamental policy on religion, which must be properly understood, and fully carried out. In doing so, we must distinguish between religious belief, and religious privileges with an exploiting system; distinguish between priests' ordinary activities and the extortion and harm practiced on the multitude; distinguish between ordinary religious persons and counterrevolutionaries who assume the cloak of religion. All feudal privileges and oppressing exploiting systems of religious houses must be done away with, and counter-revolutionaries wearing the cloak of religion wiped out. Towards the masses' religious beliefs there must be firm protection, without any interference or restraint. There is perfect freedom for the masses to believe or not, to believe this or that; to believe today and not tomorrow, or to disbelieve today and believe tomorrow.

Those present also agreed that along with putting into effect the policy of religious freedom, we must improve the work of political ideology among the believing masses, expose counter-revolutionaries wearing the cloak of religion using religion to shatter national unity and to harm the people of different races; we must also combine class struggle among the masses with production struggle, always promoting teaching of socialism and communism and of science and culture, for ceaseless raising of popular class feeling and thinking.

DOC. 40. *An Anglican Journalist Interviews the Director of the Bureau of Religious Affairs (1956)*

'The People's State Wants Cooperation, not Victims or Martyrs'

THE DIRECTOR of the Bureau of Religious Affairs is Ho Chen-hsiang, aged fifty-four, father of four children, a Communist Party member of twenty-five years' standing, something of a skeptic, and a chap to whom I took a considerable liking. Within a few minutes of our meeting, when I commented that it was surprising to find an atheist in such a job, he said, "Why not? You can imagine the outcry the Moslems would make if I were a Christian, or the fuss most Christians would make if I didn't belong to their 'party.' "

As head of the bureau, his status is higher than that of the head of a department in a Western state; although it is not exactly comparable with that of a minister in a parliamentary democracy. This indicates better than anything else I can imagine just how important religion is in the eyes of the Chinese Government.

'We Stand on Common Ground'

Ho CHEN-HSIANG is responsible directly to the Central Government Administrative Council (what we call the Cabinet) to which he has immediate access.

Mr. Ho was quite frank about the irreconcilability of Christianity and Marxism, at least in theory.

"The attitude of the Government briefly can be summarized in an old Chinese saying," he told me. " 'We stand upon our common ground, and maintain our differences.' "

"You must realize that the Christians [Protestants] and the Roman Catholics are, after all, Chinese citizens. . . .

"Not only are they Chinese citizens, they have special skills which the New China needs in the tasks before her.

"As long as they are patriotic citizens, then why should they be persecuted? It is true that they are very small in numbers; but proportionately, they are very highly trained in all kinds of things."

"In other words," I observed, "you tolerate Christianity at the moment just because some Christians are useful to your relations with other countries, too?"

"Of course," Mr. Ho said.

"Our constitutional guarantee of religious freedom is there for a very good reason, and no one in China would ever question it nowadays.

"As long as a man is patriotic, and does his share in the work of reconstruction, and as long as his religious beliefs do not operate against the People's Republic, then why should we be so stupid as to try to eradicate them by force?

"You cannot root out religion by force. Though I believe some of your Christian parties have tried to do so in old times in Europe.

"The People's State does not want victims, or martyrs.

"It wants cooperation and support.

"Between socialism and religion I do not believe there is any necessary antipathy. On the contrary.

"Our whole policy is to get individuals and groups of people to support the Government—especially religious groups. So we treat them in such a way that we can fairly and objectively speaking expect them to support us."

"And do they in fact give you that support?" I asked him.

The Religions Rally

"THE OVERWHELMING MAJORITY of all religious leaders and their followers are strongly in favor of the People's Government," he said. "Believe me, that is the truth. You need only see how the Moslems, for example, have rallied behind us in the northwest to see how true it is.

"As far as the Christians and the Roman Catholics are concerned, of course, that was not the case in the time immediately after Liberation.

"There were still so many foreign missionaries here, and there were many misunderstandings.

"But since the churches rid themselves of foreign influence, the whole position has changed. We know that they are now self-supporting and so on, and that although a section of the Roman Catholics—but not many—still entertain ideas of a return to the old system, most of the Roman Catholics and all the Christians see that they are on the correct path."

"This is all very nice," I said. "But what about the fundamental question of freedom? In the West, you often hear of clergymen and even bishops attacking their governments' policies from the pulpit. What about China?"

"Well, I can quite understand Christians overseas criticizing their governments' policies," Mr. Ho said (a trifle smugly, I thought). "But that of course is entirely your own affair, and has nothing to do with China, so I shall not discuss it.

"Here, it is not true to say that we discourage criticism. On the contrary, we are always glad of it. But criticism is different from attacking the government.

"There are many faults in China today. These can only be remedied if they are criticized. The churches have as much right as anyone to mention them. They are encouraged to do so in a constructive way.

"But it would be a different thing to attack the government, the way that some foreign missionaries used to do, encouraging all kinds of treasonable activities. They used to go about saying that the Government and all it stood for was evil. They used to tell people that all our reform programs were wrong, and that sort of thing. They used to urge the workers not to cooperate with the Government, and even to work against it.

"That does not happen now. I think the main reason is that most misunderstandings have been removed, on all sides."

'Why Are Priests Imprisoned?'

"If all is as you say, then why are there so many Christian leaders still in prison?" I asked him. "To my certain knowledge, there are four Roman Catholic bishops and three Protestants. And Wang Ming-tao and our own Bishop Kimber Den have only just been released from jail. If that is not religious persecution, then what is it?"

Mr. Ho was distinctly uneasy when I mentioned Bishop Kimber Den; but he stuck manfully to his line.

"Oh, no!" he said. "None of these cases means religious persecution.

"In each case, the man concerned committed a political offense, even though he may have used the church, the pulpit, to try to hide what he was doing, as so many did in former years."

"But that is not so, surely?" I countered. "You say that each one has committed a political offense? Then what about Bishop Kimber Den? Here is a man of fine character, who has been imprisoned without a trial for five years. Then he is suddenly released, after being kept there all that time without a trial. And now you turn around and free him and say it was all just a mistake. I can tell you that a lot of people outside China will regard that as monstrous."

"I know," said Ho Chen-hsiang. "But you have met [Anglican Bishop] Kimber Den, I believe, and you have heard what he had to say. I do not think he would have said that he was imprisoned because of his religion, or penalized in any way for it. It came about through political factors.

"I agree that the handling of his case is not at all satisfactory. I can only say that we welcome your criticisms over this, and that those who were responsible for the delays, which are the most unsatisfactory aspect of this case, have been severely punished. I should also say that the whole matter was outside my jurisdiction.

"At a former stage, everyone knows that many unfortunate things happened with regard to Christians and Roman Catholics. But if you look at it objectively, you must admit that it was a natural reaction by many Chinese people after the things that had been done against China under the guise of missionary work. It was never the policy of the Government."

Nothing I could say would shake Mr. Ho on this.

He maintained that the only intention of the Communists after "Liberation" was to ensure, as part of their responsibility for the security of China generally, that "espionage" was not carried on by foreign missionaries or Chinese sympathizers with the West.

The moment that "conditions improved so much that we knew this would not happen," he said, then the Government relaxed the very close watch it had maintained on the churches.

Contacts Abroad Welcomed

As to the effect of the attitude of the Government on Christian opinion abroad, Mr. Ho said: "We quite realize the importance of that.

"Here again, there is much more than Christian membership to consider. We have to consider relations between Chinese and other Buddhists and Moslems, all over the world.

"Frankly, now that we know these groups are not working against the People's Government, we welcome their contact abroad. We think they can all help us work towards world peace.

"You must remember that there has never been any great difficulty with Moslems. Many of them go on pilgrimages to Mecca every year.

"It is only with the Roman Catholics that our position is somewhat different. Our policy is to welcome ecclesiastical relations with the Vatican. Each diocese can directly contact the Pope; but the Government is not going to allow the Vatican to interfere in Chinese affairs.

"You must admit that the Vatican has never ceased to attack our Government. It has not shown very good manners, and it has not tried to understand our problems.

"It has just tried to use the Roman Catholic religion to undermine the work of reconstruction.

"I do not want to influence your thinking about the Roman Catholics. It is much better for you to see them and ask questions and find out for yourself. So I will only say that in my opinion they are solidly behind the Government, and they are embarrassed by the attitude of the Pope."

The position of the Chung Hua Sheng Kung Hui [the Anglican church in China], Mr. Ho said, was otherwise.

"I think the policy of your church is much more realistic and in line with the objective facts," he said. ("Objective" is a favored word!)

He said he had no doubt that a small minority in England and the United States wished to see a return to the old missionary days, despite the fact that the C.H.S.K.H. was now autonomous.

"I think the way they have maintained their autonomy must be a surprise to some people," he said.

"When you ask about the effect of our attitude to the churches overseas, that is a good example. We encourage the Anglicans to have contacts abroad, and of course we hope that in that way the truth about China will become known abroad."

I asked him whether the Government's attitude would mean that it would be possible for the C.H.S.K.H. freely to send a return delegation to Australia, and whether the Chinese bishops would be able to attend the Lambeth Conference.

He said a return delegation to Australia would be "very welcome."

As to Lambeth, "There will be no objection whatever to their going to the Lambeth Conference," he said.

"On the contrary, not only will the Government not hinder them from going, but we will gladly help if we are asked."

I then asked why, if relations between Church and State were so cordial, the membership figures of the several denominations had not increased (although I knew that there had been actual increases in certain cases).

'An Extraordinary Custom'

"THAT IS A PROBLEM for the churches themselves," he said. "But I think you will find that in some cases membership has increased, and that total membership has remained about the same, with a very slight increase."

My last question was: "If the churches are as free as you say they are under the Constitution, then why cannot they proselytize in the way they used to, with street meetings and the like? How can they possibly increase in numbers if they cannot proselytize? Are you not really aiming at restricting their membership to the present level, in the hope that they will ultimately die away?"

Mr. Ho gave me the standard answer about the possibility of disturbances following open air meetings, stressing the point that Christianity is still "foreign" and anti-Chinese in the eyes of many.

"But surely they have all sorts of legitimate avenues apart from that," he said. "They have their services. They have meetings in halls and churches, literature, personal visits, catechism classes, retreats, meetings in private houses and so on.

"They have even this extraordinary custom (at this he gave me a knowing wink) of baptizing innocent infants, who do not know what it is all about! Now, a thing like that, although opposed to reason, and however ridiculous it may seem, is harmless. We have never tried to intervene against it."

However, I had no intention of discussing infant baptism with Mr. Ho, so on that note I left him.

Section 2. Religious Policy and National Minorities

AN ESTIMATED 6 percent of China's population belongs to non-Han ethnic minorities. The importance placed on these national minorities is seen in the wealth of pictorial and written material describing their life and contribution to the national effort appearing regularly in Chinese publications.

Because Lamaistic Buddhism and Islam, the two major religions of the border regions, were intimately related to traditional social and cultural systems, the importance of a correct religious policy was early emphasized. Although a considerable body of material from Tibetan refugees and other sources charges the Chinese with systematic suppression of indigenous religion and culture,[1] the Chinese, as late as 1965, continued to speak of a policy of freedom of religious belief and of state support for the repair of monasteries, mosques and temples, and for the maintenance of organized religion. Numerous eye-witness reports, however, tell of savage attacks by Red Guard bands in 1966 on religious buildings of all kinds, and by all reports available to us, those not converted into warehouses, hospitals, dormitories and other secular uses are closed and inoperative. The 1968 report in *People's Daily*, "Mao Tse-tung Replaces Buddha in Tibet" (Doc. 110) suggests a truer interpretation of the state of Tibetan Buddhism today than the account given in Document 43.

1. See *News-Tibet*, published by the Office of Tibet, New York.

Chang Chih-yi, a high Party official, writing in the magazine *Nationalities Unity* in 1962, affirms the importance of a correct religious policy for the past, present and long-term future. The Party's policy on freedom of religious belief, he writes, is entirely compatible with the basic interests of the Party and the people of minority groups, for it leads to unity in mobilization for nation-building. Thus it is "the only correct policy" and it is a "long-term policy" which must be implemented. However, the systems of feudal exploitation and oppression linked with the traditional religions must be eliminated in order to free the people for socialist development.

The vice chairman of the Chinese Islamic Association, writing in the same year, traces ten years of progress, as he sees it, under the Party's religious policy, comparing the oppressive and divisive use of religion by feudal leaders under the old system with the liberating effect of the new regime's religious policy—a policy, he writes, which promotes unity among the people and at the same time advances the cause of local religion.

He alludes to the struggle with counter-revolutionaries "hidden in Islamic circles," and the process of educating and transforming the religious professionals. Most (but not all) of them had been won over by 1962, some even elected as labor models and "advanced workers." The "broad masses" of Moslem believers, he writes, following the victory of the mass struggle, had completely changed their spiritual outlook.

At the same time, the importance of the Party's religious policy in relations with Islamic circles in Asia and Africa was frequently pointed out. Visiting groups of Moslems from other countries were able to see that Chinese Moslems were "enjoying freedom of religious belief and leading a happy life."

Reports from China since 1966 indicate that the only place of worship kept open is a mosque in Peking, apparently primarily for the use of Moslem visitors from abroad.

DOC. 41. *Chang Chieh, Vice-chairman, Chinese Islamic Association: The Party's Policy on Freedom of Religion Further Implemented among the Islamites*

I. CHINA IS A UNIFIED multi-national country, and a country in which many religions exist side by side. Most of the people of minority nationalities believe in religions. Ten different minority nationalities, including Hui (Moslem), Uighur, Kazak, Uzbek, Kolkoz, Tatar, Tajik, Tunghsiang, Salar and Paoan, believe in Islam. It is, therefore, of tremendous significance to implement correctly the Party's policy on freedom of religious belief among these minority nationalities.

Before the liberation, the broad masses of Moslems in our country had no freedom of religious belief. At that time, imperialism colluded with the reactionary ruling class in our country in using religion as a tool with which to consolidate their rule and oppress the people of various nationalities. On the one hand, they used the people's religious belief to deceive and benumb the people; on the other, they used and fostered feudal leaders of religious sects and religious privileges among the various nationalities to carry out brutal oppression and exploitation of the people. Moreover, they used different religious beliefs and different sects in one religion to sow discord and create splits, thus leading to mutual discrimination between religions, between sects, between nationalities, and between regions. Under these circumstances, it was of course impossible for the broad masses of Moslems to have freedom of religious belief. It was not until the founding of new China when the people of all nationalities under Party leadership have freed themselves from all forms of oppression and exploitation that the broad masses of Moslems, guided by the Party's policy on freedom of religious belief, begin to enjoy real and complete freedom of religious belief.

Since the correct implementation of the Party's policy on freedom of religious belief is conducive to the strengthening of the unity among various nationalities, to the unity between the masses of people who believe in religion and those who do not believe in religion, and to the mobilization of all positive factors for the common construction of socialism, this policy has, therefore, won the unanimous support of the people of all nationalities in our country, and the unanimous support of the whole body of Moslems.

During the past ten years and more, the Party's policy on freedom of religious belief has been implemented in an over-all manner in Moslem circles and among the Moslems of various nationalities. It is entirely possible for the broad masses of Moslems to decide their own religious belief in accordance with their own free will, and the Party and government pay full respect and considerations to their religious belief and customs and traditions. All legitimate religious activities and ceremonies are not only allowed to be carried out as usual, but are also fully protected by the government.

The Party and government have helped us build our own religious body—the Chinese Islamic Association. In a number of provinces, cities and autonomous regions, local Islamic organizations have also been established in accordance with need. An Islamic institute has been set up for the purpose of training exclusively Islamic patriotic intellectuals well versed in Islamic scriptures. Well-known Ch'ing-chen monasteries located in various parts of the country have been repaired. Islamic classics have been translated and published. Annual pilgrimages have been organized. Also, the Party and government have given appropriate consideration to, and made suitable arrangements for, the patriotic, law-abiding religious professionals. All this is a full expression of the Party's policy on freedom of religious belief.

In the wake of the continuous development of China's socialist revolution and construction, the broad masses of Moslems have daily raised their ideological consciousness. But the feudal oppression and economic exploitation in Islam have been a serious obstacle to the development of various nationalities which believe in Islam. The contradiction between some reactionaries in Islam and socialism has become increasingly acute.

In response to the unanimous request of the broad masses of Moslems, a forum of Hui people was called in Ninghsia, which exposed and criticized the hideous crimes committed by reactionary Ma Chen-wu (see Doc. 56). This was followed by democratic reform of religious systems in various places, and great achievements were made in this connection.

Prior to the democratic reform of religious systems, there still existed Islamic family divine rule and the hereditary system of dictatorship of leaders of sects; also in existence were the feudal administrative systems practiced in Ch'ing-chen monasteries and the feudal ownership of land. Sectarian systems and in particular compulsory systems of religious burdens and systems of "religious" punishment which interfered with the life of the broad masses of the people still existed. All these systems were in fact systems of feudal privileges under the cloak of religion. The existence of these systems not only seriously impeded the development of socialist construction enterprise but also hampered the thorough implementation of the policy of freedom of religious belief. They were abolished through the active efforts made by the broad masses of Moslems and the patriotic and law-abiding religious professionals. This has enabled the masses to free themselves from feudal oppression and exploitation under religious cover, accorded protection to the legitimate activities of the masses, truly insured the implementation of freedom of religious belief, and at the same time reduced the economic burden of the masses, thereby greatly stimulating the enthusiasm of the masses for developing production and further improving their livelihood.

Through this democratic reform of religious systems, contradictions of two different types were further distinguished from one another. Counter-revolutionaries and wicked elements who wore religious cloaks were exposed and isolated. And patriotic and law-abiding religious professionals were won over, united with, and educated.

It is a firm and consistent policy of the Party and the Government to protect the freedom of religious belief by the people, and to win over, unite with, educate, and transform all patriotic and law-abiding people of religious circles. During the past several years, religious professionals have made great advance. In the course of struggle to eliminate all counter-revolutionaries hidden in Islamic circles and to abolish systems of feudal privileges and feudal exploitation, they were able to discern the demarcation line between the enemy and ourselves, and between the observance of law and violations of law. They have raised under varying degrees their patriotic and socialist consciousness. Most of them are willing to embark on the socialist path under Party leadership, and many of them have participated and are participating in labor and other service work of which they are capable. What is more, not a few of them have been elected as labor models and advanced workers. While taking an active part in building up socialism in the mother country, they have also raised their confidence and initiative in self-transformation. At present, under the guidance and help of relevant units, they are actively studying current policies and Chairman Mao's works. This is very encouraging indeed.

Following the victory of the mass struggle for the elimination of systems of oppression and exploitation in religion, the broad masses of Moslems have completely changed their spiritual outlook. They have rid themselves of all old conventions and rules unfavorable to production, to the development of their nationalities and to the socialist construction. They have further broken down the barriers which existed for a long time between the various nationalities, between religions, between different sects and between religious followers and non-religious people, thereby promoting the development of socialist national relations among various nationalities in our country. As a result of the reform, the broad masses of Moslem women have gained their emancipation and genuinely acquired equality of sex and freedom of marriage. Once the feudal oppression was eliminated, the broad masses of the Moslems immediately displayed a limitless potential power. Today, they are holding high the brilliant banners of the general line, the great leap forward and the people's communes, and together with the people of all nationalities in the country, are striving to build up socialism in the mother country with greater efforts and free hands.

The Party's policy on freedom of religious belief has also exerted a salutary effect in the world. During the past ten years and more, new signs have appeared in Islamic circles in our country. The skyrocketing zeal displayed by the Moslems in our country in socialist construction in our country, and the sympathy and support shown to the just struggles waged by the Asian and African peoples against imperialism and for winning and safeguarding their national independence by the Moslems and all people in our country, has been a source of great inspiration to the people of various countries in Asia and Africa, particularly to the Moslems there. Through uninterrupted mutual friendly visits, Moslems of other countries who visited this country all warmly praised the policy of our Party and government on freedom of religious belief when they saw that Moslems in our country were enjoying freedom of religious belief and leading a happy life. That is why all rumors and slander fabricated by imperialism and all reactionaries against our country on the religious question have thoroughly gone bankrupt.

II. Continuing to implement the Party's policy on freedom of religious belief correctly and in an overall manner is an important task in our work in the future.

The Party's policy on freedom of religious belief is a thorough and overall policy. The overwhelming majority of religious professionals have gained a clear understanding of it as a result of the mass democratic reform of the religious systems. However, a small number of them still entertain doubts about this policy; they think that to abolish the systems of feudal oppression and exploitation in religion is to "abolish religious beliefs among the people." We should help people who entertain this notion to study the Party's policy on freedom of religious belief further, and explain to them that freedom of religious belief is totally different from the use of religion for carrying out feudal oppression and exploitation. Freedom of religious belief concerns the question of ideological belief among the people, and the Party and government will not interfere with, but will protect, the religious belief of the masses of the people and all their legitimate religious activities. The use of religion for carrying out feudal oppression and exploitation is a violation of State laws. Therefore, the use of religion for carrying out illegal activities and practicing feudal oppression and exploitation must be resolutely checked. At the same time, as everyone is aware, how could the masses of Moslems have any real freedom of religious belief under the rule of feudal divine rights such as that of Ma Chen-wu? For this reason, abolition of the systems of feudal privileges in religion does not imply the "abolition of religious belief among the people," but is precisely aimed at genuine implementation of the policy on freedom of religious belief and at protecting the rights of the people in respect of production and livelihood.

The Party's policy on freedom of religious belief is a long-term and unalterable policy. Some people hold that after the democratic reform of religious systems, it is no longer necessary to carry out further this policy of the Party. Such an idea is unrealistic and incorrect. It must be borne in mind that the birth and development of a religion are by no means accidental, but are deeply rooted in social and ideological origins. As far as the present practical conditions of Islamic circles and the broad masses of Moslems are concerned, the question of religious belief remains one which will exist for a long time. The basic attitude adopted by the Party and government toward the religious question is this: As long as there are still people who believe in religions, they will resolutely stick to the policy on freedom of religious belief.

DOC. 42. *Chang Chih-yi: Correctly Understand and Implement the Party's Policy on Freedom of Religious Belief*

THE PRINCIPAL RELIGIONS in our country, namely, Catholicism, Christianity, Islam, Buddhism, and Taoism all command a mass following, and exert broad and far-reaching influences on the masses of people of all nationalities. Almost all the people of the many minority nationalities believe in Lamaism (within the domain of Buddhism) or in Islam.

These five different religions not only have a long history but will exist for quite a long period of time to come after the establishment of a socialist society or even of a communist society. Catholicism, Christianity, Islam, and Buddhism are all world religions. In our country, the question of religion involves the relations among the masses, the relations among the different nationalities, the relations among different classes inside the country, and the relations between China and other countries; the question therefore is very complicated. From this it follows that in the past, at present and in the future, the question of religion has been and will remain an important social question for a relatively long period of time to come. A correct handling of this social question will be of tremendous significance to the strengthening of the unity among the people of various nationalities and to the construction of our great socialist mother country.

The basic policy our Party and State have adopted toward the question of religious belief has been one of freedom of religious belief. Since liberation, they have consistently observed this policy and scored marked successes. Freedom of religious beliefs of all religious followers is respected; their legitimate religious activities and centers necessary for the carrying out of these activities are accorded protection. Among the citizens, both religious and non-religious people are entitled to equal political rights. Moreover, the State also allocates funds for the repair and maintenance of temples, monasteries and churches of historical value, and has granted property tax reduction or exemption to centers of religious activities and to the dormitories and office buildings of religious professionals.

Patriotic organizations have been set up for all these religions, and religious classics and books published and distributed. With the exception of Taoism, religious schools have been established. All this has produced a favorable political effect both inside and outside the country.

To be sure, in some places and among some cadres, there have been some shortcomings in the implementation of the

Party's policy toward religion, mainly due to the fact that the characteristics of religious believers have been somewhat neglected, and help necessary for their religious life has not been extended to them. The reason is that in the present-day conditions in our country, religion is an old superstructure left over from the old society, and is naturally at loggerheads with the new socialist economic base. Such a contradiction finds expression in the relations between one man and another and in class relations. When this contradiction among the people is exploited by the enemy, there arises the contradiction between ourselves and the enemy; moreover, these two contradictions of different nature are often interwoven. Since the religious question is so intricate and complicated and since the training of new cadres and the educational work for cadres cannot as yet keep pace with the rapid development of the revolution and construction in our country, it is inevitable that some cadres, for lack of sufficient experience, should have committed some errors in the handling of religious matters. In order to raise the policy level of the cadres and further implement the Party's policy toward religion, and to strengthen our unity with religious believers of various nationalities, we believe that it is necessary once more to propound the several principal aspects of the Party's policy on freedom of religious belief.

The policy on freedom of religious belief is a long-term, basic policy adopted by the Party toward the question of religious belief by the people. Chairman Mao said: "The Communist Party adopts the policy of protecting religion. Whether you believe in religion or not and whether you believe in this religion or that religion, all of you will be respected. The Party respects religious belief. This policy, as presently adopted, will continue to be adopted in the future."

The policy of freedom of religious belief has precisely been drawn up on the basis of a scientific analysis of the law and peculiar characteristics of religion, and therefore is entirely correct.

Another reason why our Party has adopted the policy of

freedom of religious belief is that it is entirely compatible with the basic interests of the Party and of the people of various nationalities in our country. A basic task before the people of various nationalities in our country at the present stage is this: Under the Party leadership and guided by the three red banners, to build our country into a great socialist country with modern industry, modern agriculture, and modern science and culture. To realize this task, it is necessary to unite all those forces which can be united and to mobilize all those factors which can be mobilized to serve the socialist cause. Millions of religious believers (most of whom are laboring people) constitute an important social force. It is in the interests of the Party and the people that they must be rallied around the Party and the Government as far as possible and that their positive role must be given full play to serve the revolutionary and construction undertakings. Furthermore, their consciousness is to be raised through practice in the revolution and construction.

This is the central task for religious work at the present stage. The key to achieving this lies in having a correct policy to deal with religious beliefs. Such a correct policy, as mentioned earlier, can only be one of freedom of religious belief. It is only when we thoroughly implement this policy that we shall be able to handle correctly the relations between the religious followers on the one hand and the Party and State on the other, between the religious people and the non-religious people, and between believers of different religions and sects; enhance the unity of various nationalities, the unity among the people, and the unity between religious and non-religious people; and give full play to the enthusiasm of religious followers in building up the mother country, in fighting against imperialism, and in defending world peace. It is then and only then that we can make the mass of religious followers accept the patriotic and socialist as well as scientific and cultural education, and that we can unite with, educate and transform the overwhelming majority of the religious people, isolate and split the rightists, and expose and attack the imperialist and counter-revolutionary elements.

From the above analysis, it can be seen that the policy of freedom of religious belief is the only correct policy that can be adopted by the Party and State in dealing with the religious belief of the people. It is a long-term policy as well as a positive and revolutionary one. It must therefore be implemented seriously.

In the past, our Government had punished, in accordance with law, a group of imperialist elements and traitors who carried out counter-revolutionary activities by wearing religious cloaks. This was aimed at protecting the interests of the State and the people and insuring the enforcement of State laws. Here the question of religious belief did not arise. In the future, the Government will, on the one hand, persist in the implementation of the policy of freedom of religious belief and, on the other, continue to rely on the masses (including the mass of religious followers) in resolutely suppressing all elements who use religion for carrying out counter-revolutionary and other law-breaking activities. . . .

The building of a socialist society is the common objective of the people of various nationalities in our country. Article Four of the Constitution says: "The People's Republic of China, by relying on the organs of state and the social forces, and by means of socialist industrialization and socialist transformation, insures the gradual abolition of systems of exploitation and the building of a socialist society." The building of a socialist society is thus aimed at eliminating all phenomena of oppression and exploitation of man by man. Among these national minorities, unless systems of feudal oppression and exploitation in religion are abolished, laboring people will not be genuinely emancipated, and their politics, economy, and culture will not be developed. This means that these nationalities shall not be able to develop and become socialist nationalities. That is why the Party and the Government, on the one hand, insists on implementing the policy of freedom of religious belief, and, on the other, has to rely on the masses in abolishing the systems of feudal oppression and exploitation in religion through the democratic reform. This is entirely necessary.

DOC. 43. *Freedom of Religious Belief for All in Tibet (1965)*

SINCE THE DEMOCRATIC REFORM in Tibet six years ago, the Buddhists and the emancipated serfs in the region enjoy genuine freedom of religious belief. They are now entirely free to believe or not to believe.

In Lhasa, worshipers carry on their usual religious activities, such as attending services, prostrating themselves, or turning prayer wheels in the many monasteries or along Bargor Street which encircles the famous Kokhan Monastery. The monasteries observe traditional Buddhist festivals as before. Sermons, catechisms, and services are often sponsored by such famous monasteries as Daipung, Sera, Gandan, and Jokhan, at which living Buddhas and highly accomplished lamas lecture on Buddhist scripts or expound Buddhist theology.

Before the democratic reform, the lamas, peasants, and herdsmen who wanted to make pilgrimages to Lhasa had to pay taxes or make offerings to their monasteries or manorial lords.

Seventeen research courses in Buddhist theology have been set up in the big monasteries, with an enrollment totaling some 2,000 lamas of various sects. Though they were lamas for twenty or thirty years, most of them had little chance before the democratic reform to study the Buddhist canons. In the past five years, thirty-three have qualified for the degree of "Geshe," the highest order of theological accomplishment in lamaism, and eleven others have been sent to study at the China Buddhist Theological Institute in Peking.

Living Buddha Jaltsolin, Vice-chairman of the Tibet branch of the Chinese Buddhist Association, said that before the democratic reform many poor lamas were in effect slaves in *Kasaya*, the robe of a Buddhist monk. Drudgery robbed them of any time to undertake religious activities. In a temple of Daipung Monastery, investigation by the Religious Affairs Department of the Preparatory Committee for the Tibet Autonomous

Region showed that of the 301 lamas there, 281 had been forced to become lamas or enter the monastery in place of rendering *corvée* [impressed labor]. In the old feudal serf society under the monastic-aristocratic dictatorship, a steady flow of lamas was insured by the system by which a family with three sons had to send one to a monastery. In addition, many people who were unable to pay land rent or debts were compelled to take up slave labor in the monasteries.

According to a current exhibition in Lhasa, the usurious debts owed to Daipung Monastery by its 20,000 serfs amounted to the fantastic sum of 140,000 tons of grain and 10 million yuan. The democratic reform completely wiped out the monasteries' feudal privileges, their system of oppression and exploitation, and their enslavement of the serfs and poor lamas. The monasteries are now run by democratic administrative committees elected by the monks and nuns. Irrespective of their position, lamas enjoy the same rights as the other citizens.

The policy of freedom of religious belief put into practice by the people's government follows the principle of political unity and the separation of religion from politics. This means that the people's government fully respects and protects the people's freedom to believe or not to believe, their freedom to believe in one religion rather than another, their freedom to be converted today and, if they so wish, to renounce the belief tomorrow.

Monks and nuns who were forced to take up religious duties in place of rendering *corvée* or were compelled to enter the monasteries, and who wish to leave to take up production and become reunited with their families, are given financial help and allotted a share of land, housing, and various means of production. Similarly, the wishes of those who want to stay and of those who want to enter monasteries are also respected and protected.

The aged and infirm, ailing or disabled among the monks and nuns receive government care. Like nonbelievers in need, they are provided with allowances and free medical attention. There is not the slightest discrimination against them.

The government treats all sects equally, and all the sects now have their representatives in the Tibet branch of the Buddhist Association of China. Religious disputes have become fewer and there is greater unity among the various sects.

A number of the famous monasteries with a long history have been placed under the protection of the people's government which keeps them in good repair. Several 100,000 yuan were spent and more than sixty ounces of gold used in the considerable repairs to Jokhan and Ramogia Monasteries, the temple, and the other religious institutions damaged by the rebels during the armed rebellion staged by the reactionary clique of the Tibetan upper strata in 1959.

Living Buddha Jaltsolin, who was the Dalai Lama's reader, denounced the imperialists, foreign reactionaries, and the Dalai clique of traitors for spreading the slander that the Communist Party burned monasteries, destroyed cultural relics, and suppressed religion. "It is no other than they themselves that did all these things," he declared. He also recalled that Sera Monastery had been burned down on four occasions during the past few centuries and that Daipung, Gandan, Jokhan, and Rasgren Monasteries had suffered varying damage by fire, as a result of internal strife for power, and from looting, within the ruling clique.

Section 3. Religion and Imperialism

SINCE THE TRADITIONAL RELIGIONS were thoroughly indigenized and autonomous, feudalism rather than imperialism was the focus for attack and reform in Buddhism and Islam. Even so, the Chinese press charged that the Sixth Conference of the World Fellowship of Buddhists (1961) was infiltrated by American imperialists in religious disguise bent on using religion for aggressive purposes.

The campaign to eradicate imperialist influence in Christian circles began early, in a drive for full financial and administrative autonomy to free the churches from all ties with foreign churches. Chou En-lai himself convened at least three conferences in 1950 and 1951 which formulated regulations for church life under the new government (see Doc. 24, 25, 26). The Protestant Three-Self Reform Movement and the National Catholic Patriotic Association, constituted in 1954 and 1957 respectively, centralized administrative supervision of all Christians under the Religious Affairs Bureau of the State Council and formalized the complete independence of Chinese churches from foreign control and support. By the end of 1951 most missionaries had left China and all educational, medical and other institutions had been nationalized.

A second aspect of the anti-imperialism campaign was the systematic effort to discredit the efforts of the missionaries. Historical surveys of missionary work in China catalogue charges of missionary collusion with imperialist penetration in China from the Opium War down to 1949 and later. The anti-imperialist exhibits at the Nanking Theological Seminary refer to missionary participation in the imposition of the unequal treaties, and to alleged missionary crimes of espionage, collusion with the Kuomintang, and cultural aggression through educational work.

The report from a provincial Catholic Anti-Imperialist Patriotic Campaign in Heilungkiang in 1959 illustrates the heightened politicizing of the churches following the Hundred Flowers period and subsequent rectification campaign. Local and regional religious groups across the country held protracted self-study meetings in which suspected reactionary persons were denounced, while all participants reexamined the practice and place of religion in the New China. In this report "imperialist elements in religious cloaks" were cited by name, their crimes ranging from espionage, sabotage, sowing rumors and discord, and stealing state secrets, to conspiracy. According to the report, the "broad masses" of believers and patriotic clergy were successful, after a period of struggle, in expelling the imperialistic influences. The Vatican is particularly vilified as a source of imperialist interference, an image carried over from the "rites controversy" of the early eighteenth century and enhanced after 1949 by papal encyclicals denouncing Communist policy toward the church.

A statement by five leading Protestants at the Third People's Political Consultative Conference in 1959 condemns alleged distorted reporting on Christian life in China by "American imperialists." The statement denies that Christian participation in production is "slave labor," and charges the foreign imperialists with confusing the issue in Tibet by connecting the Tibetan revolt with the problem of religious freedom.

DOC. 44. *Hsieh Hsing-yao: How Did Imperialism Use Religion for Aggression on China? A Historical Survey of Missionary Work in China*

A NATION-WIDE patriotic movement has unfolded in China since the Chinese Christians issued toward the end of July, 1950, the statement "Road for Chinese Christians in New China's

Reconstruction." The movement called upon all Chinese Christians to sever relations with the imperialists and practice self-government, self-support and independent preaching. . . .

1. Imperialism Makes Churches Tools of Aggression

CATHOLICISM WAS IMPORTED to China in 1582 but at that time saw little chance of expansion. In the beginning and the middle of the Ching Dynasty, the Manchu regime, to block the unlawful church activities in China, ordered to allow no foreigners to come to China for preaching purposes. In 1840 (the twentieth year of Emperor Tao Kuang), China was defeated in the Opium War and was forced into signing the Nanking Treaty at the point of imperialist bayonets. Since then, large batches of foreign missionaries, the claws of imperialists, flocked to China. "Things have changed and the dark days are gone" (as described in the *History of Catholic Churches in China* by Te-li-hsien). In 1844, America forced the Manchu regime to sign the "Wan Hsia Treaty," in which the right for Americans to establish hospitals and churches in the Chinese ports was first stipulated. Following the example set by America, France came to ask the Manchu regime to give protection to the French churches in China in the "Whampoa Treaty." In 1858 (the eighth year of Emperor Hsien Feng), China suffered defeat at the hands of the Anglo-French Joint Forces and the Sino-French Tientsin Treaty was concluded, in which it was stipulated that "All law-abiding Chinese willing to enter the Catholic church should undergo no restrictions whatsoever and all decrees to prohibit Catholic church activities were rendered null and void." Once the imperialist churches had secured the protection by treaty, missions were restored everywhere and the footprints of the aggressors spread all over China. Thus did the imperialists send their preachers to China by means of big cannons. . . .

Since 1846 (the twenty-sixth year of Emperor Tao Kuang), the "negotiations for the return of churches" proved to be the most serious and difficult problem of the time, the reasons being that foreign preachers, with the imperial order "of returning the old sites" as the pretext, made all kinds of unreasonable demands, as revealed by the archives. . . .

The "Nanking Treaty" marked the beginning of imperialist aggression in China and the intensive activities of foreign preachers in China.

2. Foreign Preachers' Intrusion Into the Interior and Intervention of Domestic Affairs

SINCE THE IMPERIALISTS used churches as the stronghold for aggression, foreign preachers, with the treaties as the background and money as the tool, menaced China's sovereignty and oppressed the Chinese people.

First, there was the foreign preachers' intrusion into China's interior. Although the Nanking Treaty and the Sino-American Wan Hsia Treaty stipulated that foreigners were permitted to domicile in commercial ports only and not permitted to enter the interior for religious and commercial purposes, the imperialists willfully violated the stipulations and sneaked into the interior of China. No fewer than thirty-five cases happened between 1846 and 1850, where they were arrested by the local authorities of the various provinces due to unauthorized travels to the interior, in Tibet, Szechuan, Hupeh, Chekiang, Kwangtung, Hopei, Shansi, Kiangsu, etc. . . .

Secondly, as experts on China, the missionaries plotted imperialist aggression in China. Each time an unequal treaty was signed, their participation in intrigues was seen. As is well known in China, the Nanking Treaty placed the first shackle on China. Rev. Morrison, the first Christian pilgrim to China, was the man who drew up the draft of the Nanking Treaty, while Rev. Gutzlaf prepared the draft of the Chinese text. . . .

In 1860, when the Peking Treaty was concluded between France and the Manchu regime, a French missionary acted as the interpreter for the French envoy and he unilaterally inserted the sentence, "French preachers are permitted to purchase or lease in all provinces land property and to build houses without restriction" (Chen Chi's "The Boxers' Movement"), to which the dumbfounded Manchu regime agreed. In 1858 when the Anglo-French Joint Forces invaded China, America grasped the opportunity to force the Manchu regime to sign the Sino-American Tientsin Treaty and Rev. Ting Hui-liang and Rev. Williams, two old China hands, followed American Envoy William Reed to Tientsin and helped draw up the draft. . . . At the end of the Ching Dynasty, Timothy Richards, a religionist and educator, emerged a prominent politician. He once ran a newspaper (the *Times*) and established a school (the Shansi University). All the aforementioned persons were foreign missionaries who clamed to "do to others as you would be done by" and "people come to serve God." In each important stage of China's political and diplomatic changes, there was the participation of missionaries; they not only pulled the wire behind the screen but actually played the leading role.

Thirdly, the imperialist missionaries, in general, directly meddled in China's internal affairs. In the sixth year of Tung Chih (1867), a French bishop named Hung made himself an official of Szechuan Province and ordered an official seal for his own use. In the following year, a bishop named Hu-po-li of Kweichow Province recommended citation for a local official. A Shantung missionary called himself an inspector-general. Missionaries in Szechuan and Kweichow even demanded to have local officials removed due to disputes over churches. They not only infringed upon the right of an official but the sovereignty of our nation. All this unreasonable state of affairs infuriated the masses and fully bared the imperialist missionaries' desire to rule over the Chinese people. . . .

Archives are full of instances where the missions and part of the missionaries had something to do with the aggression of imperialism and carried out secret activities in the interior. It is also not uncommon that the missionaries oppressed the good people. In one instance, a foreign missionary slaughtered over 200 people and went away unpunished. . . .

3. *Conclusion*

IT IS CLEAR that Catholic and Christian churches in China pursued the same course as imperialism. In the past hundred years, churches have been the bastion of the aggressors, while the latter served as the background of the former. Whenever chances occurred for diplomatic negotiations, missionaries came to meddle in the affairs. For instance, J. Leighton Stuart, former President of Yenching University, had posed as a religionist and educator for many years. Outwardly he acted as if he really sympathized with the Chinese; in fact, he was one of the most important secret agents for American aggression on China. Unveiling himself, he became the American ambassador to China in order to carry out America's aggressionist policy toward China. The three American spies recently arrested in Tientsin were also the dean of a college, a Catholic father, and a vice-president. But what they did in China was decidedly against the Chinese people. All this served as typical examples to show the relationship between imperialism and missionaries and is really worthy of our vigilance.

The policy on religion of the Chinese Communist Party and the Central People's Government was defined clearly, namely, the people have freedom of religion (Article 5 of the Common Program of the CPPCC), but pure belief in religion should absolutely be separated from the foreign aggressionist and counter-revolutionary activities and must not be mixed up. This point all the Catholic and Christian patriots realize today. The self-conscious patriotic movement at present developed throughout the nation by the Catholics and Christians has the warm support of the vast majority of the people.

DOC. 45. *Ch'en Ch'i-pin: Report to the Catholic Congress in Harbin on the Condition and Task of the Catholic Anti-Imperialist, Patriotic Campaign in Heilungkiang (July, 1959)*

I. ON THE QUESTION of an anti-imperialist and patriotic stand, let us recall that for a very long time in the past our churches were dominated by the imperialists and the Vatican, resulting in our churches falling into a semi-colonial status. In order to realize their conspiracy of permanently controlling our churches, they sent large numbers of "missionaries" to China. Even after the new China was established, these imperialist elements clothed in the religious cloak, ignoring the purpose of preaching for the saving of the human soul, and using our churches as a tool to serve imperialism, have even doubled their efforts in carrying out sabotage against all enterprises of the new China. For instance, in 1949, a spy ring headed by imperialist element Hu Kan-p'u was tracked down in Tsitsihar. Covering themselves with a religious cloak, they were bent on stealing our military, political and economic secrets. Although their conspiracy met with ignominious defeat, the imperialists refused to die a natural death. Subsequently, the "Legion of Mary," a reactionary organization headed by imperialists Wu Po-man and K'ung Shih-chou tried to sabotage the Catholic anti-imperialist and patriotic campaign and the laws and decrees of the people's government. But these reactionary activities went bankrupt again after they were exposed by the broad masses of laymen who had wakened up.

Later, in 1958, imperialists Lung Tsai-t'ien, Pu P'ei-hsin, Hsing Kuan-ch'i, Lo Shu-te, and others hidden in the four dioceses of Kirin, Tsitsihar, Yenpien, and Kiamussu, by taking the Shanmu Hospital in Tsitsihar as the base, under the cover of a charitable enterprise, and posing as "Christ's ambassadors," continued to spread rumors and instigated the masses. These imperialist elements spared no efforts in serving the aggressive policy of the imperialists, abused the divine rights, and sowed discord between the laymen and the government, among the laymen themselves, and between the clergy and the laity. They prevented the laymen from participating in the struggle for the redistribution of land and against the evil landlords. They did not allow the laymen to go into the army and participate in war. And they said that to love the great mother country under the great, glorious and correct leadership of the Chinese Communist Party was a "sin." These imperialists not only publicly or secretly carried out anti-Soviet and anti-communist conspiratorial activities, but they also brought up a number of faithful slaves and sent them to the church to carry out counter-revolutionary activities under the cover of religion.

For instance, imperialist element Jen Fu-wan publicly denounced the Party's policy of freedom of religious belief in the church and attacked the anti-imperialist and patriotic campaign. This was not only harmful to the construction enterprises of the mother country, but brought insult to the Holy Church. The patriotic Catholic laymen and clergymen, in order to safeguard the interests of the mother country and the people, to maintain the purity of the church, to promote the real spirit of Christ in showing love for all men, and on the righteous stand of loving one's country and religion, have been carrying out a firm struggle against these criminal acts endangering the state and the church.

The people's government, in accordance with the demand of the people, and to safeguard the interests of the country and the people, abolished the reactionary organization, the "Legion of Mary," and expelled the imperialist elements who for a long time were hidden in the church. This will enable all churches to become purely religious organizations having faith in our Lord, and they will no longer be tools directly controlled by the imperialist elements in the service of imperialism.

The patriotic clergymen and the broad masses of laymen have not only made great contributions which glorified our Lord and benefited the people in the course of struggle for expelling the imperialist elements from the church, but at the same time have also raised their patriotic consciousness in the course of actual struggle, incessantly eliminating the imperialist influences, and waging a resolute struggle against the reactionary conspiracy of the Vatican against the new China. The capitalist rightists inside the church, by taking advantage of the rectification campaign launched by the Chinese Communist Party and by ostensibly helping the Party to carry on its rectification campaign, positively fought against Party leadership, against socialism, and against the anti-imperialist and patriotic campaign. This aroused the great indignation of the patriotic clergymen and laymen throughout the province, and they then resolutely carried out a firm struggle against the rightists, and smashed all their plots. Following the great socialist educational campaign and the anti-rightist struggle, the overwhelming majority of clergymen and laymen further distinguished enemies from ourselves and right from wrong, loved even more passionately the leadership of the Communist Party, and became even more firm in taking the socialist road. The clergymen, through their participation in the anti-rightist struggle and on the basis of elevating consciousness, have surrendered their hearts to the Party and, in order to strengthen their self-education and self-transformation, have respectively devised their own plans for this purpose.

II. The great victories gained in the anti-imperialist, patriotic campaign for the past several years prove most unpleasant to the imperialists and the Vatican. Therefore they have adopted various dirty means to spread the shameless slander, made false charges, and carried out destructive activities against us. There is nothing strange about that. This is because the Vatican and the imperialists are birds of the same feather. Our stand is basically different from theirs, and it is impossible to have a common language. It would be extremely naive to ask Eisenhower, Dulles, and his servant, the Vatican, to support socialism.

After several years of study and personal experience, we have clearly recognized the reactionary nature of the Vatican in persistently using the Chinese Catholic Church to serve imperialist aggression. For a very long time, posts of bishops in the various dioceses were without exception assumed by the imperialist elements, and espionage activities were carried out under the cover of religion. Various sorts of military, political, and economic secrets were collected, which served the aggressive policy of the imperialists. When the Japanese imperialists invaded the Northeast, putting the people there in a hell, the Vatican, following in the footstep of the Japanese imperialists, recognized the puppet Manchukuo. During the Second World War, the Vatican collaborated with Germany, Italy, Japan, and France, and became their accomplice; after the conclusion of the war, the Vatican again surrendered itself to the American imperialists who were vainly hoping to dominate the world, supporting all aggressive policies of the American imperialists. On the one hand, the Vatican supports the American imperialists in their occupation of our territory of Taiwan, and collaborates with the Chiang Kai-shek clique, permitting those imperialist elements expelled from our country to carry out conspiratorial activities around us. On the other hand, by using the holy name of our Lord, it has time and again issued "encyclicals" and "orders," forcing us to oppose our beloved mother country and to "shed blood" for its political conspiracy. It prosecuted and attacked, by means of "excommunication" and other means those clergymen and laymen who adhered to the stand of anti-imperialism and patriotism; it commended those counter-revolutionaries—rebels of China—inside the church and wicked elements of the church, such as Kung P'in-mei, calling them the "most faithful bishops." This fully proves that the Vatican has wholly betrayed the holy will of our Lord, and overstepped justice and righteousness. For this reason, the question of relation between the Chinese Catholic Church and the Vatican is the question of two basically different political stands and the question of contradiction between the enemy and ourselves. Our Chinese clergymen and laymen must abide by the teachings of our Lord, and love fervently the new socialist China led by the Communist Party. They must protect the purity of the church, and perform worthy deeds in glorifying our Lord and saving the human soul. Thus they must draw a clear demarcation line with the Vatican, thoroughly break away from all its control, and change the semi-colonial status of the Chinese Catholic Church.

DOC. 46. *Strip Off the Imperialist Religious Cloak, Joint Speech by Five Protestant Leaders at the First Session of the Third People's Political Consultative Conference (May 11, 1959)*

We Oppose the Use of Religion to Interfere with Our Internal Affairs

WHAT IS VERY DETESTABLE to us is the fact that while the Chinese Christians are joyously marching on the socialist road along with the people of our nation and heartily enjoying the freedom of religious belief and other freedoms, the Christian organizations which are tools of the American imperialists, including "the China Committee" of the so-called "Division of Foreign Missions" of the National Council of the Churches of Christ in the United States of America, are playing their tricks and slandering us.

As we know, the American imperialists have always held up the shop sign of "Church Unity" in order to bring together all the sects and denominations of Christianity and organize them into a crusade for the purpose of opposing the socialist camp, the new nations and the independence movement of the colonial peoples. Today, while the Chinese Christian churches, on the basis of patriotism and opposition to imperialism, are uniting even closer according to the genuine teachings of the Bible, the American imperialists are fabricating rumors and saying that the Chinese churches are suffering "heavy blows."

On the eve of the liberation, the American imperialistic missionaries positively plotted "emergency measures," attempting to change the churches throughout China into reactionary bases for the purpose of their long-range opposition against the Chinese people. To reach this goal, they strongly advocated that the ministerial personnel should engage in production. But now, when for the purpose of self-reform and for promoting a happy life for the nation's people and for themselves the Chinese Christian workers joyously take part in socialist construction, the imperialists slander us by saying that it is "slave labor" for the church people and that it is a "blow to the church."

If the American imperialists think that they can prevent their dying fate by fabricating rumors and slandering China and the Chinese church, they are dreaming. The hatefulness and slander of the imperialists are clear indications that our actions are just and are a severe blow to the American imperialists.

As we know, new China has always implemented its policy of freedom of religious belief and has always respected the religious beliefs, customs and habits of the various nationalities in the big family of the fatherland. Under the instigation of the imperialists, the Indian expansionists and the reactionaries of the Chiang Kai-shek clique, a small group of thoroughly reactionary masters of the farmer-slaves in our country's territory, Tibet, have recently seized the Dalai Lama and staged an open rebellion. Thus they have attempted to destroy the unification of the fatherland, rend the unity of the various nationalities of our nation and restore the imperialists' enslavement of our people in Tibet so that the special privileges and position of these reactionary leaders of continuously exploiting and oppressing the Tibetan people may be maintained.

On April 18 [1959], these reactionaries issued the so-called "Statement of the Dalai Lama" which was distributed by an official of the Indian Government and which contained extreme absurdities and numerous contradictions. This is proof of interference with our internal affairs, an activity which has aroused in us the greatest indignation.

To cover up their secret plot, the imperialists and foreign reactionaries have openly confused the issue by connecting the revolt in Tibet with the problem of freedom of religious belief. We Chinese Christians will never permit any other nation to intefere with our internal affairs. We are determined to strip off the imperialists' religious cloak and expose their wolflike faces.

The imperialists' objections have nothing whatsoever in

common with religious belief. They are absolutely not "protectors" of religion. What they attempt to do is to use religion as a tool to achieve their aims of exploiting and enslaving people. Indeed, they are the true enemies of religion. Our fatherland is in an unprecedented great leap forward and the 650 million Chinese people who hold their fate in their own hands are marching heroically towards the target of socialism. We are undertaking world-shaking enterprises day and night. Internationally, socialism has become a matchless power, whereas imperialism is already like the setting sun in the western mountains. The ambition of the imperialists to rule the world and enslave humanity will never be realized.

We Christians have personally suffered from the poisons of the imperialists in our spiritual life and we must, therefore, expose the crimes of the imperialists through facts. We must, moreover, thoroughly purge the poisonous thoughts of the imperialists which have stubbornly occupied the depth of our hearts. We must unite our own people and those throughout the world to undertake a resolute struggle against the aggressive plots of the American imperialists and foreign reactionaries.

The nation's great leap forward state of affairs demands that we Christians intensify our self-reform, further mobilize our working spirit, march forward with a hundredfold conviction and make more positive efforts in our fatherland's socialist construction and for world peace, together with all the people of our nation.

DOC. 47. *Be Vigilant Against U.S. Intrigue Through Religion*
(December 19, 1961)

THE *Jen-min Jih-pao* carried today an article on the sixth Conference of the World Fellowship of Buddhists held last month in Phnom Penh. The article gives a detailed account of how the U.S. imperialists carried out dirty political intrigue in the name of religion.

The article says that the Chinese Buddhists, with great enthusiasm, sent a delegation headed by the elderly Buddhist leader the Venerable Shirob Jaltso to Phnom Penh to attend the conference. The Chinese delegation was accorded a cordial reception by Prince Sihanouk, Cambodian Government leaders and Cambodian Buddhists and laymen. In their meetings and talks, both the Chinese and Cambodian Buddhist leaders expressed ardent hopes for further promotion of friendship between the Buddhists and other people of the two countries.

"The Chinese Buddhists," the article points out, "have always devoted their efforts towards the promotion of international friendship and cooperation among Buddhists." In the past few years, remarkable progress was made in the friendly relations between the Buddhists of China and other countries. Personal visits and goodwill missions were exchanged between the Buddhists of China and other Asian countries and interflow and cooperation in the field of Buddhist culture have also taken place between China and many other countries. The Buddha-tooth relic of China was brought on invitation to Burma and Ceylon at different times and was worshipped by thousands of people of these two countries. This has, it says, greatly promoted the mutual understanding and friendship between the Chinese people and the people of Ceylon and Burma and their common cause in religion and in the defense of world peace. During this conference in Phnom Penh, the Chinese delegates had contact with delegates from many other Asian countries who expressed a sincere desire for friendship and solidarity with the Chinese Buddhists.

"However," the article continues, "dark clouds from the West appeared over the sixth Conference of the World Fellowship of Buddhists." Strange figures who had never been seen in dignified Buddhist conferences in the past made their appearance in the conference and were very active. All these people, without exception, came from the United States.

"It is not a new trick of imperialism to use religion for aggressive purposes. The Chinese people have painful experiences," the article says. "In the past they carried out their activities mainly through the spreading of Catholicism and Protestantism. Now they have sneaked into Buddhism to carry out their activities." The article points out that U.S. aggressors are now killing people in Southeast Asia and are actively preparing for massacres on a larger scale. They are trying to rekindle the war in Laos, dispatching their troops and officers to South Vietnam for intensified aggression and instigating the government of Thailand to carry out armed provocations against Cambodia. "The overwhelming majority of the people of these countries are Buddhists. The fact that these Americans in religious cassocks show such an 'enthusiasm' for Buddhism should arouse the serious vigilance of the Buddhists of Asian countries."

It is regrettable, the article says, that a small number of Southeast Asian personages were taken in by the Americans and failed to expose their intrigues in time. Consequently certain resolutions with ulterior motives were adopted haphazardly. Under American manipulations, three of the twelve newly elected Vice-presidents of the World Fellowship of Buddhists are such Americans.

"Anyone who is somewhat sober minded can see clearly that the conference was manipulated by the American plotters who had sneaked into it. This is further proved by the unjustified voting down at the conference of the Chinese delegation's proposal for cancelling the resolution of the fifth Conference of the World Fellowship of Buddhists on accepting Taiwan as a regional center. . . .

DOC. 48. *Anti-Imperialist Exhibits at Chin-ling Hsieh-ho (Union) Theological Seminary (1962)*

SINCE 1959, the Chin-ling Union Theological Seminary in Nanking has responded to the "three-self" movement appeal and carried out work in gathering historical materials concerning the imperialists utilizing Christianity to make aggression into China. At the beginning, the seminary conducted this in collaboration with the preachers in the Nanking area. During the last three years, through various forms, including recollections, visits and discussions, it compiled twenty-eight brief histories of the various churches and religious organizations in Nanking, a number of memoirs and a complete set of exhibit materials "exposing the criminal actions of the imperialists utilizing Christianity to invade China."

The exhibit materials are divided into eight sections. The first section contains confessions of the colonialists and imperialists concerning their utilizing of Christianity to carry out aggression into China. These naked confessions have proved that the missionaries were really the vanguards of aggression, that the so-called missionary movement was "a good investment" made by the imperialists in China and that Christianity became an ideological weapon, used by the colonialists to eliminate the people's resistance in the colonial countries.

The second section contains several exhibits of historical facts showing how the missionaries participated in the signing of unequal treaties. After the colonialists had opened the gates of China with the bombardment of cannons, they forced the Ching Dynasty to sign unequal treaties. In the process of signing treaties, the missionaries performed a very important function. Accordingly, the former U.S. Secretary of State Foster Dulles said that the missionaries constituted "an absolute necessity in diplomatic relations." The missionary (J. Leighton) Stuart, a well-known "China expert," had signed a list of unequal treaties with China during the three years when he was the U.S. Ambassador to China, especially the Sino-American Commercial Treaty, which stipulated that the United States enjoyed various special privileges in China. In accordance with the shameless declarations of the reactionary Kuomintang bureaucrats, even "all China's territory and enterprises are open to the United States."

The third section contains proofs of the crimes, in which the imperialist missionaries gathered various secret information from China. As a matter of fact, under instructions from the U.S. State Department, the American Embassy and consulates in China, those so-called "doctors," "professors," "theological teachers," and "gospel messengers," who had the beautiful cloak of missionaries, tried their best to gather various secret military, economic and other information from China.

The fourth section contains some materials concerning Chinling University and the Chin-ling Girl's College of Fine Arts. These materials depict a true portrait of the so-called missionary universities, so that people will have a full understanding of them. They promoted an enslaving education, trained compradores, sold American goods in China under the pretext of academic studies, stole ancient cultural objects from China and gathered various kinds of secret information.

The fifth section deals with theological education. Through the utilization of "scholarships," the imperialists won over and trained certain theological students to become tools in their aggression in China. The purpose of the theological college in offering a course in the rural church was to carry out a struggle against the Communist Party. Through "intern activities," the theological college tried to send "theological students" into factories in the liberated areas to carry out their activities.

The sixth section contains illustrations demonstrating that the enslaving education was carried out through the spreading of gospel. The exhibit materials exposed that when the Japanese imperialists invaded China's Northeast, the imperialist missionaries, "Ai-ti" and others, under the name of "evangelism," advocated "non-resistance" and disseminated the reactionary and erroneous theories that "we cannot resist the Japanese" but "we must oppose the Communist Party."

The seventh section exposes the erroneous theories advocated by "Li-k'o-fei," a "professor" of Chin-ling University and an imperialist missionary, and the strategy and tactic that were adopted by "Jui-t'ao-an" (a Chin-ling University "professor") and other imperialist missionaries, who held a meeting at Ku-ling to discuss how to utilize Christianity to oppose the Communist Party, when the Chiang bandits were launching their "fifth encirclement campaign" against the Central Soviet District in 1933.

The eighth section concentrates on the exposition of the criminal actions of "Hua-fan-yu," an imperialist. He had always collaborated with the Chiang bandits, gathered secret information and carried out anti-communist and anti-people activities.

Since the beginning of this year, the colleagues of this college have concentrated their efforts in compiling the historical materials concerning the imperialists utilizing theological education to make aggression in China. After the Yenching Union Theological Seminary united with this college, the strength for the compilation of historical materials was greatly increased. It is predicted that this college will have a further development in the compilation of historic materials.

DOC. 49. *Yankee Imperialist Cultural Aggression (March 4, 1966)*

Hypocrisy of Missionary Activities

ANOTHER WEAPON in the U.S. "ideological offensive" is missionary activities. According to statistics for 1958, out of the 29,000 American missionaries abroad, more than 15,000 were in Asia and Africa. In 1961, those sent to Africa by Protestant denominations totalled 8,500, or eleven times as many as American diplomats there. There were 3,800 in India and Japan, the two major targets of U.S. ideological infiltration. Out of the 1,100 American citizens in Southern Rhodesia, 700 were missionaries. By 1963, American missionaries overseas had increased to 33,000.

In the past, in the name of philanthropy, American missionaries have run schools and hospitals in the hinterlands of many Asian and African countries in order to poison the minds of the local people. They also used this means to gather local information and carry out subversion in coordination with the political, economic and military needs of the U.S. Government.

But now, the mounting struggle for liberation in Asia and Africa has compelled U.S. imperialism to modify its tactics and adopt more hypocritical and covert methods in its missionary activities overseas.

American missionaries today profess support for national independence and sympathy towards social progress so that they can worm their way into local mass movements, and sidetrack them into a path of "reformism" and away from anti-imperialism and revolution.

They have evolved a whole set of cunning stratagems to trap different types of local believers. Churches are deliberately given an indigenous character and religious rites a national form. Local churchmen are encouraged to take the limelight while American missionaries act behind the scenes. Ceremonies which are not easy for local believers to grasp no longer receive the usual attention, and a host of activities outside the churches are organized. Meetings are arranged and lectures on special subjects given to spread the virus of reactionary ideas.

These missionaries also use modern means of communication to put across imperialist ideas and the "American way of life." In Africa, American churches in recent years have made greater efforts to set up broadcasting and book distribution networks. What they are trying to sell goes far beyond the province of religion. By running schools, medical and health services, they try to sneak their way into the local trade union and youth movements so as to increase their influences.

Recently American missionaries have been advised by their church headquarters to preach "love" and "forgiveness" as a means to calm the anti-imperialist temper of the Afro-Asian people. Actually they miss no opportunity to engage in criminal underhand activities. The execution of the American missionary doctor-cum-special agent Paul Carlson by the Congolese (L) people in 1964 shows what is up the sleeve of U.S. imperialism in its foreign missionary operations.

DOC. 50. *Message from Chinese Christians to Mission Boards Abroad (1949)*

THE INFORMAL GROUP of Protestant leaders from which this Message was sent in December, 1949, later became the founders of the Three-Self Movement.

A NEW CHAPTER in the history of China has begun; a new era has dawned. A new "People's Government" has been born under the leadership of the Chinese Communist Party with the cooperation of all the revolutionary elements in the country, and with the avowed common purpose of putting into execution the political, social, and economic principles of the New Democracy. Historically, the new era is the culmination of a century's struggle against external exploitation and centuries of internal feudalistic oppression. It is the main milestone in the nation's struggle for national unity, independence and democracy. From now on, a new political concept, a new philosophy, a new creed and a new mode of living will be instilled into the masses of the people with a vigor that is hitherto unknown. Much of China's traditional heritage will be rigorously scrutinized and, if need be, discarded; many new and far-reaching policies will be put into execution. Likewise, much of western culture that has been introduced in recent years will be reexamined and shorn of its undesirable elements. Out of this will be born a new China, radically different from the China of old. Compared with the present moment, the change of dynasties in the 4,000 years has little significance; the revolutions of 1911 and 1927 and the war of resistance are but wavelets in the rapids of time. From such a change there is no turning, and at such a time diehardism has no place.

We Christians in China feel the urgent necessity of reexamining our work and our relationship with the older churches abroad in the light of this historical change in China. We need not reexamine our faith, for our fundamental faith in Christ is not to be shaken, and under the New Democracy freedom of religious faith is definitely stipulated in the adopted national policy. It is also needless for us to relate here what the Christian movement in China has accomplished, nor need we stress at the present juncture what share our Christian friends abroad have contributed to that achievement. These are matters of history and of our common knowledge. Whatever true achievements we had made in the past will always stand the test of time, and will be our assets as we go forward into the future. Nevertheless, many of our Christians here and many others still outside the Christian fold are not aware of this. It is our duty to see to it that they are rightly informed. But we do feel the necessity of inviting your serious attention to what is happening now to our Christian work, the challenge that is upon us, and what changes of policy and in our general relationships demand careful consideration and readjustment. Such a change as described above will affect our work in a deeper way than we realize. We should not be tempted by any wishful thinking, particularly those of you whose thinking and planning have such great bearing on what our future course will be, and how effective our future contributions might become.

Just at present, there do exist scattered abnormal conditions where religious activities have apparently been interfered with. Such is to be expected during the first days of the revolution, and can be attributed to the misunderstanding of the lower ranks of the political workers who do not have a full grasp of the real government policy in regard to religious bodies. We have the hope that this wave of abnormality will soon pass, and proper conditions will be established in due time. We are confident you will be able to adopt the same view on what is happening now and will not be swayed by the momentary eddies of the present.

In addition to these momentary surges of abnormality, there does exist some deep-rooted feeling on the part of the communists that the Chinese church has been intimately related to imperialism and capitalism. It is a fact that the Christian Church in China in the past has been entangled with the unequal treaties imposed upon China under duress; it did enjoy certain special privileges accruing from them. It is also a fact that the churches in China have had close connections with the churches in Britain and America in personnel and financial support. It is also a fact that the church life and organization here in China has been modeled after the pattern in Britain and America. Traditions of denominationalism have been imported and taken root here. Much of the church administration is still in the hands of missionaries, and in many instances church policies are still determined by the mission boards abroad. We do realize and so wish to assert that missionary work in China never had any direct relationship with governmental policies; mission funds have always been contributed by the rank and file of common ordinary Christians and church members; missionaries have been sent here for no other purpose than to preach the Christian gospel of love, and to serve the needs of the Chinese people. The central Christian motivation will not and can never be questioned, but these other social implications can very easily give rise to misunderstanding and accusation. We do also realize that many of our missionary friends and many of the leading members of mission boards have been aware of the unfortunate political involvements in the past and have done what they could under the circumstances towards their correction. We also realize that you do sincerely believe in the establishment of truly Chinese indigenous churches, controlled and administered by the Chinese Christians. The time has come for us to redouble our efforts in making our policies articulate and unmistakable, and to make concrete plans for their realization.

We are not unmindful of the challenges and difficulties lying ahead in a more fundamental way. Just how the Christian gospel can be witnessed to in a clime that is, by virtue of its ideology, fundamentally materialistic and atheistic presents a challenge stronger than ever before. Whatever the external clime may be, the burden falls upon us Christians to demonstrate the efficiency and sufficiency of the gospel as exemplified in the life of Christ. That the gospel is in itself both efficacious and sufficient will stand on its own truth. Many of the methods may be timeworn. Some of the channels to which we have been accustomed may be closed. The challenge is to find other methods that are timely and other channels that are lying open. If we are challenged in the command "Love thy neighbor as thyself" in its full practical applications of everyday individual living, in its social applications to community life, then we ought to be ready to accept that challenge and find means for its demonstration. If others are showing the way how to take up the cross of hardship and sacrifice that we have laid down, then we should be ready to take it up again. If we have allowed our petty differences to divide us, if we have been too jealous of our own prerogatives, if we have clung too hard to our timeworn traditions, then let us take up the challenge to forget our differences, our spheres of influence, and to unite our efforts in truly creative work. The banner of the Cross has never been easy to carry and it will not be easy in the new era of China. More than ever before, the genuine Christian spirit must shine forth in its true light regardless of the ornaments in which it is clothed.

Heretofore, the Chinese church has been keeping itself aloof from the political torrents that surged around it. The new philosophy considers that all phases of life must necessarily come under the influence of politics in contradistinction to the traditional Protestant view of the separation between church and state. In a world where political influences play such an important part and affect our lives and work so extensively, it is a challenge how the church as an institution and how Christians as citizens in society can perform their Christian functions and discharge their duties to society at the same time. In areas of social service and education we shall have to accept the leadership of the government and conform with the general patterns of service, organization, and administration. Just how these new adjustments are to be made, is for the Chinese churches to determine. We have our privileges as Christian believers. We also have our duties to perform as Chinese citizens and Chinese social organizations.

Specifically, we wish to invite your attention to three fundamental points of future policy:

1. The authority of policy determination and financial administration must pass over to Chinese leadership wherever it has not yet been done. Definite steps must be taken for its realization. The principle of self-support must be reiterated and steps taken for its final consummation.

2. As regards the future position of missionaries, we would like to state:

(a) There is nothing in principle which makes the future position of the missionary untenable, or renders his service unnecessary. On the contrary, there is a definite challenge to work and serve under adverse circumstances, and to bear witness to the ecumenical fellowship. Even though circumstances may render active participation difficult, the mere presence of the missionary will give articulate expression to the Christian quality of our fellowship which transcends all differences and defies all obstacles.

(b) The future contribution of the missionary will lie along lines of special service projects, and not along administrative lines. To BE, to SHARE, and to LIVE will be a significant contribution in itself.

(c) The missionary, from now on, will be living and working in a setting that is entirely foreign to the newcomer. Difficult physical and mental readjustments will be demanded from him. We deem it our duty to state some of the important adjustments so far as we can pass judgment at the present time, so that you may be properly advised in your endeavor to enlist the services of missionaries to the China field.

The missionary will be placed in a political environment much different from the one he is accustomed to. It is necessary that he should have an open mind and have due sympathy with and endeavor to understand the political and social trends now operating in China. To learn and to know is to be stressed more than ever before.

The missionary will be living in an economical environment, whose standard of living is much lower than the one he is accustomed to, and in which practice of austerity will be the rule rather than the exception for some time to come. He should be prepared to share in the general economic struggles of the people among whom he lives and whom he tries to serve.

Travel is likely to be restricted. The missionary should be prepared to be located in one place more or less permanently during his term of service. As a rule, his work will be more intensive than extensive.

Adjustment for families is likely to prove more difficult. Clear understanding should be reached beforehand to avoid difficulties arising from maladjustments.

3. Regarding financial support, there is nothing in principle that prevents its continuance. It is understood that mission funds are still welcome provided no strings are attached. It is to be stressed here, however, that such financial support should be regarded as temporary in nature, and it is the duty of the Chinese church to build up its own support as soon as circumstances permit. An understanding needs to be reached between the Chinese church and the mission boards concerned, based upon the principle of self-support on the one hand, and a realistic evaluation of the problem on the other.

The Christian movement will have its due place in the future Chinese society and will have a genuine contribution to make. Its future road will not be a bed of roses. To build a new nation on the ruins of the old will not be easy, neither will it be easy to build a genuinely Chinese Christian movement. Difficult as it is, the task will be easier if we can clear away some of the unnecessary obstacles in the way which we ourselves can remove. The Chinese church will not emerge through this historical change unaffected. It will suffer a purge, and many of the withered branches will be amputated. But we believe it will emerge stronger and purer in quality, a more fitting witness to the gospel of Christ. (Signed by 19 national church leaders.)

Section 4. Self-reliance and Autonomy

SELF-RELIANCE is a virtue stressed at every level of socialist construction in Communist China. Mao Tse-tung's teaching directs the struggle for nation-building by innovation and learning-by-doing: "On what basis should our policy rest? It should rest on our own strength, and that means regeneration through one's own efforts."

While the state's insistence that Christian bodies sever all dependence on foreign churches undoubtedly stemmed from the nation's policy to centralize control and expel foreign influence, the movement for triple autonomy (self-support, self-government, self-propagation) had begun decades before 1949 in the Chinese churches and was without doubt sincerely supported by Protestant leaders in the early Communist period. Catholics, with their ties to Rome and the world church, resisted.

Reports from the church in China up to 1966 indicate that financial support came in part from rental income on church buildings, from contributions of believers, from church-operated small industries and farms, and from government subsidy. Clergy and professional church workers, however, increasingly were forced to engage in secular employment to maintain themselves and their families.

The Christian Manifesto and Y. T. Wu's report suggest the sense of pride and independence which accompanied the movement for triple autonomy.

DOC. 51. *The Christian Manifesto: Direction of Endeavor for Chinese Christianity in the Construction of New China*

THIS DOCUMENT, adopted May, 1950, was worked out by the founding group of the Three-Self Movement in consultation with Premier Chou En-lai. It was eventually signed by at least 400,000 Protestant Christians, about half of all Protestants in China.

PROTESTANT CHRISTIANITY WAS introduced to China more than a hundred forty years ago. During this period it has made a not unworthy contribution to Chinese society. Nevertheless, and this was most unfortunate, not long after Christianity's coming to China, imperialism started its activities here; and since the principal groups of missionaries who brought Christianity to China all came themselves from these imperialistic countries, Christianity consciously or unconsciously, directly or indirectly, became related with imperialism. Now that the Chinese revolution has achieved victory, these imperialistic countries will not rest passively content in face of this unprecedented historical fact in China. They will certainly seek to contrive by every means the destruction of what has actually been achieved; they may also make use of Christianity to forward their plot of stirring up internal dissension and creating reactionary forces in this country. It is our purpose in publishing the following statement to heighten our vigilance against imperialism, to make known the clear political stand of Christians in New China, to hasten the building of a Chinese church whose affairs are managed by the Chinese themselves, and to indicate the responsibilities that should be taken up by Christians throughout the whole country in national reconstruction in New China. We desire to call upon all Christians in the country to exert their best efforts in putting into effect the principles herein presented.

The Task in General

CHRISTIAN CHURCHES and organizations give thoroughgoing support to the "Common Political Program," and under the leadership of the government oppose imperialism, feudalism, and bureaucratic capitalism, and take part in the effort to build an independent, democratic, peaceable, unified, prosperous, and powerful New China.

Fundamental Aims

(1) CHRISTIAN CHURCHES and organizations in China should exert their utmost efforts, and employ effective methods, to make people in the churches everywhere recognize clearly the evils that have been wrought in China by imperialism, recognize the fact that in the past imperialism has made use of Christianity; purge imperialistic influences from within Christianity itself; and be vigilant against imperialism, and especially American imperialism, in its plot to use religion in fostering the growth of reactionary forces. At the same time, the churches and organizations should call upon Christians to participate in the movement opposing war and upholding peace, and teach them thoroughly to understand and support the government's policy of agrarian reform.

(2) Christian churches and organizations in China should take effective measures to cultivate a patriotic and democratic spirit among their adherents in general, as well as a psychology of self-respect and self-reliance. The movement for autonomy, self-support, and self-propagation hitherto promoted in the Chinese church has already attained a measure of success. This movement from now onwards should complete its tasks within the shortest possible period. At the same time, self-criticism should be advocated, all forms of Christian activity reexamined and readjusted, and thoroughgoing austerity measures adopted, so as to achieve the goals of a reformation in the church.

Concrete Methods

(1) ALL CHRISTIAN CHURCHES and organizations in China that are still relying upon foreign personnel and financial aid should work out concrete plans to realize within the shortest possible time their objective of self-reliance and rejuvenation.

(2) From now onwards, as regards their religious work, Christian churches and organizations should lay emphasis upon a deeper understanding of the nature of Christianity itself, closer fellowship and unity among the various denominations, the cultivation of better leadership personnel, and reform in systems of church organization. As regards their more general work, they should emphasize anti-imperialistic, anti-feudalistic and anti-bureaucratic-capitalistic education, together with such forms of service to the people as productive labor, teaching them to understand the New Era, cultural and recreational activities, literacy education, medical and public health work, and care of children.

DOC. 52. *Y. T. Wu, Chairman of the Protestant Three-Self Movement Preparatory Council: Report (August 6, 1954)*

1. The Work of the Past Four Years

THE PRINCIPAL ACCOMPLISHMENT of the China Christian Three-Self Reform Movement during the past four years has been the freeing of the personnel, management, and finances of the Church from imperialistic control, the cutting off of imperialistic relations, the beginning of wiping out of imperialistic influence, and the first steps in self-government, self-support, and self-propagation.

Chinese Christian churches and institutions have basically cast off imperialistic control, and are in the process of becoming religious organizations governed by Chinese Christians.

For more than a hundred years Chinese Christianity has been controlled by western mission boards, and has been the tool of imperialistic aggression. The Three-Self Movement has changed this situation, has forced the imperialistic elements to leave China, and has forced the mission boards to close up their work. As a result Chinese Christianity has basically cast off imperialistic control of personnel and church government, and is now beginning to manage itself.

The use of mission funds has been one of the traditional methods used by mission boards to control the Chinese church. After the Three-Self Reform Movement had begun, many churches made definite plans to achieve complete self-support within a specified period. In November, 1950, when the United Nations was discussing how to prevent American aggression against China and against Taiwan, American representative Austin made a statement insulting both to the Chinese people and to the Chinese church; he spoke of these mission appropriations as a "favor" to the Chinese people and the Chinese church. His lies aroused the protest of both the Chinese people and the Chinese church. Then in December the American Government announced the freezing of all Chinese funds, both public and private, in the United States, attempting in this way to threaten the livelihood of all those working in churches and institutions which still received mission aid. But this scheme of theirs failed. Chinese churches and religious institutions immediately announced their determination to reject all further appropriations and to undertake immediate self-support. So we have gone forward by faith, and during these past years, through the generous giving of [Chinese] Christians, the willingness to endure hardship shown by church workers, and the help given through the Government in remitting church property taxes, the Chinese Christian church has basically achieved self-support. . . .

Section 5. Religion and Feudalism

SINCE ONE OF THE FIRST GOALS of the Communist regime was to destroy the power of the landlords in the rural areas, it is not surprising that the religious aristocracy of Lamaistic Buddhism and Islam came under sharp attack. Mao Tse-tung's own hostility to the power of entrenched indigenous religion has already been cited. The excerpt here from a 1964 article in *Kuang-ming Jih-pao* suggests that, despite the land reform movement against the "feudal lords in religious clothing" in the early 1950s, remnant restorationist forces were still at work. The continuing campaign against these forces was not in conflict with the Party's policy on religion, the writer said, because it dealt with a social system of oppression; only by abolishing these systems of feudal oppression in religion could a true policy of freedom of religious belief be implemented.

The public accusation of Ma Chen-wu, translated here from a 1958 issue of the *Kirin Jih-pao*, is typical of denunciation statements coming out of countless study and accusation meetings of all religions during the post-Hundred Flowers anti-rightist period (see Part II, Section 8). The importance placed on discrediting Ma Chen-wu, a leader of the potentially explosive Moslem minorities, can be seen in the range of political and criminal charges, and in the scope of the accusation meeting itself. 407 representatives of the Chinese Islamic Association from more than eight provinces covering the entire Moslem area of northwest China met for three full weeks in late summer 1958, hearing the charges and passing judgment. Ma's alleged crimes included conspiring under the cloak of religion to overthrow the people's government, armed rebellion, attempted restoration of the rule of the reactionary class, torture and murder of his opponents, exploitation of his religious role for personal gain, squeezing of "slave" labor and extortion of money from gullible religious followers, and personal profiteering from control of religious landholdings and patronage payoffs from clerical appointments. While Ma Chen-wu himself was convicted and duly punished for his alleged anti-Communist, anti-people and criminal activities, the wide public exposure of the case was used to justify tightened controls on the practice of the Moslem faith. According to this report, "A great many of the representatives . . . urged that through this struggle [with Ma] they must all learn a lesson and be determined to eliminate all the rules of exploitation and other unreasonable systems in the Islamic religion, so that an evil man will no longer have a chance to undermine socialism and obstruct the progress of the Hui people in the name of such religious rules and systems."

DOC. 53. *The Problem of Monasteries (1959)*

ALL MONASTERIES in Tibet that belong to those who took part in the rebellion shall be treated as rebellious monasteries. . . . Buddhism was originally a religion with peaceable altruistic pure doctrines; but because the feudal serf-owning class has used monasteries as means for ruling and oppressing the people, the monasteries have themselves become a complete system of feudal exploitation. The monasteries not merely have village gardens, to exploit the laboring people, they also have many special privileges, to oppress and harm them. This state of affairs is wholly different from the religious freedom provided in our constitution nor does it harmonize with the creed of that very religion, nor benefit the monasteries themselves. The Tibetan laboring people believe in religion and really love the monasteries; but because they make an excuse of religion to cruelly mistreat the masses, they are bitterly hated by the masses. Within the monasteries there is rigid stratification; poor lamas are really slaves in monk's robes, and most of them are forced to become lamas to escape life's hardships. They urgently need liberation. Under these circumstances, we feel that we must start a triple movement in the monasteries: against rebellion, against privilege, against exploitation. As regards land and loans of non-rebel monasteries, [we] also follow the policy of reduction; and when this is done, if this year's income is insufficient to maintain the lamas, the government shall supplement it.

While the monasteries are practicing the three antis and two reductions, they must honestly carry out the Chinese Communist Party policy of religious freedom, protecting patriotic law-abiding monasteries, and preserving their cultural relics. Monasteries of historical significance that took part in the rebellion, shall after this problem is settled, be preserved.

DOC. 54. *Chang Chih-yi: Correctly Understand and Implement the Party's Policy on Freedom of Religious Belief (1962)*

NOR MUST FREEDOM of religious belief be confused with the use of religion for carrying out feudal oppression and exploitation. Among certain minority nationalities in our country, apart from secular feudal lords, there were also religious feudal lords the degree of whose exploitation and oppression of the people was exceedingly appalling. Feudal oppression and exploitation, whether or not it was carried out under a religious cloak, was basically not the question of religious belief, but the question of social system of oppression and exploitation of man by man. . . .

In the view of the Party and the State, this category of systems must be reformed by relying on the masses and through the religious believers themselves. These systems are systems of feudal oppression and exploitation under the cloak of religion, and their abolition will not hamper the religious belief of religious followers. . . .

Since the reform of these systems of feudal oppression and exploitation in religion among certain nationality minorities does not mean that those religious systems which give expression to legitimate religious activities are abolished, it is in no way in conflict with the policy of freedom of religious belief. Moreover, it is only when these systems of feudal oppression and exploitation in religion have been abolished that the laboring people can genuinely acquire the right of freedom of religious belief.

Prior to the democratic reform, feudal lords and slave-owners in certain national minorities not only interfered with the religious belief of the people of their own nationalities but also used their religious privileges to interfere with the various aspects of life of their people. Forcing the people to believe in religion, they regarded religion as an invisible fetter imposed on the neck of the laboring people. Whoever renounced his religious faith or changed to another religion according to his own will would be brutally punished. It was unthinkable that under these circumstances the people of these national minorities could have freedom of religious belief. At the same time, it is only when we resolutely carry out the policy of freedom of religious belief that we can unite with the religious believers among the broad masses of the laboring people, and win over all religious people who can be won over. It is only by thoroughly abolishing the systems of feudal oppression and exploitation in religion that we can consolidate the fruit of victory of this struggle. . . .

It can thus be seen that reform of systems of feudal oppression and exploitation in religion is not at odds with, but promotes, the implementation of the policy of freedom of religious belief. It is therefore wrong to think that abolition of the systems of feudal oppression and exploitation in religion is inconsistent with the policy of freedom of religious belief. Similarly it is also wrong to think that in the course of reforming the systems of feudal oppression and exploitation or after such a reform has been victoriously concluded, it is not necessary to observe the policy of freedom of religious belief. . . .

DOC. 55. *Liu Chun-wang and Yu Hsiang: Religion and Class Struggle in the Transition Period (1964)*

Religious Feudalism

RELIGIONS IN OUR COUNTRY, especially the Lamaist division of Buddhism and Islam, have been for a long time controlled and utilized by the feudal class. In these religions there were a number of feudal lords and some extremely savage and cruel systems of feudal oppression and feudal exploitation. Religious temples and monasteries owned large areas of land, large numbers of livestock, and large quantities of other means of production. They required the masses to contribute toward their upkeep and to do labor without any compensation, and cheated the masses and extorted money from them under various pretexts. They also had their own prisons and courts of justice and meted out punishments to the masses as they pleased. After the liberation, the Party and the government led the popular masses in waging a resolute struggle against these feudal lords in religious clothing, and, through the land reform in Han nationality areas and democratic reforms in national minority areas, abolished the feudal land system in religion and other systems of feudal oppression and feudal exploitation. It was a violent class struggle, and in some places the form of armed struggle had to be adopted owing to rebellion by the feudal class. However, the remnant forces of feudalism, unwilling to go into extinction, always try to reverse the land reform, democratic reforms and the abolition of the systems of feudal oppression and feudal exploitation in religion, and to carry out activities that will put them back in power again. Some reactionary elements in religious clothing even work in cooperation with foreign countries from the inside, and carry out criminal activities aimed to split the unity of the motherland and undermine national solidarity.

DOC. 56. *Chinese Moslems Expose the Crimes of Ma Chen-wu (October, 1958)*

FROM AUGUST 17 to September 6 [1958], the Chinese Islamic Association called the Hui people to a discussion meeting at Yin-ch'uan Hsien, Ninghsia Province. Through displaying facts, reasoning from evidence, hot debate, and big headlined pronouncements, the representatives thoroughly exposed, criticized, and repudiated Chen-wu, the extreme rightist element in the Islamic religion, for his anti-Communist, anti-people and anti-socialist crimes.

Attending this meeting were Ta P'u-sheng and Chang Yu-chen, Vice-chairmen of the Chinese Islamic Association, some committee members of the same Association, and representatives of the Hui people from Shensi, Kansu, Ts'inghai, Yunnan, Kirin, Hopeh, Sinkiang, Ninghsia and other provinces. There was a total of 407 representatives.

According to facts uncovered by the representatives, Ma Chen-wu has undertaken anti-Communist, anti-people and criminal activities through his position as chief of the Cheh-hai-lin-yeh Sect of the Islamic religion, by wearing the cloak of religion over a long period of years, through his authority as the religious chief, and by utilizing certain religious rules which are harmful to socialism and are detrimental to the progress of the Hui people.

According to evidence exposed at the meeting, Ma Chen-wu has committed every possible crime and is deep in bloody debts. Before the liberation, in order to strengthen and expand his feudalistic authorities and power, he conspired with Chu Shao-liang, Ma Hung-kui, Ma Chi-yuan and others, all reactionary rulers under the Kuomintang, in killing many peasants and revolutionary cadres. In 1939, when the revolution of the Hui people in the Hai-yuan and Ku-yuan area, Kansu Province, was suppressed by the reactionary Kuomintang, Ma Chen-wu ordered his henchmen to arrest and murder many Hui peasants and leaders who had taken part in the revolution. Also, in cooperation with Yang Teh-liang, a reactionary warlord under the Kuomintang, he murdered eleven family members of one of the revolutionary leaders, Ma Ssu-i, who is now Secretary of the Ku-yuan Hui People's Autonomous Chou Committee of the Communist Party.

According to exposures at the meeting, Ma Chen-wu has, through his evil use of authority, consistently murdered and brutally treated those who were opposed to him, dissatisfied with him and were unwilling to obey his orders. He has scooped out the eyes of many people, cut off their ears and tongues, chopped off their arms and legs, pulled out the muscles from their feet and crushed their bones. For example, Ma Chan-ch'uan and Ma Hui-chung, two Hui people in the Ku-yuan Hui People's Autonomous Chou, have been brutally and permanently crippled by him in this way.

The thing that has angered us most is the fact that after having murdered some of the people with a pistol or an ax, Ma Chen-wu has dared to chop their bodies into small pieces. He has also killed other people and took their hearts out to make oil. His servant, Wang Lung-t'u, was murdered in exactly this way. Not only was his belly cut open, but his heart was also taken out.

When Ma Chen-wu heard the news that Chang Chen-kuo of Ku-yuan Hsien had married his [Ma's] forsaken mistress, he immediately murdered all the five members of Chang's family. In 1949, shortly after the liberation, Ma Chen-wu even poisoned his own son, Ma Liang-teh, for even he was opposed to his criminal deeds.

Evidence uncovered at the meeting show that Ma Chen-wu has utilized his position as the "religious chief" to issue "orders" and organize several reactionary rebellions. Before the liberation he conspired with the reactionary Kuomintang and vainly attempted to stop the Chinese People's Liberation Army from liberating the great Northwest of China.

After the liberation of the Northwest, Ma Chen-wu was firmly opposed to all the policies of the Party, thinking that the government could be deceived. Relying on his own "power" and "the support of the masses," he has secretly plotted revolts and attempted to become a local king, dreaming of "a reign over the nation for forty years."

In 1950, shortly after the liberation of the Northwest, when the People's Government had not been long established, Ma Chen-wu, in conspiracy with the counter-revolutionaries in Peking and Nanking, laid plans for the "May 8th" (May 8, 1950) counter-revolutionary armed rebellion. At the time, the counter-revolutionaries held banners with Ma Chen-wu's seals on them and incited some of the masses who had not yet obtained a clear understanding of our Communist Party to actually encircle and attack Peiping and Nanking.

In 1952, when the land reform had just begun in the Ku-yuan Hui People's Autonomous Chou, Ma Chen-wu then plotted the "April 2" (1952) counter-revolutionary armed revolt. During the revolt, his henchmen widely distributed banners of "P'i-erh-han" (i.e., letters of introduction to heaven) with Ma Chen-wu's seals on them, saying that "heaven's gate is widely open and [your] forefathers are waiting to receive you."

In April this year, when the establishment of the Ninghsia Hui People's Autonomous Region was being contemplated, Ma Chen-wu vainly attempted to usurp the leadership power of the would-be Hui People's Autonomous Region. To achieve this purpose, he despatched his henchmen to make connections in the Chang-chai-ch'uan Hui People's Autonomous Hsien, Kansu Province. While there his henchmen, under the pretext of "protecting the Kung-pei" (i.e., the tombs of leaders of the Islamic religion), instigated the "April 4" counter-revolutionary armed rebellion in which several hundred counter-revolutionaries took part. During the rebellion, they cried the "three-all" slogan, namely: "Kill all the government cadres; Rob all the grain in the granaries; and Take away all the money in the cooperatives and trading companies!"

But since the Party and the Government had already educated the Hui people for several years, their political consciousness was greatly elevated. Therefore, shortly after this armed rebellion had taken place, the Government, through the positive help of the Hui people themselves, quickly brought the rebellion to an end.

After the "April 4" rebellion was crushed, Ma Chen-wu still

would not give up. On June 1 of the same year he again ordered his henchmen, Ma-tung and Chen Ju-chin, to lead a revolt in Chen-chia-fen, T'ung-hsin Hsien. From the documents taken from the bodies of Ma's followers whom we killed during the fight we could see even more clearly the ambitions of Ma Chen-wu. On these documents was written the purpose of his revolt as being "the establishment of the Hui People's Republic in the Ninghsia area." The form of this "Republic" was to be "a unification of the party, politics, religion and military affairs." This reactionary organization was to be "the Islamic Democratic Party." The slogan was: "Avenge our Chief, Ma (Chen-wu), and glorify our Islamic religion!"

Facts exposed at the meeting show that Ma Chen-wu's tricks in threatening the people to join in the counter-revolutionary activities by utilizing the authorities of religion have been extremely vicious. His slogan has been: "Kill the family members of any man who refuses to join in our rebellion." Huo Kui-hua, a Hui woman from Hsi-chi Hsien, accused Ma at the meeting and said that during the "April 2" revolt Ma Chen-wu's bandit followers in Hsi-chi Hsien forced her father to join them. Because her father refused to comply, these bandits first cut off his legs and then burned him to death.

To accumulate strength for further revolts, Ma Chen-wu gathered around him a group of runaway landlords, counter-revolutionaries and bad elements, and harbored them by assigning them religious positions in the Kung-pei [i.e., cemeteries], shrines and mosques. By taking cover under such positions Ma thought they could undertake counter-revolutionary activities. In this way Ma Chen-wu harbored more than thirty counter-revolutionaries in the Wu-chung area alone.

During the exposure, criticism and repudiation of Ma Chen-wu at the meeting, the representatives were unanimously of the opinion that Ma's counter-revolutionary activities have directly affected the progress of the Hui people and have become a stumbling-block on the Hui people's road to socialism.

During the exposure at the meeting, representatives of all the places proved with large quantities of concrete facts that Ma Chen-wu not only has, through his "orders" and his feudalistic authority, murdered the Hui people, maltreated them and plotted a series of revolts, but has also brutally exploited them through religion. According to these representatives, Ma Chen-wu instituted many "A-mai-lis," or festival days to commemorate the dead ancestors to which the A-hungs must be invited to chant the scriptures and be treated with big feasts, thereby squeezing money out of the living for the dead. For example, he has kept a record of the days of birth and death of all the family members of his followers and has seen to it that religious services be held on such days. These include "Grandmother's Day," "Wife's Day," "Aunt's Day," and others, sixty-five of such "A-mai-lis" in a year. On the average, one of such "A-mai-lis" is held every six or seven days, among which are seven occasions of big festivals.

Whenever such a day came, Ma Chen-wu would order his henchmen to force the people to offer him "Mieh-t'ieh." From the Hui people in Hsi-chi Hsien alone he has squeezed over one million yuan annually. In 1952, after the "April 2" rebellion was put down, the Party and the Government sent the Hui people in that area a 1,200,000,000-yuan relief fund (old currency) for their rehabilitation. Of this amount Ma Chen-wu squeezed out more than 600,000,000 yuan through numerous "A-mai-lis" and "Mieh-t'iehs."

Ma Chen-wu has also, on the basis of his authority as the religious chief, instituted many systems of feudalistic exploitation. Even up till now in Hsi-chi Hsien alone he owns more than 2,500 *mou* of land. The management of this land depends, on the one hand, on the labor of his slaves and, on the other hand, on the voluntary labor of the Hui masses. The Hui People's Cooperatives in Hsi-chi Hsien have to render an annual voluntary service of over 2,600 working days and their animals over 2,100 working days. During harvest seasons, the Hui people within eighty to ninety li of his land have to put aside their own harvest work and come to do voluntary labor on his land.

The "slaves" in his household have never been paid a wage, but Ma has ordered all the Fangs (i.e., the area where a mosque and its congregation are located is called a Fang) to pay an annual fee of wages for his slaves. The fire-wood which his household consumes has also been supplied by all the Fangs.

All the A-hungs of the Islamic mosques have been appointed by Ma Chen-wu. Through the appointment of A-hungs he has squeezed a big sum of money. To please him, some of the A-hungs have done everything possible to swindle and exploit the masses. Ma has regularly, in the name of repairing the "kung-peis" [i.e., tombs], squeezed the Hui people for money. In 1954, in Ch'uan-ch'ang, Kirin Province, he swindled away hundreds of thousands of yuan from the people.

To achieve his purpose of exploiting the masses, Ma Chen-wu has considered it nothing to employ all possible mean tricks. Whenever there is a death or a remarriage of a widow, the family must send money to him. Otherwise the dead cannot be buried or the widow cannot be remarried. Ma Chen-wu has through his nephew alone, Ma Kuo-pi, sold more than one hundred widows and obtained over 5,000 yuan from these sales.

Before the liberation, Ma Chen-wu even sold his hair, beard, the dirt from the "kung-pei," his household firewood ashes, dry bread, small pieces of his ragged clothes, and even his own manure to the Hui masses as "miracle drugs" to cure their diseases. By so doing, he not only has swindled big sums of money but also has caused many deaths.

Last year he sold dirt from the "kung-pei" in P'ing-liang Hsien to members of the Miao-wan Cooperative in Ching-yuan Hsien which in turned poisoned ten children to death. He has also sold big quantities of "P'i-erh-han" [i.e., passports to heaven] to swindle and make fools of the masses. Because of Ma's severe punishment, the Hui people have been paying thirty to sixty percent of their annual income for religious services which has all landed in his own pocket.

At the beginning of the discussion meeting, Ma Chen-wu cunningly denied all these charges and refused to give a clear account of his activities. Later, after ten days' exposition, criticism and repudiation and before large quantities of factual evidences, he confessed that the four armed rebellions had all been plotted and directed by himself. By so confessing he initially gave an account of his armed rebellious activities and his crimes against the people. Meanwhile, he also confessed how he had undertaken criminal activities of feudalistic exploitation of the people through his authority as a religious chief.

According to the exposures of the representatives at the meeting, before the liberation Ma Chen-wu was an ambitious politician in the cloak of religion. After the liberation, the Party and the Government adopted the attitude of uniting with him, educating him and helping him, with the hope that he would repent of his past sins and redeem his crimes through establishing some merits.

The People's Government showed him affectionate concern and honored him with the positions of member of the Committee on Nationalities Affairs under the Committee on Political and Military Affairs of the Northwest area; Governor of the Ku-yuan Hui People's Autonomous Chou; member of the National Committee of the Chinese People's Political Consultative Conference; and Vice-chairman of the Chinese Islamic Association and so on. In all the democratic and socialist reforms, the Party and the Government were lenient toward him.

But Ma Chen-wu has always insisted on his own reactionary political stand and has undertaken reactionary activities to overthrow the People's Government by using religion as a tool. For this reason, all the representatives at the meeting petitioned the Government to severely punish Ma Chen-wu, the extreme rightist element.

A great many of the representatives, while exposing the crimes of Ma Chen-wu, urged that through this struggle they must all learn a lesson and be determined to eliminate all the rules of exploitation and other unreasonable systems in the Islamic religion, so that an evil man will no longer have a chance to undermine socialism and obstruct the progress of the Hui people in the name of such religious rules and systems. Ho Fu-ch'eng, a Hui representative from Kirin Province, demanded the elimination of Ma Chen-wu's authority to issue "orders" and "appoint A-hungs" and the outlawing of Ma's personal title to and the mosque's ownership of land and cattle. Ho also urged the representatives to thoroughly implement the Government's policy of freedom of religious belief and forbid any man to interfere and exploit the people through the Islamic religion as a tool.

Ma Yu-huai, Vice-chairman of the Preparatory Committee of the Ninghsia Hui People's Autonomous Region, made a summary speech at the meeting. According to him, Ma Chen-wu has been a big feudalistic mountain heavily imposed on the heads of the Hui people. He has for a long period of years brutally ruled, exploited, and squeezed the Hui people and has obstructed their attempts to progress in the political, economic, and cultural fields.

The exposure of the reactionary nature of Ma Chen-wu, Ma Yu-huai said, will further liberate the Hui people, especially those under his enslavement, from the remnant bonds of feudalism and enable them to positively join in the socialist construction of the fatherland.

Ma Yu-huai further pointed out, on the basis of the large quantity of facts, that Ma Chen-wu has been an extreme rightist who has consistently plotted the downfall of the People's Government, attempted the restoration of the rule of the reactionary class, and has firmly opposed the Communist Party and the People.

In conclusion, Ma Yu-huai, on behalf of the Preparatory Committee of the Ninghsia Hui People's Autonomous Region, announced the deposition of Ma Chen-wu from the membership of the said Preparatory Committee, from the Governorship of Ku-yuan Hui People's Autonomous Chou and other similar administrative offices. He also suggested that the Government confiscate Ma's money and property. Finally, Ma Yu-huai said that although they have gained a great victory in the struggle against Ma Chen-wu, it is only a beginning, and that they must continue to struggle against him to the very end.

Ta P'u-sheng, one of the Vice-chairmen of the Chinese Islamic Association, on behalf of the Association announced the expulsion of Ma Chen-wu from his Vice-chairmanship in the Chinese Islamic Association. The representatives at the meeting expressed unanimous support for the actions taken by the Chinese Islamic Association and the Preparatory Committee of the Ninghsia Hui People's Autonomous Region regarding Ma Chen-wu. They pledged that, after returning to their respective districts, they would widely report on the spirit of this discussion meeting, mobilize the Hui people to continuously expose the crimes of Ma Chen-wu, and resolutely struggle against the other evil men and bad events in the Islamic religion.

Section 6. Superstition

THE THEORETICAL DISTINCTIONS between organized religion and local superstitions were thoroughly discussed in Part I, Section 3. Shanghai's deputy mayor, writing in 1953, here directs a vicious attack on another variety of "superstition," the so-called reactionary Taoist cults, prohibited by order of the Military Control Committee, an action undoubtedly induced by the subversive record of secret societies under previous regimes. With no central organization or coordinating system, it would be impossible to bring them into a single, easily controlled body. The prohibition order is backed by the deputy mayor's public exposé of their alleged acts of treason, sabotage, and counter-revolution. The deputy mayor denies categorically that they are authentic religious groups; they swindle and defraud their followers, he declares, and lead debauched lives.

The battle against over sixty superstitious practices said to have impeded agricultural production in a border region is described in the article on Lei Shan Hsien. After a three-month-long meeting and large-scale debate the people passed resolutions reforming local customs and festivals, thereby eliminating, it was said, the loss of up to 100 working days a year. Certain cadres who "glamorized" and protected local customs are chided for wrong priorities.

Another battle with local superstitions is described in "Derive Value from Superstitions." Here the emphasis is on practical use of local resources, a "supernatural" cave filled with organic mire, rather than on theory or political study. Courageous cadres break the taboos.

DOC. 57. *Hsu Chien-kuo, Deputy Mayor, Shanghai Municipal People's Government: Why Must We Prohibit the Reactionary Taoist Cults? (Broadcast over Shanghai Radio, June 7, 1953)*

Dear Listeners:

Today I propose to take a little of the time of this broadcasting station to talk to you on one problem, the problem of the prohibition of reactionary Taoist cults. A few days ago, we must all have seen in the press the notification of the Shanghai Military Control Committee on the prohibition of reactionary Taoist cults. The notification clearly ordered the prohibition of the *Yi Kuan Tao*, the *Chiu Kung Tao*, the *Tung Shan She*, the *Lung Hua Sheng Chiao Hui* of the *Yi Sheng Tien Tao*, the *Hsi Chien Tao*, the *Lao Mu Tao*, the *Tao Te Hsueh She*, the *Tao Fa Chiao Tung*, the *Chung Te She*, among the scores of reactionary Taoist cults. The public security organs, in breaking up the *Yi Kuan Tao* and other reactionary organizations, placed under arrest a group of arch leaders who had committed very serious crimes and incurred the great wrath of the masses.

This decisive measure on the part of the People's Government obtained the enthusiastic support of the broad masses of the citizens. Indeed not a few members of the families of the arrested leaders of these cults, with full understanding of the cause of righteousness, had before the arrests actively given information, and after the arrests assisted the government in looking up evidences, traces, and also mobilizing their arrested relatives into speedy frank admissions of their crimes. Thus when the woman cult leader Chi Chao-ti was arrested, her daughter and her daughter-in-law both urged her to confess frankly immediately, while her son (a paper factory worker) also wrote to her saying that if she would not confess frankly, he would sever his relationships with her. When the cult leader Yu Yi-ching was arrested, his son also said, "In personal relationship he is my father, but from the viewpoint of class stand, he is my enemy." He proceeded to expose the crimes of the father.

These incidents are very moving, being the concrete manifestations of the further raising of the political consciousness of the people of Shanghai. However, since the backbone members of the higher ranks in the reactionary Taoist cults have been deceiving the masses under the cover of the burning of joss sticks, kowtowing before their shrines, living on vegetarian diets, and saying Buddhist prayers while in effect their organizations were actually engaged secretly in counter-revolutionary activities, there are therefore still people who do not fully understand their true nature. These people say, "There is no point in prohibiting these Taoist cults, for they all burn joss sticks and live on vegetarian diets." Some members of the families of the arrested leaders say, "It is our freedom of religion to believe in the *Yi Kuan Tao;* why should we be arrested?" We can say that these people have their eyes blinded by the black screen of the reactionary cults. We can say definitely that reactionary cults like the *Yi Kuan Tao* are absolutely not religious organizations, but counter-revolutionary organizations. Let us look into the facts relating to their criminal activities.

From the very beginning, these reactionary Taoist cults have been counter-revolutionary organizations employed by the imperialists and the reactionary ruling class in the country. The big chiefs of these reactionary Taoist cults have mostly been warlords, landlords, despots, collaborators and special service agents. As far back as in the days of the war against Japan, these organizations acted as the abettors in crime of the Japanese imperialists, sabotaged the war of resistance, conducted propaganda among the masses to serve as loyal subjects of the Japanese invaders, supported the "Greater East Asia New Order," and assisted the enemy in investigating and reporting on the anti-Japanese elements, acting as guides to the enemy, supplying information, and persecuting the Chinese people.

On the surrender of Japan, the reactionary Taoist cults immediately colluded with the special service of the Kuomintang, and were exploited by the American imperialists and the Kuomintang bandits for activities against the Communists and against the people, sabotaging the people's liberation war. The big chiefs of the *Yi Kuan Tao*, Chi Ming-chou and Chang Chin-chung, had submitted letters to the Department of Social Affairs of the Chiang bandits and the Shanghai Kuomintang Headquarters pledging their loyalty to the Kuomintang and their determination to oppose the Communists. Chao Tse-kuang and other heads of the *Chiu Kung Tao* in coordination with the anti-people's war launched by the Chiang bandits colluded with special agents in the organization of the "China Relief Charity Association," and forced members of their cult to collect intelligence reports in the liberated areas. After the liberation, they continued to establish bases in Raining Road and other points in Shanghai, to direct the activities of leaders of their cult in Soochow, Hangchow and Shaohsing. The *Tung Shan She* established connections with Wang Shih-chun, special service chief of the CC Clique[1] of the Chiang bandits, and secretly organized bases with the objective of directing insurrections in Shanghai after its liberation.

After the liberation of Shanghai, the reactionary Taoist cults accepted the orders of the American-Chiang special agents, and turned to secret activities, organizing "information sections" and "liaison stations" to carry out the "single line leadership" method for continued operations. They incited members of their cults to adopt a hostile attitude toward the people's government, prevented them from cooperation with the government, sheltered counter-revolutionaries, collected intelligence reports, and plotted for opportunities to stage insurrections and enthrone themselves emperors.

In a word, they adopted a hostile stand against the masses

1. At one time, this was a powerful clique inside the Kuomintang Party.

of the people in everything. Wherever the People's Government did something for the good of the people, they would sabotage it. Thus when in 1949 there was the typhoon which damaged the sea walls, and the Shanghai Municipal People's Government called on the masses to effect repairs to them, these cult leaders spread the rumor that "the God Neptune is doing all this havoc, and we must not act against Heaven." They also incited the backward members among the masses into drowning many cadres engaged in repairs to the sea walls. When agrarian reform was introduced in the suburban areas of Shanghai, they spread the rumor that "whosoever takes the land and property of another will have generations of his descendants condemned in Hell," to sabotage the movement. When the resist-U.S. and aid-Korea campaign was launched, they started spreading propaganda about the American atomic bomb and talked of the third world war, spreading the rumor that the Americans would land in Shanghai and Chiang Kai-shek would return. During the five-anti movement,[2] the *Chiu Kung Tao* compiled a "ghost telephone directory" of six-digit numbers, and spread rumors to sow dissension in the unity of the people. After Eisenhower came into power, the *Yi Kuan Tao* fabricated the story of a baby being born out of a bitch, spread ideas about a change in the universe, and impersonated gods and ghosts to threaten the masses in order to achieve their objective of sabotaging production and construction, and undermining social order.

It will be thus seen that these reactionary Taoist cults are absolutely not religious organizations, but every inch counter-revolutionary organizations. That they have succeeded in deceiving a small portion of the culturally backward masses has been due to their putting on the cloak of gods and buddhas to cover up their counter-revolutionary activities. When their crimes have not yet been fully exposed, they can for a moment blind the eyes of a small portion of the masses. This is also one

2. The "Three Anti-" and "Five Anti-" movements of 1951 mobilized the entire populace, first, against corruption, waste, and bureaucracy, and second, against bribery, smuggling, stealing national resources, skimping on work and material, and stealing national economic secrets.

of the poisonous and treacherous characteristics of the reactionary cults.

For the masses deceived by them, these reactionary Taoist cults are also organizations which swindle and injure the people. They fool the masses with superstitious practices, cheat people out of money, insult women. People who join the cults have to pay various kinds of fees, and it is claimed that only by "doing good" (that is, spending money) will one be spared from suffering. In the *Yi Kuan Tao*, one gold bar of ten ounces will have to be spent for holding once the service known as "ferrying a believer into immortality." The *Chiu Kung Tao* has some fifty to sixty devices of swindling its adherents on the pretext of teaching them the mysteries of the cult. The *Pao Kuang* chapter of the *Yi Kuan Tao* alone held more than 600 services for "ferrying believers into immortality" and extorted sums totalling more than 12,000 silver dollars. When an adherent falls sick, he is not allowed to see a physician but is forced to pay money to the cult and seek the help of the immortals. A packet of the ashes of joss sticks is issued and is said to be the "medicine of the gods." Besides cheating one out of his money, harm is also done to his life.

Can we thus say of the heads of these cults that they are men who believe in deities and buddhas? Absolutely no. When they talk of teaching their believers the mysteries of immortality, and hold planchette (automatic writing) sessions, everything is a secretly prepared hoax, and people are deceived by outward appearances. These people live the most debauched of lives and are most extravagant. They often drive their believers into disposing of all their property and holdings, and proceed to outside areas for "the propagation of the truth in new lands," to develop their organizations. Many people closed down their businesses, sold their land, and finally lost everything they had. . . . Only by uniting ourselves and devoting our efforts at production may we make a good job of the construction of new China. The reactionary Taoist cults fear the efforts of the people at construction. In addition to engaging directly in counter-revolutionary activities, they also produce paralyzing effects on the spirits of the people, and attempt to make people believe that their sufferings are sent down from Heaven, in the attempt to reduce the morale of the people in their fight against the enemy and their zeal in production and construction. In our determination to prohibit these anti-popular and counter-revolutionary Taoist cult organizations, we are not only taking care of the general interests of the people, but also protecting the interests of the members of the cult who have been deceived. This is very obvious. The objective of our prohibition of these cults is to destroy their organizations, purge all counter-revolutionaries, save the majority of the members who have been deceived, raise high their political consciousness, in order to remove the obstacles to production and construction of our city, and to consolidate the people's democratic dictatorship. . . .

As to the mass of members deceived or coerced into joining the reactionary Taoist cults, their treatment must be quite different from that for the chiefs referred to above. These people have been victims of deception, and have committed no crimes. Only because of their ignorance they were deceived, and we must sympathize with their ignorance, adopt the policy of patient unity and education, to assist them into awakening, call upon them to resign from the cults and to be deceived no more. We must welcome these people in taking the step of resignation from the cults, and cannot permit any action that should embarrass them. . . .

DOC. 58. *How Lei-shan Hsien Struggles to Change Its Customs (1958)*

LEI-SHAN is situated in Kweichow Province's high mountainous region; it has a population of about 56,000 people, of whom more than forty-four percent are Miao nationals. After the liberation, a great stride in the hsien's economical and cultural development has been in evidence, particularly after having victoriously gone through a socialist revolution. . . .

During the Great Leap Forward, many of the antiquated rules and customs as well as those feudal superstitions detrimental to production and constructive to thought have been abolished.

In the past, antiquated rules and oppressive customs were countless. A rough estimate showed that there were some sixty superstitious regulations contained in their folklore. For example, every year before plowing a "living guide" had to lead the way before the masses would commence farming. As a result, production was frequently delayed.

While working on the irrigation project, they were afraid to damage "dragon reins" or to provoke the mountain god, lest they bring disaster to their families. When farms were invaded by insects, farmers refused to exterminate them and contended that to do so would be against nature and their conscience. When sick, they revered ancestral spirits, prayed to their god for help, and killed lots of livestock. This custom has been very costly and detrimental to production.

In addition, there have been too many religious festivals, including many national days, during which production has been at a standstill. Because of superstition and festivals, production has been discontinued more than 100 days annually, and in some areas 138 days. As each nationality maintains different festivals, numerous conflicts arise from these divergences.

Through the various stages since the liberation, we have done quite a lot to improve these undesirable national customs and habits. This reform has been carried out in view of the particular organizational status of the masses and their degree of awareness. During the land reform in 1952, the Party actively publicized the guidance and education of the masses in changing their previous farming habits and improving their productive techniques.

In areas where the people did not know how to plow, for instance, a work team was dispatched specifically by the hsien committee to set the masses in motion and to demonstrate plowing methods to them. The People's Government issued free iron farming tools to those who could not afford to pay for farming implements. Health personnel were sent to take care of the sick. Measures of solidarity, indoctrination and reform were applied to "living guides," shamans, town elders, etc., with an aim to correct their deceitful and improper conduct.

Through many meetings in the past years, problems of reforming national customs and habits were discussed, progressive elements were praised for their conduct, and bad elements and misconduct that had upset production work through superstition were exposed and criticized. On the basis of expanded ideological awareness, several shamans were exposed for deceitful conduct.

Meanwhile, campaigns were launched among the masses to widely expose and criticize superstitions, so as to enable the people to realize their evil influence. To cite an example, in 1955 when a village in Ku-lu Hsiang suffered from a calamity caused by insects, a shaman cheated the villagers by making fifty households butcher fifteen hogs as homage to their god. While paying his respects to the ancestral spirits, the shaman agitated the people not to return to work in the fields for three days. However, three days later when the people went to the field, all the crops had been devoured by the insects.

Another example took place in 1954, at Ch'eng-kuan Hsiang where the people, to prevent the outbreak of fire, were inveigled by the shamans to kill a cow as a sacrifice. While the ritual was going on, the hsiang was on fire. As to the ceremony of eating the viscera of a bull, everyone knows that it is not redeemable for a ten-year period. By examining these concrete facts and through successful education, the people finally became embittered concerning the evils of superstitions. Having been able to distinguish right from wrong, they were willing to abolish many of their superstitious customs and rites.

However, owing to a misconception regarding national privileges and the growth of nationalism, considerable resistance was met when reform activities dealing with national customs and habits were being executed. During the national reform movement, our hsien had experienced a socialist indoctrination whose main platform involved the intensive criticism of local nationalism. A great debate extending from the highest to the lowest rung and including both the Party and the people was also held then.

At the Second Session of the hsien's Second People's Representative Conference at the beginning of this past January, proposals on reforming national customs and ceremonies were aired. Later, they were submitted to various nationals in the hsien for discussion. Three months later, after the close of the meeting, and following solidarity of the bottom levels, a vote was held to conduct an extensive reform.

A large-scale debate was also staged. Then, at the First Session of the hsien's Third People's Representative Conference on April 20, resolutions were passed by a great majority, and following careful discussion, to make a certain important reform on local customs and ceremonies.

With regard to festivals, for instance, originally there were five New Year holidays. Now only one spring festival is allowed. The spring festival has been an event common to all nations in Lei-shan Hsien.

The "harvest feast" (formerly there were four such feasts) is now completely abolished. Instead, July 15 has been stipulated as an autonomous memorial day for the Miao and T'ung nationalities in southeast Kweichow. The flute dance, being a typical Miao dance and not unwholesome in its performance, will be retained. As to their unsavory habits of singing and horseplay, it has been decided to extract the merits and to gradually abolish the defects.

Other customs such as eating the viscera of a bull, dragon-calling, slope-climbing, "retirement" of old fields, "retirement" for old cows and old horses, "Mah-yuan-ti," maiden's lot, and others have all been abolished because they are unfavorable to production and also are not meritorious. Reactions of the various nationalities to these stipulations show that they comply with the people's demands.

In correcting the customs and rituals of the nationalities, the policy adopted by Lei-shan Hsien has depended on the Communist Party members and on the active elements of the masses. Debates were held from top to bottom levels so as to facilitate a vigorous two-fold effort. Local nationalism has been the goal of opposition forces. A clear demarcation was drawn between the masses and the capitalistic class so that the masses could distinguish right from wrong.

Other measures included a thorough investigation and study of the various national customs and ceremonies, a careful analysis of these customs and rituals so as to determine their different social influences, the separation of meritorious from malevolent customs and habits, and propositions on revolutionizing them which were discussed and debated repeatedly by the masses. The masses were then educated through methods of recollection and through giving clear accounts and comparisons of the past with the present.

In correcting nationality customs and ceremonies, nationality cadres, particularly those at the highest level, should stand out and work as vanguards to resolutely overcome pro-rightist conservative thoughts.

In dealing with people such as "living guides," shamans and town elders, measures on solidarity, education and reform should be applied. In addition, they should be frequently called to attend meetings. They should be subjected to education and mobilized for use in promoting reform activities dealing with their national customs and rituals.

Reactionaries who have made it a practice to drive a wedge among the people by means of sabotage activities cloaked by nationality customs and rituals should be punished according to the law.

Nationality customs and ceremonies should be decided by conditions of the social life. When conditions of social life change, customs and habits must follow suit. Although some of the customs and habits may be wholesome, some prove to be otherwise or are even harmful as time goes by. While it's an obligation and a necessity to retain and develop good traditions, it is likewise necessary to correct some of the outdated and harmful customs and habits.

The reactionary class had in the past used these evil customs and rituals to enslave the people. In the past two years, the capitalistic class, rightists, and advocates of local nationalism have attacked the Party and socialism under the pretext of respecting nationality habits and customs.

Quite a number of nationality cadres, under the ideological influence of local nationalism, have somehow glamorized nationality customs and ceremonies and have insisted quite improperly that they should receive all due respect. These cadres have injured the socialist reform.

That nationality customs and habits can be easily taken advantage of by people with such intentions may be proved by many facts. Those who do not have an accurate knowledge of nationality customs and habits are susceptible to local nationalism. As minority nationals, we should be aware of and alarmed at these things.

DOC. 59. *Derive Value from Superstitions (1958)*

RETURNING FROM A TOUR of manure-collecting activities at the Pi-ling Cooperative of Tsing-hsi Hsien, Huang Chen-nieh, Secretary of the K'a-peh Hsiang Branch Headquarters of Lung-ling National Autonomous Hsien, Kwangsi Province, told Chairman Huang Kuo-tung of the K'a-peh Hsiang Cooperative: "Old Huang, look! I wasn't worried before. But when I saw what was going on in other areas, my pulse mounted. In other areas, cows are sheltered in barns and so are hogs. The people gather manure from the hills and from the fields. Everywhere, manure is heaped like hills. What about us?"

Speaking before a meeting of the Hsien Branch Headquarters, Huang Kuo-tung said: "Manure is available. We can have as much manure as we want if we can only open up supernatural ditches and fairy caves."

What Huang referred to was a big ditch, eighty to ninety feet long, ten feet deep, and four to five feet wide. It was dug by the villagers in 1938 to prevent drought; but the results were unexpected. Food shortages continued to plague the people. Many people emigrated, some starved to death. Hogs were diseased. The village elders complained that the ditch had cut off the dragon reins and had forced the dragon to fly away.

Thus, the ditch was associated with the disaster. The elders said that nothing further should be done to the ditch. Thereafter whenever it rained, garbage was washed down into the ditch by the rainfall. Now the ditch is filled up and people consider it a supernatural site.

After the cooperative chairman had related the story, everyone felt that those two places are indeed good sources of fertilizer. They unanimously agreed that they should start digging. Meanwhile, all the Miao and T'ung peoples living in the hsien had participated in a district mass meeting, at which the district committee secretary urged them to learn from their forerunners, to catch up to them, and to surpass them. Hundreds of the members of the K'a-peh Hsiang Cooperative were crowded into three circles to discuss how to search for manure sources. Concluding the discussion, they unanimously resolved to start digging in the supernatural ditch.

Ch'en Kwang-teh, leader of the third production group, said: "Whatever can be accomplished by others shall also be done by us. The supernatural ditch cannot assure us a living, only food can." As soon as he had finished his comment, Huang Chen-nieh confidently went up to the platform and announced their plans. Their target was to administer 80,000 chin of manure for each mou of land and to make each mou produce 800 chin of grain.

But upon returning to the village, some of the village elders were heard to say: "If you have no fear of death, go ahead and dig manure. In any case, we are old; we can die today if fate so dictates." The cooperative chairman and the secretary of the hsiang party branch each told them: "Don't be afraid. Since we want the manure from the supernatural ditch, we cadres will go there as a test. Let's see what the demons can do to us!"

Thus, the hsiang magistrate, the secretary of the hsiang party branch and the cooperative chairman all went ahead of others to the supernatural ditch.

Chang Pao-hua, a primary school teacher, working with four of his family members, dug 50,000 chin of fertile deposits in only a half day's time. The secretary of hsiang party branch, back from the ditch, reported the score of the half day's work from the top of a tree through a megaphone. In response, all the households and the various units in the hsiang got their baskets and other tools ready that very night, planning to follow the cadres to the supernatural ditch to dig the fertile mire early the next morning.

When dawn came the following morning, horns sounded the order to advance toward the supernatural ditch. Soon, the ditch was full of people, carrying hoes and baskets. Hundreds and thousands of hoes rose up and down. After a battle of four days, some 210,000 tan of fertile mire was collected and heaped up into a hill.

While the supernatural ditch was being attacked, youth assault troopers led a vanguard to the fairy cave, where they removed mire and bat manure. Some wanted to use these deposits as fertilizer for peanut growing and others wanted them for grain.

Because of the great manure-collecting victory, some of the cooperative members have written two special verses:

> The supernatural ditch has soil rich and
> good;
> Party members, cadres and masses all with
> one heart,
> With hoes and baskets used in unison, have collected
> twenty million chin of manure in
> four days.

> With the tide of production riding high,
> People rise up before dawn.
> For a bounty harvest at the year's end,
> A visit to the fairy cave brings bounti-
> ful years.

DOC. 60. *Chou Chien-jen: The Question of Breaking Down Religion and Superstitions (April 21, 1964)*

SUPERSTITIONS MUST BE ELIMINATED. Superstition refers to all kinds of stupid thoughts that stifle intelligence; they are the so-called "unreal concepts." They can obstruct the progress of society. It is necessary to break them down. Some superstitions have in fact already been eliminated. In the old days, a man had to choose a good day to set out on a journey of any distance. If the almanac said that it was "not suitable to travel" then he would not dare to start out. This sort of superstition was very common when there were no steamers, trains and other fairly safe means of transport. Of course, travel was rather dangerous in those days. The roads were not safe and robbery was unavoidable. It was rather dangerous to travel by sail when there were often storms in summer and autumn. The taboo on starting a journey on a day that was not suitable for travelling gradually spread very widely. When means of transport improved and travel became safer, this taboo unconsciously disappeared.

These superstitions had shallow roots and were fairly easy to eradicate. They were only found among the upper classes. Those who had little money with them had no cause to fear robbers. The boatman who made his living on boats did not care whether or not the almanac said it was suitable to go out, because he had to sail. Hence superstitions also have a class nature.

However, there are many kinds of superstitions, and the difficulty of destroying them varies from one superstition to another. It takes longer to break down physiognomy and fortune-telling based on the shape of a character picked at random and on the time, day, month, and year of a person's birth. Yet there are some still harder to break down. Superstitions about "luck" last longer. Luck is a mysterious force existing nowhere, yet everywhere. If a man has good luck, he will find happiness, and if he has bad luck, he will encounter adversity. Superstitions about luck have obviously decayed. However, fate and luck are related. Unless the superstition of fortune-telling is stopped, superstitions about luck will still remain. This superstition is also connected with the blind fortune-tellers. If all dealers in superstition had taken up other work and none was left, this kind of superstition would not be hard to destroy.

There are many such superstitions, which are not described in detail here.

However, superstition covers a very broad field. Religion is also superstition. It is a type of superstition with deep roots and the support of material powers. As it is on a larger scale its bad influence is even greater. Religious superstition is not the same as more superstitious fear of ghosts and foxes. There is a definite policy for the treatment of religion, and that is freedom to believe in religion and freedom not to believe in religion. This will not be discussed here. Most religious believers support socialism and take part in socialist construction in their political activities, and we should recognize this clearly. Here we are only concerned to discuss the ideological aspect. From the point of view of ideology, superstition must be broken down, and there is obviously nothing more to say. Religious and superstitious thoughts constitute a serious threat to socialist revolution and its construction. Socialist revolution aims to change the old social system of exploitation and oppression and to destroy classes. Of course this aim requires courage and revolutionary struggle. On the other hand, religion teaches people to seek happiness, solve the problems of life and reach the happiness of the afterlife through prayer. Therefore belief in religion must make revolutionary ardour fade. Marx had a famous saying, "Religion is the opiate of the people." Lenin had a similar saying, "Religion is bad alcohol which benumbs the spirit." Grape wine has some nutritional value besides a harmful alcoholic content. Bad alcohol contains only poison which has a stupefying effect. Superstition is hostile to the direct pursuit of improvement. Everybody should know this point.

Another kind of phenomenon should also be mentioned here. There is a traditional misconception that laboring people believe in superstition more than "upper class" elements. This is an erroneous way of thinking. In the past, we seemed to find from superficial observation that more fishermen and peasants believed in superstition along the coast and in areas either plagued with drought or waterlogged. However, it was obvious that their living was hard. In an age when there were only sailing junks and no weather forecasts, fishermen's lives were in great danger when they went out to sea to catch fish. Sometimes, they "came back fully loaded with fish," but when they were caught in a storm, their junks would easily capsize. Peasants had very little surplus grain, so they could not stand long droughts and incessant rains. The laboring people lived more under the threat of danger and in fear of hunger than the wealthy families who enjoyed safety in their houses and had plenty of grain in their granaries. In the old days, protection was sought from the gods and idolatrous processions were held to greet the gods before fishermen went out to sea to catch fish and when peasants encountered long droughts or incessant rains. These actions were related to the threat to people's lives. Most temples and similar structures were built by wealthy people and bureaucrats. There were also some built on imperial orders. The promoters were in fact mostly "upper class" people. It is obvious that religion was also their tool for misleading the people. Otherwise, why should they spend so much money and exert so much energy to do these things?

Why does religion still exist in our society? The reason is quite simple. Religion has a comparatively strong foundation. This foundation exists because of the presence of bourgeois elements and the continued influence which exploiting ideas have on people. This is the foundation on which religion exists. Religion has its own structures, church workers and priests, etc. This is its material instrument of publicity. Churches stand in places where Christianity exists. This is a symbol of superstition. Other temples have the same function. Sermons given by ministers in the churches, as I heard in earlier days, refer to softness overcoming hardness, as advocated by Lao Tzu. They say that the teeth are hard and the tongue is soft, but the teeth will fall out and the tongue remains sound when one is very old. Incense and candle lights in the temples as well as the activities of church workers and religious believers are also a kind of material attraction which tempts people on to the path of superstition. Religious workers continually extend church influence, and some common people who are not religious workers themselves but have a profound feeling for religion and superstition also disseminate religion and superstition.

In short, superstition is harmful and must be broken down. Speaking of ideology, we must first clearly recognize the harm of superstition if we want to smash it, and in particular we must know what superstition is. We can see that, although superstitious people believe in superstition, they do not know that what they believe is superstition. They think they are doing the right things. Scholars in old days recited "heavenly blessings and good deeds" in the morning and kept their "merits and faults" in the evening. They did not think that their action was silly, but that it was something which should be done. Learning from the past, we must therefore explain to people the harm of superstition and at the same time make clear what superstition is. Superstition cannot be broken down if people do not understand what superstitious ideas are. . . .

Section 7. One Hundred Flowers Bloom: Complaints Against Religious Policy in Practice

WITHOUT DOUBT religious leaders in the early years of the People's Republic were eager to demonstrate the solidarity of religious believers with the collective effort to unify and rebuild their broken nation. The early patriotic pledges of the various groups were not likely the result of overt coercion, although social pressures and a highly charged political milieu made consensus almost mandatory.

It was not until the "blooming and contending" period of about one month during the Hundred Flowers period in 1957 that open criticism of the regime's implementation of religious policy appeared in the Chinese press. Even this, as seen in selected documents here, appears largely as evidence cited in official counterstatements published subsequently during the anti-rightist period of 1958–59. As with criticisms of government and Party coming from other sectors of society, primarily from intellectuals, the criticisms from religious leaders had gone too far. Mao Tse-tung and Party leaders had overestimated the degree of popular consensus for state policies and Party leadership in many sectors, including the religious. Party leaders, shocked at the vehemence and volume of complaints and criticism, concluded that liberalization had been premature, that mobilization for all-out effort to build the new China demanded a political solidarity that quite obviously had not been achieved.

The brief period of "blooming and contending" was abruptly halted with an editorial in *People's Daily* warning that class differences still prevailed and that class struggle must continue—the beginning of a rigorous anti-rightist campaign directed toward ideological rectification. The "bourgeois intellectuals," it was assumed, still carried the poisons of pre-revolutionary habits and thinking, and could not be trusted. Suspected rightists were subjected to protracted "study meetings," some lasting for weeks or months, to reform-through-labor camps, or to personal denunciation at mass accusation meetings, often resulting in prison sentences or long-term assignments to thought reform camps.

In the new climate of political orthodoxy and rectification, religious leaders came under attack along with other intellectuals. Numerous personal confessions and lengthy denunciation documents appeared in the Chinese press in 1958. Official religious bodies and conferences at national, provincial, and local levels issued statements and pledges notable for their political and patriotic orthodoxy.

From this time on, down to the total silencing of religion in 1966, religious leaders would never again speak out as they did in the brief period when the Hundred Flowers bloomed.

The criticisms from religious leaders selected here came from Buddhists, Moslems, Protestants and Catholics. They spoke of interference with religious activities, of personal abuse, pressures on children of believers, anti-religious propaganda, and failure by hostile cadres to understand and implement the Party's religious policy. Citing blasphemy of God by an official, one leader said that it was "worse than reviling one's mother"; the use of a church as a stable, he said, was like "defiling our ancestors' graves."

A Protestant leader in Hunan is said to have called Party members a privileged class, saying also that socialism and the church were in basic conflict and that collectivization hampered freedom of movement, keeping members too occupied to attend services. He said that the Religious Affairs Bureau was authoritarian, undemocratic and solved no problems for the church, serving, in fact, as a kind of religious police bureau.

The "erroneous views" of Moslem Liu Sheng-ming were exposed in *Hopei Jih-pao*. He was quoted as saying that the Party's real policy was not freedom but extermination of religion, that "special care" shown to Moslems was only for the purpose of extending the state's influence, and that collaborationist imams were "black sheep" who betrayed the faith for personal rewards. Liu sabotaged national solidarity, his opponents said, by sowing enmity between the Moslems and the Han Chinese.

Lamaist leader Shirob Jaltso spoke on behalf of his people at the 1956 session of the National People's Congress, pointing out the difficulties in adjustment for Tibetan monks and believers forced too rapidly into new patterns of collective farming. He urged a flexible policy which would take into account the local customs and traditions, saying the best method is "moving slowly at the beginning. . . ."

Quite obviously these are only samples of the full range of complaints and grievances held by religious believers. Much fuller accounts of these can be found in *Documents of the Three-Self Movement*,[1] in *Religion in Communist China*,[2] and in the publication *China Bulletin*,[3] as well as in newspaper accounts and other material from that period.

DOC. 61. *Local and Provincial Complaints About Treatment of Religions (Peking, Religious Leaders) (May, 1958)*

THEY THOUGHT that there were still cadres and those among the masses who did not treat religious leaders and believers with enough respect, and even discriminated against them. Some of the Christian priests remarked that in the minds of believers there was a sort of oppressiveness; and although they went to church services, on their return home they dared not admit that they were believers. Some of the people and the police interfered with the families of these believers in devious ways; for instance, the children of believers would be called for individual interviews; some school teachers would not allow children to attend Sunday school, telling them: "If you go again, we will expel you." A priest said: "My child goes to a certain middle school; he is good from every point of view but because I am a priest his application to join the Youth League has been repeatedly turned down."

Islamic imams had much to say about intermarriage between

1. Asia Department National Council of Churches USA, New York, 1963.
2. Richard C. Bush, Abingdon, Nashville, 1970.
3. Asia Department (above).

Mohammedans and the Han—one of them said: "In particular a Han Party or Youth League member, before marrying, is obliged to join the Mohammedan religion—but this is clearly anomalous. Consequently, some Mohammedans regard marriage between Han Party or Youth League members and Mohammedans as a mockery. . . ."

A Catholic sister said: "When we walk in the streets wearing our habit, some people abuse us, shouting 'Running dogs of Imperialism,' want to tear off our hoods, and give us stony stares." Some Catholic fathers remarked that a believer at the Thirteenth Middle School (by the name of Tai) was the object of discrimination—a certain Youth League member wrote on the blackboard abusing him in all sorts of ways, so that everyone looked down on him.

During the discussion, the religious leaders held that the Religious Affairs Bureau of the Municipal People's Committee and other departments concerned showed insufficient concern for every religion, and did not help enough in solving problems. Some of the Islamic imams said: "The United Front Department of the Communist Party Municipal Committee does not maintain sufficient links with us, and its members rarely bother to meet us. The Bureau of Civic Affairs shows a lack of concern about our living conditions; and very little help has been given in connection with repairs to mosques this year."

Members of the Buddhist religion had similar feelings towards the Bureau of Religious Affairs. . . .

Some of the Catholic fathers said: "The Government advocated the self-sufficiency of religions; but the question of the Seventh Hospital and the Thirty-ninth Middle School, the estates of which belong to the Church, has remained unsolved since 1950. Are they being rented, or requisitioned, or are they on loan—we can't make out why, up to the present, not a penny has been received in respect of these few hundred houses. . . ."

Some Christian priests had much to say about newspapers publishing a great deal of anti-religious articles, but not publicizing religious policies in a favourable light. Some believers voiced views against their own religious leaders, alleging that they had, all along, failed to merge deeply with the masses, and had failed to help the monasteries, temples and churches in a concrete manner to solve their problems. . . .

DOC. 62. *Rebel Moslems in Honan Province* (*May, 1958*)

DURING THE PERIOD OF "big contending and big blooming" last year, upon the occasion of the frantic attacks on the Party by the rightists in various parts of Honan, the rightists hidden in the upper strata of the Hui [Chinese Moslems] nationality and the Islamic religious circles also became active. They disseminated reactionary views which undermined unity among the nationalities and cast a slur on the nationalities policy of the Party. Some of them even plotted riots and intended to sabotage the unity of the country by creating an independent kingdom. . . . They gave the utmost publicity to such reactionary fallacies as "All the Hui people of the world form one family" and "Religion comes before country. . . ."

These rightists, as they have always done, opposed the socialist system, hated the new society, described today's society as pitch dark, alleged that, while there were "more rich people than poor people" in the days before liberation, there were "more poor people than rich people" in the days after it, stigmatized the socialist system as the "system of starvation," and said that "the more numerous and greater the cooperatives are, the narrower becomes the road before the Hui people." They sabotaged the state's policies and decrees, privately slaughtered draught animals *en masse*, and speculated in edible oils and grains. . . .

They regarded with hostility the cadres and Party and Communist Youth League members of the Hui nationality. They stigmatized the Hui cadres as "tu-shih-man" [i.e., enemies] and "traitors of the Hui people," and described the progressive imams as "men without a religion. . . ."

Pai Ch'ing-chang, during the period of "big contending and big blooming," slandered the Party's nationalities policy everywhere, in an attempt to instigate the Hui people to more riots. Rightists Yuan Ch'ang-hsiu, imam of Ningling hsien, instigated the Hui people to fight the Communist Party, and frantically inflamed them to attack their own hsiang and cooperatives, then to attack hsien and cities, and finally to set up an Islamic state. . . .

DOC. 63. *Protestant Group Makes Trouble (February, 1958)*

THE ANTI-COMMUNIST and anti-socialist statements and actions of Kou Hsi-tien and Liu Ya-han, rightist Protestants operating under cover of the cloak of religion, were fully uncovered and criticized at the Kansu Province Protestant Representatives Conference. . . .

At the meeting this time, Kou Hsi-tien still frantically launched attacks on the Party, slandering the Party policy on freedom of religious belief. He also condemned Government cadres for their failure to understand the religious policy, as well as spread the rumor that the religious policy pursued in the province had ended "in a mess." He also rallied members of his small group to a meeting illegally called, and posted big-character newspapers on so-called "appeals from churches in twelve places" to attack cadres and intimidate the People's Government. During the meeting, he had himself illegally elected head of the "executive committee for propagation of faith in the West China section," in a futile attempt to carry out anti-Communist activities through the medium of this organization, as well as infiltrate the National Self-Administration Association to usurp the powers of the leadership and disintegrate the Self-Administration movement at its roots. . . .

Liu Ya-han, another rightist element uncovered at the meeting, was a Kuomintang member and served as a mechanic in the enemy air force during 1939–49. . . .

At the meeting this time, he viciously attacked the Party, spread anti-Communist and anti-people poison, abused the national flag and picture of the leader, attacked the campaign

against counter-revolutionaries, denounced the work of the Pro-
curatorate, defended Fang Cheng-kuang, the counter-revolutionary, spread rumors accusing the Party policy on freedom of
religious belief as "unread," undermined the self-administration
movement, and denounced patriotic members of the faith.

DOC. 64. *Defense of the Vatican by Catholic Rightists (March,*
1958)

CATHOLIC REPRESENTATIVES' CONFERENCES, study meetings, and
forums have been called recently in twenty-six provinces, munic-
ipalities and autonomous regions throughout the country to
undertake the study of socialism and to propagate the resolutions
of the Chinese Catholic Representatives Conference called in
July last year. . . .
    At these meetings, a few rightist elements hiding in the Church
launched vicious attacks on the Party and socialism. Fan
Hsueh-an, bishop of the Paoting diocese in Hopei Province,
frantically claimed that it was "sinful" to expel imperialist elements. He also accused the People's Government of "saying one
thing and meaning another," and condemned the worker-peasant
alliance as "banding together like wolves." Chang Chen-kuo, acting bishop of the Szeping diocese in Kirin Province, openly
advocated non-cooperation with the People's Government, and
used the reactionary slogan of "kneeling down to pray, and
standing up to fight" to incite Catholics to "fight" the People's
Government. Liu Chien, acting bishop of the Sichang diocese in
Szechwan Province, openly admitted in a big-character newspaper that he favored the old society and spurned the new society.
Wan Ku-ju, vicar-general of the Loshan diocese in Szechwan
Province, openly advocated disturbances, and demanded the dis-
solution of Communist Party leadership and a going over to
capitalism. Wang Keh-chien, priest, in the Hangchow diocese in
Chekiang Province, and Sung Kung-chia, Catholic layman in

Shanghai, also launched frantic attacks on the socialist system, religious policy and the campaign against counter-revolutionaries. These rightist elements also slavishly defended the Vatican's reactionary political nature.

DOC. 65. *Marcus Cheng's Speech*

ON MARCH 19, 1957, the Rev. Marcus Cheng addressed the Chinese People's Political Consultative Conference in Peking on the subject of respect for religious faith. His speech was reported in full in the March 25th *People's Daily*.

I HAD NOT INTENDED to speak at this Conference session, because our leader Y. T. Wu has already spoken, and I thoroughly endorse his recommendations. But I have found that though his speech aroused a great deal of interest, yet some people misunderstood it. They did not note his three main propositions, namely, 1. The government has been energetic in carrying out its religious policy, and its achievements in this respect have been great. 2. For this epoch-making change in Chinese Christianity (i.e., the establishment of the Three-Self Movement), we cannot but give thanks to the People's Government Party. 3. We Chinese Christians will not be led astray by imperialism; we love our glorious new China and its leaders, the Communist Party and Chairman Mao Tse-tung; we want to govern our church well; we will do our best for the socialist reconstruction of our country; with the whole world we will seek for justice and for the union of peaceloving Christians, and will work for world peace and human progress. On the basis of these three propositions Mr. Wu made some further observations. No one disagreed with him as he said, "Some churches have not been allowed to resume services; in some villages and small cities church buildings and furniture have been appropriated by various government organs, and the religious life of Christians has been interfered with. The policy has not been uniform, and some cadres have taken a hostile attitude throughout, forbidding subscribing money to the church, repairing church buildings or taking in new members. . . . Some cadres have not only not respected religious faith, but have even adopted an abusive attitude." Every one recognizes that these mistakes should be corrected. But some friends thought that Mr. Wu ought not to have raised these "vague questions about the carrying out of the religious policy," and thought that his purpose was to preclude criticism of his religious faith. On the contrary Mr. Wu said, "Believers, unbelievers and critics of religious faith all have freedom. It does not disturb us that some persons criticize our faith. A believer who is a humble seeker after truth is not afraid of criticism of his faith."

I would like to add a few words in support of Mr. Wu's recommendations. First I would like to say, the contradiction between belief and unbelief, between theism and atheism, is a contradiction among the people, and not against an external element. We are all citizens of China, and this is not a contradiction between friends and enemies of the people, but an attempt at discrimination, at finding the truth. It is a contradiction of the "hundred schools" [category].

Therefore believers have freedom to preach their faith, and unbelievers have freedom to criticize religion, and the attempt in this controversy to discover the truth should be carried out calmly, without abuse or name-calling. You speak out your atheism and I will preach my theism, and in this controversy you must not take to abusing my mother, defiling my ancestral graves or reviling my ancestors. In the eyes of us Christians, God is the Supreme Being, and the churches are His temples, the place where Christians worship Him. In the argument over theism and atheism you must not revile God, or blaspheme His name; you must not take our churches by force. For example, a letter from a minority tribesman just the other day says, "Our church is still occupied and is in terrible condition, as it is being used as a stable." This defiling of our churches is like defiling our ancestral graves, and impresses us very painfully. At the opening of a new steel bridge, an official of high rank gave an address, in which he emphasized that this bridge had been made by human effort, and was not the work of any so-called God. Then he said, "You Christians should throw your God into the dungheap." Such blasphemy of God is, in the eyes of Christians, worse than reviling one's mother. This is not criticism, but abuse of religion. Chairman Mao on November 22, 1952, in a speech in Tibet said, "The Communist Party protects religion. Believers and unbelievers, believers in this or that religion, all are protected and respected." We believers appreciated very much this word from Chairman Mao, and what especially impressed and comforted us was his statement that the Government would not only protect, but would also "respect." Now this means that you must not blaspheme the God whom we worship, nor defile the churches in which we worship Him.

On the other hand I must say that even when we are abused and our temples defiled, we can bear it and forgive, because we remember that our Christian Church has been used by imperialism as a means of aggression against China. We also remember how, especially in the Middle Ages, religion was used to oppose and persecute scientists. When astronomers said that the world was round, we thought it was not in accordance with the Bible, so we cut out their tongues so that they could not speak, and even burned some of them to death. Now science has government backing, but it does not retaliate in the same way upon us. So if we meet with a little abuse and difficulty, should we not bear it? We should realize that those who now abuse and revile us are no other than the imperialist missionaries, and therefore we should bear it gladly, for Jesus said, "Great is your reward in heaven."

I wish to say further that if in the carrying out of government religious policy there have been some mistakes we should bear it and forgive, and not hold resentment, because the Christian Church's cutting off of relations with imperialism and the establishment of a Three-Self church is a new thing, something we have never done before. With no previous experience we are groping our way, and though we do our best it is inevitable that there should be mistakes. We do not speak of the mistakes which the unbelieving cadres have made, for we Christian workers ourselves in these few years while pushing the Three-Self Movement have made many mistakes, and this old man more than any. Again, we who are members of the Consultative Conference have an opportunity to observe conditions, and we see that mistakes are constantly being made in carrying out the policies regarding education, industry, public health, and commerce. By comparison, the mistakes in carrying out the religious policy have been rather minor. In carrying out the industrial policy there have been mistakes, but one cannot say that therefore the workers do not have freedom, and so in the same way one cannot say that because some cadres have made mistakes in carrying out the religious policy therefore there is no religious freedom.

In 1948 I was in America and American pastors told me, "We do not dare to preach on peace, or we should be suspected of being Communists, and would lose our jobs," but I would not be justified in drawing the conclusion that there is no freedom of religion in America. Again, these mistakes are not surprising, for China is a huge country with a vast population, and to take a poor and backward agricultural country and change it into a glorious socialized state, is a new thing that none of us has ever done; it would be surprising indeed if no mistakes were made in the process. Our only purpose in calling attention to these mistakes is that they may be corrected. At the same time we express our appreciation of those cadres who have helped and protected us and truly carried out the religious policy. . . .

The "vague questions" which Mr. Y. T. Wu raised in regard to the carrying out of the religious policy included a reference to publications criticizing religion. Mr. Wu said that he had seen twenty-nine such books. I have seen only between ten and twenty, but yesterday I received a letter from a preacher who said that he had read more than forty such books. Incidentally I might add that he was able to add, "After reading all these books I know whom I have believed, and my faith is stronger than ever." But the point I want especially to make is that most of these books and pamphlets are just translations from the Russian and a few others are just quotations from Christian writings, in which we criticize ourselves or one another. I should perhaps explain that Christians are divided into two large schools, the modernists and the conservatives. The modernists want to use scientific methods in their criticism of the Bible. When Marx was a Christian in Germany he was a modernist, and then he gave up his faith. He believed in God and we respected him; then he no longer believed in God and we also respected his lack of faith. For we know that his earlier faith and his later atheism both were honest and sincere. Marx was very familiar with the Bible, and in his book *Capital* he quotes from it more than forty times. He also published some constructive criticisms of the Bible, criticisms which even we conservatives have been happy to accept. What he was opposed to was not Christianity itself, but to the fact that Christians did not live in accordance with Bible principles.

When we read Chinese history we see that though Chinese have believed various religions, there has never been a religious war in China. This is a special characteristic of the Chinese people.

In reading *China's Recent Revolutionary History* I find the following words: "In the old democratic revolutionary period, the Chinese people went through several revolutionary struggles, of which the most important in size and influence were the Taiping Rebellion and the bourgeois revolution of 1911 headed by Sun Yet-Sen. These two revolutions were very effective in their struggle against feudalism and imperialism" (page 6). When I who have preached Christianity for over fifty years read this history written by a Communist I have conflicting feelings; on the one hand I feel ashamed because for more than 100 years imperialism has used Christian missionaries as forerunners of their aggression, and even we Chinese Christians ourselves have either consciously or unconsciously been their stooges, and now regret deeply that we have thus offended against our Fatherland and the people. On the other hand we feel proud and happy, because the leader of the Taiping Rebellion, Hung Hsiu-chuan, and the leader of the bourgeois revolution, Sun Yet-Sen, were both of them Christians; they were both of them baptised in the Christian Church and drew inspiration from the teachings of Jesus. Their spirit of service, sacrifice and revolution came from Jesus, for Jesus taught us that the Son of Man came not to be ministered unto, but to minister, and to give his life as ransom for many.

And again, "The Spirit of the Lord is upon me, because he has annointed me to preach good news to the poor. He has sent me to proclaim release to the captives and recovering of sight to the blind, and to set at liberty those who are oppressed." Jesus's mother, Mary, said of him that he would scatter the proud in the imagination of their hearts, he would put down the mighty from their thrones, exalt those of low degree. He would fill the hungry with good things, but the rich he would send empty away." Bernard Shaw says, "This song (the original is in the form of a poem) is most revolutionary, and has had a deep revolutionary effect in European history."

I have visited the common tomb of our seventy-two famous martyrs, and as I read the inscription I discovered that many of them (some say more than half) were disciples of Jesus Christ. This was not accidental. In the January number of the *Historical Study* magazine is an article by Tsinghua University professor Lui Hai-tsung, in which, speaking entirely from the standpoint of historical science, he discusses Christianity as follows: "Primitive Christianity was a movement of protest against imperial Rome by city workers, including free artisans, slaves, and those with uncertain means of livelihood, and in later history Christianity has always been a people's movement opposing the ruling class." Engels had previously made the same point, saying that Christianity was a soocial movement directed at freeing the slaves.

After Liberation we Chinese Christians all answered the call of the Three-Self Movement and entered upon political study, studying current events and government, and some even studied Marxism and Leninism, and this led us to study our Bible anew, from which we derived the three principles of self-support, self-government and self-propagation. The last named concerns the content of our preaching, and we discovered that the poison of imperialistic, feudalistic and capitalistic thinking was mixed up in it. We are engaged in a criticism of our own faith; on the negative side we have gotten rid of our anti-Russian, anti-Communist poison, and on the positive side have established the truth and substance of Christianity on a sound biblical basis. We stress the fact that Jesus was a carpenter; the Son of God was incarnate on earth and lived here thirty-three years, of which more than twenty years was spent in common labor, both in a manual trade and in farming, so that he thereby raised the position of labor, and we who are followers of Jesus should follow Him in loving labor and the produce of labor. We have learned anew the biblical teaching, "If a man will not work, let him not eat" and "Let him who stole (and the exploitation of our fellowmen is stealing) steal no more, but let him work with his hands, so that he will have enough and to spare for those who are in need." Of course this does not mean that we no longer stress the saving grace of Christ upon the Cross; we still proclaim that his precious blood is the way of salvation. Our purpose in reexamining our doctrines is rather to enrich the content of our faith. We have also studied political economics, and have learned two principles: 1. Material production is the basis of society; if people would live they must have food, clothing and other material things. And if they would have these things they must produce them and that means that they must labor. 2. Men in material production do not work singly, but in society, and therefore their productive efforts must be correlated according to appropriate norms. When we study Christian doctrine in the light of these two principles, we find that they are taught by the Old Testament prophets, the New Testament apostles, and by Jesus himself, and that we therefore should observe them in our own lives. We gladly note the risen Jesus stood early one morning by the Sea of Galilee, and asked the seven toiling hungry disciples who were fishing there, "My children, have ye aught to eat?" And when they came ashore they found that the Lord had prepared a fire with broiled fish and cakes, and invited them to come eat breakfast. From this we see that the Lord Jesus came to earth not only to save our souls with His most precious blood, but also by labor to provide for the needs of our bodies. Therefore we Christians can say as the Buddhist delegate has already said, "It is not only our civic duty, but also our religious duty to love our country, observe its constitution, unite with its people, and take a positive part in the socialist construction of the country and the movement for world peace."

DOC. 66. *Hsin Tsung-chen: True Freedom of Religious Belief Is Possible Only Under Communist Party Leadership: A Moslem Leader's "Errors"* (*1958*)

RIGHTIST LIU SHENG-MING, long concealed within the Hui nationality in our province, has been exposed—something that calls for rejoicing. Here I wish to refute the erroneous views of rightist Liu Sheng-ming on the question of freedom of religious belief alone.

Rightist Liu Sheng-ming has said, "Although the Communist policy of freedom of religious belief is expressly put in writing, in actual practice it is not what it is represented to be. The Communist Party is not so good as the Kuomintang. The Communist Party wants to exterminate all religion." What he really means is that the policy of freedom of religious belief professed by the Communist Party is a mockery.

That is out-and-out slander. As everyone knows, the freedom of religious belief is written in the Constitution of our country as a basic right to which every citizen is entitled. Article 88 of the Constitution provides that "Every citizen of the People's Republic of China shall have freedom of religious belief." In his Political Report which he made in behalf of the Central Committee of the Chinese Communist Party at the CCP Eighth National Congress, Liu Shao-Ch'i expressly said, "With regard to the question of freedom of religious belief in national minority areas, we must carry out with perseverance the long-term policy of freedom of religious belief, and must not interfere (with such freedom) during the social reforms." As a matter of fact, Party committees and governments of all levels have been acting in strict accordance with the provisions of the Constitution and the directives of the central leadership of the Party.

After the liberation, the Party and the government have protected Islamic mosques and safeguarded the freedom of religious belief, so that we are able to manage freely our own religious affairs and lead a pleasant, religious life. Moreover, our political status has been raised to a higher level, and the miserable situation that existed in the old society, where the reactionary rulers demolished and burned down Islamic mosques at will, cooked and ate pork in the mosques, massacred innocent Imams and Moslems, and designated areas inhabited by Hui people "bandit areas" has been abolished. Where there was political discrimination against Moslems and imams, and no safeguard for personal security, the situation has been changed. Now many imams have become people's deputies or members of the People's Political Consultative Conference or are taking part in other work, having a share in the management of the affairs of the state and enjoying completely equal political rights. Under the solicitude of the Party and the government and with their help, the Chinese Islamic Association has been established. A Preparatory Committee for Islamic Association in our province was also established in 1956. In addition, the state has also helped us to establish an Islamic institute for teaching the Koran, so that imams well versed in the Koran who ardently love the socialist motherland and the people may be trained for the Islamic faith. What other government in China has done that?

Although the production of certain consumer goods in our country is still behind the needs of home consumption today, the cattle and sheep which we Moslems slaughter for our own consumption during our festivals are exempt from slaughter tax; moreover we are supplied with the necessary cooking oil and flour. Great concessions are made to the imams with regard to the cloth they use and to Moslems generally with regard to the cloth used in funerals. The Communist Party and People's Government have also helped to overcome some of the difficulties of livelihood of the Imams which they themselves could not overcome. According to incomplete information based on letters received by the Hopei Provincial Islamic Association from imams in the administrative areas of Tangshan, Kalgan, Tientsin, Shihchiachuang and Tunghsien, a total of Yuan 28,640 in relief funds from the government was received by 292 imams in 1957 alone. Had any other government in the history of China shown such concern for the livelihood of imams and Moslems?

These obvious facts show that real freedom of religious belief, equal political rights for all, and solicitude and help for all are possible only under Communist Party leadership. How can one say, "The Communist Party is not so good as the Kuomintang, because the Communist Party wants to exterminate all religion"? Could rightist Liu Sheng-ming have failed to see the facts for himself?

Rightist Liu Sheng-ming has his own underhanded political objective in slandering the Communist Party and its policy toward religion. Closing his eyes to the facts, he has charged maliciously that "the government takes special care of the Hui people and the imams because it wants to extend its influence, so that you may praise it," and things like that. He tries to instigate the masses to oppose the leadership of the Communist Party and the People's Government.

We all know that the government of today is an honest, public-spirited government which is wholeheartedly devoted to the service of the people. No other government in the history of China was mindful of the people's welfare. It has won the ardent and sincere support of the people of all the nationalities in the country. The Party and the government have always been coura-geous enough to openly examine their work for shortcomings and errors. They always welcome strict supervision from the masses on their activities so that they may discover and overcome these shortcomings and better serve the people. Our government has no need whatsoever to buy the support of some people. It is sheer slander to say that it does that.

Having slanderously attacked the Party's policy of freedom of religious belief, rightist Liu Sheng-ming also slanderously attacks those Imams who are helping the Party and the government do their work for the nationalities well, saying that these imams are "the black sheep of the Hui nationality who betray the Islamic faith in return for high positions."

Under the care and education of the Party and government, many imams have truly and greatly increased their socialist consciousness. They would use every opportunity to propagan-dize among the masses the Party's policy of freedom of religious belief, quickly transmit to the Party and government the views and demands of the Hui people, and have done much to consolidate national solidarity for the common development of the nationalities. In particular, they have actively accepted socialist transformation during the high tide of socialist transformation and helped the Party and government in doing a certain amount of work, achieving good results. They have produced good results in making closer the relations between the Party and Hui masses and the ties between the Imams and the masses. What they have done and their political-ideological progress are valuable and do honor to our Islamic faith. Moreover, it is the duty of an Imam to do what he can voluntarily to help the socialist construction of the motherland, increase the solidarity of the nationalities, and help the development of the Hui nationality. By so doing he is not harming the religion. Love for one's motherland is part of the duties of the imanis. If by so doing one is considered to have "betrayed the religion" and to have been a "black sheep of the Hui nationality," then what is it that our religion wants to do?

Liu Sheng-ming regularly disseminates the belief among the Hui people that the Han people are their eternal "tusman" (enemy). He tries to instill in the minds of the Hui people that the Han people are their enemy by constantly recounting past stories of fights and feuds between Hui and Han people engineered by the reactionary ruling class of the past. But history and innumerable facts have shown that the Hui and Han people can never be separated. The clothing, food, housing and transport of the Hui people, and even the building of mosques and management of Islamic affairs, are inseparable from the direct or indirect aid of the Han people. Had it not been for the correct leadership of the People's Government, the Hui nationality would not have today's happiness. By sabotaging national solidarity and sowing enmity between the Hui people and the government, rightist Liu Sheng-ming is trying to drag the Hui people backward and make them return to the miserable life of beasts of burden of the past. We all know that we shall not be able to manage our religious affairs unless our livelihood is assured. Obviously Liu Sheng-ming is trying to undermine the Islamic faith.

The facts are quite clear. Nothing that Liu Sheng-ming has done has anything to do with religion, nor is done for the sake of the glorious tradition of the Islamic faith. Wearing the cloak of religion and under the banner of upholding the glorious tradition of the Islamic faith, he is engaged in opposition to the Party and socialism and activities designed to split the nation. We should see clearly and sharpen our vigilance, take away the hypocritical cloak of rightist Liu Sheng-ming, and expose his anti-Party, anti-socialist scheme to wreck national solidarity. Drawing a line of demarcation between him and ourselves, we should thoroughly smash the schemes of rightist Liu Sheng-ming by resolutely carrying out the Party's policy of freedom of religious belief, upholding national solidarity, and taking an active part in the socialist construction of the motherland.

DOC. 67. *Criticism and Repudiation of Li Ch'ang-shu's False Anti-Communist and Anti-Socialist Theories: A Hunan Methodist Leader's Criticisms Denounced (1958)*

DURING THE PARTY'S moral reform movement, Li Ch'ang-shu made use of the opportunity of blooming and contending to shoot countless poisonous arrows, and madly attacked the Party. Now I will expose and repudiate his anti-Party, anti-socialist and criminal words and deeds in the following:

1. Slandering the Communist Party Members as "A Specially Privileged Class" and Opposing the Leadership of the Party

DURING THE PERIOD of blooming and contending Li Ch'ang-shu violently attacked the Party, saying: "Under the law, non-Party people are not equal with Party members. When a Party member commits a crime the Party will minimize the crime and dispose of it privately and internally. But when someone who is not a Party member commits a crime he will be arrested and sent to the Bureau of Public Security with a lot of publicity. This is a special privilege of the Party member which constitutes a basic problem. If this is not corrected, it is impossible to break down the wall between the Party members and the masses."

And he further said, in a thoroughly reactionary manner: "Moral reform must wipe out the Party members' thought of being a specially privileged class. Such a thought is the root of corruption. During the Manchu Dynasty, the Manchus often said [to the Chinese officials]: 'You are the official of our royal family.' Such a thought caused the deterioration and eventually the downfall of the Manchu Dynasty. The Kuomintang deteriorated in the same manner. If the Communist Party will not purge itself of such a thought, it will of necessity deteriorate."

Again, he declared: "By saying that Party members have a special privilege I mean that all the organizations have Party members as leaders." Please observe that such false theories of Li Ch'ang-shu are the same as or more violent than those proposed by other rightist elements of the propertied class, such as, "The Communists must leave the press offices"; and "The government representatives must withdraw from the public-privately owned enterprises." It is not hard to see that the secret motive of Li Ch'ang-shu's open "opposition to the special privileges of the Communist Party members" is to oppose the leadership of the Party.

Ever since the establishment of the Chinese Communist Party, it has always demanded its members to devote their all, even sacrifice of their lives, for the cause of the great revolution of liberating the Chinese people and the whole of humanity, and for the cause of socialist construction and of the eventual realization of Communism in the world. During all the stages of the Chinese Communist revolution its members have demonstrated the greatest revolutionary spirit and have, for the cause of the revolutionary enterprise, sacrificed their lives, shed their blood, and never retreated in the face of death. Their moving and heroic stories are too numerous to be cited here.

During the eight years since the liberation and through the five great campaigns and the three big reforms, they have achieved great results and have basically accomplished the grand socialist revolution. The faces of both the cities and the farming villages have been changed, have put on new and prosperous looks, and are still being improved daily. But Li Ch'ang-shu has dared to compare the Communist Party with the Manchu royal family and with the feudalistic and reactionary rule of Chiang Kai-shek's Kuomintang. This is nothing more than his vicious plot to oppose, slander and hate the Communist Party and demand its resignation.

Li Ch'ang-shu has slandered us by saying that "the Communist Party members are a specially privileged class." But our unanimous understanding is that the Communist Party members are not a specially privileged class as Li Ch'ang-shu has stated because the Communists have fortified their thoughts with Marxism and Leninism, have constantly elevated their own class consciousness and their working effectiveness, and have always put the welfare of the Party and the nation above their own personal welfare.

In addition, they have served the people with faithfulness and honesty, have relied on the masses, have united them, have loved them, and have accomplished the tasks which the Party and the nation entrusted to them. If we have to say that the Communist Party members have a special privilege, then it is indeed their special privilege to sacrifice their own lives courageously for the enterprises of the people. Li Ch'ang-shu's slander that the Communist Party members "are a specially privileged class" only shows his reactionary nature and his opposition to the leadership of the Communist Party.

Li Ch'ang-shu has also slandered us by saying that the "non-Party people are not equal with Party members under the law." Such slander is completely groundless. Facts have clearly shown that thousands upon thousands of Communist Party members have served the people faithfully and honestly. There may have been individual Party members who have broken the law by acting contrary to the welfare of the Party, the nation and the people but the Communist Party will never be lenient with them nor love them foolishly; instead it will punish them according to the law of the land. For instance, during the three-anti movements, both Wang Hui-mien, former chief of the Public Security Bureau in Ch'angsha, and Liu Ch'ing-shan, former Special Commissioner in T'ientsin, received the most severe punishment according to the law of the nation for their serious undermining of the welfare of the people.

Again, for example: during the present struggle against the rightist elements, Mao T'eh-fu, mayor of Hsiangt'an Hsin, and Sha Wen-han, governor of Chekiang Province, have all been removed from their posts on account of their having changed into rightist elements. Do these concrete examples not show that the Communist Party members and the non-Party people are equal under the law? Li Ch'ang-shu's slander only clearly explains that he is deliberately driving a wedge between the Party and the masses and is opposing the leadership of the Party.

II. Li's False Anti-Socialist Theories

LI CH'ANG-SHU, the rightist element has declared: "The more development socialism achieves the more difficult it will be for the church" and that the socialist-reform, socialist construction, the spreading of Marxism and Leninism, and the abolition of the special privileges of the imperialists have all brought difficulties to the church. He has also created propaganda that there is a conflict between the church and socialism and to dissolve this conflict either the church or socialism must be destroyed. Li Ch'ang-shu knows that establishing socialism is the common desire and aim of the 600,000,000 Chinese people and is what they all wholeheartedly support and positively strive to achieve. He also knows that it is impossible for him to oppose socialism openly, for the people will resolutely turn against him. To achieve his anti-socialist secret purpose, however, he has used religion as a pretext and the church as a signboard, has manufactured all types of false theories, and has exploited the religious emotions of the Christian masses to instigate resentment and dissatisfaction.

As we all know, the aim of socialism is to destroy exploitation and poverty, and lead all the people to walk the road to prosperity and happiness. This road is one which benefits the people and strengthens the nation, a bright road which brings pleasure to God and joy to man. In the past years, the great achievements of the fatherland both in the socialist reform and socialist construction have fully proved the unique superiority of the socialist system. The decision of our nation to take this road is a completely correct one.

The agricultural cooperative and the public-private ownership of industry and business have changed the system of productive material ownership and solved the basic problems of exploitation and poverty which the Chinese people suffered for thousands of years. This has greatly encouraged the positiveness of the workers and farmers in their productive labour, the unprecedented development and standard-raising of industrial and agricultural production, and the daily improvement of the life of the people, including religious followers. A new life and new look have been seen throughout the cities and the rural areas.

This is something over which the people throughout the nation, including Christians, should rejoice, but Li Ch'ang-shu, the rightist element, has said: "Agriculture has been cooperativized, industry and business have been placed under public-private ownership, and everything has been organized. [We] are not free to move, which has caused the church some difficulties." This clearly explains his opposition to socialist reform and his vain intention of preserving the unreasonable capitalist system of man-eat-man, and man-oppress-man, so that he may achieve his criminal aims of continuously oppressing and exploiting the people.

Socialism is not something that will naturally drop down from heaven, but something which can only be established by the full, positive, and creative labor of the people throughout the nation. The industrial and agricultural speedy-progress movement which is now being widely spread over all the nation is specifically designed for speeding up socialist construction, so that the day of satisfaction and happiness may arrive earlier. But Li Ch'ang-shu, the rightist element, has said: "Everybody is busy with production and socialist construction. Because people are so busy, the number of people coming to church services has decreased. In the past they were not so busy." The purpose of Li Ch'ang-shu in saying these words is to oppose socialist construction and, under the pretext of "church services," incite the Christian masses not to join in socialist construction positively, so that he may carry out his secret plots of undermining it.

Marxism and Leninism are the truth which liberates the whole of mankind. They are also the guide to socialism. If there were no Marxism-Leninism there would be no freedom and liberation for mankind, and neither would there be the peace and joy of socialism. Li Ch'ang-shu understands this point and that is why, in order to oppose socialism and oppose the propaganda of Marxism and Leninism, he has used religion as a pretext saying: "The propaganda of Marxism and Leninism has brought harm and difficulties to churches." He has thus attempted to incite the Christian masses to oppose the propaganda of Marxism and Leninism, so that he may achieve his shameful aim to undermine socialism. As we all know, the central power which leads socialist construction is the Chinese Communist Party. Although the world view of us Christians is different from that of the Marxists and the Leninists, socialist construction is in harmony with our basic welfare. Furthermore, the propaganda of Marxism and Leninism has never demanded that we give up our religious belief. Facts have proved that during the past years we, under the protection of the Constitution, have fully enjoyed freedom of religious belief. Therefore, Li Ch'ang-shu's random talk can never deceive the people.

During the past one hundred and more years the imperialists have aggressed against China through the use of Christianity. They and their running dogs, under the protection of the special privilege and power obtained from us, have acted in an overbearing and tyrannous manner in China and have brought to her great calamities. Thanks to Chairman Mao and the Communist Party, for under their talented leadership the imperialists have been driven away and the Chinese people have been liberated from hot fire and deep water. Now all the Chinese people are walking down the road to socialism and are enjoying a peaceful and happy life. Any Chinese who has a conscience must feel proud of himself and have a sense of gratitude.

But Li Ch'ang-shu, the rightist element, has lost his mind in saying: "After the abolition of the special privileges of the missionaries (i.e., the imperialists), the church has lost its protection.

For this reason the church has been faced with some difficulties."
From this we can see that Li Ch'ang-shu is determined to "bow
down and exhaust his energy until he dies" to serve the imperialists.

Not only this, but Li Ch'ang-shu, the rightist element, has
deliberately created a conflict between Christianity and socialism
and considered it impossible for them to coexist. He has said:
"There is a conflict between the church and socialism and to
dissolve this conflict either the church or socialism must be
destroyed." He has thus attempted to incite Christians to oppose
socialism. But he has made a miscalculation with his abacus, for
those Christians who have come back to their consciousness and
those who have already stood up with the people have seen
through his secret plots and cunning schemes and will not fall
into his traps, but will resolutely walk down the road to socialism.

As we know, the welfare of socialism and that of the church
and Christians are entirely the same. Only Li Ch'ang-shu loves
what the people hate and hates what the people love, and dreams
that he can stop the wheel of history from turning and block the
way on which socialism is making advances. He has attempted to
restore the rule of the imperialists and capitalists in China. This,
however, will never be permitted by the nation's people, including Christians. I tell you, Li Ch'ang-shu, you rightist element, do
not dream any more, for the age has passed and will never
return when you could become a landlord and exploit the peasants and be a running dog of the imperialists and oppress the
people with the protection of the imperialists' special privileges in
China.

III. Denying the Achievements of the Party and the Government in Carrying Out the Religious Policy

DURING THE PERIOD of blooming and contending, at a discussion
meeting called by the Bureau for Religious Affairs, Li Ch'ang-shu
openly slandered the Bureau's relation with the people of the
religious circles as having "more control, less cultivation; more
doubt, less trust; and more centralization, less democracy." Again,
he spread the following false theories: "The Government's reli-

gious policy is a closed-door policy," "The Bureau for Religious Affairs has never solved any problem for the church," and so on. He was thus deliberately denying the Party's achievement in its religious work and was madly attacking it.

As everybody knows, in the years since the liberation the Party and the Government have unusually esteemed the people of the religious circles, correctly and thoroughly implemented the religious policy, helped the religious circles undertake learning, and have assisted them in solving all the concrete problems. The Party and the Government have, further, supported the Christian church to do better in expanding its anti-imperialistic and patriotic movement, and liberated it from the control of the imperialists, and have made it a Chinese church over which the Chinese Christians themselves have direct authority.

The Party and the Government have also raised the status of the people of the religious circles. Many deputies in the Hsiang People's Congress through the National People's Congress there have been Christians, and from the Hsien and the City People's Political Consultative Conference to the national one many Christians have been many committee members. Under the education and cultivation of the Party and the Government, the level of Christians' political knowledge and their patriotic awareness has been greatly elevated. In Hunan Province alone, the Party and the Government have conducted three sessions of the Three-Self patriotic learning which have given an opportunity for political learning to more than 200 Christian ministers, and the various learning sessions sponsored by the hsien and the City People's Political Consultative Conferences have also given opportunities for representatives of the religious circles to learn. To raise the socialist consciousness of the people of the religious circles, the Party and the Government have spent big sums of money in organizing and taking their representatives on inspection tours throughout the nation to see the various great construction projects of the fatherland and have, through all types of visual education, elevated the socialist understanding of the Christians one step further.

At the same time, the Party and the Government have helped the church to solve a series of concrete problems, such as exempting taxes on the buildings and grounds of the churches and the residences of church workers, and in helping with the difficulties in the livelihood of some of the church workers. Other similar problems of the church have all been solved by the Government. Li Ch'ang-shu has enjoyed and known much of this. He cannot deny these facts which exist objectively regardless of how he obscures his conscience or how he makes random statements. The secret plots and motive of Li Ch'ang-shu in denying these achievements of the Party and the Government and in confusing right with wrong are to incite the masses to oppose the Party and socialism.

Li Ch'ang-shu has slandered the Bureau for Religious Affairs as being "the religious public security bureau which functions as a police department." This slander of his clearly explains that he is not a citizen of the People's Republic of China, but an enemy of the people. Why does he slander in this way? As everybody knows, the people's public security organizations are the ones that deal with the enemies and are, at the same time, the ones that protect the people. The people throughout the nation consider the public security organizations as those which suppress evils for the people and act as protectors of the people's welfare. They think that the public security organizations are the ones that deserve the most respect of the people, and that the public security officers deserve most of their affection.

But it is an entirely different matter when Li Ch'ang-shu views the public security organizations and their officers from the reactionary ground of their being a running dog of the imperialists. Since he considers the public security organizations and officers as the attackers of his undermining activities, he views them as the most horrible and hateful organizations and people. With his thought and psychology of hatred against the public security organizations he has slandered the bureaus for religious affairs and insulted the public security organizations. Is not his anti-Party, anti-people, and anti-socialist hideous face even more clearly seen through this?

In short, Li Ch'ang-shu, you have made a miscalculation. You thought that you, being the Chairman of the Hunan Provincial Christian Three-Self Patriotic Movement, Chairman of the Hunan

Church District of the Methodist Church, and having obtained the positions, through swindling, of people's deputy to the Provincial People's Congress and committee member of the Provincial People's Political Consultative Conference and having put on the religious and patriotic cloaks, can by blowing your whistle blindly deceive the church workers and Christian laymen into following you to oppose the Party, the people, and socialism. We tell you, your dark schemes have been ripped open and smashed into pieces by the masses. You can never deceive the masses.

Under the leadership of the Communist Party and through the various learning sessions, the five big campaigns and by the three big reforms, the ministerial personnel and Christians of new China have raised high their political awareness. We are determined to march forward with the people of the whole nation on the bright road to socialism. We ardently love the Communist Party and faithfully support its leadership. At the Hunan Provincial Christian socialist learning session, our fellow Christians and co-workers have ripped open and smashed into pieces your "religious cloak" and your "cloak of loving both the country and religion." Your anti-Party, anti-people, and anti-socialist repulsive face has been completely exposed, which has aroused the indignation of all the church workers, and fellow Christians and will arouse the people of the whole nation to curse and berate you. This then is the end of you as a thorough rightist element of the propertied class.

DOC. 68. *Shirob Jaltso, Tibetan Buddhist Leader: Attention to Special Characteristics of Minority Nationalities: Report Delivered to the Third Session of the First National People's Congress (June 2, 1956)*

NOW I WOULD LIKE to make some suggestions on the basis of certain conditions which I have recently grasped through personal contacts, and I hope that you deputies will give me your advice.

I. Pay full attention to the special characteristics of minority nationalities during the upsurge of cooperation

IT IS, OF COURSE, an undisputable truth that cooperation is the only way to improve minority people's agriculture and animal husbandry so as to follow Socialism, but owing to their different standards, the methods of following Socialism should not be the same. The key point is to pay quick attention to the religious problem of minority nationalities. Our State policy of freedom of religion is a policy which is very satisfactory to religious people, but in carrying it out, various authorities have to be careful at all times. The Tibetan lamas have the Buddhist rule and custom, whereby they cannot take part in farm work—a tradition which cannot easily be changed. While some regular religious expenses had to be met solely by the income from the farms or cattle and sheep of lamaseries and monasteries, the lamas cannot obtain remuneration by labor after these farms and animals are transferred to farm cooperatives. Therefore, the remuneration for their farmlands or cattle and sheep should still be paid to them to solve their difficulties and relieve their uneasy feelings. This is the first point.

The expenses for certain religious activities of lamaseries and monasteries had always been borne by a certain tribe, or several villages, or a single village, or several families as a matter of custom. After all of them were organised into higher cooperatives, it has become difficult to find benefactors. In future, adequate arrangements should be made so that expenses for this kind of religious activities will not be affected. This is he second point.

The Tibetans in general have a strong faith in Buddhism. Therefore when every tribe or village or family, in the past, conducted such religious activities as prayer services, and charities, it was a group of people or an individual who took the initiative. In future, such activities which have previously been launched by a group of people should be taken up by farm cooperatives and those conducted by individuals should not be interfered with, so as fully to carry out the principle of freedom. This is the third point.

There are still some monasteries and lay Tibetans who have been accustomed to private ownership and individual operation for generations and cannot quickly understand and implement the excellent system of collectivism and cooperation. Therefore, in regard to those who are unwilling to join the cooperatives at present, the correct principle of freedom of choice should be carried out, and they should not be impatiently asked to join the cooperatives or forced to withdraw from the cooperatives. In such cases, they should be given sincere assistance instead of being discriminated against. This is the fourth point.

In short, the Tibetans are strongly disposed to maintain local customs and have always been used to conservatism. Therefore there is nothing strange in that they are reluctant to accept cooperation, a new undertaking which they never heard of before. In promoting new undertakings under these objective circumstances, we should have great patience. If we want to achieve success in a hurry when the conditions are not yet ripe, it will be extremely disadvantageous to both the government and private individuals. The idea of private ownership is an old one which has existed for several thousand years, and it cannot be easily eliminated. Especially at the beginning of a new undertaking, we should go forward at a more steady pace, we should put off, for the time being, something which should be deferred, and we should not seek more figures. First of all, we should endeavor to conduct successful propaganda and education so as to set examples, establish faith and achieve gradual improvement. When the time is opportune, no doubt the people will accept reform with pleasure. This is the method of doing things slowly at the beginning but fast at the end.

If we want to achieve success in a hurry in conducting the great Socialist reform in the nationalities areas without paying sufficient attention to the special characteristics of minority nationalities and to the financial circumstances affecting their religious beliefs, it will cause inconvenience to certain religious activities of some Tibetans including the giving of alms, and create difficulties in the maintenance of some monasteries and lamaseries and in their conduct of religious activities. Thus these monasteries and lamaseries will feel financially embarrassed and will worry about a decrease in or even a complete lack of, the supply of lamas, thereby becoming dissatisfied with the government. For example, in some Tibetan people's areas in Szechuan province, the implementation of land reform, collection of commercial and other taxes from monasteries, and the handling of farmlands and livestock have recently become quite unsatisfactory, and in collecting small arms from the people, some local authorities have even taken away the weapons which were offered to the gods on the altar, thus causing some Buddhist followers mistakenly to doubt the truth of freedom of worship and arousing uneasiness among the local people. Although these conditions prevail only in individual areas, their repercussions cannot be ignored. This is the improper method of doing things fast at the beginning but slow at the end. We may say that this unnecessary and unpleasant situation could have been entirely avoided. In regard to its causes, we should, of course, give due consideration to the suspicion aroused by the concealed enemy, against whom our vigilance is needed, but the chief cause is that apprehensions actually existed in the monasteries and lamaseries and that deviations and shortcomings really appeared in the course of our work, thus providing an opening for the enemy to stir up trouble.

Section 8. Religion and Unlawful Acts

THESE DOCUMENTS, all from the year 1958, represent the range of charges brought against religious leaders of all persuasions. The crimes of rape and seduction, of embezzlement, swindling, taking rice and money from believers, inciting political dissension and harboring counter-revolutionaries are found again and again in denunciation documents. In addition to these, Abbot Pen Huan was found guilty of collaborating with the enemy during the Anti-Japanese War, of smuggling, peddling rumors, opposing land reform, using the monastery to shelter landlords and thieves, imposing feudal rule in his monastery, encouraging rape, thievery and murder, and prohibiting the reading of books by Chairman Mao.

Faith healing, exorcism of demons, secret (home) meetings, and obstructing production by religious customs and taboos (such as Sabbath rest) are other unlawful acts cited here. Unfortunately, there was no free press coverage of the accusation meetings and other judicial procedures that condemned these men. But the similarity of charges, whether Buddhist, Christian or Moslem—e.g., the frequency of the charge of rape and seduction of women—follows a common pattern.

DOC. 69. *Some Protestant Leaders in Hunan Province: Resolutely Eliminate All the Unlawful Activities in Christianity*

SINCE THE LIBERATION, there have been many unlawful activities and much confusion in the Christian church in Hunan Province. These unlawful activities have seriously disturbed the peace and order in society, harmed agricultural production, injured the health of the people, and are roadblocks in the advancement of socialist construction. Now we will expose the facts which we know according to the following four headings:

I. Spreading Reactionary Theories and Disturbing Peace and Security

THERE HAVE BEEN some bad elements of the church who, under the pretext of religious activities, have distorted the truth of the Bible and have undertaken the criminal activities of spreading reactionary theories and disturbing the hearts of the people. For instance, there is a certain preacher who has consistently manufactured rumors to deceive the masses, opposed the Soviet Union and Communism, slandered our leadership, and has incited the Christians to curse the soldiers of the militia. For example, he has manufactured rumors, saying: "The third world war will break out soon. It will be the people's calamity, for the power of the atomic bombs is very great," and so on. These reactionary words have seriously disturbed the hearts of the people, brought harm to peace and security, and has defiled the church itself.

II. Swindling Money and Undermining Production and the Central Movements

IN 1956, during the time when the members of the agricultural cooperatives in Lo-k'ou, Liling hsien, were in a hurry to do their spring rice planting, and seeing that their young plants were about to spoil, Yang Ch'i-yung of the True Jesus Church was determined to have his church members "observe the Sabbath Day," which seriously obstructed agricultural production (and he did the same with church members of the five church districts of which he is the superintendent). He also manufactured rumors, saying: "This is what God has ordained, which no one can change. This also is the freedom of religious belief which nobody can stop." Yang Ch'i-yung also caused Christians under his leadership to hold spiritual life cultivation meetings during busy harvest seasons. When the government would not permit these Christians to hold such meetings, he wrote to them and encouraged them, saying: "For the sake of the Lord you must struggle with the government to the end. I and the fellow Christians of the other church districts will pray for you." He was extremely mad!

Yang Ch'i-yung, the bad element, knows how to make money and how to make it through the Gospel. He has cleverly launched more than ten projects to threaten and swindle his church members and imposed on them the heavy burden of making contributions. What is more serious is that Yang Ch'i-yung has made unlawful decisions through the representatives' meeting of the church districts to mobilize their church to make contributions by "reducing their own consumption of rice," and has called on them to save and send to their respective church one cup of rice daily as food for their church workers. At the same time, the officers overseeing the church districts may come freely to eat at any church without a meal ticket.

Furthermore, the rice which these Christians have contributed by "reducing their own consumption of rice" must not only be used as food and daily expense of the churches in the various church districts, but part of it must be sent to the headquarters in charge of these districts. The Ta-chang Church District alone sent over 700 catties of rice to the headquarters. For this reason, many Christians have suffered shortages of food and have petitioned the government to subsidize them. This has seriously upset the planned demand-and-supply balance of food in the villages.

There are other preachers who have manufactured rumors,

deliberately aimed at undermining the Party's central tasks. For example, in May, 1955, during the time when the plague of locusts in Lien-yuan, P'ing-ti, and nearby places was very serious, the local government organized the cadres and mobilized the masses to launch a fight-the-locusts campaign. But a certain preacher of the Central Hunan Lutheran Church not only did not join the campaign, but instead gathered his church members to hold a prayer meeting and manufactured rumors, saying: "Locusts are sent down by God, and they cannot be destroyed completely. We need only to pray to God [in the day time] and, at night, sweep the devil in our homes with the branches of a peach tree, and then everything will be allright." He also obstructed his church members from positively taking part in the fight-the-locusts campaign.

Again, for example, a short time ago Li Tao-ch'un went to the Christian church in P'ing-hsiang, Kiangsi Province, to hold spiritual-life cultivation meetings while the people there were busily engaged in constructing an irrigation system. He baptized over seventy people and seriously obstructed construction work.

III. Swindling the Masses and Intimidating them into Joining the Church

IN MARCH, 1956, Yang Ch'i-yung, preacher at Liling Hsien, made random talks, saying: "I and Ho Ch'ung-sheng are all sent by the Bureau for Religious Affairs in Ch'angsha. The Bureau is a joint organization of all our Christian churches." Chang Chung-ch'i, minister of the Church of Christ in China at Lai-yang, was acting lawlessly in the villages, swindling and threatening the masses. On November 6, 1956, Chang, in Hsuan-hsia-yu, beat his rectangular badge hanging on his chest, which was given him as a certificate of his taking part in the Hunan Provincial Christian Learning Session, and said falsely to a certain farmer, Lo, in an overbearing manner: "I have come with the orders of the Provincial government. Those who are of a lower rank should obey their superiors." He thus deceived and threatened the people. There are some preachers who have fabricated rumors and deceived people to join the church. For instance, a certain preacher of the China Inland Mission Church once said to the masses: "To avoid all calamities and troubles, everybody must join the church," and so on.

In some places there are the so-called "independent preachers" who are undertaking secret activities and whose ways are mysterious. They rush to the East and then the West, creating confusion everywhere.

IV. Opposing Medical Treatment and Causing Death to the Sick

CH'EN YA, preacher at the True Jesus Church in Ch'i-ho Chen, T'ao-yuan Hsien, has swindled the Christian masses, undertaken unlawful propaganda against the use of medicine, and has given "treatment" to patients by crying "Hallelujah" and by baptizing them. He has also declared: "By joining the church, the blind can see, the paralyzed can walk, the deaf can hear, the humpbacked can stand straight, and the dumb can talk," and so on. Since the liberation, Ch'en, together with Ai Ch'eng-jen, Ai Ch'eng-feng, and Ai Kui-hua (who have all been arrested), have caused death to a girl by the name of Ting and to over ten other people in the eleventh district of T'ao-yuan Hsien, in this way.

Yang Ch'i-yung and others of the True Jesus Church in Liling Hsien have been consistently opposed to the use of medicine and prevented patients from seeing a doctor. They have insisted on curing the patients by giving them cold water to drink, thereby causing death to them through mistreatment. For instance, because the wife of Yang Kuo-tung (a Christian) who lives in Lo-k'ou-ch'ung was deceived by them she refused to take any medicine after having given birth to a baby and she died after drinking cold water for three or four days. Many other people have died in a similar manner all because they refused to take medicine after having been sick. The most unbearable fact is that when they "cure the sick" by offering prayers they make it known that "when Jesus cures the sick he will quickly restore health to those who should live and let others die faster who should die, lest both of them should suffer." They thereby deceive the Christians and push off their own responsibilities in causing people to die.

Yang Ch'i-yung and others did not care whether the weather was cold or the water was frozen when they baptized and they forced the patients to "receive baptism" in the river and caused them to die. The most cruel aspect of all is the fact that the two-year-old son of Huang Ch'i-ho, a Christian, also died on account of receiving baptism in the same manner.

There is a woman preacher at the T'ung-tzu-p'ing Lutheran Church in Yiyang Hsien who is carried in a carriage made of bamboo, and roams everywhere to manufacture rumors, swindle the people, heal the sick and exorcize demons. She has deceived the people by saying: "This carriage is given to me by the local official who wants me to use it to make rounds to heal the sick and exorcize the demon."

The facts exposed above are only a few examples of the unlawful activities which have been carried on in the churches of our province. Even these few examples will sufficiently show how extremely serious the criminal deeds of the bad elements in the church have been. We Christians must concern ourselves with these problems, must understand the harm these unlawful activities will bring, must know the boundaries of the religious policy, must realize that these are not problems having to do with religion but political ones, and we must make clear in our minds that these are criminal activities against the nation's constitution. Moreover, we must stand firm on the ground of the people, strengthen our patriotic and law-abiding education, resolutely purge all the unlawful activities in the Christian church, struggle to the end against the bad elements, and we must also petition the government to outlaw such activities and punish the offenders according to the law.

DOC. 70. *Counter-Revolutionary Nature of Buddhist Abbot Pen Huan Unmasked (1958)*

ACTING ON INFORMATION given by the broad masses and following investigations leading to corroborative evidence, the public security organ of the Shaokwan Administrative District ferreted out Pen Huan, abbot of Nan Hua Monastery and a counter-revolutionary operating under the cloak of religion. He was recently arrested.

According to facts on hand, Pen Huan was originally a collaborationist and rascal who infiltrated the Buddhist faith. During the Japanese aggression in China, he was associated with a Japanese puppet organization. His counter-revolutionary duty was to conduct investigations into the condition of our guerrilla columns. He also consistently undertook traitorous propaganda. When he came to Nan Hua Monastery, he did not change his reactionary stand. He consistently spread disquieting rumors and provoked ill feelings between the monks and the people. He also used his religious position to perpetrate illegal deeds, such as smuggling, disposing of smuggled items, and buying food grains and gold without authorization.

According to information furnished by Buddhist followers and investigations conducted by the public security department, Pen Huan consistently fabricated rumors in the monastery attacking various Party policies, particularly the policy on religion, as well as alienating Buddhist followers from the Communist Party and the People's Government. Since the People's Government carried out the policy on freedom of religious belief over the past years, the Nan Hua Monastery freely conducted various kinds of religious activities. Pen Huan, however, covertly smeared the motherland before monks and before Buddhist devotees from abroad, claiming that there was no freedom of religious belief in the country. In an effort to safeguard and preserve religious relics and treasures, the government over the past years appropriated several thousand yuan annually for renovating the Nan Hua

Monastery. Pen Huan, however, spread the rumor claiming that the People's Government had not done anything to repair the monastery.

Over the past years, the monastery on numerous occasions held services for initiation of novices into the Buddhist priesthood, while Pen Huan himself recruited forty to fifty disciples. Pen Huan, however, accused the government of forbidding him to conduct "initiation" rites and recruit Buddhist followers. He also resorted to the practices of conducting "secret initiations" and withholding the issuance of initiation certificates to novices who had already been initiated into Buddhist priesthood in order to mislead and incite the Buddhist faithful to harbor dissatisfaction against the People's Government. Although Pen Huan kept thousands of "initiation certificates" in his room, he gave out that such certificates had now to be issued by the government, in an attempt to attack the government policy on freedom of religious belief.

To help ease the livelihood difficulties of the monks of the Nan Hua Monastery, the government allocated them farmland and offered them medical care at state expense, as well as issuing monthly living allowances to Pen Huan. The latter, however, treated monastery property as his own and freely squandered it away on the one hand and lied about the miserable life of the monks on the other in an attempt to incite the monks to harbor dissatisfaction against the People's Government.

On the occasion of the birthday of the "Sixth Patriarch" in June, 1954, many people visited the Nan Hua Monastery for the worship. In the interest of maintaining social order, public security officers summoned Pen Huan and others to obtain their help in doing a good job of public security work, and to attend to the registration of visitors in accordance with census regulation. Upon his return to the monastery, Pen Huan told the monks with malicious intentions that it was a trap laid by the People's Government and that freedom of belief was false.

Pen Huan also had consistently spread rumors and fallacious remarks to attack various political movements. He strongly resented land reform, saying that "it is difficult to forget this hatred in a lifetime." He also personally visited Nanhsiung Hsien to understand the "miserable condition" of a landlady (she became a nun later), and has since vociferously championed her cause. During the high tide of agricultural cooperativisation, Pen Huan again spread the big lie, claiming that "participation in higher grade agricultural producer cooperative leads to nowhere." He also used his religious position to obstruct the monks from joining cooperatives. When the entire body of monks and nuns realized that they should be on their own and should actively take part in labor production, Pen Huan, in his capacity as abbot, sternly reproached the monks for caring only about production and disregarding the practice of Buddhist devotions. He also spread reactionary utterances pointing out that "there was no need to work under the Kuomintang rule" and that "the present is a far cry from former days." At the time when bourgeois rightist elements were frantically launching attacks on the Communist Party and the People's Government last year, Pen Huan was so elated that he provokingly told Buddhist followers: "The Communist Party is too dictatorial and overbearing." He also indicated he would concentrate his attack on Communist weaknesses.

According to facts uncovered by Buddhist followers, Pen Huan used his position in the monastery to shelter large numbers of counter-revolutionaries and other types of bad elements. Among Buddhist followers recruited by him, there were over ten counter-revolutionaries, reactionary bureaucrats, landlords, village despots, and petty thieves. Of these, three were counter-revolutionaries. Using these people as his trusted underlings, Pen Huan obstructed the Buddhist faithful from cultivating close association with the People's Government and watched and dealt blows to progressive Buddhist disciples, as well as built up his own power to counter that of the People's Government. He also connived in the misdeeds perpetrated by his followers, even encouraging them to rape women, steal money and property, and commit other crimes.

Furthermore, Pen Huan imposed a feudal and barbarous rule on the monastery, and introduced numerous illegal practices. He prohibited the Buddhist faithful from reading new books and newspapers, threatening them that they would have to give up the Buddhist priesthood should they persist in reading "Selected Works of Mao Tse-tung." He often struck and swore at the monks and nuns, as well as infringed on their personal rights. He was even mean enough to flirt with the nuns. For this reason, the monks then all felt they dared not speak what was on their minds or get something off their chests. After Pen Huan was arrested, they cheered and exclaimed in high spirits: "Only now have we been completely emancipated!"

DOC. 71. *Kiangsu Provincial Christian Conference Victoriously Concluded (1958)*

FROM FEBRUARY 26 through May 13 [1958], the Christian circle in Kiangsu Province held a conference in Nanking. A total of 240 Christian delegates and observers attended the conference, including ministerial personnel and responsible leaders of the Christian Three-Self Patriotic Movement from all parts of the Province, plus all the faculty members and business staff of the Nanking Union Theological Seminary.

Through big bloom, big struggle, and big debate, the conference exposed several rightist elements of the propertied class hidden in the Christian church. All these rightist elements have centralized their attacks on the leadership of the Party, the people's democratic dictatorship, socialist democracy, the socialist system, the Soviet Union, and on the foreign policy of our government. They have declared: "Obedience to the leadership of the Party will affect [our] 'personality' and 'independent thinking'"; "the Party should not lead the religious circle, for it is impossible for amateurs to guide the professionals"; and "the socialist system of today is inferior to the system in the past." These rightist elements have also greatly distorted, slandered, and attacked the [government's] implementation of the religious policy. They have attempted to make use of the so-called "religious emotion" to incite Christians to shoot at the Party, saying "the religious

policy is a fake and there are several sets of it." They slanderously say that denouncing the imperialists is "denouncing [our]
religious belief," thus attempting to disapprove and wipe out the
achievements of the Chinese Christian Three-Self Anti-imperialistic and Patriotic Movement.

All of these rightist elements have had thousand-fold political
and thought relations with the imperialists and the reactionary
group of the Kuomintang. Shao Ching-san, Yang Ching-ch'iu,
Tsang An-t'ang and the rest have all been faithful slaves fed and
brought up by the imperialists. After the liberation, they have
consistently insisted on their reactionary stand, resisted reform,
and, under the cloaks of religion or of "progress," have done
everything possible to slander and undermine all the policies of
the Party and the Government and the various political movements under the leadership of the Party. Last year, during the
time when the rightist elements throughout the nation, under the
pretext of "for the sake of the church" and "for the sake of
religious belief," were madly attacking the Party and the people,
Shao Ching-san dared to support openly the minority of rightist
elements at Nanking University in launching the so-called "democratic stream" which was an anti-Party and anti-socialist movement. At the present conference he has again, making use of the
opportunities of blooming and booming, spread many reactionary
theories and once more attacked the Party and the people. The
anti-Party, anti-people, anti-socialist, and reactionary words and
deeds of these rightist elements have aroused the extreme indignation of the delegates. These delegates have, on the basis of a great
quantity of facts, exposed the ugly and hideous faces of the rightist elements and solemnly criticized and repudiated their shameful
and slanderous words. The majority of the rightist elements have
been forced by facts and truth to make confessions and bow to
the people.

The conference has also exposed unlawful activities of the
church such as faith healing, exorcising demons, causing death to
people, secret meetings, unlawfully establishing churches, self-
styling of preachers, seduction of women, exploitation and extortion, manufacturing rumors, undermining the government,
deceiving the masses and others. According to initial estimate, in

the past few years, the bad elements and reactionaries in the church have caused death to many people through faith healing and exorcising of demons. For example, Chang Chung-hsin, the bad and rightist element who has commissioned himself as the preacher of the church in Chiang-p'u Hsein, himself alone has directly or indirectly caused death to more than twenty people. There have been even more deaths caused by delay through faith healing and being prevented from seeing doctors. There are churches in some districts which, in addition to being impure in organization and undertaking widespread unlawful activities in faith healing, exorcising demons, causing death to people, extortion and exploitation, have raped and insulted women through "spiritual dance," "spiritual love," and other evil practices. In individual churches there still are people who regularly conspire with counter-revolutionaries, rightist elements, and others who hate the new society and the Communist Party, and, under the pretext of "family meetings" and "Bible classes," spread reactionary theories and undertake unlawful activities, thereby bringing serious harms to the welfare of the nation and the people.

Through this conference, all of us have understood that in the past few years the Christian circle in our Province has achieved definite results in the anti-imperialistic and patriotic movement. But there are still serious problems to be faced. Not only unlawful activities still widely exist in the church but the thought influences handed down by the imperialists and the reactionaries of the Kuomintang and the power of the remnant counter-revolutionaries and rightist elements who still control some of the churches are still to be further exposed and liquidated. Aside from these, the political awareness of the church's ministerial personnel is also far behind the development of our fatherland's socialist construction.

For these reasons, the conference has passed the following resolutions: (1) Christians must honestly support the leadership of the Communist Party and firmly walk down the road to socialism. The Christian circle everywhere must continue to go deeper in spreading socialist thought-education and, on this basis, expanding the hand-the-heart-to-the-Party movement. (2) They must go one step further in intensifying the anti-imperialistic and patriotic movement throughout the whole province and in reorganizing the Christian organizations. They must also thoroughly purge themselves of the thought-influences of the imperialists and be vigilant at all times against the attempt of the imperialists in using Christianity to advance their secret activities. (3) Christians of the whole Province must observe the Constitution and all the policies and decrees of the government. They must positively take part in all the patriotic activities and resolutely wipe out all the unlawful activities and confusions of the church. (4) To participate directly in the socialist construction enterprises, to achieve better the goal of self-reform, and to solve the problem of self-support, all the ministerial personnel must take active part in production and voluntary labour.

The conference has also passed "A Proposal Concerning the Elimination of the Confusions and all the Unlawful Activities in the Church." The proposal makes the following recommendations: no church should undertake the activities of faith healing and demon exorcising, and all the practices which are harmful to the health of the people's bodies and spirits must be stopped; all the so-called "churches," "worship halls," and "family meetings" which have been established without the permission of the government must be dissolved; with the exception of personal religious life, all the meetings must be held in the church; church organizations and personnel must be reorganized and redistributed; the offerings of the Christians must be voluntary and nobody is permitted to ask for contributions from church members; no ministerial personnel should manufacture false "witness" or spread the poisons of the imperialists and the counter-revolutionaries; ministers must not speak any words which are harmful to the welfare of the socialist fatherland, and when they hear any slanderous words they must not spread them but must report them immediately to the government. The conference, in addition to guaranteeing the carrying out of all these resolutions, expresses hope that ministers and Christian laymen throughout the nation support its actions.

DOC. 72. *How to Hold a Successful Accusation Meeting*
(1951)

ACCUSATION SPEECHES were delivered in specially called mass
denunciation meetings, often with the accused forced to sit or stand
on the platform. In order to give local church authorities guidance
in the proper way to hold such a meeting, YMCA Secretary Liu
Liang-mo wrote an article on *How to Hold a Successful Accusation
Meeting*.

ONE OF THE CENTRAL TASKS at present for Christian churches and
groups across the nation is to hold successful accusation meetings.

Why do we want to accuse? Because for more than a hundred
years imperialism has utilized Christianity to attack China, therefore we want to accuse it of its sins. As a result of the longtime
influence of imperialism, many Christians have the old-fashioned
idea of "being above politics"; therefore we must hold accusation
meetings to educate everybody. Big accusation meetings consti-
ture a most effective means of helping the masses of believers to
comprehend the evil wrought in China by imperialism, to recognize the fact that imperialism has utilized Christianity to attack
China, and to wipe out imperialist influences within the churches.

Accuse what? We must accuse imperialist elements and their
helpers as well as other bad elements hidden in the churches. We
want to expose their sin of utilizing the churches to attack China
and deceive believers. For example, many Christians in Tsingtao,
Shanghai, Hangchow and Peking have accused America's political
agent, Ku Ken-en, of wearing the cloak of religion to engage in
counter-revolutionary activities, and even rumor-mongering and
swindling, raping women and killing sick people. Christian leaders
such as Ts'ui Hsien-hsiang and Chiang Ch'ang-ch'uan have
accused imperialist elements, Frank Price, etc., who take the name
of missionary to carry on special agent activities, and other special
agents of America and Chiang who hold high positions in the
churches.

How shall we hold a successful accusation meeting? First, we must remove the thought barriers of many Christians. Some Christians suppose that they ought to "hide evil and display good" or that they ought not to accuse. And yet Jesus's reprimands to the scribes and Pharisees of that time were certainly accusations. Some Christians feel that they are "unable to accuse of some things"; they ought then to participate more in the big accusation meetings of people from all walks of life and the public trials of counter-revolutionaries. The anger and charges of the masses of the people towards imperialism, bandits, and wicked tyrants will arouse the righteous indignation and accusations of Christians towards imperialism and bad elements in the churches.

Second, if we want to hold a successful accusation meeting, we must first do well the preparatory work. Every church and the city-wide church federation ought to first organize an accusation committee. They should first study whom they want to accuse, and whom to invite to do the accusing. After this they should invite those participating in the accusation to attend a meeting to mobilize accusations so that they may understand why, what and how they should accuse. The second step of the preparation work is to hold in every church and group preliminary accusation meetings. In these meetings we should urge everyone to enthusiastically express his opinions and accuse. In this way we shall be able to discover a few people who accuse with the greatest power and invite them to participate in the large accusation meeting and can also correct certain weaknesses in their speaking, for example, making briefer the speeches which are too long, making clearer the speeches which are unclear, and making fuller the content of those which are insufficient.

Third, what can be considered to be a successful accusation meeting? According to the experience of Ts'ui Hsien-hsiang, who accused Frank Price, accusations (1) ought to be according to facts; (2) must break through all sentimentality; (3) must in every sentence be spoken from the depths of the heart; (4) must be thorough-going, outspoken, sincere, and uninhibited; (5) must hold firmly to the position of the people. Bishop Chiang Ch'ang-ch'uan of the Methodist Church, when he accused the bad element of the church, [Bishop] Ch'en Wen-yuan, said, "I am determined to purge my church in the spirit of unmitigated punishment of offenders, no matter who they are, definitely cleaning out thoroughly all elements like Ch'en Wen-yuan; if there is one, remove one, if there are ten, remove ten!" This sort of accusation moves people very deeply.

Fourth, the atmosphere of the meeting must be dignified when carrying on a local church or city-wide accusation meeting. The order of arrangement of the accusers is very important; they should be arranged as follows: first high tension, then moderate, then another of high tension, etc.; only so can the accusation meeting be a success. When the accusations have succeeded in deeply stirring people, clapping and applause may be used as a form of expression. Throughout the whole process of preparation for the big accusation meeting, we ought to invite the Religious Affairs Bureau of the local People's Government or other related offices, democratic political groups and other concerned parties to come and advise. The texts of outstanding accusations ought to be recorded and given to local papers for publishing, and also mailed to the Preparation Committee of the Chinese Christian Oppose-America Assist-Korea Three-Self Reform Movement Committee (address: 131 Museum Road, Shanghai). If there is evidence of specific crimes of imperialist elements or bad elements in the churches, such as correspondence, pictures, weapons, radios, etc., these must be reported to the local police office; and after obtaining the agreement of the police office, we may open a local exhibit of concrete materials, or mail them directly to the Preparation Committee of the Chinese Christian Oppose-America Assist-Korea Three-Self Reform Movement Committee for use in a nationwide exhibition.

What about after the accusation? After the accusation the patriotic fervor and political comprehension of the masses of believers will be raised and they will have a much clearer understanding of imperialism. We ought to encourage the whole body of workers and fellow-believers in the church and all Christians to carry out the following tasks: (1) Strengthen study of current affairs; (2) Continue promoting the Three-Self Reform Movement; (3) Continue cleaning out all imperialist and bad elements within the churches; (4) Participate in local and national movements for the suppression of counter-revolution; (5) Actively participate in the Oppose-America Assist-Korea movement.

To hold a successful big accusation meeting is one of the important tasks that every church must do well to wipe out the influences of imperialism!

Section. 9 Religion and Socialist Construction

THE HEIGHTENED TEMPO of national mobilization and political conformity that swept the nation in the Great Leap Forward campaign of 1958–59 is reflected in the reports of three religious leaders. Shirob Jaltso's speech to the 1960 session of the CPPCC, unlike his frank remarks of 1956, has only words of praise for the "new appearance of Buddhism." As a result of political study there is, he says, a new mentality of Buddhists, a heightened political consciousness; they no longer reject the world but welcome participation in worldly activity. No longer do lamas and nuns live parasitically off the labor of others; by joining in manual labor with the people former class distinctions are abolished and new friendly relations between clergy and believers prevail. He catalogs the restoration and promotion of Buddhist culture, Buddhist studies, and Buddhist publications. The laity are active in pilgrimages to holy sites and increasingly seek Buddhist services. All these, he declares, are evidence of full freedom of worship, a freedom that must be clearly distinguished, however, from the use of religion for counter-revolutionary activities. These must be resolutely rooted out.

Catholic, Protestant and Moslem reports from this period maintain a similar tone of untempered enthusiasm for the government's treatment of religion. Just a few short years before the total suppression of all open religious practice, no hint of criticism or impending trouble appears in the statements of these religious leaders.

DOC. 73. *Shirob Jaltso, Buddhist Member, CPPCC National Committee: New Appearance of Buddhism in China—Speech Delivered at Second Session of Third CPPCC National Committee (April 15, 1960)*

SHIROB JALTSO SPEAKS of three features in the new appearance of Buddhism: first, a new political consciousness and patriotic identity, most clearly seen in the abandonment of monastic seclusion by the clergy and participation in collective labor; second, the revival of Buddhist culture; third, the widespread practice of Buddhist religious services.

In 1960 Shirob Jaltso said, "In dealing with differences between political and religious matters we should follow the Party, not the religion, in respect of those Buddhist teachings which run counter to the policies of the Party and which are not vital to Buddhism. . . . But, in respect of those Buddhist teachings which do not affect the policies of the Party at all and which are vital to Buddhism, we should exercise our right to freedom of worship. This is exactly what our Government is doing."

But by late 1966, judging by all reports available, all religious services had ceased, *Modern Buddhism* was no longer published, and the Chinese Institute of Buddhist Studies as well as the Chinese Buddhist Association had ceased to function.

PRESIDENTS, DEPUTIES, and Committee Members—I hereby voice full support for the reports by Vice-premiers Li Fu-ch'un and Li Hsien-nien and undertake to act accordingly.

The first thing I should mention in the new appearance of Buddhism in China is that the mentality of the Buddhists has undergone a change, as a result of which customs and habits are different from what they used to be. Since the liberation, under the leadership of the Party and as a result of political studies and several movements, the Buddhists have incessantly increased their patriotism and heightened their political consciousness. In this way, they have gotten rid of the "negative feeling of weariness of this world" which was handed down from the past and which in the past made the Buddhists tolerate what they could tolerate and consider themselves as above and beyond this world; the "positive feeling of being a part of this world" has been induced in them and has made them heroic and strong and led them onward courageously; and their mentality has been completely changed.

Take an example. Having studied the rebellion of the reactionary bloc of the upper social strata in Tibet which occurred in March last year, all the Buddhists in the nation were able to understand fully that the rebellion was in substance a rebellion staged by the all-evil reactionaries at home and abroad in the name of Buddhism, a counter-revolutionary plot aimed at splitting the motherland apart and at perpetuating the slavery of the Tibetan people. The Buddhists distinguished right from wrong over this important issue, understood the policy of free worship more fully, further increased their patriotism, got rid of the so-called "above and beyond this world" attitude which in the past made them indifferent to the affairs of the state and the conditions of the people, were able to stand firmly on the side of the people when right had to be distinguished from wrong over an important issue, and supported the correct measures of the Government for quelling the rebellion.

At the same time, as a result of political studies and the several movements, the Buddhists have gradually come to think and believe that one should subsist on one's own labor. They have also come to understand that labor is something glorious and noble and beneficial to oneself and to others. They actively got organized for taking part in production under different forms. Using their intelligence and their hands, they have created wealth for the people and material conditions for their own spiritual improvement and the spread of their faith. Whereas they used to live by exploiting others, they have discarded such a shameful parasitic life. Their view on society has been completely changed.

Take an example. The monks on Wut'ai Mountain have given up feudal exploitation through land relations. In autumn harvesting last year, when the masses were busy, over 200 of them went down the mountain to help. Later, the masses set apart several hundred mou of farm land for the monks and nuns to cultivate. There was thus mutual assistance.

Whereas in the past the relations between the monks and nuns on the one hand and the masses on the other were those between the exploiting and the exploited, such class contradictions have now been removed. Class friendship based on common laboring has been founded between them. Owing to the change in the mentality of the Buddhists, a change has also occurred in their other conditions: they are no longer discriminated against by society or without any political status at all as they were in the past. They now enjoy the due respect of society and the due trust of the people, with whom they have won equality. In all parts of the country, the monks and nuns are given the same remuneration as the workers or peasants doing the same jobs, and politically enjoy the rights to be elected to youth congresses, political consultative conferences, and people's congresses and to work in the Government. They are allowed to express their opinions not only on Buddhist matters, but also on ordinary matters, and importance is attached to the opinions they express on all occasions. The above fully shows that the Buddhists in China, after being reformed, have assumed a new appearance and that customs and habits are now different from what they used to be.

Secondly, I should mention the reglorification of Buddhist culture. The spread of Buddhism during the past two thousand years or so left behind a treasure of highly artistic things and things of academic interest. These precious legacies were utterly destroyed by the reactionary rulers before the liberation. After the liberation, the Party and the Government took steps to protect them. The Chinese Buddhist Association was founded in Peking to help the People's Government enforce the policy of free worship and to promote the teachings of the various Buddhist sects. The China Institute of Buddhist Studies was opened; apart from making research in the Han language section of Buddhism, it has also been unfolding work for research in the Tibetan language section and the Pa-li language section of Buddhism.

The monthly magazine *Hsien-tai Fo-hsueh* [*Modern Buddhism*] was founded. It has been promoting the political and religious studies of the Buddhists and taking an active interest in national construction and world peace. *The Buddhist Encyclopedia* was compiled. And the Buddhist religion in China was systematically reorganized. These projects represented definite contributions toward the work of inheriting the past of Buddhism in China and paving the way for its future. . . .

The third thing I should mention is the regular holding of religious functions. In the monasteries on Wut'ai Mountain in Shansi, the monasteries on T'ient'ai Mountain in Chekiang, and Yüwang Monastery in Ningpo, there are usually holy monks explaining Buddhist teachings and precepts and making spiritual improvement. During my pilgrimage, I, too, was asked to explain the teachings on "faith," "the mind," "the three ways of Buddhism," and "the four doors" in Chingan Monastery in Shanghai, Yüwang Monastery in Ningpo, Ch'ien Monastery in P'ut'o, Paot'ung Monastery in Wuhan, Ch'ungshan Monastery in Taiyuan, and Hsient'ung Monastery, Shihfangt'ang, and Kuang-chi Mao-p'eng on Wu'tai Mountain. My audience frequently numbered 300 or 400.

Many are also those asking for Buddhist services. In Shanghai, there are so many requests for Buddhist services that the monasteries are unable to satisfy all of them. Though they engage in production, the monks and nuns in all parts of the country say their morning and evening prayers as usual. In all the monasteries where I stayed in my travels, I heard bells in the morning and drums in the evening; all of them were filled with delight in Buddhism. These magnificent yet prosaic religious functions and the quiet life of the Buddhists fully show that there is full freedom of worship in our socialist country.

Concerning the economic life of the monks and nuns, since, as said above, they are engaging in production, they are receiving a steady and better income and leading a better life. As for the old, weak, and disabled among them, who either cannot labor at all or are earning too little to support life, they are well taken care of in the same way as the "five guarantee" families. The above shows fully that the Buddhists irrespective of age in the new China have each found a proper place for themselves, and all of them are leading perfect and happy lives. Let the rumor-mongering experts at home and abroad, who are envious of us, shut their mouths!

It is also clear from the above that freedom of worship for the Buddhists in the new China is fully protected. We do not at all try to conceal those unhappy incidents of the past which had to do with our religion. For instance, at the instigation of the imperialists, the reactionary bloc of the upper social strata in Tibet rebelled, burned, killed, and plundered. Damage was thereby caused not only to the people but also to the Buddhist religion. The reactionaries who took part in the rebellion were the enemies not only of the people but also of the Buddhist religion. In the interests of the people and the Buddhist religion, they had to be exterminated. The policy of free worship of the Chinese Communist Party is very clearly worded. Every Chinese is entirely free to believe in a religion or not to believe in any religion, to believe in any religion he likes, to believe in a religion today and to renounce his faith tomorrow, and to believe in no religion today and to believe in one tomorrow.

The enjoyment of this freedom must be strictly distinguished from the reactionary activities of the counter-revolutionaries. While freedom of worship must be protected, the Buddhists must be deprived of all their freedom to engage in counter-revolutionary activities in the name of Buddhism. This is not a contradiction at all. As the sayings go, "Unless the weed is removed, the crop will not grow well" and "Unless the enemies of Buddhism are exterminated, Buddhists will not be able to go to heaven." In our country, every clean Buddhist and clean monastery is protected by law. For believing in Buddhism, no good monks or nuns have ever been discriminated against, and no good monasteries have ever been damaged. It is only when the Buddhists, made use of by the counter-revolutionaries, engage in counter-revolutionary activities against the Party, the people, and socialism and engage in these activities to such a frantic extent as makes them beyond hope of remedy, that the People's Government will, in consideration of the interests of the people, be forced to take suppressive measures against them. The People's Government has the duty to destroy the bad and to give peace to the good. It does not allow the public enemies of the people to remain unpunished.

Besides, the measures taken to destroy the bad and to give peace to the good are taken in the interests not only of the people in general but also of the Buddhist religion and its followers. Since those who engage in counter-revolutionary activities in the name of Buddhism are not genuine Buddhists but are tumors of Buddhism, to show mercy to them means to nourish tumors; only by quelling the rebellion militarily, suppressing the black sheep in the Buddhist religion, and removing the tumors is it possible to restore the original goodness of Buddhism. Thus, the principal thing for the Buddhists to do is to realize that there are no contradictions between political matters and religious matters, to stand firmly on the side of the people, and to eliminate completely the black sheep in the Buddhist religion who are harmful to it. . . .

We do not deny that there are differences between political matters and religious matters, but we hold that these differences do not prevent religion from serving the people. In dealing with these differences, we should follow the Party, not the religion, in respect of those Buddhist teachings which run counter to the policies of the Party and which are not vital to Buddhism. We should give up these Buddhist teachings and absolutely obey the policies of the Party. But, in respect of those Buddhist teachings which do not affect the policies of the Party at all and which are vital to Buddhism, we should exercise our right to freedom of worship. This is exactly what our Government is doing.

DOC. 74. *P'i Shu-shih, Chairman, Catholic National Patriotic Association, Archbishop of Shen-yang: Life of Catholics in China (1960)*

IN CONTRAST TO THE BUDDHIST LEADER, Shirob Jaltso (Doc. 73), China's chief Catholic leader, writing on the occasion of the new government's tenth anniversary, passed quickly over the religious situation of Catholics, stressing instead the material progress, social reforms and collective solidarity of the people under the new regime. Catholics were active, he said, in politics and in socialist construction at every level, and the teachings of Jesus were being implemented in the elimination of social evils and mass suffering due to poverty.

But by late 1966 the celebration of the Catholic mass, by all reports, had ceased throughout China. P'i Shu-shih, no longer heard from, could no longer praise the People's Government for having "consistently and without fail carried out the policy of freedom of religious belief."

THE YEAR 1959 will see the tenth anniversary of the founding of the People's Republic of China. Looking back at the past ten years and the way traveled by our great motherland, I am full of joy and gratitude. The old China, owing to imperialist aggression and the corrupt rule of the old Chinese government, was impoverished and backward; but within the short space of ten years, incredible and great changes have happened under the correct leadership of the Chinese Communist Party and Chairman Mao Tse-tung. The new China is prosperous and vigorous; not only industry, agriculture, culture and science have made flying leaps forward, but the material life and spiritual aspect of the people have also undergone radical changes. Like the rest of the Chinese people, Chinese Catholics are proud of being able, and feel it a supreme honor, to live in such a great country and such a great era.

For the past ten years, the 3,000,000 Chinese Catholics, like the rest of the Chinese people, have been living a democratic, free, and increasingly happy life. We have become masters of our own country and are taking part in state affairs. According to incomplete statistics of 1957, more than 400 of our bishops, priests, sisters, and lay members of the Church have become deputies to People's Congresses at the national, provincial, municipal, hsien, and ch'ü levels and members of CPPCC at various levels. In April this year, six Catholic bishops, one Catholic priest, and two Catholic laymen attended the first session of the Second National People's Congress and a conference of the Third National Committee of the Chinese People's Political Consultative Conference; they discussed state affairs together with over 2,000 people's deputies and CPPCC members who had come from all parts of the country. There is also a large number of the Catholic clergy, sisters, and Catholic laity who have been elected members of the Federation of Democratic Youth and Federation of

Women at the national, provincial, municipal, and hsien levels. In addition, a large number of members of the Catholic laity are occupying government posts. For instance, T'ung Shao-sheng, vice-governor of Szechuan, is a Catholic.

Most of the Chinese Catholics are workers and peasants. In the old society, they, like the rest of the working people of the country, regularly suffered the pains of privation and unemployment, and led a kind of life worse than that of draft animals. After the liberation, they have been given jobs and are living an increasingly better life.

The religious belief of Chinese Catholics is fully protected by the laws of the state. Article 88 of the Constitution of the People's Republic of China expressly provides that "Citizens of the People's Republic of China have the freedom of religious belief." The Chinese Communist Party and People's Government at all levels have consistently and without fail carried out this policy of freedom of religious belief. All members of the Catholic clergy and Catholic laity in all parts of the country freely live their religious life, and the important rite of offering to the Lord—the Holy Mass—has never ceased. Take for instance St. Joseph's Church in Peking. Two masses are celebrated here every morning during weekdays, and during Sundays and feast days three masses are celebrated in the morning and an evening mass is specially celebrated for the workers and other employees. The important feast days are celebrated with even greater fervor.

But freedom of religious belief does not mean in the least "freedom" for those who belong to some religion to damage the interests of the people of the motherland or freedom to break the laws and violate the policy of the state or sabotage socialist construction. Unfortunately, we have a number of black sheep in our Catholic Church who have done many evil deeds to jeopardize the state and the people under cover of religion. Kung P'in-mei, formerly bishop of Shanghai, is one of them. He sabotaged the agrarian reform, ordered Catholics who were peasants not to recognize their ownership right of the land distributed to them, and helped landlords to conceal large numbers of title deeds in the vain hope of "reversing the account." More contemptible still, Kung concealed Teng Chia-chun and other

Kuomintang "special service" men, who owed many debts of blood, in Tungchiatu church in Shanghai so that they might continue to engage in counter-revolutionary activities; he also secretly ordered Catholics and the clergy not to inform against or accuse the counter-revolutionaries. He turned the holy church into a "bandits' lair." He is a traitor to the country and a black sheep of the Church. His arrest by the government according to law was fully in accord with the interests of the state and the 600,000,000 people (including Catholics). That is a political question which has absolutely nothing to do with the question of freedom of religious belief. After Kung P'in-mei's arrest, religious activities in the Shanghai diocese have never been restricted in the least as a result, but on the contrary have been helped by the government. For instance, the belfry of Siccawei church in Shanghai was blown down during a typhoon in 1956, but was rebuilt with funds appropriated for the purpose by the government.

The Chinese Catholic clergy and laity realize from their personal experience that in the new China, not only their material life has improved, but it is easier for them to save their own souls. In the new China, social morality is quickly rising and occasions of sin are greatly reduced. Opium smoking, gambling, and prostitution, which had induced countless people to follow the road to their own undoing in the past, are now completely wiped out. Drug addicts, gamblers, and prostitutes have all become productive workers. Singing their praise of the new society, people often say, "The old society turns human beings into devils, but the new society turns devils into human beings." That is quite true. In the old society, many robberies, thefts, murders for money, cases of seduction of women, abductions, cases of deception, and other crimes occurred every day; and quarreling and fighting were often seen in the streets and in houses. In the new society, what we often hear of and see are noble acts of respect for the aged and love for the young, mutual aid, and courtesy; and moving cases of lost property being returned to the owners, rescue to the distressed, and help to those in suffering; and people trying to protect property of the state and the people at the risk of their own lives. In public organs, schools, the streets, and the parks, one may often see cadres, students, and ordinary people of the Han, Mongol, Tibetan, Uighur, and other nationalities working and playing together. They are close to one another and are like brothers and sisters to one another. The new China is really a big family in which there is unity and friendship among all nationalities and groups. The ideal state which has always been cherished by the Chinese people since time immemorial, in which "the aged have somewhere to go, the young are taken care of, and widows and widowers and people who are alone have someone to depend upon for support" and in which "lost property is not taken away [from the rightful owner] and doors are not closed at night," is being gradually realized in the new China today. How can people not love such a society?

Owing to their love for the new society, Chinese Catholics, like the rest of the people of the country, have a high degree of political fervor and production activism. At present, under the leadership of local people's governments and the clergy, Catholics are taking an active part in all branches of socialist construction of the motherland and the movement in defense of world peace together with the rest of the people. We fully realize that to work hard for the ample clothing and feeding of the 600,000,000 Chinese people and for peace and happiness of the whole world is to carry out the teaching of Jesus to love mankind and to love Jesus Himself. Jesus says, "You who have done something for the youngest of my brothers have done something for me." We also realize that in a socialist society in which the working people are the masters, labor is no longer done in order to gratify the greed of a small number of landlords and capitalists, but for the sake of the happiness of all the people, that is, for the sake of our own happiness. As a result, we have skyrocketing zeal and have produced many model laborers and advanced workers.

Ten years is only a short time to our ancient country. But in this short space of ten years cataclysmic changes have taken place in our great motherland. The new China is going forward in gigantic strides. Here new buildings rise every day, new factories and mines go into production every day, new people and new things appear every hour and every minute, and countless new books and songs are everywhere. Really "one hundred ruins rise again" and "one hundred flowers bloom." Here there is no national oppression or religious discrimination; instead, there is mutual respect and mutual aid. How can one be unhappy in such a society? Therefore, the 3,000,000 Catholics in China, together with the rest of the nation, are greeting the tenth anniversary of the founding of the great motherland—the People's Republic of China—with positive action to fulfill and overfulfill the national economic plan of 1959. We firmly believe that after some years of hard struggle, China, an economically and culturally backward country which has in the past suffered a great deal from imperialist aggression, will be built into a great socialist power with its highly developed modern industry, modern agriculture, and modern science and culture. Together with the rest of the nation, we are determined to fight to the last in order to achieve this great end!

DOC. 75. *Chinese Moslem Leader on Religious Freedom in China (1965)*

ALL MOSLEMS in China today enjoy full religious freedom, declared Burhan Shahidi, President of the China Islamic Association, at its Third National Conference which closed here today.

Reporting on the work of the association, he said that an unprecedented, speedy development in political, economic, and cultural fields has been registered in the areas of China where Moslem minority nationalities live in compact communities. The Moslems have taken part in the socialist construction with unparalleled initiative, and their living conditions have improved gradually, along with the rapid growth of production.

The Chinese Islamic Association has made big achievements in its work of helping the government carry out the policy of freedom of religious belief, of organizing Islamic theological study, and of strengthening exchange of friendly visits with Moslems of other countries, he declared.

The Chinese Communist Party and People's Government have

consistently pursued the policy of freedom of religious belief, the Chinese Moslem leader said.

On Mohammedan festivals, the government granted special leave to Moslems in government offices, factories and schools, and State trading organizations supplied the followers of Islam with special food and other commodities needed for the occasions.

Burhan Shahidi said that with the financial help from the People's Government, a number of famous mosques have been thoroughly repaired. They include the 800-year-old Niuchieh Mosque in Peking, the Kwangta Mosque in Canton, the Fenghuang (Phoenix) Mosque in Hangchow, and the big Ipoerhanlin Mosque in Kashgar of the Sinkiang Uighur Autonomous Region.

Touching on the work of the Chinese Institute of Islamic Theology, Burhan Shahidi said that since its founding in 1955 it has trained many imams and Islamic scholars of Hui, Uighur, Kazakh, Uzbek, Khalkha and Sala nationalities. To foster intellectuals highly learned in Islamic theology; the institute gave special research classes where students from all parts of the country took courses in the Koran, the Hadith (the doings and sayings of Mohammed), the Figh (Islamic law), Chinese Islamic history, world Islamic history, and Arabic.

The Chinese Islamic Association, which was founded in 1953, has issued two editions of the Koran as well as many other Islamic theological works.

Burhan Shahidi continued, stating that the association organizes annual Chinese pilgrimages to the holy city of Mecca.

The Chinese Moslems, he said, firmly support the people of Asia, Africa, and Latin America in their just struggle against imperialism and for national liberation and independence. In the past years, they sent delegations to make friendly visits abroad on many occasions. They warmly received more than 330 Moslems from twenty-eight countries and regions. The exchange of visits has greatly strengthened mutual understanding and friendship.

Concluding his report, the Chinese Moslem leader declared that Chinese Moslems would rally still more closely around the Chinese Communist Party and Chairman Mao Tse-tung, the great leader of the people of all nationalities of China, and take an active part in the socialist construction of their country.

Section 10. Religion and Labor: the Great Leap Forward

NATIONAL MOBILIZATION for greatly expanded production goals during the Great Leap Forward period involved every citizen able to work—even the aged and handicapped: "Old but not weak; crippled but not useless." Religious professionals were called out from their places of spiritual retreat and religious activity and charged with their duty to join in the collective effort. A report from Inner Mongolia describes how lamas, through classes, meetings, discussions, debates, and study, received "systematic education in socialism" which clarified their thinking. Subsequently they drew up programs for productive labor, some pledging up to 300 days a year. Other goals were collectivization of nomadic agriculture, and self-support through labor for the lamas as traditional sources of financial support dried up.

Laymen also joined the production campaign. The Yangchow Patriotic Cellulose Factory, the Kweilin Red Light Pickle Factory, and a Foochow organ factory were among several church-run factories reported from this period. Christian women in Kweiyang celebrated Women's Day in 1958 by digging maggots, taking part in a sanitation cleanup, planting trees and fighting the four pests (flies, rats, mosquitoes, sparrows).

Religious groups frequently adopted pledges of patriotic support such as that of the Chekiang Protestant "patriotic speedy-progress meeting," and the combined Buddhist-Taoist "systematic socialist learning session" on Mount Nan-yueh. These pledges faithfully reflect the total preoccupation with production goals of the Great Leap Forward, making no reference to customary religious needs or activities. Here no mention is made of the Party's policy on freedom of religious belief, or of needed protection for religious activities in the midst of the frantic production campaign. Normal religious activities, already greatly restricted, were further inhibited by demands on the time and energy of clergy and laymen.

DOC. 76. *Buddhists and Taoists at Mount Nan-yueh Welcome the People's Communes (1958)*

THIS YEAR, under the correct leadership and support of the Party and the Government, we Buddhists and Taoists in Nanyueh have gone through a systematic socialist learning session. Through this learning session we have elevated our socialist awareness, have clearly understood the struggle between the two roads, and have completely overcome capitalism on the economic, political, and ideological fronts.

We have also expressed wholehearted support for the great movement of the people's communes, which are guaranteed to do the best job possible in the present phase of industrial and agricultural production, and we are determined to welcome the establishment of them. Now we want to present the following production pledges as a glorious salute to the establishment of the people's communes, as well as a friendly challenge to all religious followers throughout the country:

1. We will respond to the call of the Party and the Government to undertake before the establishment of the people's communes, universal propaganda within and outside the cooperatives and repeatedly explain to the masses the nature of the people's communes as well as the purpose of establishing them. We will also call meetings of various sizes to mobilize the masses to freely bloom and discuss how to establish the people's communes and learn about their superiority.

2. Through hard work during three days and three nights we will build three steel refineries and reach the goal of producing forty tons of steel by the fourth quarter of this year. We will also reach the target of letting the cooperative members contribute the basic raw materials and of letting the members themselves learn the techniques for refining steel.

3. Within five days we, the members of our cooperative, will complete the harvest of the second rice crop in the forty-nine mou rice field, fertilize the field for the sixth time for the late crop of rice, and uproot the vines and weeds in the field of sweet potatoes for the third time.

4. We will organize the religious followers in our cooperative who are between forty-five and sixty-five years of age to undertake sideline production and cooking according to their individual physical strength, so that they may become laborers of different degrees.

5. During the fourth season of this year we will expand supplementary production on a big scale.

6. To increase production and speed up the establishment of the people's commune, we will increase our participation in work from forty-five percent to over sixty percent of [available] manpower.

7. We guarantee that as soon as we join a people's commune we will thoroughly carry out the principle of laboring with diligence and frugality and refrain from eating expensive food and other wasteful enjoyments, so that we may accumulate production capital for the commune through centralization of material and the saving of money.

Having started our pledges, we will definitely carry out what we have pledged. We present these pledges as a congratulation to the Communist Party Committee, as a salute to the people's communes, and as a friendly challenge to religious followers throughout the nation.

(Signed by the whole body of
cadres and members of the
Buddhist-Taoist Agricultural
Cooperative in Nan-yueh,
September 13, 1958.)

DOC. 77. *Inner Mongolian Lamas Advancing; Report in Nei Meng-ku Jih-pao (Inner Mongolia Daily) (1958)*

II. . . . SINCE THE LIBERATION, the lamas in our ch'ü, as each socialist enterprise rapidly expanded, have raised their socialist consciousness, and have obtained big results in the reconstruction of political thinking. Especially since the Party central committee appealed for nationwide reform, the lamas under Party and government guidance, through conferences, classes and report meetings, current events conversations, and discussions in villages and pastures, and teaching on socialism, have been given widespread, deep, and systematic education in socialism. Through self-expression, bulletins, and debate, the following problems were clarified: Party guidance and walking the socialist path; racial amity; racial growth and prosperity; the cooperative plan in herding areas, and the policy of religious freedom and law-abiding patriotism. In clarifying knowledge, raising awareness, the ethical issues were defined, self-enemy lines were demarcated. On this foundation, they themselves exposed, condemned, and fought against lamaist bad characters who under the cloak of socialism worked against socialism. Thus, all the lamas in the ch'ü, like other people, in every way and place were educated in socialism.

Thus, most of them, entirely of their own free will, asked about joining a movement of dedication to the Party. From the end of June until now, incomplete figures show for the whole ch'ü, 1,588 lamas in the movement, trying to make it deep, thorough, true, and quick. Many lamas commented: The Communist Party is like father and mother, saving us for a new life; to respond to its kindness, we offer all our strength to serve in the building of socialism.

Through education in socialism and dedication to the Party, the lamas drew up programs for production and construction, for strict frugality, attention to health, eliminating the four pests, creating forests and so on; and for each man to have thought-reconstruction, take part in productive labor, learn modern culture and science, and get into social activities. Some lamas in the Hu-lun Pei-erh League laid down in the program that each man should take part in labor 200 days a year, most wanting to share in herding labor 300 days. They put these plans into challenges as between temples, and banners, and leagues, with responses; and they decided on regular inspection and comparison, so that the progressive might become more so and the backward catch up, all going forward together in a socialist leap forward.

DOC. 78. *Lamas in Chao-wu-ta League Participate in Increased Labor and Production*

Report from Jehol Province (1958)

EVER SINCE THE LAUNCHING of the cooperative movement and after having gone through socialist self-reform, the followers of Lamaism in the Chao-wu-ta League [Jehol Province, Inner Mongolia], have eagerly plunged themselves into the high tide of joining cooperatives and of taking part in labor production. The overwhelming majority of the 1897 lamas in the whole League have already joined the agricultural and livestock production cooperatives. For instance, of the 357 lamas in the Wang-nui-t'e District [i.e., a constituent unit of the league], 339, or over 94 percent, have joined livestock cooperatives. Again, among the 357 lamas, 340 have participated in physical labor and 10 others have taken part in mental labor, giving a total of 98 percent labor participation.

The 48 lamas of the Ta-ch'eng-tzu Temple in Ning-ch'eng Hsien have all joined cooperatives and have taken part in productive labor. And in the Pa-lin-yu District, where there has not yet been any fully organized cooperative movement, 52 percent of the lamas joined pastoral cooperatives. Those lamas who have not joined any cooperatives are undertaking physical labor in a Mutual Aid Group.

Some of the lamas have been elected chairmen of the cooperatives or group leaders, not only because they have positively joined the cooperatives and actively taken part in productive labor, but also because they have fulfilled leadership functions. . . .

Because of their participation in productive agricultural labor and an increase in income, the vast majority of the lamas have basically become self-supporters. For example, ever since the 79 lamas of the Hou-chao Temple in Pa-lin-tso District organized themselves into a Mutual Aid Group in 1956 they have stored surplus grain each year. In 1956 alone, in addition to their own consumption, they sold to the Government over 10,000 catties of grain. Meanwhile, because these 79 lamas have done an excellent job in planting and protecting trees, they as a group have been judged to be a model unit in forestry.

During the last three years, they have planted over 10,000 trees, pruned and protected more than 5,000 other trees in the mountains, and have experimented in planting fruit trees. They organized themselves into cooperatives this year (1958), and are planning to sell to the Government more than 20,000 catties of surplus grain by the end of this year.

Especially since the launching of the Leap-Forward Movement, lamas in all places have shown even greater enthusiasm in productive labor. For instance, every one of the 48 lamas in the Ta-ch'eng-tzu Temple in Ning-ch'eng Hsien has joined in physical labor. Among them, the younger ones are taking part in the construction of a water reservoir and the older ones are taking turns boiling drinking water day and night for those who construct the reservoir.

The aged lamas in the San-tso Society do not want to sit and enjoy the Government's five guarantees [i.e., food, clothing, housing, transportation and burial]. They have, through the help of the cooperatives, established for themselves a "Lama Paradise." This has been established entirely by the aged lamas who have security under the five guarantees, but all of them have voluntarily joined productive labor in the "Lama Paradise."

Among them, the sixty-four-year old lama, T'ieh, is in charge of raising bees and the duty of lama Ao Li-sheng is to feed hogs. Even the eighty-seven-year old lama, Cha-la-ssu-lai, will not sit idle. He voluntarily goes out to guard the houses of people who undertake productive labor elsewhere.

To increase production, a great many lamas, in addition to participating in collective productive labor, have learned to do supplementary production. For instance, over 90 percent of the 48 lamas of the Ta-ch'eng-tzu Temple have undertaken supplementary work. Some of them raise bees, others raise long-haired rabbits, and most of them have planted fruit trees.

Because the lamas have joined cooperatives and taken part in productive labor, their life has taken on a new meaning. Firstly, they have universally elevated the level of their political thought, accepted the leadership of the Party and the Government, and have strengthened their unity with the people.

Next, they have given up the traditional way of life which they enjoyed without having labored for it. In fact, they have truly become self-supporters because they have joined in productive labor and have increased their income. This not only has reduced the burden on the broad masses of people, but has also brought guarantees and protection to their own life. Especially since they have joined the cooperatives, a great many lamas who are of advanced age or physically weak have enjoyed the cooperatives' "five guarantees" in full, while others have enjoyed them in part.

DOC. 79. *Christian Women Contribute Labor, Kweiyang*
(1958)

Kweichow—Christian women in the churches of the city of Kweiyang celebrated the "March 8th Women's Day" in an unprecedented manner. On March 6, six of the women Christian workers went to the countryside and dug out three catties of maggots; on the 7th all of the Christian women took part in the patriotic sanitation big cleanup work; and on the 8th, with the exception of some of them who attended the Women's Day celebration, all the other Christian women in the city took positive action in their respective church activities which were centered on planting trees and eliminating the four pests. On the evening of the 9th, the Three-Self Patriotic Movement held a discussion meeting for Christian women to exchange their experiences in establishing in their families diligence and frugality and their understanding of the socialist speedy-progress movement. Chao Yu-kuang and Ma Wen-hsin, two of the five-superior positive elements made speeches on their accomplishments as woman models. Over fifty Christian women were present.

Also, these Christian women positively thrust themselves into a campaign which was to "make Kweiyang a city of four-absence through a ten-day bitter fight." Sister Liu Chu-ying alone led the masses and dug out more than seventy-two catties of maggots on the 12th. On the morning of the 14th over thirty Christian women joined one hundred and more other women of the religious circles and submitted to the Party five written pledges.

DOC. 80. *Yangchow Church Workers Build Cellulose Factory, Yangchow (Kiangsu) (1958)*

UNDER THE LEADERSHIP of the Religious Affairs Bureau in Yang-chow [Kiangsu Province], the Christian churches of the city held a joint meeting to discuss the establishment of a productive business. All of the people present at the meeting mobilized their thoughts and contributed their opinions. Finally, through debate, they decided to establish a cellulose factory, which would fulfill the requirement for an industry that would "produce more, bring more profit, employ more people, and [have] raw material readily available." They decided to build such a factory and named it the "Patriotic Cellulose Factory."

Through three mobilization meetings, the working spirit and determination to struggle of the whole city's patriotic Christians rose very high. Every one of them submitted personal letters of firm pledges, vowing to support and join the factory construction work with full effort. The slogan of the Christian masses was: "Those who have money contribute money, those who have strength contribute strength, and those who have material contribute material." Over 90 percent of the Christians contributed money for construction of the factory, in amounts according to their individual financial strength. Some of them offered their jewelry and articles of gold which they had valued and kept for years. Others said: "Although I have no money, if the factory needs anything which I have I will offer it immediately." Some folks over seventy years of age and busy housewives also voluntarily signed their names in the book as voluntary laborers. Others contributed on more than one occasion their brass, iron and tin articles. By such methods the problems of a construction fund, labor, and tools have basically been solved.

At present, our Technique-learning Group has gloriously accomplished their mission of learning how to make rush, hemp, and cotton products. And now, the members of the group in Ch'angchow are learning the techniques of spinning and weaving hemp.

Members of the Material-purchasing Group, in addition to busily supplying and transporting construction material to the factory site, have been rushing back and forth to T'aichow, Kaoyu, Paoying, Hsinghua, Wuhsi and nearby places to buy the major construction and supplementary materials.

The Labor-supply Group commands an army of long-term, alert, and voluntary laborers who work with special enthusiasm. Under the encouragement of the labor slogans: "Old but not weak," "Crippled but not useless," and "Do not retreat from the battle front if injured slightly," the great majority of Christian adults have . . . positively and selflessly joined in the labor. They transport bricks, pull wagons, carry water, and mix cement, like streams busily flowing without stop. Even when the weather is burning hot the number of volunteers working here has never been less than sixty daily. Our fellow Christian Fan Li-hua has well said it: "What we are doing is not only constructing a visible factory; it is also, in reality, a test of whether we Christians can stand such a labor."

At present, Christians of the entire city are speeding up the construction of the almost completed "Yangchow Patriotic Cellulose Factory" with the highest spirit and one hundred percent confidence. They guarantee that, with another twenty days' hard work, the factory will start production before the Mid-Autumn Festival and will salute the government with brand new hemp products on National Day [i.e., October 1st].

DOC. 81. *March Courageously on the Road to Socialism, Patriotic Speedy-Progress Mass Meeting, Chekiang (1959)*

Chekiang—The religious circles of Wenchow [Chekiang Province] held a patriotic speedy-progress mass meeting at 2 P.M., 3 April, in the Ch'engsi Church. Attending the meeting were over 1,200 representatives of the various religious bodies of whom more than 900 were Christians. The mass meeting showed the following slogans: "Surpass Ningpo, repress Hangchow, and battle against Shanghai; compare patriotism, contest progress, and purge the three poisons." The meeting was officially opened with the playing of military songs and the Reverend Hsieh Sheng-t'ao, Vice-chairman of the Interreligious Learning Committee, made an opening speech. In his speech, the Reverend Hsieh pointed out that since socialist construction had pushed forward the speedy-progress of production with a force that would move a mountain and overturn an ocean, the people of the religious circles must catch up with the tide and be its promoters, and each religion must mutually compare its patriotism and its progress in contests.

Liu Mei-chai, representing the Wenchow Metropolitan Christian Three-Self Patriotic Movement, read the speedy-progress plan. The plan sets forth, among other things, the following decisions: the Christians are determined to reach the goal of "the three nos"—no waste, no poison, and no confusion and unlawful activities—break down routine practices, eliminate bad habits, and exert efforts to achieve production progress; never hold services whole days on Sundays, but only on Sunday mornings; never hold meetings or conduct activities during the weekdays (services may be held on Sunday evenings for members who have productive work to do during the day time on Sunday); and never hold revival meetings or Sunday preaching in the rural districts.

It also declared that the Wenchow Metropolitan Christian Three-Self Patriotic Movement was determined to establish a pasture so that the Christian workers might strive to be self-supporting. The plan further provided for raising 200 rabbits, 2 milks goats and 2 milk cows in 1958; the goal for 1959 is 500 rabbits, 7 goats and 3 cows, and for 1960 is 1,000 to 1,500 rabbits, 20 goats, and 8 cows. Each Christian worker must labor more than 100 days in the pasture.

At the meeting the Reverend Hu Kui-yeh, and the Mssrs. P'an Yuan, Lu Li-min, Hsiao Ch'ing-yuan, Wang Ch'eng-hsin and others gave speeches, in which they expressed support for the proposals in the city's Christian Three-Self Patriotic Movement's plan, and accepted the challenge of the Methodist Church and unanimously insisted on comparing patriotism and contesting progress with members of that body.

Representatives of the other religious bodies also read their speedy-progress plans at the meeting.

The meeting also invited Director Wu of the Wenchow People's Committee's Bureau for Religious Affairs to make a speech. Finally, Chairman Hsieh Sheng-t'ao made a summary speech, mobilizing all the representatives to exercise their full energy, make up their minds, and prove their words with concrete actions. The meeting was concluded with the playing of military songs.

Section 11. Clergy Reform Through Labor and Study

PARTICIPATION IN MANUAL LABOR was long an important method for transformation of class viewpoint in Communist China. Even now (1970), in the aftermath of the Cultural Revolution, millions of educated urban youth are being shifted to labor assignments in the rural areas. In the post-Great Leap Forward period leaders and clergy of all religions took part in countless "socialist learning" sessions directed by Party cadres. These "Hand hearts to the Party" campaigns resulted in personal confessions, testimonies of personal transformation, and "patriotic compacts," which pledged personal and group support for socialist production, setting goals for productive labor by clergy and believers consonant with new proletarian points of view learned during political study.

In an eighty-two-day learning session in Chekiang over 100 Christian clergy "all voluntarily handed our hearts to the Party." Some, it was said, broke into tears during small-group discussions as they realized that they did not belong to the worker class but were "second-class exploiters" and "propertied class intellectuals." Manual labor was designed to break down class distinctions and lead to solidarity with the working people.

After sixty days of socialist learning in their monastery under Party leadership, Buddhists in Kiangsi corrected former "mistaken viewpoints." Through productive labor "the thoughts of the Buddhists in the Yun-chu Mountains have been liberated."

An ecumenical "Religious Circles Leap Forward Farm" in Shantung brought Moslem, Protestant, Catholic and other clergy together. Through farm labor, they said, they learned the value of labor and the necessity of self-discipline and reform through labor. Some said, "Labor has enabled us to experience more joy in life."

Yangchow Buddhists helped build a reservoir and discovered that labor, contrary to traditional Buddhist doctrine, was the greatest Buddhist virtue. A Shanghai pastor, moved to self-revelation by socialist learning, recognized his privileged background and determined to become a laborer in order truly to bear witness among workers.

DOC. 82. *A Buddhist "Lo-han Corps" Formed in Yun-chu Mountains to Support Agricultural and Industrial Production, Kiangsi Province (1958)*

FROM MAY 24 TO JULY 21, a period of sixty days, the whole body of Buddhists in the Yun-chu Mountains, Yung-hsiu Hsien, Kiangsi Province, undertook socialist learning in the monastery. During the learning session, the local Party and government organizations gave directions and support. Through free blooming, big debate, wall posters, and other methods, some of the mistaken viewpoints of these Buddhists were corrected. They were enabled to accept the leadership of the Party and the People's Government and understand its religious policy. On this basis, their political awareness has been elevated.

Through this learning session, all of these Buddhists have realized the great strength and power of our fatherland and have understood that because of the leadership of the Party the people of the whole nation have stood up on their own feet and have been liberated from political and economic bondage. They have come to understand that because of the shining light of the Party's main line it has been possible for our fatherland's industrial and agricultural construction to make flying progress. They have also realized that only under the leadership of the Party will it be possible for the 600,000,000 Chinese people, including the Buddhists themselves, to lead an increasingly happy life.

Through this learning session and on the basis of their political understandings, all of these Buddhists have joyfully signed a "Socialist Patriotic Compact." In this patriotic compact they have expressed their determination to support the leadership of the Party, to walk down the road to socialism, and to join actively in labor for agricultural production and for the conservation of trees in the Yun-chu Mountains.

In the compact they also expressed their determination to give help to the industrial and agricultural productions in the neighboring cooperatives and to undertake selfless labor for the nation's socialist construction.

Through productive labor, the thoughts of the Buddhists in the Yun-chu Mountains have been liberated and their working spirit has also been strengthened. In addition to their own labor for agricultural production and for planting and protecting trees, they have extended their help to their neighboring cooperatives.

For example, between July 28 and August 10, fifty of these Buddhist monks gave voluntary help to the Hsiang-chia-p'ing Cooperative in the Yun-chu Mountains in a race against time in harvesting and planting. The farming masses were grateful to them and awarded them a red banner and gifts. The farmers said: "In the past, the monks in the Yun-chu mountains only knew how to recite the scriptures. They even had to hire laborers to work in their fields. But today they are different, for they have given us great help."

In response to the call of the Yung-hsiu Hsien People's Committee to "Produce one million catties of charcoal each day to support the nation's steel production leap-forward campaign," these Buddhist monks organized a "charcoal producing corps" consisting of over sixty members. The members of this "Lo-han Corps" marched in a great procession to the Tiger's Valley in the Yun-chu Mountains. As soon as they set up their tents, some of them immediately went to cut trees on the mountainside while others began to build furnaces for burning wood into charcoal. Their working spirit became increasingly furious.

After struggling for thirteen days and nights, they built ten furnaces. Of the ten furnaces, two are big ones which produce 4,000 catties of charcoal per day and the other eight are small ones which altogether produce 2,000 catties of charcoal per day. They cut trees in the daytime and burn them into charcoal at night. Now they are crying another slogan: "We will build five more furnaces, produce more charcoal, and provide more fuel for steel production!"

DOC. 83. *Greatest Buddhist Work Is Taking Part in Voluntary Labor, Yangchow (1959)*

ON FEBRUARY 20 Yangchow religious circles proposed taking part in the labor of building the West Lake reservoir. This lake is a famous sight at Yangchow, formerly a poet's paradise, but now that the people are masters, it is being made a reservoir. When completed, it will prove very useful for irrigating paddies along the hills to the west. Yangchow's religious people readily responded to the local party's call, and proceeded to take part in this free glorious labor. These circles, including us Buddhists, enrolled eighty-one for short-time free labor. Fifteen days were allotted for digging and moving 400 kung fang of earth; in nine days 500 were finished, getting reward and praise from masses and officials. After this job, the Buddhists said: "In past days in the temples we moved water and fuel, burned incense and swept floors, worked at planting vegetables and trees, thinking to lay up happiness; now we know that 'purifying the land, solemnizing the land, enriching all life' are greater Buddhist works." So all considered that labor was the greatest virtue among Buddhists. A sixty-year-old woman Buddhist mendicant, vice-chairman of the Yangchow Buddhist Society, was the first to register for this job, and she worked hard at it; the chairman, an old monk Sung-t'ao, coming out to cheer the workers, began to carry earth and in spirit won the "hundred yard dash," boosting everybody. All asked to have part in any more such free labor, determined to seize the opportunity.

DOC. 84. *Tsinan Religious Personnel: Leap Forward Farm*
(1959)

EVER SINCE THEY VICTORIOUSLY accomplished their tasks of steel refining and coke making last year, the Christian ministerial personnel in the city of Tsinan [Shantung Province], under the leadership of the City Bureau for Religious Affairs, have quickly moved from the industrial front to the agricultural battle line. On February 3, 1959, under the enthusiastic support and encouragement of all the people in the city, the Christian ministers, Catholic priests, Islamic ahungs and others established a "religious circle leap forward farm."

The farm has an area of over seventy mou of hilly land. As soon as you walk into the farm you will see tender and green-leaved saplings neatly planted on every part of the land. After three years, these small trees will produce large quantities of plump apples. Since at the present time the trees are still young, we have made use of the land space between them to plant all sorts of high-productive crops suitable for growth on hilly land. On the lowest level, we have planted sorghum, corn, and vegetables.

On the mid-level we have planted millet, and on the higher level we have planted a vast area of cotton, sweet potatoes, peanuts, and a variety of melons and beans. We have also planted sunflowers, caster oil plants, medicinal herbs, and flower-grass on the edges of the farm, on the roadsides and on the sloping areas. In addition to these, we have a variety of sideline activities. At present we are raising more than 500 chickens, over 10 sheep and some rabbits. We are also planning to raise bees.

To better organize our productive power and mobilize for production, we have divided all of our comrades on the farm into four teams, each with a commander and an assistant commander. All of our farm land has also been divided among the four teams. Under the leadership of manager and assistant manager of the farm, each team takes its own necessary steps to guarantee a bumper production of their crops. To encourage the spirit of production, the farm has made some red banners. In the Autumn harvest season, the team which produces the most will win the red banners.

Although we feel quite pressed in our labor, all of our comrades have always kept a full working spirit and enthusiasm. At the beginning, all of us did positive work in accumulating manure and then deep ploughing the field. Now we have completed sowing and some of the seeds have already shot out tender sprouts. The faces of our comrades are daily becoming sunburnt and their hands stiff, but what we have gained are strong muscles and a joyful spirit. We feel truly happy, as if our hearts are blooming, especially when we see that the seeds which we have personally sowed are sprouting.

Aside from productive labor, we have three study sessions each week (including political and agricultural studies). In addition to the cultural and recreational activities which are carried on during our daily rest periods, we see movies once every month and learn to sing great leap forward songs regularly. We are truly enjoying a happy life and laboring happily.

We comrades of three different religious beliefs are united by one heart. We respect each other's religious belief and we enforce and learn from each other. We have set up a brilliant and glorious perspective before us. We have all said: "We want the people in the city of Tsinan to eat the big apples produced here on the Leap Forward Farm."

We have planted all kinds of flowers, grasses and trees on the roadsides in order to decorate our farm into a multicolor and beautiful garden. Some of our comrades have said: "The more we labor the more we love to labor. In the past when we said we wanted to construct our fatherland we were merely crying empty slogans, but now we have a farm and therefore an opportunity to contribute our strength. This is indeed the correct road on which we should walk!"

Through labor, all of us have come to feel more strongly about the preciousness of labor and the necessity of self-discipline and reform which is attainable through productive labor. From now on we must change the life of exploitation which we practiced in which we enjoyed things without laboring for them, and we must also change our strong capitalistic thinking and ways of doing things. Some of us have said: "Labor has enabled us to experience more joy in life."

The reason that we are able to achieve these great results is entirely due to the correct leadership of the Party. During the manure collection campaign, Director Ch'en Chung of the Tsinan Bureau for Religious Affairs personally pulled a wagonful of manure to our farm as a gift to us. This, plus his encouragement and concern about our labor, has deeply moved us. In a discussion meeting our comrades said: "We must labor hard and do a good job on the farm so as to repay the encouragement and concern of the Party and government officials."

DOC. 85. *Shanghai Pastor Reforms to Become a Laborer (1958)*

THE SHANGHAI ministerial personnel's socialist learning has been pushed continuously from one high tide to another. The socialist self-revolution has deepened its effect in the minds and souls of the individuals.

Through the implementation of the handing-hearts-to-the-Party movement, many fellow-workers were determined to break away from their old selves. During the periods of analysis and cricitism of their errors in thinking, words and deeds, they were faced with a basic problem: To which class do the Chinese clergy belong?

As an individual, I can not help thinking of my own family background and experiences. Both my grandmother and my grandmother-in-law were evangelists in American imperialist-controlled churches. Hence, my parents were "trained" by the imperialists, having attended missionary schools. My father, having worked for the church, was provided with an opportunity to go abroad. As for me, I have been brought up in missionary surroundings from the time I was a primary student until I completed college and theological education. During the whole process, I have never experienced any ups and downs in life. My abandoning of plans of "going abroad" was due to the liberation of the fatherland.

Upon completing my theological study, I worked at a so-called "self-supporting church" in a parish. The church was financed basically by the members of the exploiting class.

Soon, the three-anti and five-anti movements started. My church, like many other churches in Shanghai, had undergone periods of irregular developments. Some of the unlawful capitalists and frustrated elements came to the church in quest of "consolation." At that time, I sympathized with them and often preached to them on "peace." In return, they presented me with extra "gifts" during festivals.

What I depended on in the past were imperialists and the exploiting class. The imperialists had robbed China of wealth and sucked the blood and sweat of the Chinese people; whereas the exploiting class had exploited and suppressed the laboring people. But in the past, I clung to them, sharing their gains through exploitation. Actually, by doing so I had become a member of the exploiting class. I feel ashamed whenever I think of this.

Now I am working in the headquarters of the Episcopal Church. The education I received from both the Party and the Three-Self movement over the past years has encouraged me to contribute voluntarily my share to the fatherland. However, what I have been able to do is indeed too little when compared with the contribution from the laboring people on various fronts. This is especially true in the face of today's great leap forward in socialist construction, in industrial and agricultural production and in the developments in medicine, communications, commerce, and education. I have not contributed to these achievements but have enjoyed the achievements of the people. I am deeply ashamed of myself.

The light of the great socialist education has dawned on me. If the church wants to walk down the socialist road, it must reform its previous financial dependence on the exploiting class. If the ministerial personnel want to walk on the socialist road, they must reform their ideological stand and participate in labor, thereby enabling themselves to be members of the laboring people. Only by doing so can we contribute our share to the construction of the great socialist mission of our fatherland, and exert our effort toward the well-being of the people. Likewise, only by so doing can we truly bear witness among the laboring people.

Our Lord, Jesus Christ, was a carpenter. Peter and John were both fishermen. They were all brought up as laboring people. Historically, reform movements were brought up from the church's low level. Participants in these movements frequently were people who had lived through a collective laboring life. The leaders did not depend on others for their livelihood. But whenever the church mingled with the exploiting class, ministerial personnel built their enjoyment on the sufferings of the laborers, thus separating themselves from the people. Henceforth, as laborers, we not only are enabled to be worthy of the socialist age but also are loyal to the primitive and pure religious life. I want to be a vanguard in the socialist construction, and also a labor-loving preacher.

DOC. 86. *To What Social Class Does a Preacher Belong? (1958)*

THESE ARE TWO LETTERS written to the Protestant magazine *T'ien Feng* in 1958 in response to the editors' request for comments on the question, "To what social class does a preacher belong?"

Seeing the Preacher's Social Class Through the Hand-the-Heart-to-the-Party Campaign of the Christian Workers in Chekiang Province—by Hao

RECENTLY, OVER ONE HUNDRED ministerial personnel of Christian churches in Chekiang province held an eighty-two-day socialist education-discussion meeting in Hangchow. To better reform our political stand, at the meeting all of us voluntarily handed our hearts to the Party and drafted our personal concrete plans for speeding up self-reform, so that we might catch up with the present-day trend of the speedy-progress movement and serve the cause of socialist enterprise.

At the meeting, we gained an important understanding through handing our hearts to the Party. It is that we came to a profound realization, through the black hearts we handed to the Party, of the evil and repulsiveness of our original capitalistic nature. At small-group discussions, some fellow workers burst into tears and confessed how in the past they had returned goodness with hatred, and thought or did many things which were offensive to the Party and the people. It was on the basis of this understanding that these Christian leaders firmly made up their minds to speed up the reform of their class stand.

Before the "Hand-the-Heart-to-the-Party" Campaign, we had been unclear about the fact that the ministerial personnel belonged to the propertied class. During our discussion on the report of comrade Liu Shao-ch'i, which he had made at the Second Session of the "Eighth National Congress" of the Chinese Communist Party, in which he mentioned that there were two laboring classes and two exploiting classes in China, some fellow workers thought that the ministerial personnel belonged to the laboring class. They declared: "We come from families of poor farmers"; "We do not own any store and we do not rent our land"; "We have no property and we live a hard life." Others said: "Among our church members many are working people and we are their servants"; and still others remarked, "In the past we were above politics and did not belong to any class." It was only after we had handed our hearts to the Party and through debate that we began to see clearly that the ministerial personnel do not belong to the class of the workers, nor do they belong to that of the farmers or any other laboring people (with the exception of a few of the voluntary preachers who are farmers by profession), but are the intellectuals of the propertied class and are second-class exploiters of the exploiting class through and through.

Here I wish to explain this question from three angles:

*1. Seeing the Preacher's Propertied-class
Nature Through His Family Line, Education,
Thought, and His Affection*

THE ORIGIN OF Christian preachers is very complex. Some of them came from the families of the landlords and rich farmers, others from those of the capitalists, and still others are members of the lower propertied class. It is even easier to see the political faces of those people who have been traitors, officials and reactionary military leaders, and who have taken the profession of preachers during the political changes in the past.

Some co-workers have said: "I came from the family of a poor farmer or working man. I led a hard life when I was young and suffered exploitation by the landlords or capitalists." We cannot deny that among the preachers there are many who have come from the families of poor farmers, working men or other types of poverty-stricken people. But these preachers are those who, after having received a slave education from the propertied class and, especially, from the imperialists, have revolted against their own original class, have followed the imperialists, the feudalists and the bureaucratic capitalists, and have been exploiters, solely serving the interests of these three classes of big enemies. They are the same as those of the propertied class and their thoughts and affections have long been different from those of the people. Though they visit the laboring people in their homes, they dislike them as being filthy. Many preachers considered going to a seminary and becoming "a preacher" as an escape from labor production and as a good opportunity for "promotion." This so-called "promotion" is in reality a revolt against their own working class and an embracing of the propertied class. Their class status has thus been changed.

The preachers' change of class status has intimate relations with the kind of education they have received. Our co-workers, in addition to receiving a general education of the propertied class, have received a special and profound slave-education which the imperialists have given them through Christian schools and theological seminaries.

While handing out his heart [to the Party], a young minister said that in the past he was once a shop clerk and was bitterly hateful of the owner and opposed to his exploitation of all his employees. But after he became a minister, he naturally came over to the propertied class and has ever since been sympathetic with all the shop owners. The reason why he has thus revolted against his own class is because he has received the imperialists' slave education.

2. Seeing the Preacher's Exploiting Nature Through the Sources of His Income

IN THE PAST, the majority of church workers in China depended on the imperialists' financial support for their livelihood. The salaries of some of them were provided entirely by the imperialists, while others, claiming to be self-supporting, were in reality financially supported by the imperialists through a variety of ways. Take the Church of Christ in China as an example. After the Sino-Japanese war, the preachers of its churches throughout the nation were without exception receiving money from the Restoration Fund, the Child Education Fund, the Medical Fund, the House Repairing Fund and other such funds set up by the imperialists. Aside from these, they also received relief goods and the little favors and gifts which the missionaries were accustomed to give. These are also the reasons why the thoughts and affections of the preachers have been attached to the exploiting class.

In addition to these financial sources, the livelihood of preachers in the cities had another source, namely, that from the propertied class and its intellectuals. The trustees, deacons, elders, and treasurers of the church were mostly these people. The Board of Trustees of the Episcopal Church in Ningpo was in the past always controlled by four capitalists, of whom one was a compradore, one a member of a special agent's family, and the other two were all counterrevolutionaries. The ministers were thus always in the company of these reactionary and exploiting elements, bowing to them, serving them, and listening to their commands.

In the past, preachers in the rural area depended mostly on the landlords and rich farmers for their financial support. It was very seldom that a poor farmer could become a deacon, an elder, or a treasurer of the church. Many church buildings were "contributed" by the landlords and rich farmers. Other churches depended on the money of the landlords and wealthy farmers which they obtained through hoarding and monopolizing of goods, lending money on usury, and through buying and selling. The church of Ta-t'ung-ch'iao in Chia-shan Hsien is an example. It is precisely because of this reason that, during the land-reform, the masses called the minister of that church the tail of the landlords. Some churches were entirely the territory of the landlords. For instance, among the members of the Ch'ien-hsiang Christian Meeting Place in Tung-yang Hsien there were more than 20 landlords. The congregation of the Nan-hung Methodist church in Hai-chen Hsien always held their meetings in the house of a landlord and the church's finance was also supported by him. After the land-reform the meeting was moved to the house of a wealthy farmer. The minister of that church thus completely became property of the exploiting class.

There are other preachers who once owned materials for production and undertook direct exploitation, such as holding shares in shops, buying stocks, and doing speculative business. In the rural area, some preachers even bought land and collected rent on it, others lent money on usury. A minister of the Episcopal Church in Fu-yang Hsien, in addition to receiving subsidies from the imperialists, acted as a landlord to rent out his land and lend rice on 50 percent interest. There are many more preachers who used to live such a life.

3. Seeing the Preacher's Class Nature Through the People Whom He Serves

DURING THE TIME when we were handing our hearts to the Party, our co-workers cited many examples showing how in the past they had served three classes of enemies and the exploiting class. Here I mention only a few of them:

(A) A great many preachers were bitterly hateful of themselves because they had in the past served the imperialists and the reactionary government. They said in those days that their evangelistic work in the prison was no more than spreading the "merits" of the reactionary government. At the time when the members of the Kuomintang were withdrawing from Tinghai Hsien, the local preachers collected contributions for them and consoled them with kind words. When Chiang Kai-shek withdrew to Fenghua, there were some preachers in Ningpo who made a special trip to preach to him and asked him to sign his autograph. A certain so-called evangelistic band which had long claimed to be transcending politics also went to join the procession to "welcome" him. And during the war of liberation, all the preachers offered prayers to God that the liberation army might not cross the Yangtze River.

(B) Many preachers admitted that in the past they had consistently taken the people of the propertied class the landlords, and the wealthy farmers as their main objects of service. During the new year's day or other holidays they would hold thanksgiving services for these people and bless them. But they had insisted that those poor and laboring Christians should love others without regard to principles and taught that troubles and difficulties were blessings, often citing the story of Lazarus to persuade them to endure hardships. By doing so these preachers were causing the exploited to forget their troubles and give up the class struggle.

(C) There were also a number of preachers who told how, after the liberation, they had expressed sympathy for the landlords, the wealthy farmers, and the people of the propertied class during all the campaigns, crying out that these people were wronged and giving them encouragement. A woman evangelist said that, during the land reform, when she saw that some Christian landlords were undergoing reform through labor in the field, she and the other Christian women who were with her passing by the field began to sing: "In the world ye shall have tribulation: but be of good cheer; I have overcome the world" (John 16:33). They purposely let the landlords hear these words and receive comfort.

Another preacher said that during the land reform, he returned the furniture articles of the landlords which had been distributed to him, saying: "These are ill-gotten gains, I cannot keep them." Still another preacher returned the rice which he had paid to the landlord as rent but the landlord was ordered to reduce and return. During the Three-Anti and the Five-Anti Movements, a great many of the preachers defended the capitalists and some of them preached on the Book of Job to comfort and encourage them. These have all shown that the preachers were all standing on the side of the exploiting class and serving its interests.

In short, through this Hand-the-Heart-to-the-Party Campaign, our co-workers thoroughly analyzed and clearly understood the question of their being in the exploiting class in the past. Their decision for reforming their stand was, therefore, a very earnest one. In addition to their determination for learning, all of them were willing to take part in labor production, adopting the thoughts and affections of the laboring people through labor, and to serving them.

The Preacher is an Exploiter—by Hsin K'uo

To WHAT SOCIAL CLASS does a preacher belong? This is a question whose clear answer is what many of the preachers urgently need to know.

Some preachers are extremely indignant when people call them exploiters. They feel that although they have not directly taken part in labor production, they work hard for the church, serve the Christian masses, and should not be called exploiters. They ask: Are we not public servants like the government cadres and school teachers? Thus they refuse to admit that they are exploiters.

Some of them have even said: "We have no land and house property, neither do we have materials for production. We are 100 percent proletariats and belong to the proletarian class."

There has thus been a variety of opinions and the question cannot be clearly answered. Now I wish to state some of my own humble opinions and discuss them with the readers:

1. Like the other intellectuals, the preachers are not a class by themselves. They are attached to a certain class, living on it, are trained by it, and are serving the interests of it.

In the past, the church was controlled by the imperialists and the people of the propertied class. Preachers in those days were naturally attached to the imperialists and the people of the propertied class and serving their interests. After the liberation, the imperialists were driven out of China and the Chinese church also cut ties with them, but the church was fallen entirely into the hands of the bourgeoisie.

Although most of the members of the city church were laboring people, the bourgeoisie being in the minority, the majority of the church deacons, elders, trustees, and committee members were nevertheless rich and propertied-class people. The important business, policies, and ways of carrying them out were all controlled and decided by the people of the propertied class. The preachers were always obedient to these people and followed their footsteps. In their preaching, they always pleased the propertied-class people and defended their interests, beautifying and legalizing their exploiting activities and saying their properties were the blessings of God. In visiting their church members, they naturally went more times to the homes of the propertied-class Christians, but very few times to those of the laboring ones. Therefore, the preachers were always serving the interests of the propertied-class people.

The control of the rural church by the landlords was similar to the monopoly of the city church by the propertied-class people. In the past, preachers in the rural area were attached to the class of the landlords and were serving their interests.

2. Next, let us see what type of education the preachers have received. In the past, all the schools were the places where the ruling class trained its slaves and servants. Therefore, once even a son of a laboring man entered school and received such slave-education, his thoughts and affections would gradually undergo change and would eventually revolt against his own class, with his mind filled the thoughts of the people of the propertied class. The large majority of preachers received their education from such schools and accepted such thoughts. Some of the preachers

have even received their training from Christian schools and theological seminaries, which were established by the imperialists as tools of cultural aggression, and have been deeply poisoned by the imperialists. For this reason, their stand, thoughts and viewpoints are necessarily those of the exploiting class.

3. Finally, let us look at the preachers' way of life: The laboring people leave for work at dawn and come home after dark. They produce wealth and serve the people all day long. The preachers, on the contrary, are free, unorganized, and are idle all the time. They have no discipline of work and their livelihood depends on support from their church members through contributions. The preachers thus gain without labor and sit to enjoy the fruits of others. Even up till now, there are churches which sustain themselves through collection of house rent and undertake exploitation.

From the actual way of life of the preachers, we can see that they are exploiters who either gain without laboring for it at all, or gain more with less labor. Seeing the situation from the three above angles, we know that preachers have been educated and trained by the imperialists and the people of the propertied class, have attached themselves to them, and have faithfully served their interests. We conclude, therefore, that preachers belong to the exploiting class. To thoroughly reform ourselves, we must demand opportunities for physical labor.

Section 12. Religion and the Cultural Revolution

THE OPENING SECTION of the August, 1966, *Decision of the Chinese Communist Party Central Committee Concerning the Cultural Revolution* defined the terms and made clear the aims of the campaign which closed the schools, turned against countless Party functionaries, challenged the assumptions and style of the educational and cultural sectors, and called on the people to "transform the spiritual aspect" of society by discarding surviving remnants of tradition and creating an entirely new proletarian culture. While religion is not specified among the "four olds" under attack, it evidently was seen as part of the "superstructure which is incompatible with the socialist economic base," for all places of religion were forcibly closed by roving bands of Red Guard militants in the fall of 1966. Red Guards also invaded the homes of believers, destroying religious scriptures, art, and literature, and harassing believers. Aside from a single mosque used by foreign Moslem visitors in Peking, until 1971 no evidence pointed to the survival of any public practice of religion throughout China.

At the same time no official policy statement either supporting or nullifying the constitutional guarantee of freedom of religious belief has been issued. In fact almost nothing on religion has appeared in the Chinese press since 1966. The Red Guard attack on the Confucian scholars (Doc. 99) came in 1967, and the Red Guard posters (Doc. 96–98) date from that year as well.

Four attacks on alleged Soviet accommodation with Christianity appeared inexplicably, and without reference to the domestic scene in China, in the Chinese press at the height of the Sino-Soviet border confrontation in 1969. In the midst of his bitter attack on Soviet revisionist collusion with Christianity, however (in Doc. 100), the *Red Flag* writer reiterates the standard guarantee of freedom of religious belief, quoting Chairman Mao rather than the constitution: "All believers in Protestantism, Catholicism, Islamism, Buddhism, and other faiths enjoy the protection of the people's government as long as they are abiding by its laws."* In his own words the writer continues, "We consistently advocate protection of the freedom of religious belief and the freedom of not believing in religion." Paradoxically, he repudiates idealism, monasticism, and "all kinds of religious superstition."

DOC. 87. *An Australian Observes the Cultural Revolution (I)*

A NUMBER OF FOREIGN VISITORS to China during the Cultural Revolution raised questions about religion with Chinese in casual encounters. Invariably the questions provoked amusement or firm testimonials to the secular faith of the new China. Neale Hunter, a young Australian English teacher in China 1965–67 recounts his experience.

WHILE VISITING the famous White Horse Temple in Loyang with a group of foreigners, a monk was questioned, through interpreters:

"And what do you monks do with your time?"
"We work in the field," he replied. "And we meditate."
"Meditate?" asked one of the foreigners. "What do you meditate on?"
The monk did not hesitate:
"I, myself," he said, "am working on the problem of *who* eats when *I* eat, *who* talks when *I* talk."

* Doc. 100.

This answer, which would be perfectly comprehensible to Buddhists anywhere in the world, was the source of much embarrassed and apologetic amusement among the interpreters— Shanghai students brought up almost entirely under the new regime. At first, they said the monk's words were unintelligible. When some of the foreigners insisted on a translation, they gave one but made it clear that such ideas were completely strange to them.

DOC. 88. *An Australian Observes the Cultural Revolution (II)*

AT ANOTHER BUDDHIST MONASTERY Hunter asked their guide, a woman who was obviously bored with lofty halls filled with gilded religious figures, what she thought of it all.

"BUDDHA BELONGS to the past. He has nothing to do with our society today."

I took the plunge and disagreed with her, suggesting that the word Buddha simply meant 'enlightened one,' and was a name for a person who understood all things with perfect clarity.

"Why," I went on, "Chairman Mao, if you like, is a kind of Buddha."

She swung round on me then, with a look of utter horror on her face, and snapped:

"Chairman Mao and Buddha have nothing whatever in common!"

DOC. 89. *An Englishman Observes the Cultural Revolution*

IN 1967, A BRITISH VISITOR to the People's Republic of China reported a conversation with his guide-interpreter as they walked down a mountain in Shantung Province.

I MENTIONED HOW much I enjoyed the stillness and the beauty of the view from the old Buddhist monastery we had just visited. "It is a monastery no more. It belongs to the people," she said. This was very true; hundreds were enjoying it.

"I wonder what contribution Buddhism has shown us from Universal Truth," I asked. "None," she declared. "Only Chairman Mao understands Universal Truth." Could not the Buddhist philosophy have taught us something about inner peace, or the principle of non-violence? "Certainly not. Revolution is our aim and purpose." The mountain was not as still as it had been.

Surely, I suggested, is not Love fundamental to Universal Truth, the love of God for men and man for man.

"When I first went to school and was very young, I believed in universal love. But I have learned better. There is no such thing. For instance, I hate . . . I hate the Top Party Person in authority taking the capitalist road. I hate all bosses, landowners, and reactionaries. . . ."

"But you do not believe in trying to think well of a person even if you do not see eye to eye with him, and even if you think there is something wrong in his nature or outlook?" This was impossible. To hate the sin and love the sinner was Western deviationism. . . .

DOC. 90. *A Japanese Observes the Cultural Revolution*

ANOTHER VISITOR, a Japanese journalist, describes a picture series displayed in the People's Art Museum in Peking, depicting Army rescue operations after an earthquake in Hopei Province. One picture, with an explanatory caption, shows an old woman destroying a statue of a boddhisattva.

WHEN THE EARTHQUAKE occurred, it was not the Buddhist saint but Mao Tse-tung who helped her. The old woman realized that the Buddhist saint did nothing for her. The next picture showed her destroying the old charm to give place to a portrait of Mao

Tse-tung, and a new portrait of smiling Mao in military uniform was hung in the old family Buddhist shrine. The next picture showed a soldier feeding an old blind woman, with a caption reading, "The warm sentiment of the class excels mother-and-child love." The picture was followed by a poem to praise Mao Tse-tung, which was composed by a girl.

> If you do not study Chairman Mao's writing for a day,
> The food will not taste good and the night will be unsleepable.
> If you do not study Chairman Mao's writing for two days,
> You will feel as though your eyes are being covered with scales.
> If you do not study Chairman Mao's writing for three days,
> You will be lost in direction and your mind will be dim.

DOC. 91. *Decision of the CCP Central Committee Concerning the Great Proletarian Cultural Revolution*

1. *A New Stage of the Socialist Revolution*

THE CURRENT GREAT PROLETARIAN cultural revolution is a great revolution that touches people to their very souls, representing a more intensive and extensive new stage of the development of socialist revolution in our country.

At the Tenth Plenary Session of the Eighth Central Committee of the Party, Comrade Mao Tse-tung said: In order to overthrow a political regime, it is always necessary to prepare the public opinion and carry out work in the ideological field in advance. This is true of the revolutionary class as well as of the counter-revolutionary class. Practice proves that this assertion of Comrade Mao Tse-tung is entirely correct.

Although the bourgeoisie have been overthrown, yet they attempt to use the old ideas, old culture, old customs, and old habits of the exploiting classes to corrupt the mind of man and conquer his heart in a bid to attain the goal of restoring their rule. On the other hand, the proletariat must squarely face all challenges of the bourgeoisie in the ideological sphere, and use its own new ideas, new culture, new customs, and new habits to transform the spiritual aspect of the whole society.

At present, our aim is to knock down those power holders who take the capitalist road, criticize the bourgeois reactionary academic "authorities," criticize the ideologies of the bourgeoisie and all exploiting classes, reform education and literature and the arts, and reform all superstructure which is incompatible with the socialist economic base in order to facilitate the consolidation and development of the socialist system.

DOC. 92. *Red Guard Paper: Reject Revisionist Religious Superstition, Hung Wei Pao (Red Guard News) (March 9, 1967)*

. . . CHAIRMAN MAO teaches us we must never forget the dictatorship of the proletariat, never forget class struggle. However, the revisionists wipe out the concept of class nature, agitate for "humanitarian ethics," "freedom," "universal love," so-called "humanism," "peace," and "don't repay evil with violence." But we affirm that "there was never a savior of the world, nor do we rely on a 'sacred dragon' or emperor. To build up happiness for all mankind we must rely entirely on ourselves." Moreover, the revisionists disseminate the so-called metaphysics of "god-and-devil," "heaven-and-hell" to dissipate the will for struggle of the people.

Whatever we destroy, whatever we establish, whatever we criticize, whatever we carry forward, we never depart from the position of the proletarian masses, we never leave the class viewpoint of Marxism-Leninism. We must destroy whatever is unprofitable to the people; whatever benefits the people must be established. Without this, how can we carry forward our culture? Can it be that the proletarian revolutionary faction can both criticize and perpetuate the religious superstitions of the exploiting class? [The answer is] no!

DOC. 93. *Red Guard Paper: Old Feudalist (Canton Mayor Tseng Sheng), August First Combat Newspaper (August 14, 1967)*

THIS "OLD LORD" mayor customarily shows a progressive public image, constantly warning others to root out feudalistic thoughts, but his own mind is filled with such things. He is quite completely an old feudalist. In 1962 his mother was gravely ill, so he quickly called Chang Shou-yang, Director of Civilian Affairs, and the secretary of the Municipal People's Council, requesting them to order a good coffin to be made. But he still was uneasy, so he himself went to the coffin shop to supervise the work. After his mother died he heard that the reconstruction project at the Culture Park had some very good lumber, so he decided against the coffin already made, and specially ordered another instead in order to give his mother a beautiful resting place in "hades" (*yin chien*). To demonstrate his filial piety he also asked someone to beautify her cosmetically, to put on gold earrings, gold rings, and several sets of new clothing before burial. This filial son then burned incense and candles and kowtowed in worship before the altar of his mother. He also held a service for her. He still felt he had not sufficiently shown gratitude toward his mother, so each year at Ching Ming Festival all his family members went out in government cars to sweep the grave. This truly is the ultimate in filial piety! In 1964, on the pretext of visiting the old revolutionary bases, he returned to the family home, climbed the mountain to worship at his father's grave, and held a ceremony at the grave site and prayed. Who would think that a Communist mayor in fact is one who holds to "heaven's grace and ancestors' virtue" (*t'ien en tsu te*)!

DOC. 94. *Red Guard Paper: Tao Chu, Chief of the South-Central Bureau, Promotes the Capitalist Counter-revolutionary Line, Hung Wei Pao (Red Guard News) (January 22, 1967)*

DURING THE CULTURAL REVOLUTION Tao Chu and the South-Central Bureau published "Ideas Concerning Certain Questions During the Cultural Revolution" (July 21, 1966). These "ideas" dealt with public policy during the "four clean-up" period, and policy to be followed during the Cultural Revolution. One of these items deals with religious policy.

. . . ON JULY 15 [according to *Hung Wei Pao*] Tao Chu said, "For the time being don't interfere with religion, and don't touch cultural relics. Since the question of religion is quite confused, we should not open this battlefront at the leadership level at this time. We should pay attention to 'Don't destroy cultural relics.' If necessary, they can be [protectively] sealed off. The demand of the masses to completely get rid of these must be delayed to the end of the campaign. After investigation and authorization, then they can be dealt with."

From the above facts, the people can easily see that the South-Central Bureau's "ideas" are by the representatives of the capitalist, counter-revolutionary line, and are controlled and plotted from behind the curtain by Tao Chu. . . .

DOC. 95. *Red Guard Paper: The Spiritual Life of a Despotic Southern Chief, Hung Ch'i P'in Hsia Chung Nung (Red Flag Poor and Lower-middle Peasant) (October 1, 1967)*

THIS WRITER ATTACKS Tao Chu for the feudal style, and for promoting the personal image of Tao Chu. For example, it is said that he had four words in his own calligraphy duplicated three stories high at the site of a new reservoir, at a cost of JMP 1,000 each.

"Tao Chu and the 'God of White Eyebrows'" [*Pai Mei T'ai Kung*]

. . . AT THE TIME OF THE "four clean-ups" (1964–65) "Robber" Tao ordered the remodelling of Lo Feng Monastery, insincerely instructing them to throw out all of the buddha figures except "Pai Mei T'ai Kung." "Pai Mei T'ai Kung" was a Sung Dynasty high-ranking official and big tyrant named Chung. But Tao said, "This old ancestor should be protected." This kind of love for a feudal bureaucratic despot, and this kind of hate for the poor and lower-middle peasants, precisely expose his class nature.

DOC. 96. *Anti-Buddhist Red Guard Posters*

TWO WALL POSTERS displayed at Lu-yung Buddhist Temple in Canton demanded that the temple cease to function as a religious institution. One poster, which proposed that the government should confiscate the temple for use as a "Red Guard Kindergarten," said:

> Why should socialist Canton tolerate the existence of this feudal and superstitious Lu-yung Temple? Why use such spacious ground to house those dead wooden idols? The revolutionary action of the Red Guards in pulling down those dead wooden idols is indeed most pleasing.

Authors of the other poster preferred that the temple should be assigned to the Chien-hsin Cardboard Box Makers. They also recalled how in 1965 the Cardboard Box Company had, "by means of productive labor reform, helped transform the Buddhist monks of Lu-yung Temple into 'new men under socialism'" and suggested that now the use of the monks' labor for the company's production purposes should be intensified.

DOC. 97. *Anti-Moslem Red Guard Posters*

POSTERS WERE SEEN in Peking in autumn 1966 calling for the abolition of Moslem customs. One poster proposed that the authorities should:

Close all mosques;
Disperse [religious] associations;
Abolish Koran study;
Abolish marriage within the faith;
Abolish circumcision.

Another poster listed a ten-point program for the eradication of Islam. Included were:

Immediate abolition of all Islamic organizations in China;
Moslem priests must work in labor camps;
Moslem burial practice must be replaced by cremation;
Abolish observance of all Moslem feasts and holidays.

DOC. 98. *Anti-Christian Red Guard Poster: To All Catholics, Protestants, Buddhists, and Moslems, Reported by an Australian Observer in Peking (August, 1966)*

ANOTHER POSTER WAS ADDRESSED to all "Catholics, Protestants, Buddhists, and Moslems," and started off, "You rolling eggs, religious people," going on to accuse them of deceiving the people, sheltering spies, and opposing Chairman Mao's thought. Outside a Catholic church I found an exhibition of anti-Christian propaganda, showing missionaries as the vilest of hypocrites. In one of the few instances I encountered of direct rudeness I was told by a surly youth to move on, as the pictures on the wall were "China's internal affair."

DOC. 99. *Respect for Confucian Virtues Is Now a Crime: What Poison Was Spread by Monsters and Demons at the Forum on Confucius, Jen-min Jih-pao (People's Daily) (January 10, 1967)*

UP TO THE TIME of the Cultural Revolution Confucius and his teachings had shakily survived the socialist remolding of man and society. In 1966–67 Red Guards locally attacked the Confucian heritage with the same vigor directed to the uprooting of all "olds." Red Guard critics, in this document, went back five years to a "Forum on Confucius" held at that time, defining the wrong thinking of the Confucian scholars. Their crimes? They called for "benevolent government," "respect for others," "love of people," "improving human relationships," and "doing to others as you would be done by." The scholars' stress on individualism—"When individuals live in harmony, without deceiving each other but forgiving one another, then there is a state of loving and supporting"—was anathema to the Red Guards. Their reply: "The struggle between [classes] is a life-and-death struggle—totally devoid of the idea of 'loving one another.'"

1. The Confucian "Demons"

FOR MORE THAN TWO THOUSAND YEARS, China's reactionary ruling classes regarded Confucius as what they called a "holy man" and consistently tried to use the reactionary concepts of Confucius to deceive and fool laboring people in order to maintain and consolidate their rule. Thus Confucian ideas became heavy spiritual fetters imposed on the working people.

After the whole country was liberated, the overthrown exploiting classes together with their agents in the revolutionary camp sought to regain their lost "paradise." To do so, they tried in every possible way to uphold and spread the old ideas and the old culture of the feudal classes in the ideological domain; thus they allowed emperors, kings, generals, ministers, scholars, and beauties to dominate our cultural scene.

At the "Forum on Confucius," counter-revolutionary revisionist elements, teaming up with reactionary bourgeois "authorities," openly advocated the idea of "showing reverence to Confucius and reviving that which is ancient." This big crime is being committed by them with the aim of restoring capitalism in China. In our Socialist new China, there is absolutely no room for Confucian concepts and capitalist and revisionist ideas which serve the exploiting classes. If these ideas are not uprooted, it will be impossible to consolidate the dictatorship of the proletariat and build Socialism and Communism. In the great proletarian cultural revolution, one of our important tasks is to pull down the rigid feudal corpse of Confucius and eradicate thoroughly the completely reactionary Confucian concepts.

As the vanguard for destroying Confucian ideas, some young Red Guard fighters—with the close cooperation of the broad masses of workers, peasants, and soldiers—have achieved considerable results in this regard. Let us hold high the great red banner of the thought of Mao Tse-tung and hit hard at a small handful of persons in power within the Party who are taking the capitalist road, pull them down and completely discredit them. Let us sweep away all the old ideas, old culture, old customs, and old habits of the exploiting classes and throw them into the garbage heap of history.

In the high tide of the great proletarian cultural revolution, we of the Chingkangshan Combat Group of Red Guards in the study of *The Thoughts of Mao Tse-tung*, Peking Normal University—cherishing the determination to protect Chairman Mao, safeguard his great thought, and foster his ideology as absolutely authoritative—set out for Chufou, Shantung [Confucius's birthplace], to rebel against the old feudal den of Confucianism. Because Confucius was the patriarch of the completely reactionary scholars of the Confucian school, our class enemies have always tried to make use of the idea of "showing reverence to Confucius and reviving what is ancient" to bring about a counter-revolutionary restoration.

In the seventeen years since liberation, the overthrown exploiting classes have never for a moment stopped trying to influence public opinion in order to achieve the object of restoring capitalism.

The "Forum on Confucius" was a big rally for openly and wantonly shaping public opinion in favor of launching a counter-revolution. . . .

Those monsters and demons who attended the "Forum on Confucius" blatantly advocated what they called "benevolent government" and "rule by moral virtues" to attack the Socialist system and the dictatorship of the proletariat, apart from openly provoking a counter-revolutionary restoration. They shouted at the tops of their voices, saying: "Those who are benevolent love people." They also remarked: "Confucius practiced benevolence with all the people in mind. If people put into practice the moral virtues of benevolence and righteousness as expounded by Confucius, there will be no strife on earth. People living peacefully do not deceive or guard against one another. They are tolerant of one another, loving and supporting each other."

Chairman Mao said long ago: "There is no such thing in the world as love or hate without reason or cause. With regard to so-called human love, there has been no such unified love since mankind was divided into classes. In the past all ruling classes were fond of promoting this concept. Many so-called saints and sages also did the same thing. However, so far no one has ever truly done so, because in a class society this is impossible."

Evaluating those monsters and demons in terms of what Chairman Mao has said, we can see that the object of their advocating "benevolent government" and "rule by moral virtues" is to blur the class boundary and resolve class contradictions. What they have drummed up is nothing but a copy of Khrushchev revisionism—"the Party of all the people" and "the State of all the people." Openly attacking the dictatorship of the proletariat for not being "benevolent," monsters and demons attending the forum talked rubbish, declaring that the proletarian dictatorship "has intentionally or unintentionally violated other people's survival." These elements of the bourgeois rightists have considered using "benevolence" to cause the disintegration of our proletarian dictatorship. This is as impossible as "ants trying to shake a big tree, only to find they have overreached themselves ridiculously." In no way can we give "benevolent government" to our class enemies. We can only permit them to behave themselves and prohibit them from saying and doing anything as they please. If they do so, we shall immediately stop and repress them. . . .

II. The Confucian Debate

To LET THE PUBLIC see clearly the vicious counter-revolutionary characteristics of these people, a few samples of their reactionary fallacies are given below:

The Confucian Scholars said:

The word "greatness" can be applied to Confucius unreservedly. Confucius was a great philosopher, statesman, and educator par excellence of the ancient world. It is by no means accidental that even today some of his theories radiate brilliance. Confucius was indeed the holiest and wisest of all philosophers. What Confucius said—even a word or two—has a bearing on the happiness of mankind.

Why does China have such an important position in the world? How did she come into being? . . . Confucius, in my opinion, played a definite positive role. Just think, for as long as two thousand years and within a perimeter of tens of thousands of miles, people have generally regarded books compiled by Confucius as "the classics." Is that a trivial matter? As a matter of fact, people already had a unifying center and have since developed a common language and common ideas, feelings and living habits among themselves. Is this not of great importance to the formation of the solidarity of the Chinese nation?

Red Guard comment:

These people have lauded and glorified Confucius practically to the point of hysterical frenzy. Their object is all too clear. They want to establish the absolute authority of Confucius in the vain hope of using Confucian ideas and concepts to unify the thought, language, feelings, and habits of 700 million people. They employ every conceivable means of disparaging and attacking Mao Tse-tung's thought, hoping thereby to induce a counter-revolutionary restoration. Under no circumstances should this be permitted to happen. We will certainly and thoroughly overthrow Confucian ideas and establish the absolute authority of Mao Tse-tung's thought!

The Confucian Scholars said:

What is the highest criterion of politics? It is to conduct a "benevolent government"—"using moral virtues and the dictates of propriety as the criteria for judging people" until they "have a sense of shame and know the standards for comparison."

What is meant by self-restraint? . . . The practice of the dictates of propriety, of course, entails respect for others and the treatment of people on an equal footing. It definitely does not lead to oppression and destruction and mass slaughter of other people.

The meaning of the word "benevolence" does not in any way merely imply "love of people." Rather, it means improving relationships between individuals. . . . It is to think of others at all times. Doesn't this mean "do as you would be done by"? Doesn't this imply "help others if you want to help yourself"? In this way, the relationship between one individual and another will not be any cause for complaint.

The further the wheel of history moves ahead, the less will be the hostility between countries at the same level. This could be a sign of progress. On the other hand, the more the countries are on an unequal footing, the more will be the hostility toward one another, and the more there will be wars and chaos in the world. This could be a sign of retrogression.

Red Guard comment:

The dictatorship of the proletariat can only give democracy to the people and impose dictatorship over all reactionaries. Therefore the reactionaries denounce us for not being "benevolent." They want a "benevolent government" from us and this means doing away with proletarian dictatorship. If their plots are successful, our Party and our country will be ruined and then the revolution will end in failure and the people will be doomed.

The Confucian Scholars said:

Doing things blindly and recklessly is entirely prompted by insatiable desires. If one does things according to what one desires one will do things badly. Doing things subjectively without regard to objective conditions will not get things done properly. If one insists on pursuing an erroneous course and if one permits one's greed to go unchecked, one will get more and more bogged down until one commits graver errors and reaps greater evil consequences.

Those who are so conceited that they claim they know half the things in heaven and everything on earth do not necessarily know everything, nor are they truly omnipotent. On the contrary, their insight and knowledge may be very small.

Red Guard comment:

Under the wise leadership of Chairman Mao and guided by the three red banners our people have won brilliant victories in the Socialist revolution and construction. They, however, denounce us for "acting blindly and recklessly" and for "bringing about the evil consequence of a house in ruin." Chairman Mao teaches us: "We should uphold what the enemy opposes and oppose what the enemy upholds." The more these people attack us, the higher we should hold the three red banners.

The Confucian Scholars said:

In fact, what Confucius meant by "benevolence" . . . [he] had all the people in mind. It is essentially characterized by "benevolence to the people." In plain language, "benevolence" means "love of people"—a recognition of man's right to survive. Before establishing one's own imperishable features, that is, one's virtue, one's merit, and one's words, one should also help others to do so. . . . These words mean that before being good in all aspects, one should help others to be good too.

"Benevolence" means "to get along well with others." When individuals live in harmony, without deceiving each other but forgiving one another, then there is a state of loving and supporting one another.

While Confucius's "love of people" subjectively means to love the ruling classes, in objective effect it means love of "the masses."

"Those who are benevolent toward others love people." These words by Confucius summarize his highest evaluation of "benevolence." To put "love of people" into practice, one must in a negative sense strive to "save others from what one wishes to avoid oneself" and, in a positive sense, "help establish others if you want to establish yourself."

We can hardly say that "benevolence" is not needed in our time and in our society.

Red Guard comment:

The relationships between slave-owners and slaves, between land-lords and peasants and between capitalists and workers, are those of exploiters and the exploited. The struggle between them is a life-and-death struggle—totally devoid of the idea of "loving one another" and "embracing one another." In a Socialist society in which classes and class struggle still exist, the primary reason why these monsters and demons have openly propagated the idea of "loving and embracing one another" is to blur the class boundary line and to repudiate class struggle. Aren't these people singing the same tune as that of Khrushchev revisionists?

DOC. 100. *Yu Fen: Degeneration of Soviet Revisionist Renegades as Seen from Their Concoction of "Communist Christianity," Hung-ch'i (Red Flag) No. 8 (August 1, 1969)*

NOT LONG AGO, a small farce was staged on the outskirts of Moscow under the "auspices" of the Soviet revisionist chieftains. Bishops and priests as well as monks and imams, religious chiefs numbering more than one hundred from all over the Soviet Union, attended a conference boisterously to discuss what they called "essential problems of our epoch." A bigwig of the Soviet revisionist renegade clique sent the conference a personal message wishing their performance a success and bidding them "to make contribution to the noble cause of consolidation of universal peace."

This is an extremely reactionary step taken by Brezhnev and the handful of other Soviet revisionist renegades who vigorously advocate religion and superstition in a vain attempt to fool the people of the Soviet Union and the world and to use the frocks of the bishops and priests to cover up the crimes they have committed at home and abroad.

The great Lenin severely denounced the revisionists of all shades and hues as hens among dung heaps in the backyard of the working class movement. They would peck at anything, however filthy, so long as it could keep them alive. The Soviet revisionist renegade clique, beset with difficulties at home and abroad, has long sought the service of the reactionary religious forces in carrying out its counter-revolutionary revisionist domestic and foreign policies. The Soviet revisionist renegade clique has long been a disgusting sycophant of the Vatican, bulwark of the most reactionary religious forces in the world, and the Pope, the loyal defender of capitalism. The notorious Khrushchev shamelessly praised the Pope as a "great man" "devoted to world peace." After Khrushchev, a new Soviet revisionist chieftain made a "pilgrimage" to Rome in the capacity as head of State and sought audience with Pope Paul VI. At home, the Soviet revisionist renegade clique does all it can to inflate the arrogance of the religious forces. It vigorously carries out reactionary religious propaganda through its press and news agencies, shamelessly trumpeting that religion, an opiate, is "beneficial," and clamoring for the restoration of religious education in schools. The religious forces have become daily more rampant and all-pervasive in the Soviet Union. The number of religious rites held in the Soviet Union in the past ten years increased threefold or fourfold, the number of churches and parishes increased day by day, and the number of religious believers reached dozens of millions. Many theological seminaries have been set up to train "successors" to the church.

Of late, the Soviet revisionist renegade clique has cooked up the reactionary fallacy of "communist Christianity" and published lengthy articles in the press advertising the "evolution of the modern Russian Orthodox Church." In the fifth issue of the journal "Science and Religion," a hired "candidate doctor of philosophy" went so far as to allege, in the typical tune of a priest, that the Russian Orthodox Church is an "instrument for transforming social relations," that "Christianity is harmonious, fitting, and in coordination with the process of transforming social relations on socialist and communist principles" and that Christianity has developed into "communist Christianity." Like revisionism—the sham Marxism-Leninism mouthed by the Soviet revisionists, this "communist Christianity," so it was said, is most enthusiastic in "calling on the believers to take part in the struggle for socialism and socialist construction." Brezhnev and company can now most conveniently find in "communist Christianity" a blue-print for "building communism." They have even thrown to the four winds their Marxist-Leninist garb because "in the Russian Orthodox Church, the building of the kingdom of Christ on earth is more and more associated with communist transformation of the world." It was amidst such loud trumpeting for "communist Christianity" that the church heads in some areas flagrantly called meetings in public places, conducted propaganda among the inhabitants, and "recruited supporters." What miasma!

Where can one find anything more shameless!

In the eyes of the Soviet revisionist renegades, they have only to put the label "communism" on Christianity and they will be able to deceive the people at home and the revolutionary people of the world and provide themselves with a fig leaf to cover up their all-round restoration of capitalism by making use of the church and their pursuance of social-imperialist policies. In fact, this precisely reveals that their so-called "building of communism" is the same stuff as the "building of the kingdom of Christ," that they are taking the most reactionary idealist stand of the big landlords and big bourgeoisie in making use of religion and that their program is the same as the deceitful propaganda about "communist Christianity."

The proletariat is determined to overthrow completely the bourgeoisie and all other exploiting classes, replace the dictatorship of the proletariat, defeat capitalism with socialism, and eventually realize communism. "Religion is opium for the people." It is a spiritual weapon of the exploiting classes for oppression, enslaving and exploiting the laboring people; it fetters the oppressed classes, preventing them from rebelling against the oppressors. Scientific communism and religion are antagonistic. The struggle for the realization of the ideals of communism in the whole world and "the building of the kingdom of Christ on earth" are incompatible with each other like fire and water.

The "Manifesto of the Communist Party" solemnly declares that the communist revolution's "development involves the most radical rupture with traditional ideas." Since the great theory of scientific communism came into being, it has been frantically resisted by the reactionary religious forces represented by the Pope. Lenin pointed out: "We must combat religion—that is the ABC of all materialism, and consequently of Marxism." The Party and Soviet state led by Lenin and Stalin waged a resolute struggle against the reactionary religious forces. Now, the gang of Soviet revisionist renegades who claim to be loyal to the behest of Lenin have shamelessly alleged that Christianity and communism are "harmonious, fitting and in coordination" with each other; they have combined communism and Christianity into one and flaunted the black flag of "communist Christianity." This shows to what despicable depth they have sunk. Listen, bigwigs of the Soviet revisionist renegade clique! You want to act as Christian "bishops" to dupe and hoodwink the Soviet people and the people of the world and at the same time you want to crown yourself with the wreath of "communism" so as to whitewash your treacherous acts. Don't you find this too ugly a farce?

Since the emergence of Marxism in the world, all the reactionary forces and revisionists of various descriptions have tried in vain to "combine" communism with religion. This was the tactic used by the "god-building" school severely denounced by Lenin. The so-called "evolution" of religion in the Soviet Union and "socialization" of religion as well as the "association" of "the kingdom of Christ" with communism, and so on and so forth—all this is sheer deceitful religious propaganda. Many fashionable theologians are now busily engaged in "reforms." They rack their brains every day in search of a "more effective form of expression" of Christianity from theological theories. They oppose what they called "flagrant infringement of atheistic materials and communism upon human dignity"; they wildly clamor for "extending the kingdom of Christ to the very limit of the earth," and "propagating gospel" among the proletariat. However, all these tricks fail to match those of today's Soviet revisionist renegade clique. The Soviet revisionist renegades have come out as "communist" theologians to prove that the ideals of Christianity had been translated into reality in their sham communism. Why is it that the Soviet religious bosses now consider it possible to give energetic support to the political and philosophical propositions of the Soviet revisionist renegade clique? They have let the cat out of the bag themselves. It turned out that they support the political "principles" of the Soviet revisionist renegade clique because "these principles accord with the needs of Christianity." It was none other than Khrushchev, Brezhnev, and their gang who, after coming to power, have turned the bourgeoisie's "hope of restoration" into "attempts at restoration," usurped the leadership of the party of Lenin and Stalin and turned the world's first state under the dictatorship of the proletariat into a dark fascist state under the dictatorship of the bourgeoisie. The reactionary religious bosses found such a "process" of capitalist restoration very "harmonious, fitting, and in coordination" with their desires and that is why they have applauded it and strained themselves to serve the Soviet revisionist renegade clique.

In playing up "communist Christianity," the Soviet revisionist renegade clique has lauded religion as an "instrument for transforming social relations." Such brazen utterance can only show up more clearly the heinous features of the Soviet revisionist renegades who are accelerating all-round capitalist restoration with the help of the reactionary religious forces. In class society, religion has always been an instrument of the exploiting classes for dominating, enslaving, and poisoning the minds of the laboring people. Karl Marx, the great teacher of the proletariat, said: "The social principles of Christianity had justified ancient slavery, extolled medieval serfdom, and, when necessary, will also defend, although with a look of pity, the oppression of the proletariat." Therefore, all the reactionary ruling classes in history supported and made use of religion. This was done by the slave-owners of slave society, the landlords of feudal society, and the capitalists of capitalist society. The Soviet people will never forget how the old Tsars always used the Russian Orthodox Church as an instrument for maintaining the sanguinary rule in their feudal empire. Right after the founding of the Soviet power, the overthrown reactionary ruling classes, with a view to seizing back their lost paradise, organized an anti-Soviet "crusade" with the help of the reactionary religious forces and in coordination with international imperialism to subvert the first socialist state. Still less will the Chinese people forget how the imperialists used religion as an instrument for cultural aggression and, later, military and political aggression against our country, turning her into a semi-colonial and semi-feudal country. Immediately after the founding of the great People's Republic of China, the imperialists made use of the reactionary religious forces as their instrument to poison the minds of a section of the people who were backward and to subvert and undermine our country. A handful of counter-revolutionaries, under the cloak of Catholicism or Protestantism, has always been an anti-communist, anti-people task force of imperialism and an imperialist instrument for aggression. That the Soviet revisionist renegade clique uses the Russian Orthodox Church as an "instrument for transforming social relations" is nothing new. This is merely a mantle inherited from the old Tsars and a piece of shop-worn junk picked up from US imperialism.

While creating the reactionary theory of "communist Christianity," the Soviet revisionist renegade clique, which is capable of committing every evil and scandal, openly lauded in its press the Russian Orthodox Church heads for carrying out its "international policy" and supporting its "efforts in ensuring international security." It has thus confessed to its counter-revolutionary aims in making use of the reactionary religious forces to push its social-imperialist policy. At present, the Soviet revisionist renegade clique is stepping up its collusion with US imperialism, intensifying its suppression of the revolutionary struggle of the people of various countries, and strengthening its control and exploitation of the East European countries and the People's Republic of Mongolia. These criminal activities of the Soviet revisionist renegade clique prove that the "international policy" of the Soviet revisionists has become an imperialist policy of mustering all reactionary forces to carry out expansion abroad.

While incessantly making intrusions into the territory and air space of our country and shooting to death empty-handed Chinese fishermen and herdsmen, the Soviet revisionist renegade clique has been making use of religion to carry out counter-revolutionary subversive propaganda through its radios beamed toward China's Sinkiang Province in an attempt to split the unity of our motherland and disrupt the national solidarity of our country. The old Tsars used religion to carry out divisive activities in Sinkiang, and now the Soviet revisionist renegade clique is doing the same. This fact has enabled the people of the world to see clearly once again that this handful of renegades are downright social-imperialists and out-and-out new Tsars. We sternly warn the chieftains of the Soviet revisionist renegade clique: You will come to no good end in using reactionary clergymen to carry out counter-revolutionary activities!

Chairman Mao, the great leader of all the nationalities of our country, pointed out in his work "On Coalition Government": "All religions are permitted in China's liberated areas, in accordance with the principle of freedom of religious belief. All believers in Protestantism, Catholicism, Islam, Buddhism, and other faiths enjoy the protection of the People's Government so long as they are abiding by its laws. Everyone is free to believe or not to believe; neither compulsion nor discrimination is permitted." We consistently advocate protection of the freedom of religious belief and the freedom of not believing in religion. Communists follow a policy of freedom of religious belief; but towards religious believers "We can never approve of their idealism or religious doctrines." We must repudiate idealism, monasticism and all kinds of religious superstition. We are convinced that the time will come when the religious believers will become awakened and cast away the "gods." To maintain its counter-revolutionary revisionist rule, the Soviet revisionist renegade clique has completely betrayed the rudimentary principles of Marxism-Leninism, acted perversely, and gone so far as to concoct the reactionary fallacy of "communist Christianity." This shows to what depth they have degenerated politically and ideologically, reflecting at the same time their mortal fear of the doom confronting them.

Has not the Soviet revisionist renegade clique told the religious heads under its pay to discuss the so-called "essential problems of our epoch"? The essential problem of our epoch, as pointed out by Vice-chairman Lin Piao in his political report to the Ninth National Congress of the Communist Party of China, is: "The contradiction between the oppressed nations on the one hand and imperialism and social-imperialism on the other; the contradiction between the proletariat and the bourgeoisie in the capitalist and revisionist countries; the contradiction between imperialist and social-imperialist countries and among the imperialist countries; and the contradiction between socialist countries on the one hand and imperialism and social-imperialism on the other. The existence and development of these contradictions are bound to give rise to revolution." US imperialism, Soviet revisionism, and all reaction in the world can never survive this great storm of people's revolution, nor can "communist Christianity" save the Soviet revisionist renegade clique from its doom.

Owing to the fact that the Soviet revisionist renegade clique is carrying out the dictatorship of the bourgeoisie over the Soviet people and pursuing a social-imperialist policy of expansion abroad, acute class differentiation and bitter class struggle are taking place in the Soviet society. The Soviet revisionist chieftains merely indulge in daydreaming and are wasting their efforts in trying to use the religious forces to benumb and disintegrate the revolutionary fighting will of the Soviet people in rebellion against the Soviet revisionist renegade clique. It can only promote the daily awakening of the Soviet people and arouse them to greater resistance; it can only enable the people all over the world to see more clearly the depravity and shamelessness of this gang of renegades. Now, the revolutionary movement of the proletariat of the world and the people of all countries is surging forward vigorously and the struggle of the Soviet proletariat and the broad masses of the Soviet people against the Soviet revisionist renegade clique is developing in depth. The imperialists, revisionists and reactionaries are heading step by step for their graves. As pointed out by Chairman Mao, the great leader of all the nationalities of our country, "Working hand in glove, Soviet revisionism and US imperialism have done so many foul and evil things that the revolutionary people the world over will not let them go unpunished. The people of all countries are rising. A new historical period of struggle against US imperialism and Soviet revisionism has begun." The Soviet revisionist renegade clique is seeking help from the reactionary religious forces to wage a last-ditch struggle. This can only bring them to a quicker and more miserable defeat. This is also the will of "god." This "god" is none other than the proletariat and revolutionary people of the world, the Soviet people included.

PART III

Ideology and the Maoist Vision:
The Religious Analogies

TWO AMERICAN SPECIALISTS on contemporary China wrote in 1966, "The Chinese Communists won their revolutionary struggle and carried out their programs of socioeconomic construction through ideology and organization. Ideology is a systematic set of beliefs about the world and how men act in it. The Chinese Communists' ideology is in part a theory of history, a vision of the past and future, and in part a set of principles for building organization, creating a new society, and changing men spiritually."[1] An adequate definition of dynamic religion at its best needs not much more than this.

In the process of transforming the social, economic, and political institutions of their country the Chinese Communists have sought to transform individuals, to "change men spiritually." A significant contribution of Mao Tse-tung to Marxist theory and practice is his emphasis on the human factor—on *man*, not man power or technology. The Great Proletarian Cultural Revolution (1966–69) laid stress on changing culture and people, on replacing traditional culture with a new proletarian culture, on transferring leadership from traditional or neo-elitist patterns to a new leadership of the masses.

Basic social and cultural institutions and traditions—the family,

1. F. Schurmann and O. Schell, eds., *The China Reader: Communist China,* (New York: Alfred A. Knopf, Vintage Book edition, 1967, p. xiv.)

parent-child relations, status of women, traditional rites and ceremonies, patterns of authority, religion—were radically affected by
the general attack on the "four olds" (old culture, customs, habits,
and ideas). The breakdown of old patterns among the religions has
already been documented in Parts I and II: the reordering of lines of
authority; the accommodation of theology and doctrine to patriotic
and ideological demands; the outright attack on unacceptable liaisons
with "imperialists," "feudalists," or other bad elements; the systematic program of thought reform through political study, manual
labor, and other means.

The Chinese Communist concept "to transform thinking" (*szu-
hsiang kai-tsao*), a secular version of religious conversion, grows
from the Maoist conviction that a totally new man is needed to
eradicate and replace the old society, which is seen as evil and
corrupt. Using a medical analogy, Mao Tse-tung speaks of "diseases
in thought and politics" which require "an attitude of saving men by
curing their diseases." A student of the psychohistorical forces at
work in China today speaks of thought reform as "group psycho-
therapy to save your soul." What critics have called brainwashing,
the Chinese Communists present as a "morally uplifting, harmoniz-
ing, and therapeutic experience."[2] While only a state with powerful
central authority could implement thought reform on a mass scale,
there is also a powerful ideological movement, vividly personified by
the charismatic Mao Tse-tung, a "pseudo-religious mystique which
creates both the demand and the emotional fervor."[3]

In the process of group political study-and-criticism sessions,
denunciation of authority figures, such as one's father or religious
leader, has a profound effect on personal orientation. The presenta-
tion of new goals and values, new morality, new authority demands
and group disciplines—the challenge of a great crusade, a vision
and plan for a new society for China and for the depressed masses
of the world, brings the individual face-to-face with a personal crisis
decision that can radically alter his sense of inner identity as well as
his external life style. "Thought reform makes use of a powerful
combination of emotional forces in the total manipulation of the
individual participant. It employs no theologians, but it closely
resembles an attempt at induced religious conversion—saving souls,

2. Robert J. Lifton, M.D., "Peking's 'Thought Reform'—Group Psycho-
therapy to Save Your Soul"; in Schurmann and Schell, eds., *The China
Reader*, p. 138.
3. Schurmann and Schell, eds., *The China Reader*, p. 138.

stressing guilt and shame, demanding atonement, recantation, and rebirth."[4]

The substitution of new personal goals, values, vision, and commitments for old ones requires reinforcement from new rites and ceremonies, new liturgical forms, new acts and deeds of commitment. Documents selected for this section illustrate the ways in which Chinese authorities have dealt with the persistent human need for socialization of inner emotional or spiritual feelings, even in a totally non-religious context. People have birthdays, get married, graduate from school, leave home for distant places, die. Weddings, funerals, anniversaries, important events call for ritual and ceremony. Secular China, now almost devoid of the rich heritage of religious ritual and folk custom once intrinsic to Chinese culture, has created its own substitutes. But the question persists: Can cultural patterns be objectively controlled, altered, or created *de novo*? Can a cult of Mao, a dedication to secular, man-made goals and values without religion, provide the spiritual vitality essential for a living, spontaneous and enduring popular culture?

According to observers, in 1971 the widespread liturgical practices centered on Mao Tse-tung and his thought reported in Documents 110–112 were diminishing. Posters of Mao's sayings, his pictures, the once-ubiquitous lapel pins, the red book of Mao's quotations itself were less in evidence.

4. Schurmann and Schell, eds., *The China Reader*, p. 144.

Section 1. Reforming Old Rites and Customs

DOC. 101. *Chao Chien-min, Secretary of Secretariat, CCP Shantung Provincial Committee: Reform Funeral Customs, Encourage Thrifty Burials Without Coffins and Graves Without Sepulchral Mounds (1958)*

FUNERAL RITES AND CUSTOMS are part of the social superstructure. Like the rest of the social superstructure, they owe their genesis to a certain economic basis and social system, which they serve, and will inevitably change with the change of the social economic basis. We have already successfully built considerable superstructure adapted to our socialist economic basis. Such superstructure is helpful to the development of the current socialist production and serves our present socialist economic basis. It should be admitted, however, that some of the superstructure we have built is not yet perfect, that vestiges of the feudal and capitalist superstructure have not yet been supplanted by our new superstructure, and that a contradiction still exists between them and the new economic basis, hindering the present development of productive forces. The old funeral rites and customs which are still observed by the rural population belong to these vestiges of the feudal and capitalist superstructure.

*Old Funeral Rites and Customs Have Become a Spiritual
and Material Burden on the Masses, Seriously
Impeding the Development of Our Socialist
Construction*

THE PRESENT FUNERAL RITES AND CUSTOMS in the rural areas
have already been simplified and changed, following the changes
in the social structure that have taken place in the several years
after the liberation and as a result of the increased consciousness
of the masses. But through lack of planned leadership and systematic reform, such vestiges of the old feudal funeral rites and
customs have not yet been thoroughly reformed, and the feudal,
superstitious content and old clannish moral viewpoints still exert
considerable spiritual pressure on the working people. The masses
in the rural areas still generally follow the old feudal, superstitious rites whenever a death of some aged and senior member of
the family occurs. For instance, they would still "announce the
death in the ancestral temple," have a priest "lead the soul of the
deceased," provide a wooden coffin and a lavish funeral, give
dinners to relatives and friends who have come to mourn, and
make frequent sacrificial offerings to the dead. Those who do
not observe these old funeral rites and customs and do not provide wooden coffins and a lavish funeral for the dead are liable
to be censured by their own friends and relatives and even by
public opinion. These old funeral rites and customs have become
a heavy spiritual and material burden on the masses, seriously
impeding the development of our socialist production and construction. The system of graves and tombs, for instance, has not
only caused serious wastage of land, but also raised great difficulties in the way of merging of land, building of irrigation systems
and the use of new-type farming implements (particularly the
use of tractors). The custom of providing wooden coffins and
lavish funerals for the dead and the feudal, superstitious rites
have caused serious waste of timber, cotton cloth, paper, and
money. As Marx says in the *Communist Manifesto*, "Unless the
proletariat, the lowest layer in the modern society, completely
overthrows all the superstructure above it formed by the classes

and layers that constitute the society proper, it will not be able to stretch its back or raise its head." Therefore, the reform of the old feudal, superstitious funeral rites and customs and establishment of a set of new funeral rites and customs adapted to the socialist system and its economic basis is very necessary and pressing, particularly today, when there is a great leap forward in production.

Since the agricultural cooperativization early in 1956, work has begun in Shantung on surveys and research in connection with the reform of funeral rites and customs. A field team has been organized and sent to the administrative districts of Liaocheng, Linyi, Laiyang, Huimin, and Tsining, where typical surveys have been made in eighteen hsiang and chen carefully selected from plains and mountainous, littoral and suburban areas. Meanwhile, several forums have been held on funeral rites and customs, attended by members of the provincial-level departments concerned, historians, and members and advisers of cultural-historical institutions. The findings of the surveys and research show that the question cannot be ignored and must be solved. The following are some of the findings of the surveys made in the eighteen hsiang and chen.

(1) There are in the eighteen hsiang and chen a total of 74,698 tombs, occupying a total of 3,202 mou of arable land, or 1.98 percent of the total area of the cultivated land. If the surrounding sepulchral land is included, the tombs actually occupy more than 3 percent of the cultivated land, all of which is good land. The existing tombs which occupy the largest area of cultivated land are found in suburban areas of cities and chen. For instance, the tombs in the eastern suburbs of Laiyang occupy 7.2 percent of the cultivated land; in general, tombs in the plains and in mountainous areas occupy about 3.5 percent to 4 percent of the cultivated land, while tombs in the littoral areas occupy only 0.11 percent of the cultivated land. It is calculated from the surveys that existing tombs in the province occupy at least 3 percent of the total acreage of cultivated land, or about 4,170,000 mou. Assuming that the average annual output (of grain) is 300 catties per mou, the province loses about 1,250,000,000 catties of grain a year, sufficient for the consumption of about 3,200,000 people for a whole year. According to statistics compiled by the

Statistical Bureau of Shantung for the years 1952–56, the average annual mortality rate of the population of Shantung is 1.2 percent. It may be calculated from this figure that there are 644,000 deaths in the province a year. If 20 percent is deducted for infants and young children, there will still be 80 percent, or 515,200 people, who need tombs. Every year the new tombs will take away 5,152 mou of land and reduce the total output of grain by more than 1,540,000 catties. The importance of the reform of the burial system in order to save land is thus quite apparent.

(2) According to the figure mentioned above, about 80 percent, that is 515,200, of the deaths in the province every year will need coffins. As each coffin uses at least 0.4 cubic meter of wood, a total of 206,080 cubic meters of timber is thus consumed every year in the province. More than 200,000 dwelling units may be built with this amount of timber, which is also sufficient for sleepers for over 2,000 kilometers of railroads. Due to the shortage of timber, coffins are expensive. The price is Yuan 50 for the cheapest, about Yuan 100 for the ordinary make, and Yuan 600 for the most expensive.

(3) According to a survey made in Chiuchai hsiang, Mengyin hsien, covering the period of three years, an average of 48 ch'ih of cloth and 3 catties of ginned cotton is required for the funeral clothes of a dead person. It may be calculated on this basis that a total of 24,730,000 ch'ih of cotton cloth and 1,545,600 catties of ginned cotton is used for making funeral clothes every year in the province.

(4) According to the surveys, the minimum funeral expenses for a dead person are about Yuan 100 (including money for the coffin, funeral clothes and other funeral expenses). Thus the yearly expenditure on funerals in the province is about Yuan 51,500,000.

Such serious waste of land, timber, cotton cloth and money is a heavy burden on both cooperatives and individuals. The obligations imposed by such feudal funeral rites and customs have caused, and are still causing, great difficulties for the masses. There are numerous cases in which funerals have caused difficulties to production, hardships to the living, and even bankruptcies to whole families.

*The Masses, Fed Up With the Calamities Caused by Feudal
Rites and Customs, Urgently Demand Reform of the Old
Funeral Rites and Customs and Hope That the Party
and the Government Will Propose New Measures*

BECAUSE THE MASSES have long endured the calamities caused
them by feudal rites and customs, and as their political consciousness has been greatly increased following the establishment of the
socialist system and collective economic basis, they are urgently
demanding reform of the old funeral rites and customs. The
masses are generally aware that the old funeral rites and customs
are wasteful, superstitious and troublesome, but are perplexed by
the absence of new rites that will replace the old. Some of them
are afraid of being censured by their relatives and friends if they
do not observe the old rites and customs. So they hope that the
Party and the government will formulate a new set of rules
governing burials. The masses say, "There are already too many
tombs, but new tombs are being added every year. If this goes
on, there will be less and less land left for cultivation purposes.
The government must think of a way to check this." Others say,
"If all the good land is occupied by corpses, what can the living
do to raise food?" Many agricultural cooperatives have adopted
the slogan, "Let us compete with Heaven; let us save land from
graves and tombs; let us fight against nature; let us rely not on
the gods and Heaven, but on our own hands, for more production!" Some of the people say, "A man dies just as a lamp goes
out, and it is superstitious to burn joss sticks and paper for him
and talk of feng-shui.* Now that we have our cooperatives, we
are prosperous and have nothing to fear. If there is any feng-shui
at all, the Communist Party and the cooperatives will be good
enough feng-shui."

So, with the consciousness of the masses greatly increased and
as a result of the needs of production and livelihood, cases have
occurred in a number of places where tombs were levelled in
order to make room for cultivation. For instance, in Makuan-

---

* Geomancy.

tun Hsiang of Liaocheng Hsien, Chiuchai Hsiang of Mengyin Hsien, and four other hsiang, 952 tombs (mostly unclaimed) were levelled in 1957, adding almost 100 mou to the total area of cultivated land. Formal suggestions have also been made for the levelling of tombs at local people's congresses and through letters addressed to the government. In October 1957, a peasant of Wangchiamiao Tsun, Mengchuang Hsiang, Liaocheng Hsien wrote a letter to Chairman Mao Tse-tung proposing the building of public mausoleums. He wrote a poem in which he gave his reasons why public mausoleums should be built:

If we want to build our country well, we must build public
   mausoleums.
The big trees will no longer go to make coffins, but will
   be used for building factories.
Good land will not be used for tombs, but will produce
   more grain.
Our fathers will not be buried underground,
They will not endure mishaps in the ground,
But will live in tall buildings, instead of lying under
   a heap of earth.
The public mausoleums must be well built,
So that they may add to the glory of our country.
At the Ch'ing Ming Festival,
Joyous visitors will come to the accompaniment of beating
   of gongs and drums,
There they will line up and bow thrice, and the dead will
   be glad.

Encouraged by the socialist system and in order to expand production and improve living standards as fast as possible, the masses are reforming the old funeral rites and customs of their own accord or are proposing such reform. That is inevitable and quite right. But our leadership thinking has been lagging behind the objective realities; we have not adequately assessed the consciousness of the masses. We have been held back by too many fears, and have not dared to openly advocate and propagandize such reform. There is lack of organized leadership and no concrete measures for such reform have been suggested or taken. As a result, the reform of old funeral rites and customs so far undertaken has been negligible and slow.

Conditions Are Now Ripe for the Reform of the Old Funeral Rites and Customs and Setting Up of New Rites and Customs Adapted to the Socialist System and Its Economic Base

IN VIEW OF THE above-mentioned facts, I think that the time has come and conditions are ripe for us to lead the masses actively and systematically in reforming their old funeral rites and customs. While reforming these old funeral rites and customs, new funeral rites and customs adapted to the socialist system and its economic basis should be established. These new funeral rites and customs which we favor are essentially different from the old funeral rites and customs. The old funeral rites and customs were created to serve the exploiting classes, to fool the people, and to instill such feudal and superstitious ideas into their minds as "a man has a soul, which lives on after he is dead" and "filial piety is the supreme virtue." Our new funeral rites and customs, on the other hand, are designed to serve socialist production and construction, to commemorate the dead and encourage the living, and to educate the people with Communist ethical standards. We also support filial piety. We should take good and loving care of the aged and our elders, so that they may have comfort in the evening of their life and may be assured of a livelihood. After they are gone, we should express grief for them and remember them; and posterity should be exhorted to emulate their good points and achievements, so that posterity may take heart, and grief for the departed may be turned into strength. In his speech, "Serve the People," which he made at a memorial service held in 1944 by central Party organs in honor of the late Comrade Chang Ssu-te, Chairman Mao Tse-tung said clearly, "In future, when someone of our own ranks dies, no matter whether he was only a cook or a soldier, we should attend his funeral and hold a memorial service for him, if in his lifetime he has rendered some meritorious service. This should become a practice. It should also be introduced among the people. When someone in the village dies, a memorial service should be held. In this way we shall show our grief for the departed and unite the whole nation."

The reform of the old and setting up of new funeral rites and customs should be based on the principle of combining the universal truth of Marxism-Leninism with concrete practice, and reference should be made to the dictum of Marx in *Capital*: "Owing to countless different experiences, natural conditions, racial relations, and externally acting historical influences, the same—that is, the same according to the principal conditions— economic basis may have endless variations in its outward appearance and different gradations." I think that, while criticizing and abolishing the feudal and superstitious contents of the old funeral rites and customs that run counter to the principle of industry and economy and hinder production and construction, we should realize that these old rites and customs have a history of several thousand years and have acquired the force of habit among the masses. Therefore, with regard to the non-essential appearances and outward forms, the masses should be encouraged to create in accordance with their history, customs, habits, and natural conditions, and various measures may be taken to suit local conditions, so that the new rites and customs may be easily acceptable to the masses and may be popularized.

*Abolition of Wooden Coffins; Deep Burials and Thrifty
Funerals; Graves Without Mounds; Disposal of Existing
Tombs; and Gradual Introduction of Cremation*

THE FOLLOWING are some concrete suggestions for reform of funeral rites and customs:

With regard to the question of abolition of wooden coffins, I suggest that some kind of substitute coffin may be universally adopted at first. For instance, the wooden coffin at present universally used may be replaced by a new type of coffin made of wooden frames and grass stalks mixed with mud or other materials. The Department of Forestry of our province has already experimentally produced two types of substitute coffin. One type, suitable for new burials, is made of a wooden frame with walls of grass stalks mixed with mud and concrete. It has the same outward appearance as the old type of wooden coffin—a concession to the custom of the masses. Its advantages are that a lot of timber may be saved, as the same amount of wood for a wooden coffin would be sufficient for the wooden frames of five or six substitute coffins, and that it is economical and durable, as each substitute coffin costs only about Yuan 10 and is as durable as a wooden coffin. The other type, used principally for reburials, is made of clay in the shape of a box or an urn with a lid. Each costs about Yuan 5 (which may be further reduced if instead of using clay, grass stalks mixed with mud are used). Furthermore, the masses may be persuaded to dispense with coffins altogether, and to bury their dead in earthen, brick or stone-lined pits. In due course of time, the substitute coffin may be abolished.

With regard to the method of deep burials, thrifty funerals, and graves without mounds, I suggest that, under the unified planning of the local governments or cooperatives, some poor land or mountainous sites may be set apart for public cemeteries, which would not hinder production and construction. Bodies should be buried deep underground without the customary mounds above ground (a tablet or tree may be planted above the grave or at some distance by the roadside as a marking), so that the ground above may be cultivated as usual, or trees or orchards may be planted. In this way the countryside may be made green, the graves or burial places may be beautified, and at the same time income may be increased. In mountainous and hilly areas, the method of burial in deep pits may be adopted where it does not interfere with farming and afforestation.

Now for the disposal of old and existing tombs. The masses may be urged to level or destroy tombs which are not claimed or which are more than five generations old. Tombs which have owners and are less than five generations old, but which interfere with production and construction, may be levelled or removed on a voluntary basis by the masses after education, in order to enlarge the area of cultivation.

As to the tombs of martyrs and ancient tombs of historical or cultural value, they should be carefully preserved. Requests by the masses for the building of tombs, planting of trees, and setting up of memorial stones for dead contemporary people who have made valuable contributions to society, worker or peasant models, and other progressives should be granted, and assistance should be given in carrying out the work.

Cremation should be introduced gradually and at important centers. Crematories should be built first in the cities and culturally developed areas where the masses have a high degree of consciousness, in order to popularize cremation.

Thrifty and simple funeral rites and customs should be encouraged. New sets of funeral rites and customs should be created in accordance with Communist ethical standards and local conditions. For instance, such methods of commemorating the dead as preserving their likenesses and relics and compiling their works and histories should be encouraged. When a cadre, an employee, a worker or a peasant dies, a memorial service may be held by the organ, factory, workshop, street, village, cooperative, or production team to which he belonged, as the circumstances may warrant. No new funeral clothes need be made for the dead; they may be buried in their old clothes. Mourning clothes need not be made for the children and friends and relatives of the dead. They may wear an arm-band of black or white, or a white border may be sewn on the hems of their clothes, as has been done in many places. Days for sacrificial offerings should be greatly reduced. Two or three days a year, preferably at Ch'ing Ming and during the Spring Festival, should be chosen for making sacrificial offerings to the dead, in accordance with local conditions and customs. Those making the offering should bow to the dead and stand in silence, and the practice of kowtowing in front of the graves should be gradually abolished.

Among the national minorities, great care should be taken in reforming their funeral rites and customs. These reforms may be put off in some areas, and the national minorities should be allowed to carry out their own reform in accordance with their own customs and habits.

These measures for reforming the old funeral rites and customs were propagandized while a survey was being carried out in the suburban districts of Laiyang and in Holo Hsiang. They were not only accepted, but also welcomed, by the masses. (However, most peasants would not accept the idea of cremation of the dead.) They say that the reform would have four big advantages:

(1) The cultivated area would be enlarged and output would be increased.

(2) Irrigation work and use of tractors would not be hampered.

(3) Money would be saved for production and construction.

(4) Feudal and superstitious thinking would be eliminated.

For the sake of caution, experiments should first be made and experience gained before the methods mentioned above are adopted, with modifications by the masses if necessary. While the experiments are made or when the methods are adopted, the masses should be ideologically well prepared and mobilized. The principle of volition must be observed, and any one who does not want to accept the new methods should be allowed to go on observing the old customs. The experiments and adoption of the new methods must be carried out in conjunction with the central tasks of production and rectification. In short, reform of the old funeral rites and customs and setting up of new rites and customs has become an urgent demand of the masses. Our Party should further strengthen its leadership and promote the movement. I believe that, after experience has been gained from the experiments and adoption of the new rites and customs in Han areas, the broad masses will be able to shed the heavy spiritual and material burden imposed on them by the old funeral rites and customs, and their thinking will be refurnished.

DOC. 102. *Liu Hou-ming, in* Chinese Youth: *Meeting of the Three Clowns (1963)*

THIS SHORT DIDACTIC DRAMA lampoons old-style religious and superstitious practice while extolling the common sense attitudes of revolutionary youth.

IT IS SPRING in a North China village. Mother Chao comes to light incense before the Kuanyin shrine. She has been busy for days and has not had time to come. She thinks that this is why her small grandson has caught a fever.

Suddenly Hsiu-yu, her daughter, comes upon her and blows out the match with which her mother is about to light the incense. Hsiu-yu sings:

The clay Buddha statue only knows how to deceive people.
Lighting incense and kowtowing is making trouble for yourself.
How many times have I told you
To break off all relations with that thing!
We are an army family and I am a cadre.
We should take the lead in destroying superstition.
Trees have roots and water has a source.
The only way to cure sickness is to call a doctor.

Hsiu-yu takes her baby to see the commune doctor. As soon as she has gone, Mother Chao lights the match again. In spite of her daughter's words, she kneels and beseeches Kuanyin to restore her grandson to health.

Ironmouth Sun is a fortune-teller who has fallen on hard days since the Communists came, but there are still a few families that believe in his magic. He has heard that Mother Chao's grandson is ill and so he comes to see her, hoping to badger some of her food tickets. He is rather hesitant because he fears Hsiu-yu, who has exposed him at a commune meeting as a "blowfly spreading superstition."

Sun tells Mother Chao that the doctor will not be able to cure the child. He asks for money to offer to the "heaven-master" so that he can find out what will happen. When Mother Chao gives him the money, he says that she must take the child out forty-nine steps in an eastward direction the following morning, to remove him from the influence of the evil star that is causing his illness. Mother Chao thanks him and asks him to continue to worship the "heaven-master" on her behalf. Sun says that he is afraid that the "heaven-master" will not stay with him much longer as he has nothing to give him to eat. Mother Chao then goes to fetch some rice for him.

While Mother Chao is away, Third Auntie Chien arrives. She often pretends to be a medium for a spirit in order to get more money for clothes and cigarettes. Afraid of meeting Hsiu-yu, she first calls out for her from the gate. Should Hsiu-yu be at home she will say that she wants to be given some work for the commune.

Sun, sipping tea, hears someone calling out "Hsiu-yu, Hsiu-yu!" and is terrified. He hides under the table. When Mother Chao comes back with a bag of rice, Sun is nowhere to be seen. She goes to answer the gate. Third Auntie Chien asks if the tea is poured out for her. "Why, yes," replies Mother Chao politely, "your spirit came before you."

At once Third Auntie Chien starts to shake and cry out. Mother Chao hurriedly kneels down and welcomes the spirit. Auntie Chien talks in half-riddles, saying that the spirit needs "three feet of red cloth and two of blue, a pig and a bottle of wine" before the baby can be freed from the ghost that possesses it. She also demands money and the bag of rice lying on the table. Ironmouth Sun mutters furiously from under the table but dares not show himself. Auntie Chien takes the incense from in front of Kuanyin and gives it to Mother Chao as a medicine. Finally she recovers from her fit and pretends to ask what happened. She demands more money from Mother Chao and drags her off to open the money-chest.

Hu Yinyang comes by the house and notices a new barn built alongside. Hu specialized in geomancy before the liberation. Now he decides to tell Mother Chao that her baby's illness is due to the position of the barn.

Third Auntie Chien hears someone at the gate and decides that she had better hide under the table. She bumps into Ironmouth Sun. They have no time to argue over the bag of rice but both crouch under the tablecloth. Mother Chao lets Hu in and he immediately says that the barn must be pulled down. He offers to read from his book on geomancy if she will give him five dollars. Mother Chao confesses that she does not know what to do, as she has been given so much different advice.

Hu Yinyang starts to call Sun and Third Auntie Chien names, and then stops suddenly. He sees the table moving as though inspired by a ghost. The other two "clowns" emerge and wrangle with each other over the best advice and who should have the bag of rice. Auntie Chien sings:

Yinyang Hu, the old tomcat,
It's bad luck for a house when he goes there!
Longlegs Wang got his son a wife
And built a beautiful three-roomed house to the north.
Then Yinyang Hu did some divining
And insisted that the new house be pulled down for the sake of
the couple's future.
Longlegs listened to Yinyang Hu
And pulled down the three-roomed house in a hurry.
The young bride was furious when she heard it
And said that a superstitious household was no good!
Hu Yinyang, the old tomcat;
Ruined the three-roomed house
And spoilt a romance!
Never believe him.
I am better than he is!

Ironmouth Sun sings:

Third Auntie Chien's belly is full of ghosts
Fighting to give incense ash to the sick!
Widow Wang in our village sprained her leg when she went out
And she gave her incense ash to eat!
She ate three packets with no result
And still hobbles about with a stick.
Neither of them are any good,
You had better believe in me!

Hu Yinyang sings:

Ironmouth Sun is a greedyguts
And all he knows about fortune telling
Is 'Spirit-star in the West, go to the West,
Spirit-star in the East, go to the East.'
If you do as he says
It will be the death of your grandson!
I know more than any of them,
And you must do as I say!

Auntie Chien is on the point of throwing another fit when
Hsiu-yu arrives with the child. His temperature has gone since
the doctor gave him penicillin. Mother Chao asks the three
whether she should still follow their advice and they hurriedly

withdraw it. Hsiu-yu then recalls their hard life before the liberation and explains that talk about "fate" was meant to stop poor people like them from rising against the landlords. Mother Chao sees how useless and wasteful superstition is, and turns over the incense pot and the Kuanyin statue. Mother Chao and Hsiu-yu sing:

> Many old ways of thought have been left by the old society and the old systems,
> Only when the old ways of thought have been torn out by the roots can we be really liberated.
> Do not believe in spirits or ghosts; down with all feudal superstitions!
> Burn up old ways of thought and old customs like paper boats and lanterns!
> Obey the voice of Chairman Mao,
> Look ahead when you walk,
> Resolve to do away with the old and set up the new,
> And always follow the Communist Party!

Hsiu-yu then takes the three "clowns" to the production brigade for punishment.

DOC. 103. *Liang Yu-ken, an Old Poor Peasant: Throw the Buying-and-Selling Type of Matrimony Into the Rubbish Dump of History (1970)*

"BY ORDER OF THE PARENTS, and according to words of the matchmaker" was an invisible rope of the doctrines of Confucius and Mencius which had tied up our women. In the old society, in their marriage the women could only obey the order of their parents and rely on the words of the matchmakers. They had not the slightest chance to make their own choice; like cargo, they were sold. How many women were strangled by this invisible rope! The evils of the doctrines of Confucius and Mencius were indeed beyond description.

All exploiting classes always oppress, discriminate against, and vilify women. The renegade, hidden traitor, and scab Liu Shao-ch'i, to subvert the dictatorship of the proletariat and restore capitalism, made his best efforts to peddle the doctrines of Confucius and Mencius, and even promoted to run "offices of matchmaking" for the young people. Indeed, it was rotten to the core, and reactionary to the extreme.

Though the Confucian "Inn" has been overthrown, its ghost is still around. [The "Confucian Inn" refers to a group of scholars who continued to support Confucian teaching and values well into the Communist period. With Confucianism now completely rejected, the "Confucian Inn" scholars have been denounced for "feudalistic" and "revisionist" thinking. This same group is linked politically with Liu Shao-ch'i, the now-disgraced President of the nation, whose handbook, *How to Be a Good Communist*, is now said to advocate outmoded Confucian values.] Though Liu Shao-ch'i has been swept into the rubbish dump of history, the lingering pernicious influence of his counter-revolutionary revisionist line is still far from being totally eliminated. At present the class enemies are still making use of the ghost of the doctrines of Confucius and Mencius and lingering pernicious influence of Liu Shao-ch'i's counter-revolutionary revisionist line to put up resistance in the corner, engage in the buying-and-selling type of matrimony, and bring back into life the "four old things." In our commune, an unreformed landlord has spread openly such reactionary nonsense as "parental care is like the grace of heaven," and "giving away your daughter without asking for money is valuing a human being as cheap as mud." He instigated those who gave away their daughters by marriage to ask for so-called "gift money" and "silver for her person." This is the new trend of the class struggle. We must heighten our vigilance.

Our great leader Chairman Mao showed his greatest concern for the liberation of women. Chairman Mao said: "The day when women get up throughout the country will be the day of victory of Chinese revolution." "Unite, take part in production and in political activities, and improve the economic status and political status of women." Thanks to the concern of Chairman Mao, and to the education and fostering of our Party, after the liberation, the broad masses of women have gained their emancipation. Politically and economically, they are enjoying the same status as men. Through their tempering in the great proletarian cultural revolution, they further develop a thoroughgoing revolutionary spirit and have smashed to pieces the spiritual yoke which the exploiting classes put on them. However, it is not easy to annihilate all the old ideas and the force of old habits; they are still swaying and corroding some people. We must continue to repudiate the reactionary ideology of the bourgeoisie and all exploiting classes, repudiate Liu Shao-ch'i's counter-revolutionary revisionist line, and resolutely smash to pieces the "four old things" and totally discredit them.

DOC. 104. *Letters to the Editor in Chinese Youth: What Shall We Do When Parents Are Engaged in Superstitious [Religious] Activities? (1966)*

Comrade Editor:

In the beginning of the lunar tenth month of this year, my mother went downtown and brought back several catties of paper money to burn for her dead ancestors. At the moment of her return, I was so angry that I was unable to speak a word. All at once, I tore into pieces these superstitious things she had brought back. Mother was very sad. She did not eat food for a few days, nor did she speak to me. Later on, some of my fellow commune members learned of this incident and said that I was a fool. They were cold whenever they saw me. I was very distressed because of this incident. What, after all, should I do when my mother is engaged in superstitious activities?

> Kuo Sui-ch'eng, Kao-chuang Brigade,
> Kuo-chi Commune, Pi-yang County,
> Honan

Comrade Editor:

My mother has been ill lately. Somebody said that there were ghosts or spirits residing in my mother's body and wanted to invite a "sorceress" [lit.: "supernatural woman"] over to treat my mother. My father thus went out secretly to invite a "sorceress." It cost him nearly ten dollars. Mother's illness does not seem to have improved, however. One day, father consulted me about inviting the "sorceress" over again. I was greatly infuriated. I am a member of the Communist Youth Corps. How did it come about that there have been superstitious activities in my own family? I propounded a number of rational explanations to my father. But he rebuked me as "an unfilial son." What should I do?

Wu Chen-fu, Tang-ch'iao Brigade,
Shuo-chi Commune, Fu-ning County,
Kiangsu

[Editor's Reply]
Comrades Sui-ch'eng and Chen-fu:

We, as members of the Communist Youth Corps and as youths of the revolution, should perform the active function of propagating science and breaking up superstition. In order to help the masses break up superstition effectively, it is essential that [we] should start by helping the masses raise their consciousness. If the masses' consciousness is raised, they will rise themselves and destroy superstition. While the masses are still not awakened in their consciousness, we should continue positive propaganda work, waiting patiently for the masses to awake in their consciousness. That is to say, we should be dauntless and not cease propaganda work simply because some people oppose us. Otherwise it should be impossible to raise the masses' consciousness. Nor should we adopt simple methods to solve problems simply because the masses are not yet awakened. In that case, the hostility of the masses would be aroused and the goal of breaking up superstition would not be attained. We hope that, based on this kind of spirit, you will pursue the task of breaking up superstitions in the villages. Such things as inviting the "sorceress" over to treat illness are important matters that concern people's life and health. While continuing the propaganda work toward the masses, [you] should insist on inviting a medical doctor to treat the illness so that the patient will not be impeded in her recovery.

Editor

Section 2. New Liturgical Forms

DOC. 105. *Fukien Radio Broadcast: A New Style Wedding Ceremony: Be Leading Persons in the Revolution, Destroy the Four Old Things, and Make New Merit (1970)*

THE FOLLOWING is the story of some cadres and members of a commune, who have studied and applied Mao Tse-tung Thought in a living way, armed their minds with Mao Tse-tung Thought, bravely destroyed the four old things and boldly established the four new things. [See Doc. 91.]

At Machi Production Brigade under Cheng-kuang Commune in Changpu County, Comrade Wu Yung-cha, Vice-chairman of the Brigade Revolutionary Committee and a member of the Communist Party, held his wedding ceremony by destroying the old things and establishing the new things, and received profound praise from the commune members. The broad poor and lower-middle peasants said: "He has taken the lead very well, and has done the correct and good thing."

Young Communist Wu Yung-cha and Comrade Chen Pai, member of the Communist Youth League, had fallen in love. The parents of both sides were exceedingly satisfied. Later, as the young couple wanted to hold their wedding ceremony by destroying the old things and establishing the new things, the parents on both sides began to have dissatisfaction. Chen Pai's mother complained: "It is a great event to give away my daughter in marriage. At present, our life has become good. We have means to provide her with a proper dowry. From the bumper harvest, I have grain and money. I must arrange the wedding of my daughter on a grand scale so that nobody will say that I am stingy." Therefore, the parents of both sides got busy to make elaborate preparations.

Comrade Wu Yung-cha thought to himself: "I am a Communist and a revolutionary cadre. I should be a leading person in destroying the old things and establishing the new things." Comrade Chen Pai thought to herself: "I am a member of the Communist Youth League. I should not allow the four old things to bind me up as fetters. I must take the lead for all the young girls."

They exchanged their own views, and came to an agreement. Together they studied Chairman Mao's great teaching, "Be prepared against war, be prepared against natural disasters, and do everything for the people." With this teaching of Chairman Mao's as a mirror, they compared the ideas and actions of their family members, and began to feel increasingly wrong. How to help their parents to raise their class consciousness? Through mutual consultation, they decided to see Secretary Tsai Wei-pang of the Brigade Party Branch for assistance. Comrade Tsai Wei-pang gave them warm support and encouraged them by saying: "You have thought and done well. You must maintain your stand to take the lead properly for the young people." At the same time, he helped them to organize a Mao Tse-tung Thought study class to study Chairman Mao's great teaching, "Be prepared against war, be prepared against natural disasters, and do everything for the people" and "Make revolution by practicing economy." They simultaneously carried out study and, by joining with what their family members were thinking and doing, could judge whether or not these things were in conformity with Chairman Mao's teachings.

By recalling the sufferings in the old society, they felt all the more that these things were wrong. Chen Pai's mother said: "I remember that when I got married I could not have a pair of new shoes. On my wedding day, we even had no white rice to eat, and had no money to buy dowry, to entertain guests, and to give gifts. Now we have good days, but should not forget our sufferings in the past. I am very forgetful, and cannot face our benefactor Chairman Mao. Now I understand that in destroying old things and establishing new things, we have nothing to do with money; it is a great problem of whom we should follow. We poor and lower-middle peasants should follow closely our great leader Chairman Mao, and be leading persons in destroying old things and establishing new things."

Wu Yung-cha's father, having heard her "fighting self and repudiating revisionism," said immediately: "I should be blamed for all this because I did not make effort to study and apply Mao Tse-tung Thought in a living way, and was poisoned seriously by the renegade, hidden traitor, and scab Liu Shao-ch'i. She said that we wanted to hold the wedding on a grand scale and with feasts. This is not the true color of our poor and lower-middle peasants. We should follow Chairman Mao's teachings and be leading persons in changing old customs and habits." Through the study, all members of both families unanimously agreed to hold the wedding ceremony in a new style.

On the day of their wedding, Wu Yung-cha and Chen Pai went on foot from the home of the bride to the home of the bridegroom. All the way the commune members praised them continuously: "They are making a good start. It is a good example for us to copy." When the newly wedded couple walked into the village, all villagers, men and women, young and old, came out to give them welcome. The girls led the bride around the village and to the fields to look over production and the water-conservation construction. In the evening, the production team held a forum and invited the couple to tell their experiences in the living study and application of Mao Tse-tung Thought. The wedding ceremony was not only simple but also gave prominence to politics. The older generation was deeply impressed. They said: "In the past when we got married, it took us three years to repay our debts for our marriage. Now, how nice to carry out such a wedding ceremony as that held by the Wu family!"

The young people said: "Communist Wu Yung-cha and Communist Youth League member Chen Pai have given us a good example. They held their wedding ceremony by destroying old things and establishing new things. We should learn from them such good ideas of practicing diligence and frugality."

DOC. 106. *The Educational Significance of Handling the Funeral of a Party Member (April 25, 1964)*

CHIN SHIH-HSIEN, a Party member of the First Production Team, Yümin Brigade, Tungkang Commune, Huinan Hsien, Kirin Province, died of illness on January 26 this year.

Opinions differed as to the way the funeral for the deceased should be handled. Some people said that since Communist Party members did not believe in spirits and gods it would be all right to buy a coffin and send him away in it. However, Chin's relatives and friends insisted that the funeral should be conducted according to established customs. There were also others who suggested holding a memorial service to commemorate the deceased.

The Party branch called a meeting to discuss this matter. Ch'i Kuei-fa, secretary of the Party branch, said: "Comrade Chin Shih-hsien was among the first group of Party members in our branch. Since he never forgot Party work when he was well, he was a good comrade worthy of our commemoration. Making funeral arrangements for Comrade Chin is not merely a personal affair but is a matter of major importance related to social customs and practices. We should conduct the funeral rites in such a way as to give them educational meaning. Therefore, I suggest a memorial service."

At the meeting, Kao Te-feng was the first to give his approval. Chang Chu-han suggested sending Comrade Chin a wreath in the name of the Party branch. After discussing the matter fully, the thinking of all the members of the Party branch was brought closer together.

Then, Chang Chu-han told the leader of the production team what the Party branch had in mind about the funeral arrangements. Later, poor peasants and lower-middle peasants of the commune were assembled to discuss this matter. Ch'i Kuei-fa called on Li Chang-fu, a relative of the late Comrade Chin, to explain to him the benefits of conducting the funeral rites not in keeping with established customs and practices. It happened that Li Chang-fu had just killed a chicken and prepared some wine in preparation for appeasing the soul of the late Comrade Chin according to old customs. After Ch'i Kuei-fa had convinced him by patient persuasion, Li Chang-fu realized that a dead man had no soul and that burning paper was wasteful. He also realized that these old customs and practices were tricks used by the feudal ruling class to mislead the masses. Finally, Li Chang-fu also approved of the idea of holding a memorial service for the deceased.

DOC. 107. *Old Aunt Wu Celebrates Her Birthday, Nan-fang Jih-pao, Canton (January 21, 1970)*

AT THE HSIA-PU BRIGADE's Lou-hsiang Production Team of Chingtang Commune in Szu-hui County, poor peasant member Wu Chin-hou is a member of the Communist Party. This old woman of 59 has, under the nurture of Mao Tse-tung Thought, became increasingly red in her heart with the increase of her age.

One day at noon, old Aunt Wu returned home from her work in the field. When she entered the house, she saw that a crowd of relatives were seated in her room, and gifts were piled on the table. She was bewildered by this scene. The wives of her nephews were surprised to see their aunt smeared with mud spots and her pants still rolled up to her knees. They asked: "Auntie, don't you know what day it is? In the past score of years, you have never stopped doing your work one day; you don't even want to take a rest on your birthday!" They reminded her of the occasion. Old Aunt Wu then began to realize that her relatives came to celebrate her birthday.

After deep consideration, she thought to herself: As a member of the Communist Party, I should follow Chairman Mao's great teaching, "Be prepared against war, be prepared against natural disasters, and do everything for the people, vigorously grasp the revolution and promote production, make more contributions to the Chinese revolution and world revolution for burying completely imperialism, revisionism and reaction in all countries, and never be extravagant and wasteful, and never participate in the 'four old things.' " Then, old Aunt Wu said: "Will you please wait for a little while?" She went to the field, and came back with a bundle of wild greens which she had collected from the field.

On that day, for lunch old Aunt Wu did not kill a chicken or a duck, nor did she prepare dishes of pork or fish. She cooked the wild vegetable and invited all her relatives to share a "meal of remembering past bitterness." When all of them took up their chopsticks to eat the wild vegetable, old Aunt Wu took some of it with her chopsticks and gave them a lesson on "remembering past bitterness and thinking about present sweetness," and also relentlessly repudiated the counter-revolutionary revisionist black stuff of the big renegade Liu Shao-ch'i. She said with profound emotion: "We should forever follow Chairman Mao's teachings, never forget the bitterness of the old society, nor lightly enjoy happiness, and make revolution by practicing economy, producing more food grain, supporting world revolution, and liquidating imperialism, revisionism, and reaction in all countries." In this way, old Aunt Wu turned this celebration of her birthday into a vivid lesson on class education.

This revolutionary spirit of old Aunt Wu in resolutely breaking away from the "four old things" greatly moved all the others. They unanimously made the pledge: "In the future, we must follow Chairman Mao's teachings, destroy the old things and establish the new things!"

DOC. 108. *Raymond L. Whitehead: Liturgical Developments in China's Revolutionary Religion (Excerpts)*

Morning and Evening Ceremonies: Tien An Men (Peking)

EVERY MORNING AT SUNRISE People's Liberation Army soldiers, Red Guards, and workers go to Tien An Men, the great public square in Peking and one of the sacred places of the revolution. They come in orderly groups and "full of vigor and vitality" they stand on the Golden Waters Bridge facing the bright sunshine of early day. With a "serious and respectful attitude" they seek daily instructions from a spiritually present Chairman Mao. At evening time they return to Tien An Men to "report to Chairman Mao" their new achievements in "grasping revolution and promoting production."

This kind of daily seeking for instructions from Chairman Mao and reporting to him in the evening goes on throughout the country. It is not surprising that it has become a daily ritual at Tien An Men, where memories of the great ceremonies of national celebration are so keen. One poet has described his feelings waiting at Tien An Men for the appearance of Chairman Mao.

Suddenly, like the eruption of a volcano,
Like the crashing of thunder in spring,
Before Tien An Men
Joyful shouts burst from our throats:
"Long live Chairman Mao! Long, long life to him!"
Chairman Mao has come!
Chairman Mao has come!
To the strains of "The East is Red,"
Chairman Mao and Vice-chairman Lin Piao
Mount the Tien An Men rostrum—
The highest peak in the world!
And now, the red sun rises over Tien An Men,
The Five Continents and the Four Seas are shining red!
I have seen Chairman Mao,
I have seen Chairman Mao!
The hearts of the Red Guards
. . . find it hard to contain
This overwhelming joy,
Chairman Mao, oh, Chairman Mao!
You are the lighthouse by the misty sea,
The bright lamp showing us the way;
You are victory,
You are light!
We will follow you. . . .[1]

1. *Chinese Literature*, No. 9, 1967.

A description of Shanghai reminds one of European peasants called to prayer by the church bells:

> The chimes of "The East is Red" from the tower of the Customs Building by the Whangpoo River heralds the dawn of a new day over the port of Shanghai.
>
> In factory workshops, commune fields and in classrooms, in army barracks, on airfields and aboard fighting vessels, the first thing workers, peasants, fighters and young Red Guards do is to stand before a portrait of the reddest red sun in their hearts to wish the great leader Chairman Mao a long, long life.[2]

2. *Peking Review*, No. 3, 1968.

Tientsin Station

IT IS REPORTED that the railway station in Tientsin has been converted into a "Thought of Mao Tse-tung Lecture Hall." After the municipal Revolutionary Committee was formed there was mass action to remove and dismantle all pictures and paintings of flowers and birds and fish, and all advertisements from the waiting room and platforms. A huge statue of the "great leader Chairman Mao" and more than one hundred portraits of him were set up, along with three hundred posters with quotations from Chairman Mao. Now at the train station waiting travellers can "creatively study and apply" the thoughts of Mao Tse-tung, "criticize the enemies" and compare "past bitterness" with the "sweetness" of the new situation.[3]

A Remote Village

A LIBERATION ARMY "Thoughts of Mao Tse-tung Propagation Team" went to carry out their work in a remote valley. After visiting three homes they still had not come across a portrait of Chairman Mao, which seemed to them very strange. One of the team asked an old "aunt" in the village if they did not want to see Chairman Mao. She replied: "Yes. We poor and middle

3. *Wen Hui Pao* (Hong Kong), March 28, 1969.

peasants want to see our great leader Chairman Mao every day, every moment. Two years ago we walked fifty miles down the mountain hoping to buy a portrait of Chairman Mao but were unable to get one." The next day three of the young fighters from the propagation team returned to the valley. They taught the villagers to sing "The East is Red" and also hung bright portraits of Chairman Mao in the houses of the poor peasants. "It was like the red sun rising over the mountains." When the villagers saw the portraits they gathered around one, and all the men and women, young and old, called out loudly, "Long life, long life to Chairman Mao! We wish Chairman Mao a boundless long life, a boundless long life."[4]

In Factories

A HONG KONG CHINESE language paper reported that according to a Hunan Radio broadcast in January, 1969, factories in that province have established such things as "Respect Rooms" and "Loyalty Rooms" and "Treasured Book Platforms." The last is a special table or platform on which to respectfully place the Four Volumes of the *Selected Works* of Mao Tse-tung. These centers (with Mao portraits) are there to provide the workers with a place to carry out the system of seeking guidance in the morning and reporting at night, and to read Mao's work daily, to struggle against selfishness and the Liu Shao-ch'i line, to engage in living study and application of Mao's thoughts and to declare loyalty to him.[5]

District Reports

IN CHINGKANG SHAN the whole district has responded well to Mao Tse-tung study classes. Almost 2,000 courses have been run attended by around 200,000 people. On the average each person attended ten classes. In every home on Chingkang Mountain

4. *People's Daily*, Feb. 12, 1969.
5. *Ming Pao* (Hong Kong), Feb. 7, 1969; and NCNA, May 10, 1968.

there is a "Treasured Book Stand." The Chingkang Shan people "study Chairman Mao's books, listen to his words, follow his instructions and are his good fighters."

In one area in Kwangsi Province there are four hundred families. Each family has a portrait of Mao and each also has a "Treasured Book Platform" on which are placed the *Selected Works*. One poor peasant's house is full of Mao portraits. He said:

> "When I see the glorious picture of Chairman Mao,
> I feel unspeakable sweetness in my heart and gain unlimited strength."[6]

The Meal of Bitter Remembering

PERHAPS THE MOST INTERESTING liturgical development so far is the meal of bitter remembering. It comes the closest to carrying the sense of a religious sacrament as it is known in the West. Basically it consists of eating a meal of wild herbs and vegetables as a method of recalling the days before liberation when such was often all the poor and starving people could eat. An interesting photograph of a group partaking of this kind of meal appears in *China Pictorial*.[7]

The exact form that such a meal takes is varied. One example comes from a county in Kwangtung Province where eight elderly women organized a group to support the People's Liberation Army (PLA) men. They picked wild herbs and walked forty miles to a military camp to deliver them to the PLA men. As the soldiers ate the bitter herbs the old ladies, eyes full of tears, recalled the old society and the bloody history of their own families' experience. This way the young soldiers were helped to remember past bitterness and the present sweetness.

Another report describes a family study course of Mao Tsetung's thought. In the study the father finally comes under certain criticism for not taking the struggle against selfishness

6. NCNA, Feb. 11, 1969, and Jan. 17, 1969.
7. No. 2, 1969.

seriously enough. Finally the criticisms from the children convinced him that they still need to maintain vigilance in repudiating revisionism and fighting selfishness. He confesses his error. The father continues to describe the situation as follows:

> It was already late at night and the children were hungry. I asked my wife to prepare a meal of bran and wild herbs to represent the past and a dish such as we eat now as a token of our present happiness.
>
> After the meal the whole family stood before a portrait of Chairman Mao and made this pledge: "From now on we will conscientiously study Chairman Mao's writings, follow his teachings, act according to his instructions. . . ."[8]

The institutionalization of the liturgy is suggested by a report which was made by the vice-chairman of a production brigade's revolutionary committee in Hopei Province. He listed four practices which were established by his family: (1) on every New Year's Day, every birthday, and every festival they hold a "meal of recalling and comparing" (recalling the bitterness of the past and comparing it with present sweetness); (2) the "four firsts" which are done every day; (3) a learning and application session every week; and (4) regular participation in class struggle and collective labor.

One of the best descriptions of the sacramental meal appears in a report called "Aunt Liang's Dinner Party." Aunt Liang is a simple villager. She invites the young people who have come to the countryside to have dinner with her. Everyone puzzled over what Aunt Liang would serve. When the students arrived she began to describe for them the bitterness of the old society and then the joy of liberation. The youth were moved by the stories of suffering. "Then dinner was served—wild vegetable soup, steamed bran and husks. The students understood what the dinner meant at once. Aunt Liang looked around and said with deep emotion: 'Children, take and eat. . . .' " The writer goes on:

> The new commune members had had a vivid lesson in class education. They were deeply moved as they ate the soup and

8. NCNA, Nov. 28, 1968.

bran and husks. No, what they ate was not simply a kind of food. It symbolized the blood and tears of the laboring people and their deep hatred for the old society.[9]

DOC. 109. *Wei Yueh-hsiang: Mao Tse-tung's Thought Is Our Guide in Building a New-Type Family (1968)*

I AM A COMMUNIST Youth League member, and deputy company commander of the militia in our Nansu village production brigade of the Gujiao People's Commune, Sinchiang County, Shansi Province.

To describe how my family's Mao Tse-tung's Thought study class began, I must start from the beginning. In 1965, the whole family started studying Chairman Mao's work in real earnest. Following Chairman Mao's teaching, we held regular meetings to review our family life in a democratic spirit and to make self-criticism and criticisms of each other.

In February, 1967, a number of PLA comrades came to our brigade to help agriculture and they lived with us. That was really fine. They had the deepest love for Chairman Mao and constantly studied his works. They helped us in our studies, too, and turned our family meetings into gatherings where each of us told of our experience in the creative study and application of Mao Tse-tung's thought.

When Chairman Mao issued his great call to "fight self, repudiate revisionism," Mao Tse-tung's Thought study classes were organized at the county, commune, and production brigade levels. My family got together and discussed the matter, and we decided that we, too, could run such a study class. So we plunged right in and the class got started.

It is our experience that running a family study class is the best way to implement Chairman Mao's latest instructions swiftly

9. *Chinese Literature*, No. 12, 1968.

and build a new type of revolutionary family. It is the ideal battleground for annihilating self-interest.

"Three Constantly Read Articles" Unify Our Thinking

OUR WHOLE FAMILY studies the "three constantly read articles" —*Serve the People, In Memory of Norman Bethune,* and *The Foolish Old Man Who Removed the Mountains*—practically every day. Whenever self-interest clashes with public interest, we use Mao Tse-tung's thought to eliminate the former and foster the latter and remold our world outlook.

When Father-in-law was looking after the draft animals for the collective, many people thought him most responsible in his work and wanted to elect him production team leader. In our family study class, we touched on this question. Mother-in-law held that becoming the team leader could mean more trouble, even offending people sometimes, so she was against it. To help her, Father-in-law got her to study the "three constantly read articles" with him. He said: "People want to elect me team leader because they think I can do some work for the collective. We shouldn't be choosy about what job we do as long as we're working for the revolution." After studying, Mother-in-law came round and finally said: "What you say is true. We mustn't pick and choose in matters of work. If we poor and lower-middle peasants don't hold the leadership in the team, who should? I'm going to follow the old rule: Follow Chairman Mao's teachings. Whatever he says, we should do." Later, when Father-in-law did become team leader, he showed himself wholeheartedly devoted to the collective and did very fine work.

One day, when I went to work in the fields, I saw the plants in one of the team's plots turning yellow. My first thought was to fetch the manure we had at home and put it on this plot. But on second thought, I remembered that no fertilizer whatever had been spread on my family's own household plot as yet. What should I do? I turned to Chairman Mao's works for the answer. Chairman Mao says in *In Memory of Norman Bethune*: "We must all learn the spirit of *absolute selflessness from him. With this spirit everyone can be very useful to the people.*" I decided then that all the manure at home ought to be taken to the team's plot.

After work, when I told my young sister-in-law about this, she said: "Of course it's a good thing to give the team's land more fertilizer; the only trouble is: What shall we put on our own land?" I replied: "We mustn't be of two minds about anything that concerns the collective. Giving the fertilizer to the team means increasing production and aiding our country's construction." Then the two of us studied this teaching of Chairman Mao's: "*At no time and in no circumstances should a Communist place his personal interests first; he should subordinate them to the interests of the nation and of the masses.*" My sister-in-law quickly saw things in the right spirit. At meal time, we asked the elders what they thought about this and they too agreed with us. That night, we sent all the manure at home, twelve cartloads, to the team's plot. And we all got together to compose this poem:

If for a single day we fail to study the works of Chairman Mao,
  Selfish thoughts will raise their heads.
By studying Chairman Mao's works every day,
  Public interest will take firm root, and self-interest will make way.
Studying Chairman Mao's works together, our family will go quickly forward,
On the broad road to ideological revolutionization.

Section 3. Religious Analogies

DOC. 110. *Mao Tse-tung Replaces Buddha in Tibet: A New Era in Which One Million Emancipated Serfs Are Grasping Mao Tse-tung's Thought*

WITH REVOLUTIONARY FERVOR and citing ample facts, cadres at or above the regimental level assigned to the Tibet Military District in the southwest frontier of the fatherland have hailed the great proletarian cultural revolution initiated and led by Chairman Mao in the course of studying the communique of the twelfth plenary session of the Eighth CCP Central Committee. This has created a new situation in which one million emancipated serfs are directly grasping Mao Tse-tung's thought.

The cadres said: The tempest of the great proletarian cultural revolution has smashed the efforts made by the big renegade Liu Shao-ch'i and his agents in Tibet to keep Chairman Mao's voice from reaching the Tibetan people. The Mao Tse-tung's Thought propaganda teams organized by PLA units in Tibet have helped spread the invincible thought of Mao Tse-tung wider than ever in the cities and mountain villages and in the farming areas and grasslands. The brilliance of Mao Tse-tung's thought illuminates the hearts of one million emancipated serfs inhabiting the highlands and has aroused them in a more deep-going way than ever before.

The comrades cited numerous facts before and after the great cultural revolution to illustrate by contrast the tremendous and profound changes that have taken place in social conditions in

344

Tibet and in the outlook of its people. Whereas previously clay Boddhisattvas were worshipped in most families, they are now replaced by Chairman Mao's portraits. Whereas statues of gods and spirits filled villages and streets, they are now replaced everywhere by quotations from Chairman Mao. Whereas previously the Tibetan people carried bundles of Buddhist scriptures, everybody now holds the "red precious book." Charms imploring Buddha's blessings are now replaced by red bags holding *Quotations from Chairman Mao Tse-tung.* Greetings wishing Chairman Mao boundless life are now exchanged between the Tibetan people who previously wished one another "good fortune." Whereas before the Tibetan people burned joss sticks, worshiped the Buddha, and chanted lamaist scriptures, they now seek the advice of Chairman Mao every morning and report to him every evening, and sing "The East is Red" every day before Chairman Mao's portrait.

Since the great proletarian cultural revolution was launched a mass campaign to study and apply creatively Mao Tse-tung's thought has spread far and wide in both urban and rural areas of Tibet. The million emancipated serfs who suffered deeply before the great cultural revolution have such profound class feelings for Chairman Mao that they are keenly studying Chairman Mao's works.

The wife of the head of a hsiang peasant association in Mo-t'o Hsien lost her sight because of maltreatment by the vicious serf-owner of the old society. She now often asks other people to read to her Chairman Mao's works and his latest instructions. She said feelingly: "Chairman Mao is our greatest savior. I cannot see, yet I can hear what Chairman Mao teaches. . . ."

A narrow path winds more than 200 meters on a seven-odd-meters-high cliff on the way between Geliangsi Hsiang and the hsien along the Kinsha River. In the course of the great cultural revolution, the emancipated serfs in the hsiang drew immense courage from Chairman Mao's "three constantly read articles." They said, "Since the foolish old man could remove mountains, we will make the mountains give way!"

They set out to build a broad road over the cliff, encouraging themselves by repeating this passage: "Be resolute, fear no sacrifice and surmount every difficulty to win victory." With the support of the hsien revolutionary committee, they completed the job after a little more than two weeks of hard work.

On the day the road was completed, the masses shouted again and again: "Long life, a long, long life to Chairman Mao!" The older people were moved to tears. They bent down to touch the broad, even road, saying: "What happiness Chairman Mao has given us!"

The herdsmen inhabiting the northern Tibet grasslands have used Mao Tse-tung's thought to overcome havoc wrought by extraordinary snowfall. The Nachu area, for instance, was hit by exceptionally heavy snows between last winter and this spring. The temperature fell under forty degrees below zero, and in some places the snow drifts were over a meter high.

The herdsmen recalled that when such a thing happened in the old society, poor people would have had to flee their homes and go begging, or would simply die. But with the help of the PLA Mao Tse-tung's Thought propaganda teams, the local herdsmen this time studied the "three constantly read articles." Defying the heaven and the earth, they battled against the snow with resolution and overcame the severe havoc, thus safeguarding both the lives of the people and their herds.

A seventy-five-year-old herdsman said with feeling: "Our victory is entirely due to Chairman Mao! With Mao Tse-tung's Thought we dare to struggle even with God. We can even win against God" (lao tien yeh).

DOC. 111. *Alberto Moravia: China Is an Immense School (Excerpts)*

[PEKING] As the flag moves closer to us, we can see the whole procession. The marchers are boys and girls, Red Guards, as we can guess from the scarlet bands they wear on their arms. All of them in blue trousers, white shirts, boys and girls alike, each with the little book of Mao clutched in his hand. At their head marches the standard-bearer, the flagstaff thrust into his belt. Then come two girls, carrying a portrait of Mao, framed in gold and decked with red festoons. And behind the portrait come the demonstrators, single file. This is the typical demonstration; describing this one, we describe them all. It need scarcely be said that the style of these processions, like that of the propaganda shows with their songs and music and dancing, is religious, in the traditional peasant pattern of religion. In place of the red banner, set the standard of Confraternity, replace Mao's portrait with that of the patron saint of the village, and you'll scarcely be able to see any difference: basically, nothing has changed. The Red Guard is certainly the most modern political movement in the Communist world; but its style cannot help being Chinese, peculiar to a country like China in which the peasants are the majority of the population.

The Thoughts of Chairman Mao

AND NOW, let's draw a trial balance. We have been talking about the Cultural Revolution, but not on the ideological and political level. We have confined ourselves to a description of its more visible aspects. And yet, even from these superficial aspects we can draw some interesting information. First of all, the Cultural Revolution consists of only two components: the leader and the masses. It ignores, overruns, or gets around any and all bureaucratic, party, or intellectual intermediaries. In their place it is attempting to use the radio, the poster-papers, and the demonstrations to esablish a direct and immediate relation between Mao Tse-tung and the people. In the second place, and this is an even more important point, this people, although it is the whole people, is primarily the younger, under-thirty portion of the people. This means that in order to touch off his Cultural Revolution, Mao turned to the portion of the Chinese population that is least expert, least endowed with critical faculties, most violent, most inclined to deny and destroy, and most easily carried away by enthusiasm.

Lastly, one other very important fact: the relationship between Mao and China's youth is not based on pure and simple admiration and devotion of the sheep towards the shepherd. It centers on the book of Mao's quotations, on Mao's thinking. And so we are not too far from the truth when we say that the Cultural Revolution, besides being a great number of other things, is a kind of political school, with theoretical lectures and practical exercises, in which the Red Guards are the pupils and Mao is the teacher.

In Mao Tse-tung's "red book," Confucius and Mao go hand in hand. In the pages of what has become the daily breviary of millions of Chinese, the dictator of the People's Republic has fused and redirected the thinking of two very distant and different philosophers. In the last six months, the little volume has become a tool for a system of ritual behavior. Here is a personality cult quite unlike the one the Russians had for Stalin.

". . . the best way would be to learn the more important phrases by heart, for purposes of constant study and application." Learning by heart for constant study and application: there's the whole perceptual and normative nature of the book, underlined in this simple piece of advice. Nobody learns the works of Marx or Lenin by heart, because their works were not written as guides to behavior. But Mao's book was.

The book consists of short selections culled from the complete works of Mao. Like all Communist leaders, Mao has written a great deal. But unlike the other Communist leaders, he has written about everything, because in his long career he has done and been just about everything: politician, agitator, military leader, lawmaker, philosopher, poet, economic organizer, and on and on. He has been, at one and the same time, the Lenin, the Trotsky, and the Stalin (but the Mayakovsky, too) of China. That's why it was no difficult task to put together a book in which, under a few chapters with meaningful titles, Everyman's whole life is covered. But you mustn't think that Mao's book can be consulted and found helpful in solving what might be called private problems. We've said that it covers man's whole life: let us add at once that the life belongs to a very special kind of man, the man of the Cultural Revolution, for whom the individual, intimate, personal life must absolutely not exist. In his book Mao himself damns that sort of life under the negative seal of liberalism.

The book, in a word, has two functions: to guide the individual in his daily life, and at the same time to inculcate even more firmly in that man the notion that daily life is not and cannot be anything but political life.

Mao as a writer is typically a politician and typically Chinese. On the first count, you can't help noticing that his book possesses the two qualities a book must have to become a handbook of civic conduct: first of all, it has the quality of an authority that might be termed scientific; it is not a book of propaganda slogans, not a batch of catchwords and generalities based on enthusiasm, but a book of reflections and affirmations drawn from experience. In the second place, it has the quality of accessibility, thanks to extreme simplification and careful, easy explanation of the material. Thus the book is the fruit of a vast and complex body of experience extending over many years, and that fruit is made available to all. Also worth stressing is the educative effectiveness of such a book, in which the lessons, so to speak, seem involuntary and natural. Which goes to show, if nothing else, that from the very beginning Mao has been a consummately skillful politician with a vocation for teaching.

Still more important than the Confucianization of Marx's thought as Mao has performed it is the Confucianization wrought upon this already transformed and translated Marxism which is Maoism by the instinctive and spontaneous action of the Chinese masses. This is no intellectual operation of the sort we have been talking about in Mao's case, but generally speaking, a religious one. We have already said that the little red book has, in six months, become the cardinal point in a system of ritual behavior. Now there is no doubt that no State, no matter how tyrannical, can force a whole people to transmogrify a book of recollections and politico-military musings into a handbook for conduct. The reception given the book by the masses was truly enthusiastic, and probably far beyond the expectations of those who compiled it. On the other hand, it would be well to stress once again the meaning of Lin Piao's advice to learn the book by heart for constant study and application. This is precisely what was done for centuries with the maxims of Confucius: competitors in the government's civil service examinations were called upon to complete, by rote, an unidentified excerpt from Confucius. Even then, it went without saying that it was more important to remember than to understand, or that at the very least mnemonic skill was a form of intelligence. But what is the meaning of this preference for memory? Obviously, it lay chiefly in the fact that memory holds and preserves whatever cannot and should not be subject to criticism and thus to change. In other words, memory is a mental process that serves to confer authority, to embalm something we do not wish to be corrupted.

The Confucianization of Maoism is thus primarily a transformation into authority, by means of memory, of a personal experience, the experience of Mao. But what does this mean except that the traditional body of precept is being replaced with another more modern which, in its way, embodies and annexes the enormous body of European culture? Mao has read Marx of course. But for the Chinese masses, it will be enough to read Mao.

Who is to say they are wrong, if, partly out of gratitude to the man who has finally provided them with order and unity, partly out of the power of the old Confucian tradition, they choose to attribute to the thought of their dictator a stabilizing, religious power? Furthermore, there is no real contradiction, no real conflict between the permanent revolution Mao preaches in his book and the masses' need for order and unity. A revolution that must be made every once in a while is worrisome and upsetting. But a permanent revolution becomes something liturgical, canonical, stable, habitual—*permanent.*

DOC. 112. *Robert J. Lifton: Revolutionary Immortality (Excerpts) (1968)*

I SHOULD LIKE TO SUGGEST that much of what has been taking place in China recently can be understood as a quest for revolutionary immortality. By revolutionary immortality I mean a shared sense of participating in permanent revolutionary fermentation, and of transcending individual death by "living on" indefinitely within this continuing revolution.

The Revolutionary "Family"; Salvation by Works

APPLYING THESE MODES of symbolic immortality to the revolutionary, we may say that he becomes part of a vast "family" reaching back to what he perceives to be the historical beginnings of his revolution and extending infinitely into the future. This socially created "family" tends to replace the biological one as a mode of immortality; moreover, it can itself take on an increasingly biological quality, as, over the generations, revolutionary identifications become blended with national, cultural, and racial ones. The revolutionary denies theology as such, but embraces a secular utopia through images closely related to the spiritual conquest of death and even to an afterlife. His revolutionary "works" are all important, and only to the extent that he can perceive them as enduring can he achieve a measure of acceptance of his own eventual death. The natural world to which he allies himself is one that must be transformed by revolution while continuing to contain all that revolution creates. And his experiential transcendence can approach that of religious mystics, as a glance at some of the younger participants in China's Cultural Revolution confirms.

What all this suggests, then, is that the essence of the "power struggle" taking place in China, as of all such "power struggles," is power over death.

Thus, for a man in Mao's position—of his age and special commitments—the affirmation of a sense of immortality becomes crucial. *The overwhelming threat is not so much death itself as the suggestion that his "revolutionary works" will not endure.*

Cultural Revolution as Death-and-Rebirth

THE ACTIVIST RESPONSE to symbolic death—or to what might be called unmastered death anxiety—is a quest for rebirth. One could in fact view the entire Cultural Revolution as a demand for renewal of communist life. It is, in other words, a call for reassertion of revolutionary immortality. . . . A cultural revolution anywhere involves a collective shift in the psychic images around which life is organized. In Maoist China, however, it has meant nothing less than *an all-consuming death-and-rebirth experience, an induced catastrophe together with a prescription for reconstituting the world being destroyed.*

From the beginning the battle cry was the triumph of youth over age, of "the new" over "the old." Hence the Red Guard's announced early goal of totally destroying the "Four Olds" (old ideas, old culture, old customs, and old habits); and the similar stress upon smashing the "old educational system" in its entirety. . . . The Red Guards themselves were heralded as young people who had "declared war on the old world." But in their attack upon old age and decay they were, psychologically speaking, declaring war upon death itself.

I would suggest that this new community, in a symbolic sense, is a *community of immortals*—of men, women, and children entering into a new relationship with the eternal revolutionary process. An event of this kind is meant to convey *a blending of the immortal cultural and racial substance of the Chinese as a people with the equally immortal Communist revolution.*

Purity and Power: the Ascetic Ideal

WHAT I AM SUGGESTING is that this ascetic ideal, much like the Calvinist equivalent Meisner also mentions, is bound up with a transcendent involvement. While the Calvinists sought to "establish the Kingdom of God on earth," the Maoists seek a Kingdom of eternal revolution.

But it [the Cultural Revolution] can also be seen as a last stand of another less recognized entity—one we may call "militant rectitude"—a state of politicized straight-and-narrow moral earnestness pursued with unrelenting passion. Militant rectitude is an existential style that seems oddly old-fashioned during the latter part of our diffusely absurd twentieth century. Its model is the Chinese version of the "new revolutionary man," but we readily recognize Confucian and Christian, as well as communist contributions. During the Cultural Revolution (or at least its early phases) its exemplar was the totally mobilized, self-negating Red Guard, unswervingly dedicated to living out the immortalizing vision. What threatens militant rectitude is a very different kind of contemporary being I speak of as "protean man."

A key to the momentum of the Cultural Revolution is the merging of purity and power. We may define "purity" as encompassing such things as self-denial (or even self-surrender) on behalf of a higher cause, the urge to eliminate evil, and ideological single-mindedness. And we may speak of "power" as either the ability to make decisions and take actions that exert control and influence over others, or as the sense of inner strength and capacity.

The great dread is that the Revolution will be devoured in this fashion, that China will "change color" and take the capitalist-revisionist road. But since it is an ultimate confrontation between good and evil—"a life-and-death struggle on which the fate of the world depends"—a sense of ultimate purity and ultimate power beckons to the individual participant. Even if he cut himself off from all but the most ritualistic Maoist images, he could feel a new autonomy as he merged with his people, his history, his revolution.

Life-and-Death: Revolutionary Martyrs

WESTERN STUDENTS of Mao's thought have had some difficulty explaining the sources of its power. While often disagreeing on the question of whether Mao has demonstrated originality as a Marxist, most have rightly stressed his persistent preoccupation with themes of "struggle" and "contradictions" and "rectification" and reform. But what has not been adequately recognized, I believe, is a characteristic quality of tone and content that, more than any other, shaped the psychic contours of the Cultural Revolution. I refer to a kind of *existential absolute, an insistence upon all-or-none confrontation with death.* Mao always further insists that the confrontation be rendered meaningful, that it be associated with a mode of transcendence. One must risk all, not only because one has little to lose but because even in death one has much to gain.

Underneath the assumption of oppression being worse than death is a characteristically Maoist *tone of transcendence*, a message to the revolutionary which seems to say that death does not really exist for him; he has absolutely nothing to fear. Mao put forth this message as early as 1919 in the midst of the stirrings of cultural and political revolution associated with the epochal May Fourth Movement:

> What is the greatest force? The greatest force is that of union of the popular masses. What should we fear? We should not fear ghosts. We should not fear heaven. We should not fear the dead. We should not fear the bureaucrats. We should not fear the militarists. We should not fear the capitalists.

Thought of Chairman Mao: the Way, the Word

THE THOUGHT OF MAO becomes not so much an exact blueprint for the future as a "Way," a call to a particular mode of being on behalf of a transcendent purpose. Behind this Way are two psychological assumptions long prominent in Mao's thought but never so overtly insisted upon as during the Cultural Revolution. The first is an image of the human mind as infinitely malleable, capable of being reformed, transformed, and rectified without limit. The second is a related vision of the will as all-powerful, even to the extent that (in his own words) "the subjective creates the objective."

And the key to psychic malleability and power—the central theme of the thought reform process—is the replacement of prior modes of immortality (especially the biological one provided by the Chinese family system) with the newer revolutionary modes: those of the biosocial revolutionary "Family," of enduring revolutionary "works," and of transcendent revolutionary enthusiasm.

The thought itself is sacralized—spoken of as "a compass and spiritual food" of which "every word . . . is as good as ten thousand words." The writings of Chairman Mao become

> the best books in the world, the most scientific books, the most revolutionary books. . . . There have never been writings even in China or abroad like the writings of Chairman Mao. . . . They develop Marxism, Leninism, they are The Peak in the modern world of Marxism-Leninism. There are peaks in the mountains but the highest peak is called The Peak.

And this sacred quality of Maoist thought is in turn directly associated with the desired revolutionary totalism:

> One has to be totally revolutionary. There are total and non-total revolutionaries. Some men are like that. You cannot say they are not revolutionaries; but they are not fully revolutionary. . . . They are half revolutionary, half non-revolutionary. . . .

The Maoist corpus is elevated to an all-consuming prophecy: it nurtures men, predicts their future, and changes the world to accomplish its own prediction; it sets in motion spiritual forces against which nothing can stand.

DOC. 113. *Donald E. MacInnis: Maoism: the Religious Analogies (Excerpts)*

[SOME OBSERVERS PERCEIVE] during this time of total suppression of all organized religions, a man-made spiritual drive in the cultural revolution. Derek Davies, editor of the *Far Eastern Economic Review*, writes, "The idealistic—one might almost say spiritual—vision of Mao is enshrined in the description of the communist man he is desperately trying to create—a man unbesmirched by individualism and the crude hunt for personal profit. It is essentially a religious vision."

There is faith, a system of belief and practice, a dogma. This faith is elucidated in the canon, primarily the *Selected Works of Mao Tse-tung*. Works by other Party leaders are, for the time at least, part of the canon. Lin Piao's *Long Live the Victory of the People's War!*, written in commemoration of the twentieth anniversary of victory in the Chinese People's war of resistance against Japan, is one of these. Liu Shao-ch'i's *How to Be a Good Communist*, however, for years a basic textbook in the fundamental spirit of Chinese Marxism, has come under bitter attack during the past year. The expression, "the thought of Mao Tse-tung," was introduced at the Seventh Party Congress in Yenan in 1945 by Liu Shao-ch'i and appeared in the Party Constitution as proposed by Liu. But the cult of Mao, based on the thought of Mao, did not appear until after 1960, and did not mushroom until after August, 1966, the beginning of the Cultural Revolution. Since then 30 million sets of the four-volume *Selected Works* and countless millions of the "red book"—the *Sayings of Chairman Mao*—have been distributed.

Maoism resembles any religious orthodoxy—fundamentalist Protestantism for example—permitting no deviation and determined to maintain purity of faith and practice. Liu Shao-ch'i is reported to have made at least two confessions in the past year, both admitting to an independent mind-set and lack of faith in the central doctrine of the dogma, the "mass line." According to

Japanese correspondents one confession, copied from a wall poster in December, said (in part), "I did not understand the meaning and development of the cultural revolution. The sixteen points [of the Central Committee's 1966 communique] determined that it should follow the mass line, should mobilize the masses, that the masses should educate themselves [in revolutionary action], that the rebel spirit should be promoted. I did not believe in the masses and did not believe that the masses could educate and liberate themselves; I believed I was afraid of chaos and disorder, of great democracy. I was afraid of counter-revolution."

Religious orthodoxy tolerates no heresy. Not only the heretical doctrine, but the heretic himself must be purged. Revisionist members of the Liu Shao-ch'i faction have been relentlessly isolated and attacked since the formal launching of the Cultural Revolution in August, 1966, with the publication of the "Decision of the Eleventh Plenum Chinese Communist Party Central Committee Concerning the Great Cultural Revolution." Item V of this document's sixteen points, called "Party's Class Line Must Be Executed With Resolve," begins by asking, "Who is our enemy and who is our friend? This question is a primary question of the revolution. . . . Forces should be concentrated on attacking a handful of extremely reactionary bourgeois rightists and counter-revolutionary revisionists. Their anti-Party, anti-socialist, and anti-thought-of-Mao-Tse-tung crimes must be fully exposed and criticized. . . . The focus of this movement is on the purge of those power holders within the Party who take the capitalist road."

This was no mere power struggle among Party leaders. It was truly analogous to a religious campaign—Cromwell's righteous army, the Reformation prairie fire, Calvin's Geneva. In the words of a Peking news release, "The workers hold that everyone has the right to sweep away the influence of the old, not only in the streets, but in factories, enterprises, government institutions, and the recesses of people's souls."

Despite considerable grounds for a theory of beatification, even deification, of Chairman Mao, based on the prevalence of

Mao images, portraits, sayings, lapel buttons, posters, songs, drama, even Maoist "worship" services on trains, planes, and street corners, the God-substitute in the ideology of Maoism is the people, the peasants and workers, the revolutionary masses. In the three short essays most widely studied during the Cultural Revolution, the *Lao San P'ien*, the focus is on the people. "The Foolish Old Man Who Removed Mountains" was determined to move two mountains—imperialism and feudalism—with his bare hands (see Doc. 11). In the ancient Chinese version God was moved by the old man's determination and sent two angels who carried the mountains away on their backs. In Mao's version the old man concludes, "We must persevere and work unceasingly, and we too will touch God's heart. Our God is none other than the masses of the Chinese people."

This proletarian mystique dominates the dogma and program of the current campaign and runs like a red line through the history of the Maoist revolution. The Cultural Revolution began with an attack in 1965 on a group of intellectuals centered in Shanghai and Peking who were accused of writing historical allegories that indirectly mocked and criticized the Party line. The sins of this group were: denigration of the cult of Mao, playing down the class struggle, supporting elitist and neo-capitalist ideas, and preaching reconciliation with the Soviet Union. In the religious analogy, these are fundamental sins, cutting at the heart of the faith, while much of the Red Guard attack was a more superficial moralism.

In a revealing interview with Edgar Snow on January 9, 1965, Chairman Mao seemed like a man "reflecting on his rendezvous with death," confessing grave concern about the long-run future of the revolution. He talked about the death of persons close to him through the years, including his first wife, both of his brothers, and a son, and remarked on his own narrow escapes, saying, "It was odd that death had so far passed him by," and that he was "getting ready to see God very soon"—immediately adding that of course he did not believe in God. His concern for the course of the revolution exposed his uncertainties about the future.

The spiritual dimension of the crisis facing the revolution was clearly recognized. The dynamic movement was in danger of crystallizing, even of reverting to pre-revolutionary customs, habits, ideas, and culture. As with religious movements, the institutionalizing process betrays the movement, becomes static, confines men liberated by the revolution, as post-Reformation Lutheranism and Calvinism came to resemble the church from which they had broken.

The dilemma of "red or expert" is paralleled in the history of the church, the periodic swings from charismatic genesis to sterile scholasticism, formalism, rationalism, relativism, and bureaucratism. The debate among frontier churchmen in this country over the merits and dangers of an educated ministry is paralleled in the current debate on education in China. If the Maoists prevail, standard academic curriculum will be reduced to a minimum and ideological remolding will take precedence. School admission standards will be based on class background and political record rather than academic achievement or intellectual potential.

Two recent visitors to Mao's China discerned the religious analogies. One, Ian Thomson, observed that the main target of the present campaign was "to build a new folk culture, religion, personal faith, call it what you will, and base the focus upon Mao." The other, Masao Takenaka, a Japanese Christian theologian, sees the struggle as a massive effort to create a "new man" on the basis of Mao Tse-tung's thought, an "integrated people capable of disciplined hard work necessary for the up-building of a socialist country. . . . Here I believe [he writes] it is not economic doctrine as in classical Marxism, nor political strategy as in the case of Lenin and Stalin, but rather the spiritual, ethical element that is understood as the determining factor in shaping world history." Can the revolution hold its youth through the present period of ideological regeneration, or is second-generation recidivism inevitable for secular religions too?

Section 4. Conversion and Dedication

DOC. 114. *Conversion Experience of a Young Intellectual: Resolutely Follow the Road of Integration with the Workers, Peasants, and Soldiers*

AMONG THE NUMEROUS TECHNIQUES used toward the goal of leveling class and privilege differentials, one of the most pervasive, evidently affecting all able-bodied intellectuals, has been reform through manual labor. One consequence of the Cultural Revolution has been the mandatory shifting to rural labor assignments of millions of educated urban youth. While purely pragmatic reasons for this rustication policy can be adduced, such as the need to clear the cities of a glut of educated youth, the ideological rationale is the one most frequently seen in the Chinese press. The urban "intellectual aristocracy" needs, the leadership believes, the transforming experience of living and working with the real people of China, the rural masses.

The following article is the personal testimony of a young intellectual concerning his conversion experience. Following the standard form, this article opens with a description of the subject's wrong attitudes prior to conversion; his internal struggle aided by study of the works of Chairman Mao; his gradual self-recognition followed by subjugation of the ego and of selfish desires for a personal career, security, status, etc. to a description of the painful wrenching that accompanies the final transformation to a proper proletarian outlook. The process is aided by the humiliating yet exhilarating experience of personal involvement in mucky, smelly and (formerly) demeaning manual labor. In most articles of this kind recalcitrant members of the family (in this case, the wife) are later led to a conversion experience by the new convert. Finally, there is usually a triumphant "success against odds" struggle with a pragmatic problem in production, often accompanied by risk-taking and suffering; but the risks and heroic struggle are justified in a triumphant victory—in this case the trial-and-error invention of a more economical way to prepare cooked pig feed. The one-time proud intellectual has proved in practical demonstration the authenticity of his proletarian conversion.

Great leader Chairman Mao pointed out in his shining work, "The Orientation of the Youth Movement": "Intellectual youths and young students must integrate themselves with the broad masses of workers and peasants." Chairman Mao's great instructions pointed out to us intellectual youths the orientation for the realization of ideological revolutionization.

I am a graduate of the Foshan Veterinary Institute of Kwangtung and came to a certain PLA production base last August to undergo tempering in labor. The past eight months' practice of struggle has enabled me to realize: For intellectual youths to break away from the revisionist line of education totally, transform their old ways of thinking thoroughly, and become the type of people welcomed by workers, peasants and soldiers, the only way is to follow the road of integration with workers, peasants and soldiers, honestly receive reeducation from them, and incessantly launch fierce attacks against the old ways of thinking deep in the soul.

Is It a Question of Personal Interest or Is It a Question of Class Feeling?

ONCE WHEN I WAS WORKING with a PLA comrade he said to me after he heard that I studied veterinary medicine: "It is a good thing to study veterinary medicine; you can serve the poor and lower-middle peasants." I said: "Veterinary medicine is the subject I hate most." Hearing this he retorted bluntly: "It is not that you don't like veterinary medicine, but that you don't like the poor and lower-middle peasants and don't have feeling for the poor and lower-middle peasants." Upon hearing this sharp criticism my face turned red and my heart felt very uncomfortable. Is the matter of liking veterinary medicine or not a question of class feeling or is it a question of personal interest? A violent ideological struggle unfolded itself in my head.

I opened Chairman Mao's works after I got back to the dormitory. Chairman Mao said: "If we do not rid ourselves of old things and replace them with a proletarian world outlook, we shall have a viewpoint, standpoint and feeling different from those of the workers and peasants. In this way we shall never be able to become congenial with the workers and peasants."

When I was going to middle school under the influence of the counter-revolutionary revisionist line of education, I considered becoming an engineer or an expert as my "ideal." Later I felt very unhappy when I was admitted into the veterinary institute, because I thought a veterinary has to work with animals day in and day out and the job is dirty and without future. This profession did not suit my ideal or interests.

But after studying Chairman Mao's teaching I began to understand that ideals and interests too have a class background. To want to become famous and expert sitting on top of the workers and peasants as a bureaucrat is only a bourgeois ideal and interest. From the viewpoint of the proletariat, to serve the people wholeheartedly and to struggle for the liberation of all mankind and the realization of communism is the highest ideal and greatest interest. The broad masses of poor and lower-middle peasants want veterinaries who do not mind dirty work. I hated dirty work and disliked the veterinary profession. Why did I think differently from the poor and lower-middle peasants? It was not a question of "personal interest" but a question of having a viewpoint, standpoint and feeling different from those of the workers, peasants, and soldiers.

Lights went out, but I was lying in bed wide awake. Scenes of the past flashed by one after another and question marks pounded my head one after another. The old society took away the lives of my father, my two brothers, and my sister. At seven I was already forced to work for the landlord to repay our debt. Our life was worse than that of an ox or horse. Without Chairman Mao I might not have been able to survive, much less go to school. Now this son of a poor peasant is fed and clothed by the workers, peasants and soldiers; but why doesn't he have feeling for the workers, peasants and soldiers?

Here I felt very painful, and a sense of hatred toward renegade, traitor, and scab Liu Shao-ch'i was aroused in my heart. It was he who, for long periods of time, pushed forward the counter-revolutionary revisionist line of education and used the decadent bourgeois way of thinking to poison our souls. It was he who made us betray Chairman Mao's teaching and embarked upon the dangerous road of becoming seriously divorced from the workers, peasants, and soldiers. It was he who turned this son of the working people into a political fool who pursued personal fame and profit and forgot the working people, the dictatorship of the proletariat and the revolution.

I made up my mind to listen to Chairman Mao, follow the road of integration with workers, peasants, and soldiers pointed out by Chairman Mao, cultivate my feeling for workers, peasants, and soldiers, and establish the idea of wholeheartedly serving them.

Am I To Move Back Or To Stay?

THE ROAD TO REVOLUTION is a rugged one. To change over from the state of being divorced from the workers, peasants, and soldiers to the state of integrating with them and from having bourgeois feelings to having a feeling for workers, peasants, and soldiers, one has to go through a painful process of transformation. I made up my mind to go through the most painful and most practical struggle to cultivate my feeling for workers, peasants, and soldiers and to transform my past bourgeois idea of disliking veterinary medicine and unwillingness to serve the poor and lower-middle peasants. I indicated my determination to the Party branch, resolutely asking to serve as a pig tender, and moved my belongings to the fodder house by the side of the pig sty. Noticing my determination the Party branch and comrades accepted my request.

The fodder house was a shabby shed; it could only keep away the sun but not the rain and there was a pig sty and a manure pool in front of it. There was no flooring, so I put some hay on the ground and slept on a mat. One day it was very cold and the north wind came into the shed through a breach in the wall bringing in the bad odor from the pig sty and the manure pool. Rainwater was leaking into the shed leaving a pool of mud on the ground. When I came back from the kitchen I found several small pigs fighting in my bunk, messing up my bedding and mosquito net. I was so angry that I almost wanted to beat them up in revenge. Facing the breach which brought in the cold wind, a violent struggle again took place in my head: What shall I do? Am I to move back into the spacious and clean dormitory or am I to stay in this dirty and leaking shed?

At night, with this problem of going or staying in my mind I opened the shining works of Chairman Mao under a dim kerosene lamp. Chairman Mao said: "For intellectual elements to integrate themselves with the masses and serve them, they must go through a process of mutual understanding. In this process there will be much suffering and friction. But as long as one has determination one can always meet this requirement."

Chairman Mao's instructions lit up my mind and I realized: To integrate with the workers, peasants, and soldiers and thoroughly transform old ways of thinking I must experience many painful tests. In the face of a stringent test I must advance bravely with determination to be able to persist in Chairman Mao's revolutionary line and in the correct orientation of integrating with workers, peasants, and soldiers. If I retreat in the face of difficulties it will be tantamount to retreating from the road of integrating with workers, peasants, and soldiers.

Late at night finally I stood in front of Chairman Mao's portrait and pledged: Although thousands of mountains are between me and Peking, I shall follow you closely and advance resolutely along the road of integrating with workers, peasants, and soldiers.

Right at this moment my wife came to visit me. Discovering that I was living under such conditions and was mixed up with pigs all day long, she said my work was very unbecoming. But knowing that I was doing as Chairman Mao taught me I was very happy and proud. At night I studied with her a series of Chairman Mao's latest instructions concerning the integration of intellectual youths with workers, peasants, and soldiers and told her about my own experience. After studying we realized: To meet the challenge of the test of difficult conditions self-consciously on the road of integrating with workers, peasants, and soldiers is an important lesson in intellectual youths' process of attaining ideological revolutionization, a glorious affair, and a proud thing. If an intellectual youth is unwilling to give up his airs and dares not throw himself into the bitter struggle to cultivate himself and has to be led along the road of integration with the workers, peasants, and soldiers, he would be most unglorious and most unbecoming. My wife was then enlightened and began tending pigs together with me. She also encouraged me to study and apply Chairman Mao's works creatively, advance steadily in the bitter struggle, and become a revolutionary fighter forever loyal to Chairman Mao.

Serving the People
Under the Leadership of the Correct Line

THE ROAD OF INTEGRATION of intellectual elements with workers, peasants, and soldiers is the road of serving the people. I was able to contribute to a certain extent to the service of the people because Chairman Mao leads us to advance along this revolutionary road and because the workers, peasants, and soldiers reeducated me. I deeply realized: The workers', peasants', and soldiers' feeling of loyalty to Chairman Mao is deeper than mine and their spirit of serving the people is stronger than mine, therefore they are good examples and good teachers to me.

This March a PLA pig tender discussed with me modifying the fodder oven to reduce coal consumption so as to respond to Chairman Mao's great appeal, "Practice economy and make revolution," with practical action and greet the convocation of the Ninth Party Congress. At that time I thought: It is not an easy thing to modify the oven because I have neither the technical know-how nor do we have any expert to help us. There are bound to be difficulties and setbacks in the work. Comrades will be unhappy with me if I do a bad job in modifying it and bring about bad effects on the feeding of the pigs. When I told the PLA pig tender about this he gave me a latest instruction from Chairman Mao: "Practice economy and make revolution" and said: "Kuo, we must not consider a chin or a liang of coal something trivial. Practicing economy is a fine tradition of our Army and a virtue of the revolutionary fighter."

At night I could not sleep; a struggle over this question was going on in my head all the time. Why do I always think differently from the workers, peasants, and soldiers in these questions? What they think about is always how to respond to Chairman Mao's great appeal resolutely and how to serve the people, while what I think is always my own gain. Modifying the oven is for the benefit of public interest, while not modifying it is for self-interest and for the retaining of old ways of thinking. I must not be defeated in this question; I must learn from the PLA comrades.

Then the struggle of modifying the oven began. There were no materials, so we looked all around for them. There were no experts, so we humbly asked PLA comrades and even went to ask old workers in a factory several li away. After more than a month's hard work the comrades and I overcame one difficulty after another. After changing the modification plan several dozen times we finally completed building a new oven with new features on the eve of the convocation of the Ninth Party Congress [April, 1969] and reduced the daily coal consumption from several dozen chin to several chin. Later, encouraged by the good news of the opening of the Ninth Party Congress, the comrades and I again modified the oven of the army kitchen and reduced the coal consumption from one and a half chin per person per day to 2.7 liang per person per day.

I realize that the attainment of such achievements was only a new starting point on my road of integration with workers, peasants, and soldiers. In the future I shall ride on the strong east wind of the Ninth Party Congress, honestly receive reeducation from the workers, peasants, and soldiers, and become an intellectual youth forever welcomed by them.

DOC. 115. *Yang Chih-an: Chairman Mao is Dearer than Any Parent*

The sky above is cloudless and blue
As the postman smilingly enters our billet,
A letter from home's a cheering thing,
It's like ma was standing right here beside me.
I open the letter and see the sun,
Red and glowing, lighting up my heart,
Ma has sent me a colored picture
Of our dear leader, Chairman Mao.
". . . Received your letter asking for my photo,
The whole family sat down and talked it over,
Chairman Mao is dearer than any parent,
Consider him to be your own pa and ma.
"Chairman Mao saved us from our sea of sorrows,
Never forget it, good child of mine.
Neither mountains of knives nor seas of fire
Should stop you from following Chairman Mao."
I hold Chairman Mao's picture to my chest.
Memorizing the words my ma has said.
Chairman Mao's road is the one we're travelling,
For ever and ever towards the sun.

DOC. 116. *Seaborne Cultural Work Team, Kwang-chow: Long Life to You, Chairman Mao (1969)*

Over the surging waters
Of the great Yangtse,
Ten thousand li, and more,
Rises a bright red sun,

Riding over the waves,
Shaking the earth!
The bold and stately mountains
Straighten out;
The rippling waters
Sing a joyful song:
Chairman Mao!
Our most respected and beloved leader
Chairman Mao
Enjoys good health;
Enjoys good health!
Chairman Mao
You give us
Faith and strength illimitable;
With your encouragement
Comes the realization of our great ideals;
We give of our best,
Aim high;
We will follow you for ever!
We will advance
Through storm and hurricane!
We bless you, Chairman Mao;
Long, long life to you.

Through a vast sea
Of clouds
Breaks a red sun;
Through the misty clouds
It shines
in every village;
All over the earth
Red flags are unfurled
By militant people;
They take up arms!
Chairman Mao!
Our great teacher
Chairman Mao
Enjoys good health;
Enjoys good health!

Chairman Mao
You have opened up
A revolutionary route for us;
You have led us towards
The liberation of mankind!
With hearts now red
And with discerning eyes
Our spirit has become militant!
We will follow you for ever;
We will advance through storm and hurricane!
I bless you, Chairman Mao;
Long, long life to you!

DOC. 117. *Hsiung Tao-keng, Young Woman Frontier Worker: A Letter to Mama*

By the Heilung River, under the Lesser Khingan Mountains,
Like a scroll the wind unfurls our scarlet banner;
As the wild goose flies up the blue sky,
Our fighters' songs soar to the bright clouds.
Tomorrow our red detachment of women
Pack up and go to cut wood in the forest.
Before our departure,
I must write a reply to my mother.
Heart throbbing with exhilaration,
So many words jostle for expression:
Shall I tell how the political instructor and myself
Together creatively study and apply Chairman Mao's works,
Fight self, repudiate revisionism and decide to strike root here?
Shall I tell how we launched mass revolutionary repudiation,
Brandishing iron fists on the bourgeois headquarters of Liu
    Shao-ch'i?
Shall I tell her how Grandad Han and I became "a red pair,"
Deepening my feelings for the poor and lower-middle peasants?
Shall I tell her how Aunt Chu recounted old bitterness,
And with her we think of today's sweet life,

So that for ever we will imprint in our hearts,
Hatred for the old society?
Dearest mama,
Six months ago,
Revolutionary determination in my breast,
The four treasured volumes in my hand,
Along the road where intellectuals must become one
With the workers, the peasants, and the soldiers,
I came to settle down here close by the frontiers.
Serve the People is our first lesson on joining up,
The spirit of Chang Sze-teh* makes its mark on our minds.
Our commander explained the Eighth Route Army tradition,
And in my hand he placed a hoe.
Where the summer weeding has begun,
There I went with my big hoe,
Trickles of sweat dripping, dripping.
"Come on, Hsueh-mei, get on with it!"
"Oh dear, I've dropped so far behind."
My face burning like fire,
Hands tightly gripping the handle,
I hoed and hoed with desperation,
"Plop!"
A young plant dropped beneath my hoe.
Ashamed and very much annoyed, I asked,
"Am I really useless with a hoe?"
Grandad Han came quietly to my side,
"Don't get flustered, girl,
You'll learn in time, in time.
Let's talk awhile as we work together."
"I want to tell how when I was seven,
Unable to pay his load of usurious debt,
My father was killed by the landlord's deadly club.
I was dragged away in payment for the debt,
Slaved for the landlord and sweated blood.
Enduring bitterness for which I find no words,
I struggled in a sea of misery,
My stomach never full, my body ever cold.

* hero-martyr.

The landlord's whip bit like poison fangs.
Lacerating flesh, drawing blood,
My tattered shirt all crimson dyed. . . .
It is Chairman Mao who led in making revolution,
Saving us poor urchins from the pit of misery.
Born in the new society, Hsueh-mei, you grew up
Under the red flag, knowing nothing
Of the bitterness of old.
Chairman Mao makes the call:
'*Educated young people—go to the countryside*'
So that they can revolutionize their thinking.
But that renegade, traitor, and scab Liu Shao-ch'i
Would have us dragged along the capitalist road.
Child,
You must always follow Chairman Mao's teachings!"

What Grandad Han said kindled
Hot hatred of oppression in my breast.

The fervent hopes of this poor peasant,
I must take for my own and always share.
From this moment Grandad Han I made my teacher,
And determined now to strike root in the countryside.

My dearest mama,
I am no longer a spoiled child, as when at school
I'd scan myself before the mirror to flick off
The least bit of dust on my clothes.
Now I spread manure with my hands,
And thick calluses have grown on my palms.
My revolutionary purpose comes clearer to me.

The latest instructions of Chairman Mao light
A beacon for intellectuals to rebuild themselves.
I will embrace the reeducation given me
By the workers, peasants, and soldiers,
Strike root and blossom in the countryside.
Dearest mama,
Just you wait for news of my endless victories!

Conclusion

QUITE POSSIBLY THIS BOOK raises more questions than it answers. Certainly both reader and author are baffled by the paradoxical response of China's leaders to the question implicit in the book's title: What is the real religious policy, in practice as well as in words, of the Communist leadership? Moreover, a further question is raised by the deep divisions within the Party exposed by the Cultural Revolution: *Which* leadership group determined religious policy at any given time?

As has been suggested in the introduction to Part I, Section 3, the exhaustive public examination in the nation's press of the theoretical bases for Marxist and Maoist religious policy by thoroughly trained scholar-theoreticians during the years 1962–65—the years when the less-radical policies of the "moderates" under Liu Shao-ch'i were in force in all sectors except the PLA—presented two distinct views of how to treat religious believers under the constitutional guarantee of freedom of religious belief. Ya Han-chang, representing the moderate position, held stubbornly to the view that believers in genuine religion (as contrasted to superstitions) should not be harassed or coerced in the practice of their faith.

The abrupt termination of this series of debates immediately followed the secret meeting of the CCP Central Committee in late 1965 at which Mao Tse-tung's challenge to the Liuist group was first made. One explanation for the total blackout of public discussion of religious policy since then is that the uncertainties regarding policy in almost every field during the ensuing struggle between the "two lines" simply ruled out further writing on religion and many other sensitive topics.

But during the entire period from 1937 to 1966, long before any hint of conflict between Mao and Liu, there was ambiguity in Party policy and practice toward religious believers: on the one hand, the record of these past twenty years shows a consistent adherence to orthodox Marxist dogma on religion in all theoretical analyses and doctrinal statements, while holding to the equally consistent adherence in official statements and theoretical discussions to the constitutional guarantee of freedom of religious belief; yet in practice, with some ambivalence from period to period, religious believers have suffered increasing constraints on the practice of their faith down to the total suppression of open religious activity by Red Guard militants in 1966–67.

Do China's present leaders really see the religious folk of their country as a potential political or ideological threat to the regime? Evidence could be adduced, based on the considerable attention given to organized religion in the 1950's, that such was the case at that time;[1] yet the total absence of official pronouncement on religious policy in practice since 1966 suggests that the leaders in Peking have simply ignored religion—the surviving remnants of the various religious groups being too insignificant, it would seem, in both numbers or influence to merit even a word in the sixteen-point Cultural Revolution *Decision* of August, 1966, or in subsequent directives and communiqués from Chairman Mao or others in the leadership group. Perhaps the leaders aren't even aware of the extent to which believers have been terrorized and intimidated by Red Guards and local extremists.

One can surmise that the split within the Party leadership,

---

1. There were an estimated one million Protestant Christians, three million Catholics, and ten to fifty million Moslems (depending on definitions) at the beginning of the Communist period. Buddhists are not easily identified, since no membership statistics are kept, but it can be assumed that most of China's peasants outside the Moslem areas, and many of her city dwellers acknowledged some faith in Buddhist canon or practice in 1949.

dramatized since 1966 by relentless and continuous attacks on President Liu Shao-ch'i and the hosts of "capitalist roaders" who allegedly followed his counter-revolutionary line, was not healed by the conflict and turmoil of the Cultural Revolution period, or by the steps toward restructuring of Party and government following the Ninth Party Congress in 1969. The struggle between the "two lines," judging by numerous reports in the Chinese press, continues to the present. It may be that accommodation and compromise for the sake of unity and restored momentum in the economic and other basic sectors of national life will gradually moderate extremist attitudes toward religion and other sensitive cultural areas.

On the other hand, the Maoist group now firmly in power, having successfully established their political authority and ideological line, may be continuing the ideological attacks simply for the sake of struggle itself—since "struggle" is seen as intrinsic and beneficial to the ongoing revolution. With their authority and confidence restored, with the factional fighting among local "rebel revolutionary" groups brought under the control, with the migration of millions of former "revolutionary youth" to the rural areas, and with the need for renewed collective effort in socialist construction, the present leaders may begin to feel less need for tightly restrictive policies in dealing with minority groups such as religious believers.

The same reasoning applies in the area of international relations. Where provocation and alienation of friends, neutrals, and foes alike characterized China's foreign relations at the height of the Cultural Revolution, she now actively seeks friends on the world scene and is moving rapidly toward normalized relations in her dealings with the nations of the world. If, as it appears, China is truly more conscious now of world opinion, she will certainly be increasingly alert to the sensitivities of religious elements in the Moslem, Buddhist, and Catholic nations of Asia, Africa, Latin America, and the Middle East. There have already been reports of complaints to Chinese authorities by visitors from such nations who could not find place for worship while traveling in China. Considerable attention was given to international religious relations in the 1950's, primarily between Chinese Moslems and

Islamic nations, and it can be expected that reactivation of the Religious Affairs Bureau in 1971 signals a return to these concerns. But aside from all such practical considerations, domestic or international, it seems clear that organized religion in China has been so thoroughly neutralized, the ranks of believers and clergy so scattered and decimated by attrition, death and superannuation with few replacements from a new generation, that even the control mechanisms used so effectively in the 1950's and early '60's would scarcely be necessary now.

The lack of access to information and to individuals in China, and the volatile nature of Chinese politics even now, rule out the possibility of any meaningful speculation on future developments in religious policy and treatment of believers. But the record of religious patriotism and support for socialist construction, and the successful mobilization of religious people for implementation of Party and state policies of autonomy and self-reliance, of opposition to feudalism, superstition, imperialism and other unlawful acts and wrong attitudes, and the enlistment of all clergy and believers for collective action toward the goals of Party and nation have surely eliminated, with the possible exception of the ethnic Moslems in certain areas and the Tibetan Buddhists, the possibility of religious groups retaining any "dangerous" group identity. Now would be the time, it would seem, when religious believers can again be allowed at least minimal freedom to meet and worship together.

In startling contrast to the situation prevailing in China, an article in the July, 1970, issue of the theoretical journal, *Hoc-Tap*, North Vietnam's (DRV) counterpart to China's *Red Flag*, speaks directly to the "mandarin bureaucrats" in DRV Party leadership, denouncing them for "narrow prejudices toward religious believers" and reminding them that the "choice of religious freedom is a democratic right" like any other political, economic or social right guaranteed by the constitution. Those "levels and branches [of Party and state] responsible for the guaranteeing of democratic rights have been guilty of negligence." Believers and non-believers alike "must be noticed and their right to freedom of conscience guaranteed." Party cadres must nurture qualities, virtues and abilities which will facilitate rapport with the masses, including believer-compatriots. Neither religious belief nor unbelief can serve as criteria for judging political consciousness. "To think that a believer is incapable of having a revolutionary spirit is wrong and dangerous. . . ." Believers themselves are encouraged to "fight for, protect and develop their democratic rights."

Nor should emergency wartime priorities interfere with the "political rights and religious freedom of believers." Any discrimination against believer-compatriots must be avoided. Criticism of Party cadres and self-criticism by the people go hand-in-hand. At all times believers must be allowed full participation in the collective national effort.

"President Ho Chi-minh has said, "For the body, our Catholic compatriots are concerned to satisfy hunger, for their souls, to enjoy freedom. In order to attain this objective we must reinforce the collective work, develop production, and increase returns to each cooperator. At the same time we must guarantee religious liberty. However, practice of religion must not obstruct production nor obstruct the policies and the laws of the State" —a straightforward statement with reasonable conditions.

If this small nation fighting an all-out war can allow its religious minorities freedom to practice their faith within the limitations imposed on all citizens, surely the Chinese can follow the reasonable policy toward religious believers set forth by their own leader. Mao Tse-tung, in *On Coalition Government* (1945) said: "All religions are permitted . . . in accordance with the principle of freedom of religious belief. All believers . . . enjoy the protection of the people's government so long as they are abiding by its laws. Everyone is free to believe or not to believe: neither compulsion nor discrimination is permitted."

List of Documents By Source

Abbreviations Used in Notes

sw   *Selected Works of Mao Tse-tung*, Volumes I to IV (Peking: People's Publishing House; Chinese edition 1960, English edition 1961).

jprs   Washington, D.C.: Joint Publications Research Service.

ncna   Peking: New China News Agency.

Documents   *Documents of the Three-Self Movement* (New York: Asia Department, National Council of Churches USA, 1963).

ncccusa   National Council of Churches of Christ, USA.

cb   *Current Background.*

scmm   *Survey of China Mainland Magazines.*

scmp   *Survey of China Mainland Press.*

flp   *Foreign Language Press* (Peking).

uri   Union Research Institute (Hong Kong).

Documents

1. Edgar Snow, *Red Star Over China* (London: Victor Gollancz, Ltd., 1963), pp. 7, 9.
2. *Report on an Investigation of the Peasants' Movement in Hunan* (Feb., 1927), SW, I (1965), pp. 44–47.
3. Schram, Stuart R., Political Thought of Mao Tse-tung (New York: Praeger, 1970), pp. 184–85, 188.
4. SW, II, p. 312.
5. "On New Democracy," SW, II, p. 381.

378   *Religious Policy and Practice in Communist China*

6. Ibid., pp. 361–62.
7. *Four Essays on Philosophy* (Peking: Foreign Languages Press, 1966), pp. 84, 86–87.
8. "On Coalition Government," SW, III, p. 306.
9. *Jen-min Jih-pao* [*People's Daily*], Peking, November 22, 1952.
10. "On the Correct Handling of Contradictions," *Four Essays*, p. 109.
11. SW, III, p. 322.
12. André Malraux, *Anti-Mémoirs* (New York: Bantam Books, Inc., 1970), pp. 438, 448, 465–67.
13. C. Brandt, B. Schwartz, and J. K. Fairbank, *A Documentary History of Chinese Communism* (Cambridge: Harvard University Press, 1952), pp. 220, 223.
14. Ibid., p. 225.
15. Snow, *Red Star Over China*, pp. 369–70.
16. CB No. 9.
17. *Constitution of the People's Republic of China*, English edition (Peking: Foreign Languages Press, [FLP] 1961), p. 39.
18. *Decisions on Some Problems in Agrarian Reform* (Peking: People's Publishing House, 1964), p. 28.
19. *Tibet 1950–67*, (Hong Kong: Union Research Institute, 1967), pp. 20, 22.
20. From China News Service, April 15, 1959; reprinted in *Buddhism in China 1949–67* (Hong Kong: Union Research Institute) Document No. 1, trans. Donald E. MacInnis.
21. *Che-hsueh Yen-chiu* [*Philosophical Research*] No. 1, February 15, 1958; translated in CB 510 June 15, 1958.
22. Peking: Foreign Languages Press, 1954, p. 35.
23. "Implications of China's Cultural Revolution," p. 5. From *China Notes*, July, 1966, p. 5.
24. From NCNA; reprinted in *Documents of the Three-Self Movement* (New York: Asia Department, NCCCUSA, 1963) pp. 22–24. (Hereafter referred to as *Documents*.)
25. *Documents*, pp. 27–28.
26. From NCNA; reprinted in *Documents*, pp. 29–33.
27. *Report*: "Socialist Revolution and Peoples Democratic Front," Section 2 (NCNA, December 30, 1964, SCMP, January 5, 1965).
28. *Jen-min Jih-pao*, August 8, 1963; in SCMP August 27, 1963.
29. *Hsin Chien-she* [*New Construction*], February 20, 1964; in SCMM April 20, 1964.
30. *Kuang-ming Jih-pao*, March 21, 1964; in SCMP April 20, 1964, pp. 2–6 *passim*.

31. *Hung Ch'i* [*Red Flag*], February 26, 1964; in SCMM March 31, 1964.
32. *Hsin Chien-she*, December 20, 1965; in SCMM April 18, 1966.
33. *Kuang-ming Jih-pao*, June 30, 1965; in SCMP July 21, 1965.
34. *Kuang-ming Jih-pao* March 7, 1965; in SCMP March 29, 1965.
35. *T'ien Feng*, May 8, 1951; in *Documents*, pp. 41–43.
36. CB Vol. I, No. 119; in *Documents*, p. 26.
37. *T'ien Feng*, September 3, 1954; in *Documents*, pp. 87–95.
38. *Che-hsueh, Yen-chiu*, loc. cit.
39. *Tsinghai Jih-pao*, July 9, 1959; in JPRS October 23, 1959.
40. Alfred Francis James, *Reports on Deputation of Australian Churchmen* (New York: Far Eastern Office, NCCCUSA, 1957), pp. 10–11.
41. *Min-tsu T'uan-chieh* [*Nationalities Unity*], No. 4 (April, 1962); in SCMM July 16, 1962.
42. *Min-tsu T'uan-chieh*, loc. cit.; in SCMM June 18, 1962.
43. NCNA September 3 and 4, 1965; in *China Notes*, January, 1966.
44. *Jen-min Jih-pao* and NCNA; in CB April 18, 1951.
45. *Heilungkiang Jih-pao*, July 25, 1959; in CB January 15, 1960.
46. *T'ien Feng*, May 11, 1959; in JPRS December 21, 1959.
47. NCNA, December 19, 1961; in SCMP December 27, 1961.
48. *T'ien Feng*, August 25, 1962; in JPRS March 6, 1963.
49. *Peking Review*, March 4, 1966, pp. 16–17.
50. *Documents*, pp. 27–28.
51. *Documents*, pp. 19–20.
52. *Documents*, pp. 87–95 passim.
53. From "Report on Chief Problems of Policy is Our Present Task," *Tibet Jih-pao*, July 5, 1959; in JPRS October 23, 1959.
54. *Min-tsu T'uan-chieh*, April 1962; in SCMM June 18, 1962.
55. From "Religion and Class Struggle in the Transition Period" pp. 4–5 SCMP April 20, 1964.
56. *Kirin Jih-pao* and NCNA; in JPRS April 17, 1959.
57. *Chieh-fang Jih-pao* [*Liberation Daily*], Shanghai, June 8, 1953, and Shanghai Radio June 7, 1953; in JPRS August 11, 1953.
58. *Min-tsu T'uan-chieh*, June 14, 1958; in JPRS May 11, 1959.
59. Ibid.
60. *Kuang-ming Jih-pao* April 2, 1964; in SCMP May 26, 1964.
61. *Kuang-ming Jih-pao*, May 29, 1958; in Rodney MacFarquhar, *The Hundred Flowers* (London: Stevens & Sons, 1960), pp. 249–50.

380   *Religious Policy and Practice in Communist China*

62. *Jen-min Jih-pao*, May 16, 1958; in MacFarquhar, *The Hundred Flowers*, p. 251.

63. *Kansu Jih-pao*, Lanchow, February 22, 1958; in MacFarquhar, *The Hundred Flowers*, pp. 251–52.

64. NCNA March 14, 1958.

65. *Jen-min Jih-pao*, March 25, 1957; translated in CB August and September 2, 1957; in *Documents*, pp. 151–56.

66. *Hopei Jih-pao*, January 11, 1958; in CB June 15, 1958.

67. *T'ien Feng*, April 1958; in JPRS March 5, 1959.

68. NCNA June 27, 1956; in CB September 21, 1956.

69. *T'ien Feng*, April 1958; in JPRS March 5, 1959.

70. *Wen Hui Pao*, Hong Kong, June 13, 1958; in CB June 15, 1958.

71. *Hsin-hua Jih-pao* (*New China Daily*), Nanking, October 5, 1958; in JPRS February 6, 1959.

72. NCNA May 15, 1951; in *Documents*, pp. 49–51.

73. *Jen-min Jih-pao*, April 15, 1960; in CB April 9, 1960.

74. China News Service (Peking, September 9, 1959); in CB January 15, 1960.

75. NCNA November 8, 1963; in SCMP November 14, 1963.

76. *Hsien-tai Fo-hsueh* [*Modern Buddhism*], November 13, 1958; in JPRS March 11, 1959.

77. *Nei Meng-ku Jih-pao* [*Inner Mongolia Daily*], November 16, 1958; in JPRS October 23, 1959.

78. *Hsien-tai Fo-hsueh*, in JPRS October 23, 1959.

79. *T'ien Feng*, March 1958; in JPRS March 5, 1959, p. 10.

80. *T'ien Feng*, September 1958; in JPRS March 11, 1959.

81. *T'ien Feng*, April 1958; in JPRS March 5, 1959.

82. *Hsien-tao Fo-hsueh*; loc. cit.

83. *Hsien-tao Fo-hsueh*, July 13, 1959; in JPRS October 23, 2959.

84. *T'ien Feng*, May 25, 1959; in JPRS December 21, 1959.

85. *T'ien Feng*, July 14, 1958; in JPRS March 24, 1959.

86. *T'ien Feng*, August, 1958; in JPRS March 11, 1959.

87. C. Mackerras and N. Hunter, *China Observed* (Melbourne: Thomas Nelson, 1967), p. 86.

88. Ibid., p. 87.

89. Ian Thomson, "Inside China Today" (October, 1967); in Donald E. MacInnis, "Maoism and Religion in China Today," *The Religious Situation: 1969* (New York: The China Institute), p. 3.

90. K. Takahashi, "Religion and the Cultural Revolution" (June 11, 1967); in Donald E. MacInnis, op. cit., p. 4.

91. SCMP, August 16, 1966.
92. Hong Kong: Union Research Institute Collection, No. 617, trans. Donald E. MacInnis.
93. URI No. 1167, trans. Donald E. MacInnis.
94. URI No. 42, trans. Donald E. MacInnis.
95. URI No. 1747, trans. Donald E. MacInnis.
96. Nanking Radio, September 6, 1966; in *China Notes*, April, 1967.
97. *Ceylon Daily News*, November 12, 1966; in *China Notes*, April, 1967.
98. C. Mackerras and N. Hunter, *China Observed* (Melbourne: Thomas Nelson, 1967), p. 141.
99. *Jen-min Jih-pao*, January 10, 1967; in SCMP 3863, January 19, 1967.
100. *Hung Ch'i*, August 1, 1969; in *China Notes*, Fall, 1969.
101. *Jen-min Jih-pao*, June 17, 1958; in CB 510.
102. *China's Youth*, December 14, 1963; trans. in *Ching Feng* Hong Kong, Vol. VIII, No. 1, 1964.
103. *Nan-fang Jih-pao*, Canton, February 6, 1970; in *China Notes*, Fall, 1970, trans. URI.
104. *China's Youth*, No. 8, 1966; in *China Notes*, Spring, 1969.
105. Fukien People's Radio, February 1, 1970; in *China Notes*, Fall, 1970, trans. URI.
106. *Jen-min Jeh-pao*, April 25, 1964; in SCMP 3217.
107. *Nan-fang Jih-pao*, February 6, 1970; in *China Notes*, Fall, 1970, trans. URI.
108. *China Notes*, Summer, 1969.
109. *Peking Review*, October 4, 1968.
110. *Jen-min Jih-pao*, November 19, 1968; in *China Notes*, Spring, 1969.
111. From *Corriere della Sera*, Milan, July, 1967; translated in JPRS September 11, 1967.
112. *Revolutionary Immortality: Mao Tse-tung and the Chinese Cultural Revolution* (New York: Alfred A. Knopf; Vintage edition, 1968).
113. "Maoism: the Religious Analogy," *Christian Century*, January 10, 1968; and *China Notes*, July, 1968.
114. *Jen-min Jih-pao*, May 4, 1969; in SCMP May 13, 1969.
115. *Chinese Literature* FLP, Peking No. 9 (1968).
116. Ibid. No. 4 (1969).
117. Ibid. No. 6 (1969).

Glossary

WEIGHTS AND MEASURES

1 mou	1/15 hectare or 1/6 acre
1 liang	1 ounce
1 catty (chin)	1/2 kilogram or 1.1 pounds
1 ch'ih (foot)	1/3 meter
1 li	1/3 mile
1 tan (picul)	50 kilograms
1 yuan	U.S. $ .40

ADMINISTRATIVE UNITS

ts'un	hamlet
hsiang	village
chen	market town
hsien	county
ch'ü	district, region

TERMS AND ABBREVIATIONS

ahung, imam	Moslem clergyman
feng-shui	geomancy
four pests	flies, rats, mosquitoes, sparrows (sometimes bedbugs)
four olds	old habits, ideas, culture, customs
Three-Self Movement	Christian churches' triple autonomy: self-support, self-government, self-propagation
PLA	People's Liberation Army
CPPCC	Chinese People's Political Consultative Conference
CCP	Chinese Communist Party

Index

*Howard, 10 weeks
with
Chinese
Bandits*